Wilson Duff

WILSON DUFF

DUFF Coming Back
A Life

ROBIN FISHER

HARBOUR PUBLISHING

Harbour Publishing Co. Ltd.
P.O. Box 219, Madeira Park, BC, VON 2H0
www.harbourpublishing.com

Edited by Noel Hudson
Indexed by Robin Fisher
Dust jacket design by Anna Comfort O'Keeffe
Dust jacket image: *Eagle—Full Circle*, in memory of Wilson Duff. Image courtesy of
    Roy Henry Vickers
Text design by Carleton Wilson
Printed and bound in Canada
Text printed on 100% recycled paper

Harbour Publishing acknowledges the support of the Canada Council for the Arts, the Government of Canada, and the Province of British Columbia through the BC Arts Council.

Library and Archives Canada Cataloguing in Publication
Title: Wilson Duff : coming back : a life / Robin Fisher.
Names: Fisher, Robin, 1946- author.
Description: Includes bibliographical references and index.
Identifiers: Canadiana (print) 20220151806 | Canadiana (ebook) 20220151881 |
    ISBN 9781550179750 (hardcover) | ISBN 9781550179767 (EPUB)
Subjects: LCSH: Duff, Wilson, 1925-1976. | LCSH: Anthropologists—Canada—Biography. | LCSH: Museum curators—Canada—Biography. | LCSH: Anthropology—Canada. | LCGFT: Biographies.
Classification: LCC GN21.D84 F57 2022 | DDC 301.092—dc23

For
Marnie, Collyne and Patricia,
who made it possible,
and Kerry Howe
because I am you.

Table of Contents

Preface

Wilson Duff once said, speaking about two Tsimshian stone masks that he did much to make famous, that they were, at one level, a self-portrait of the artist.[1] In the same way, biography is partly autobiography. So let me begin, as a biographer should, by laying some cards on the table. When I came to British Columbia in 1970 to study the history of Indigenous people and their interactions with Europeans, I very quickly made contact with Wilson Duff. When I first met Wilson I had a lot to learn and, in the years that followed, much of what I did learn, I learned from him. At the University of British Columbia I began to learn about First Nations cultures and history, like hundreds of others, by sitting in on his course Anthropology 301, Indians of British Columbia. I was drawn in by his brilliance, wit and the pleasure that he took in playing with ideas.

I clearly recall sitting near the back of the large, tiered lecture hall in the Buchanan Building, listening to Wilson Duff talking about the Carrier Indians, as they were then known, of northern British Columbia. A hand went up in the front row and a student asked why they were called Carrier. Wilson carefully explained the mortuary custom of a widow carrying the ashes of her deceased partner for several months. The student reacted with loud guffaws, and Wilson asked, Why the laughter? The student's response was that he just could not understand why anyone would do such a thing. To which Wilson responded, quick as a flash, "Well, I guess there are no prerequisites in anthropology."

My last conversation with Wilson was in the spring of 1976 in the coffee line outside Images Theatre during a conference at Simon Fraser University. He had just given what I thought was an exciting, innovative paper. I asked, naively as it turned out, if he would be willing to come to one of my classes and talk about his ideas. His response was an uncharacteristic and curt no. It was, I now know, the last thing he wanted to be asked to do. I wish now that I had known that then. That is sometimes the discomfort of learning about history, particularly when it is your own.

Between these two recalled moments, Wilson was a supervisor of my PhD dissertation in history. I remember walking into my dissertation defence with Wilson and him asking me if I was ready for "the gentle ritual." He later allowed that the discussion had turned out to be a good deal more spirited than he had expected. I had a startling research moment when I read in Wilson's papers a page of notes that he had written during the debate on my dissertation, and I learned that his mind was going in directions different from anyone else in the room. The dissertation later became a book titled *Contact and Conflict: Indian-European Relations in British Columbia, 1774–1890* and it is dedicated to Wilson because he was a huge influence on my thinking about First Nations cultures and history.[2] Sometimes people have asked me if I have thought of writing volume two of *Contact and Conflict* to take the history forward from 1890. This biography might be seen to be a partial answer to that question. Certainly, in the writing of it, I have had my own sense of coming full circle. Yet, for all of Wilson's help, I still have a lot to learn. This biography was written, and should be read, in that light.

Throughout my life since knowing Wilson I had thought from time to time that his biography would be an interesting project. Then, through the good offices of Richard Mackie, I met Wilson's daughter, Marnie Duff, over lunch at the Oystercatcher in Ganges on Salt Spring Island. Looking at Marnie when we met, I could see Wilson again. She was interested in finding someone to write her father's biography. There had been some writing about Wilson since his passing, but Marnie felt that the full story had not been told and that something more accurate should replace the fiction and the academic gossip. So I agreed to start work on this biography. We have since had many, many conversations and Marnie has strong views about some things, but she has not in any way attempted to impose them on me. She keeps insisting that it is my book.

I should note, particularly for my historian colleagues, that I have contemplated the question of whether, given my personal connection with

Wilson, I am the right person to write this biography. Am I, even now, too much Wilson's student to be objective enough? On the other hand, I cannot imagine spending several years working on a biography of someone for whom I do not have some admiration. And having known the person can be an advantage for a biographer. I knew Wilson well enough to be sure that he would not have wanted an adulatory and uncritical version of his life to be told. I still smart from, and also cherish, an absolutely devastating critique that he wrote for BC *Studies* of a draft article that I had submitted. Again, as a biographer should, I have entertained these thoughts, then let go of the search for that unattainable grail of historical objectivity and forged ahead.

Wilson himself once wrote, "There is autobiography, but there is also biography."[3] So, while I am the filter, this book is a life of Wilson Duff. I have tried to write about Wilson Duff's life, as much as possible, in the context of his time rather than ours, in an effort to avoid the worst effects of presentism—the fallacy of applying contemporary standards to the past. The presentist presumption works in two ways on Wilson's life and work. The first is the impulse to judge the work of historical figures by today's standards. In the effort to take history to the cleaners, people from the past are found to be wanting by our current doctrines. The second comes from the loss of historical memory that leads to the claim today that ideas and approaches are new, when in fact they were developed by those who went before. The very people found wanting by the first presumption are more subtly denigrated by the second. Both of these fallacies have been applied, and have done a disservice, to Wilson Duff's contribution to making the cultures of the First Nations people of British Columbia known to newcomers. He learned, practised and wrote about anthropology from the late 1940s through to the 1970s. As a scholar in his time, he was alive to the currents of thought in his day. He should not be held to account according to standards and ideas that came later.

Toward the end of his life, Wilson Duff's thinking about meaning in Northwest Coast Native art was innovative and, therefore, controversial in academic circles. His ideas attracted both admiration and derision.

Academics, as is their wont, have also engaged in a good deal of gossip about Wilson Duff, some of it accurate and much of it not. I have tried to counteract some of the false stories by presenting at least a version of the truth. As an intensely private person, Wilson Duff would, I know, not be entirely happy about this biography. At the same time, he once wondered if his wisdom would return after he died.[4] I hope that at least some of it will unfold here. In the end, I simply think that his story deserves to be told.

I should add a word about words. The names of people and places have changed since Wilson's time as Indigenous people have decided for themselves what they shall be called rather than using words attributed to them by newcomers. Yet *Indian* was the word universally used for the Indigenous people of British Columbia in Wilson's time. It is still sanctioned by some First Nations people. Wilson himself understood that it was a colonial imposition and yet, unlike many others, used it with the greatest respect. I have used the word *Indian* when referring to Wilson's work, just as some other scholars have continued to do when writing about the past.[5] I acknowledge that it has been replaced among many, but not all, by other words: *First Nations, Indigenous, Aboriginal* and, sometimes, even the formerly pejorative *Native*. I have taken the same approach to the names of places and groups and used the words prevailing at Wilson's time while providing the more current version where appropriate: thus *Kwakiutl* (Kwakwa̱ka'wakw) and *Ninstints* (SG̲ang Gwaay). Some names, like *Haida*, have not changed. Wilson once pointed out that, given different sounds in Indian languages and English and various orthographies, there is no reliably accurate version of Indian names in English.[6]

Through the research and writing of this biography I was fortunate to receive generous help from many people. The book is dedicated to the three, Marnie Duff, Collyne Bunn and Patricia Trick, who were constant co-authors. Very little history is written without the expert help of dedicated archivists. As institutions, archives have changed over the years (I am no longer given a carrel in the stacks and the freedom to select manuscripts for myself at the Provincial Archives), but the service given by archivists remains exemplary. I could not have written this book without the help of several. Alissa Cherry, Ann Stevenson and Katie Ferrante at the Audrey and Harry Hawthorn Library and Archives, University of British Columbia Museum of Anthropology, were always hospitable and helpful far beyond the call of duty. Across campus the people at the University of British Columbia Archives were also very helpful. Genevieve Weber at the British Columbia Archives gave me access to Wilson's papers even as she was in the midst of reorganizing them. Her colleagues at the BC Archives and Grant Keddie at the Royal BC Museum were unfailingly helpful. Many thanks also to Benoit Thériault and Jonathan Wise at the archives of Canadian Museum of History, and Laila Williamson at the American Museum of Natural History in New York. Thanks to Annette Vey-Chilton, the then principal of Vancouver Technical Secondary School, and her staff for giving me access to the school's records.

Several people read all or part of the manuscript in progress. My life-long friend Kerry Howe read all the chapters as they were written. His commentary was clear and helpful when things needed to be revised and generous when they did not. When Kerry and I were both working on master's degrees at the University of Auckland, we had the same supervisor. Judith Binney taught us much that we have remembered and valued throughout our careers: as Kerry recently remarked, we are both "Binney trained and operated." Judith Binney and Wilson Duff were two big influences on me as a historian. In a friendship renewed, David Dowling brought his keen editorial eye to bear and persuaded me to let go of some of my historian's caution. Bob McDonald, before he left us, read and commented on the early chapters. Wendy Wickwire gave reassurance toward the end and read a complete draft and suggested improvements. Ira Jacknis also read and commented on the manuscript. As a historian writing about anthropology, I am grateful for Wendy and Ira's suggestions and improvements. Others who gave help and advice along the way were Colin Browne, Bob Brooks, Keith Carlson, Sharon Keen, Jeff Keshen, Tony Marcano, Daniel Marshall, Patricia Roy, Keith Sorrenson, Jon Swainger, Allan Wade and Michael Nicoll Yahgulanaas. Thanks to the

Noshers for their encouragement, the Collings Foundation for the Liberator ride and Bluewater Adventures for the trip to SG̱ang Gwaay. As those who know me well would expect, I did not follow all of the advice that I was given about writing this life of Wilson Duff and for that I bear the responsibility. It was a pleasure to work with the people at Harbour Publishing as they turned my manuscript into a better book. My thanks to everyone involved for also navigating through the pandemic and bringing this book into harbour.

I am also extremely grateful to all those who gave me their time to meet and talk about Wilson. As I was interviewing those who knew him, I felt like I was following his example of ethnography by talking to people. Each person that I spoke to added a piece to this picture of Wilson coming back in this biography. Their names are in the bibliography with my sincere thanks. Some of those that I spoke to have since passed on and we are the worse for that. Each one was a "bright tile" in the mosaic that made up Wilson's world.[7] Among the many conversations I was fortunate to do a wonderful, insightful interview with the First Nations artist Roy Henry Vickers. At the end of the conversation, as he was getting up to leave, Roy turned to me and said, "You know, you will figure out a lot about Wilson, but you will not figure it all out."[8] He was absolutely correct. This book is my version of the story of Wilson Duff as best I can tell it. In the writing of it, I often said to myself, and sometimes to others, "If it is not interesting, it is not Wilson's fault."

Eagle—Full Circle, in memory of Wilson Duff.

Image courtesy of Roy Henry Vickers

1. Vancouver Boyhood

Just inside the front door of Roy Henry Vickers's Eagle Aerie Gallery in Tofino there was once a magnificent screen print dedicated to the memory of Wilson Duff. The print was called *Eagle—Full Circle*. Its form was in the classic Northwest Coast style: black formlines, red features, split *U*s, ovoids and salmon-trout heads. The eagle's head with a curved beak encircled by its wings is central to the image. Below the eagle is the face of a woman, a mother, for it is with her that we all begin. For the artist, the print represents how, in our journey through life, we continue to complete circles.[1] Wilson would have appreciated the form and, even more, the meaning of the image. It is an idea that he would have loved since he too would come to know that life is a cycle. As he put it himself in two lines that he called "Spirit Quest":

> When at last I got all the way there
> What I found was myself coming back.[2]

Wilson's own spirit quest circle began and was completed in Vancouver, British Columbia.

For one so brilliant, creative and, in the end, complex, Wilson Duff came from ordinary beginnings. He grew up in a working-class family in the Cedar Cottage neighbourhood of South Vancouver. Born to the Northwest Coast, he lived most of his life there. There were sojourns away: three years across Canada and then to India as a young man, and a year at the National Museum in Ottawa as an anthropologist. But for the rest of his life Wilson lived on and loved the Northwest Coast. He devoted most of his life to understanding its First Nations people and communicating that knowledge to others.

Wilson, the Vancouver boy, grew up in a city of mostly British immigrants working to make their way on an economic roller coaster that, when it plunged, as it did in the 1930s, created much anxiety for the parents of a growing family. Wilson's parents came to Canada from the Celtic fringe of Great Britain: his father from Ireland and his mother from Scotland. Wilson Duff Sr. was born in Liverpool in 1886, but his parents were from Islandmagee on the east coast of County Antrim, just north of Belfast. Like many Irish they had probably gone to Liverpool looking for work, but they returned to Islandmagee where Wilson Duff Sr. did most of his growing up. As a young man he apprenticed in the Belfast shipyards. Wilson's mother, Annie (who was later known as Nan) Hislop, was born in 1894 in Stirling, on the southern edge of the Scottish Highlands, but she lived with her family in Edinburgh before coming to Vancouver.

Like many Vancouver immigrants at the time, Wilson's parents both arrived while they were still single: Wilson Duff Sr. just before, and Annie Hislop just after, the First World War. They both came with other family members, and both had members of their extended family already on the West Coast, so while they were single, they each had family around them. Single immigrants often came to Vancouver from Britain for two reasons: for the potential for jobs and for marriage partners. Wilson and Annie found both. They met and courted while they were both living in the Jericho area of Point Grey. Wilson lived with his parents, Hugh and Martha, near Jericho Hill School, where Hugh was the head steward— Wilson was a plumber and pipefitter, working on new houses. Annie and her mother both lived and worked in the mansion home of the Spencers; the family owned a chain of department stores, including the big flag-ship store in downtown Vancouver. Annie worked as a seamstress for the Spencers. Wilson and Annie were married in the summer of 1921, when he was thirty-five and she was twenty-seven. They were of an age that they wanted to start a family, and so they set up house on Windsor Street in South Vancouver.

Their first son, Wilson Duff, was born on Monday, March 23, 1925. He was the middle child of the family: he had an older sister, Winifred, who was three years older, and a younger brother, Ron, who arrived two years later. Family memory has it that Ron was intended to be a boyhood mate for Wilson, but growing up and throughout his life Wilson was actually closer to his sister, Win. As the eldest son, Wilson was given the family name that he shared with his father, although it came not from his father's father but from the distaff side of the family. Wilson's great-uncle, Wilson Dick, had not immigrated and still lived on Islandmagee, but the young Wilson would visit him in his late teens. Presumably to avoid confusion in the Duff household in Vancouver, Wilson growing up was called Junior.

*

The Vancouver of the mid-1920s that Wilson was born into was a city in the midst of booming growth. The Vancouver economy had taken a few years to bounce back after the First World War and the boom would not last very long. In the mid-twenties the economy was roaring, jobs were available and the city was building and spreading out. Home ownership was possible even for those without a lot of money, and so Vancouver was a city of single-family houses at all levels of the social scale. In the growing suburbs of South Vancouver, British immigrant working-class families lived in smaller houses called *cottages*. The Cedar Cottage area lay between the cities of Vancouver and New Westminster. The growth of the area was connected to two major transportation lines: the British Columbia Electric Railway's interurban tramway ran through Cedar Cottage and, later, when the automobile became the preferred method of transportation, the Westminster Highway, now Kingsway, was the major thoroughfare. The British Columbia Electric Railway also ran the street-car system on the north–south streets that connected South Vancouver to the City of Vancouver. The logic of these transportation links was realized when South Vancouver was amalgamated into the City of Vancouver in 1929. In the 1920s Cedar Cottage was accessible: building lots were avail-able and relatively cheap, and so the area attracted young working-class families who looked hopefully to the future. The year 1929 was, alas, sig-nificant for another reason.

Early in the development of Cedar Cottage, someone had built a roller coaster near the business centre around the 3500 block of Commercial Drive. It did not survive long, but it can still stand as a metaphor for the ups and downs in the area. The dizzying heights of the 1920s were only accentuated by the deep plunge into the Depression of the 1930s, as bright optimism faded into shades of anxious grey. The Great Depression was devastating for Vancouver and the Duff family along with it. As prices for goods plummeted, thousands were thrown out of work or saw their income drastically reduced. Through much of the 1930s more than a quarter of the Vancouver workforce was out of work. The single unemployed were the largest group but, by the fall of 1930, 4,503 married men had applied for unemployment assistance and there were undoubtedly others who were too proud to ask for help.[3] Married men who were unemployed or underemployed usually had families to worry about, which only added to their stress. For them, providing for one's family was the measure of a man. Many could no longer afford their houses and, though the population of the city increased over the decade, the value of building permits dropped to a fraction of what it had been in the twenties. No area of the city was hit harder than working-class suburbs like Cedar Cottage.

Like most of Vancouver's workers, Wilson's father was employed through the 1920s. He worked as a plumber for Kydd Brothers Hardware and later for Murray Brothers, a heating contracting company. The *British Columbia Directories* suggest that he was not working for a firm after 1929,[4] presumably because the house construction sector had collapsed, and so he was underemployed for most of a decade, working on houses when he could. The Duffs were not destitute, but making ends meet certainly was a struggle. Like building permits, housing lot prices had dropped to a mere fraction of what they had been before the crash, so Wilson Sr. bought two at the corner of Lanark Street and East Twenty-First Avenue. Working with a contractor friend, he built two very similar houses that were also not unlike the house where they were living on Windsor Street: fairly straightforward construction with the roof ridge running front to back and a dormer window on one side. They may well have been built following one of the pattern books for workers' cottages that were readily available. The houses were built as spec houses, to be sold, but under the depressed conditions they were only able to sell one, so the Duff family moved the few blocks from Windsor Street into the corner house. On Lanark, they lived among working-class families, many of whom were British immigrants, living on streets with names like Inverness, Dumfries and Culloden. They were a block away from what is now Knight Street and the growing commercial centre on Kingsway. Their house was not pretentious: two storeys with a basement for the furnace, and each floor made up of small, enclosed spaces. There was a living room with an open fireplace and a small kitchen from which everything had to be carried to the dining room for meals. A narrow, steep set of stairs led up to small bedrooms on the second floor. It was here, amidst his own family and a community of families coping with challenging times, that Wilson spent his school years. By today's standards the house was cramped, with little space for five people to have much privacy. His need for solitude would become an issue for Wilson.

The house on Windsor was right across the street from Charles Dickens Elementary School, where Wilson may have done part of his first school year. After they moved to Lanark Street, all three of the Duff children continued to attend Charles Dickens, even though they were slightly outside its catchment area. Crossing Knight Street, they walked the few blocks to the school. Most children were taken to their first day of school by their mothers, and big sister Win would also have been there to show Junior the ropes. A child's expectations of school were instilled by parents and older siblings: Wilson's parents placed great value on education as a path to a better future in uncertain times, and sister Win did very well at school so was a role model. In Wilson's day, Charles Dickens was an imposing brick building like many built in Vancouver, designed to impress the community with the gravity and importance of schooling. The population growth in Cedar Cottage required the school to be expanded in 1925 to twenty classrooms, with a gymnasium that could accommodate close to five hundred pupils.[5] The teaching within, however, was formal and uninspired.

Even an effort by the provincial minister of education to overhaul the elementary curriculum in the mid-thirties made little difference in the classroom. Teachers at Charles Dickens followed traditional, formal practices. Learning was largely by rote and involved constant drills on grammar, arithmetic and the facts of history and geography. Few teachers had the education or the opportunity to convey the joys of intellectual activity to pupils. Teachers faced salary cuts through the 1930s even though class sizes were large, and got larger, while Wilson was at Charles Dickens. Teachers often paid little attention to the needs of individual students. Discipline was rigid and enforced with corporal punishment if necessary. Nevertheless, it quickly became clear, even in this constrained school environment, that Wilson was a very bright student. He skipped all or part of grade two. His younger brother, Ron, who became a schoolteacher, later wondered whether Wilson, because he was now younger in his grade and a bit of an outsider, as well as being the eldest son, learned to be very competitive at school.[6] Certainly A was a regular grade on his record, and he was often the first- or second-ranked student in his class. IQ tests were becoming popular in North American schools, and when Wilson took such a test in his last year at elementary school he produced a score of 144, which by the standards of the day would put him in the very gifted or genius range.[7] On the other hand, Wilson's father, who firmly believed in education for practical purposes, would not have been pleased with his son's Cs in Manual Arts. In the future there would be no doubt that Wilson was blessed with a creative intellect and was capable of imagining original ideas, but these characteristics were not developed through his elementary education. The system discouraged independent thinking and provided little opportunity to be creative. Another student with an excellent academic record later recalled that they "just regurgitated."[8]

At home on Lanark Street, Wilson grew up in a household where the parents lived according to well-defined, traditional gender roles. Family life was structured and disciplined, father ruled the roost and no one dared sit in his armchair by the radio in the front room. His accustomed chair no doubt provided a measure of security, but Wilson Sr. also had his challenges. Being without paid work was a source of social, economic and psychological insecurity. Providing for his family was a struggle in difficult times, and he was a man of strong and definite views that were only made stronger by that experience. "My father was a competent, thoughtful man with a straightforward way of looking at life," recalled Ron, the younger and more easygoing son.[9] Wilson Sr. had worked hard to become a skilled tradesman and, like many others in the Depression, he correctly felt that the capitalist system had let him down. It is not surprising that he had socialist and perhaps communist leanings. While politics were one thing, religion was another. Wilson's father had seen its divisive effects in Ireland and had no time for organized religion. Some of Nan's family regarded him as an irredeemable atheist. Nan's mother, on the other hand, was a member of the Plymouth Brethren and was dogmatic and insistent about the importance of religion, constantly beleaguering the family about church attendance. Since she lived close by, both she and religion were sources of conflict in the family. Wilson's mother attended the United Church, but his father was clear that the children were not to be coerced on religious matters, so they were not regular churchgoers. Wilson's father also had health problems that seemed to have come from the workplace. He had a lung disease that would not have been helped by his persistent smoking of roll-your-own cigarettes all his life. At one point, while the children were still in elementary school, his lungs were so bad that the only treatment was complete bedrest. The family spent a summer in a cottage at Crescent Beach, on Boundary Bay in Surrey, a popular getaway for Vancouverites. The children had to be very quiet, so they played outside on the beach while their father recovered. By the end of the summer he was breathing normally again, but the lung disease would return. Life on Lanark during the Depression was no easy street for Wilson Sr., but in spite of that, or perhaps even because of it, he was a strong presence in the home. Wilson's father was a hard man, obdurate and demanding of his children.

Nan Duff, Wilson's mother, was the softer side of the family. She was the homemaker who cared for her children day to day—which was also not an easy task. Father provided and mother made do with what was provided, and what was provided was not always plentiful, so making do was hard work during the Depression. The children never went hungry or went to school in rags, as some in the neighbourhood did, but the care and nurture of three children was certainly a full-time job. Nan had that reputedly Scottish talent for making a penny go a long way. She cooked meals without any waste, made bread and canned fruit and vegetables. The Vancouver area offered opportunities for food-gathering outings that the children later recalled with pleasure. They picked blackberries at the University of British Columbia, gathered clams and crabs on the beaches and sometimes took Sunday outings to the log booms on the North Shore to go fishing. They never ate at a restaurant. Nan's skill as a seamstress went a long way toward clothing her children. Nan was strong in her way, and part of that strength was in providing for her children both physically and emotionally. In later life Wilson would speak of his mother with great affection, and she became his model of what a mother should be. She was a warm, caring person who was also the one who maintained contact with her wider family, on both the Duff and Hislop sides.

One member of Annie Duff's extended family was Wilson's cousin Mervyn, who was five years older than Wilson and who sometimes was around at Lanark Street. Against firm family advice, Annie's sister, Joyce, had married a doctor from Ceylon who had treated their father when they were still in Scotland. After the First World War the couple moved to India, where Mervyn Samarasinha was born in 1920. His father, now an army doctor, went to treat a typhus outbreak in a village, but he caught the disease himself and died. Mervyn and his widowed mother came to Vancouver, but Joyce seemed unable to cope with bringing up her child. Mervyn lived in foster homes, even after his mother remarried and he became Mervyn Davis. His loneliness and alienation at being passed around among foster parents, and growing up with the consequences of his mixed cultural background, may have been mitigated somewhat by visiting his cousins in the Duff family. He is present in photos of the extended family. Mervyn experienced the dirty thirties first-hand when the man who lived in a crowded tenement across the street lost his white-collar job and, after months of unemployment, took his own life. He watched the man's surviving family living in grinding poverty until the Depression was relieved by the Second World War. Mervyn witnessed the violence at Ballantyne Pier in 1935, when striking dockworkers seeking union recognition and improved conditions clashed with police. He also watched on Bloody Sunday, as unemployed protesters were forcibly evicted from the Vancouver Post Office after the police filled the building with tear gas in 1938. Mervyn developed the sense that much was amiss with the status quo in Depression-era Vancouver, and he became more involved with the left-wing movement.[10] As he grew into a young man, Mervyn related to Wilson Sr.'s progressive social and political ideas. Wilson Jr. and Mervyn's lives would intersect again in the future.

Wilson's own memories of childhood were mixed. As an adult he would describe a traumatic experience at the age of two when his mother went to the hospital for the birth of Ron. He was taken along as well, to have his tonsils out and to be circumcised. He remembered being taken away from his parents by a nurse, yelling and screaming. But was it a real memory or a reconstruction based, say, on later family conversations? A particularly bright child—and Wilson certainly was that—might have a genuine memory from the age of two, but it would be unusual. Whether it was his own memory or reconstructed after the event, it was real and lived in him as a moment when he felt abandoned by his parents. That memory and its recall both represented and nurtured Wilson's fragile sensitivity, which was always a part of his makeup and which became more apparent in later life as, increasingly, achievement became a thin disguise.

As a child growing up, Wilson received encouragement on many things from his parents. The Duffs were a family of readers. Wilson's father had a strong mind and was constantly turning over thoughts. He devoured books and he encouraged, indeed probably insisted, that his children read a lot. They owned very few books, but once a week their mother took the streetcar to the Carnegie Library at the corner of Main and Hastings Streets and came home with an armload of books for the family to read. They read mostly biographies, travel books and social commentary. Sometimes they even read at the dinner table, though it was a practice that Win objected to. Reading led to discussion, discussion to debate, and debates became arguments that were often intense and noisy. Politics, religion, schooling, work and how to make ends meet were all on the table, where father dominated and mother mediated. At times it became too much for Wilson. As he grew older he needed to retreat from the commotion of five people in a tight space to find privacy and solitude. He set up a table and chair for himself down in the basement near the coal chute, where he could read, study and think in relative peace and quiet. Down in the seclusion of the coal cellar, Wilson took refuge in excellence and striving for perfection in his schoolwork. The need to seek the bliss of solitude never left him.

The Duff kids did have some fun. Wilson's brother, Ron, the youngest of the three, certainly had fond memories of his family and everyone's place in it. Entertainment came from the radio, a big 1927 Kolster that sat in the front room. They listened to comedy shows like Jack Benny and Fred Allen, radio plays, music and the news. *The Shadow*, with its opening line, "Who knows what evil lurks in the hearts of men?" came on at noon, and the boys would rush home from school to listen as they wolfed down their lunch before they ran back to school. They had an organ in the front room and Win took lessons for a while, so there was music in the house.

And then there was the outdoors, which was another world. Although its suburbs had spread expansively in the previous decade, in the 1930s Vancouver was still a city of green spaces and undeveloped areas. Between Vancouver and South Vancouver there were still open green spaces. For Cedar Cottage people, Trout Lake was popular: kids went skinny-dipping in the summer and, if it froze over, skating in the winter. Another boy who grew up in South Vancouver recalled the back lanes as his territory and how they came alive with "honey bees and darning needles, garter snakes and blackberry bushes, pebbles and puddles" and there was very seldom any traffic to inhibit boys at play. The only traffic in the lanes were the intermittent delivery men coming to the back doors with milk in glass bottles, coal to go down the chute, wood for the fire or vegetables for sale.[11] Wilson and Ron had a bicycle, one between them, so like Knights Templar sharing their steed in hard times, they charged around the unpaved streets and back alleys of their neighbourhood. They would also have played the schoolyard games of the day such as Kick the Can, Nobbies (loosely related to lacrosse), and Duck the Rock. On outings together, the family seemed to gravitate to the shoreline, perhaps because Wilson Sr. grew up on Islandmagee, which, though it is actually a peninsula, is almost completely surrounded by the sea. Family day trips were often to the beach, and the summer spent at Crescent Beach was great fun for the kids. The connection with the sea was reinforced when Wilson's father acquired a piece of land across the American border on Point Roberts, perched on the cliff overlooking what is now the Salish Sea. He carved out a building platform and built a cottage facing the sea, where the family would spend time in the summer and on weekends. The area became much more accessible from Vancouver with the completion of the Pattullo Bridge at New Westminster in 1937. Point Roberts was a place where the family could relax together, creating memories of happy times when they gathered on the beach and ate crabs picked out of the sea. For the rest of his life, the beach cottage at Point Roberts was a refuge where Wilson Jr. could find a measure of solace above the storm tides of life.[12]

*

As he became a teenager, Wilson continued to shine at school and felt the pressure to do so at home, particularly from his father. He already had a drive for knowledge and a passion for learning, but for his father, learning for its own sake, as an intellectual activity, was a luxury. Rather, schooling was about preparing for a practical job and a secure future. Though she did very well at school, there was no question of his daughter heading toward university, so Win was sent to Grandview High School of Commerce, where girls learned to be secretaries. His father expected that Wilson would take up a trade like plumbing or perhaps become an engineer.

In accordance with his father's wishes, after he turned thirteen, during his last term at Charles Dickens, in the fall of 1938, Wilson went on to Vancouver Technical High School. Entering that school, he might well have raised his eyes above the front door and reflected upon the relief sculpture there, which depicted two rather buxom angels greeting several male representatives of various trades, presumably at the gates of heaven.

Today there is a plaque in the front foyer that tells us the school was founded by J. George Lister, described as the father of technical education in British Columbia. The school's modest beginnings were in 1916, in the basement of King Edward High School, but under Lister it was soon moved to downtown Vancouver, into a space at the Labour Temple. Even after that move, Lister had bigger and better things in mind. These plans came to fruition in 1928, when the school moved into a very substantial purpose-built building on Broadway, at the corner of what is now Penticton Street. With more space, the school grew and became the largest technical school in western Canada. Lister was the principal at the Broadway location for two years before he passed away and was succeeded by James Sinclair, who led the school when Wilson was a pupil. While his father prescribed the trades, Wilson moved to the matriculation stream in his second year at high school, which would allow for other options, including the possibility of university, after graduation. Trades were then the prerogative of men and so, when Wilson started at Van Tech as it was known in 1938, the school was, as it always had been, for boys only. That policy would soon change, with lifelong effects for Wilson.

Through the four years that Wilson was studying at Van Tech, the patterns of family relationships at home were subtly shifting. By the fall of 1938, when Wilson started high school, the Depression was beginning to lift a little in Vancouver and work became more readily available. After the outbreak of the Second World War in 1939, Vancouver became a major centre for shipbuilding to supply merchant marine and naval vessels. Wilson Sr. got a steady, well-paying job in 1940 as a foreman in a shipbuilding plant. Things became easier financially for the family and, as a result, possibilities began to open up. There were many families in

Cedar Cottage who could not afford to have their children complete high school, let alone go to university, but that was not so for the Duffs—or at least for the boys. The parents also felt that they could afford to make trips to "the old country." Wilson Sr. went in 1938 and Nan took the trip in 1939, narrowly missing the outbreak of the war as she came back across the Atlantic. Wilson would not have enjoyed having his mother away and his father as the sole parent. He was constantly instructing Wilson to get on and do things. Ron recalled that Wilson was always on the go, not only at his father's behest but also because that was his nature. At the same time, Wilson felt that he was striving to meet his father's expectations and failing. He was also increasingly uncomfortable with being known as Junior, denoting as it did a clear relationship to his father. Wilson always felt that, no matter how hard he tried and whatever he achieved, he never measured up to his father's expectations. He later recalled 1939 as the year that he "wrote off" his father, adding that the trouble with being a father figure "is that people have to pull free of their fathers and often end up hating them."[13] Perhaps in reaction to his father, Wilson remained very close to his mother, the parent of the softer, caring side of his character. Rejecting his father was not complete in a single year, and he would continue to be Junior for some time. There would also be other father figures in his future. Nonetheless, as a fourteen-year-old teenager, Wilson was certainly kicking over the traces of paternal expectations.

He was growing up, things were changing at home, and Wilson threw himself into all aspects of school life with verve and enthusiasm. In contrast to the insecurities and failure that he felt at home, Wilson was outstanding in all that he did at school. The Van Tech ethos was made clear in the 1939 yearbook, where the headmaster addressed those who were leaving. The boys had been taught by "manly teachers" in an atmosphere of fair play in sport. He noted that physical strength is all well and good, but much more important is "strength of mind, strength of will, strength of purpose—strength of mind to set a course, strength of will to persist in that course, and strength of purpose to see the end in view and keep striving to attain it."[14] We can safely assume that Wilson read these words and took them to heart during his time at high school. During his first two years, Wilson took a range of subjects both academic and technical, but in his second two years, following his interest and his strengths, he took mostly academic subjects. In his graduating year he was in the top of seven streamed grade twelve classes. Most final grades were designated by letter, and Wilson had six As and two Bs in his eight subjects. Two other technical subjects had numerical grades and, while they were respectable, things like woodworking were clearly not his forte.[15] His high school grades reflect that Wilson was focused on the academic side of schoolwork. He always completed his homework. In the subjects that he preferred—English, Social Studies, Science and Mathematics—his grades got better and better through his high school years. Clearly, he set the course, persisted and strove to attain it. What is less clear, however, is whether his success at school did much to diminish his sense of inadequacy at home. Ron, who was two grades behind Wilson when he got to Van Tech, remembered that his brother was so driven and accomplished that Ron despaired of ever being able to emulate him.[16] At high school Wilson studied hard, and he also played hard.

The competitive side of Wilson Duff came out on the sports fields of Van Tech, where he was a force to be reckoned with. He excelled in track and field. In grade eleven he set a new school record in the broad jump, placed second in the 100- and 400-yard sprints, and tied with another student as junior champion. In his final year his broad jump was even longer, he came second in the 100- and 200-yard races, and he won the 400-yard dash. These athletic achievements made him Van Tech's champion athlete in his final school year. In that year he was also on the senior rugby team. He played at wing three-quarter, a position that often calls for individual flair, raw speed and fancy footwork, as well as defensive ability. At the end of the year he reflected that he wished that he had been able to get more than a ten-yard run on the rugby field, meaning that either the ball was not getting along the back line to him or the other team's defences were always closing him down. Nevertheless, he was as much on the ball on the rugby field as he was in the classroom; in the notes about Wilson in his graduating yearbook he was simply described as "our track and rugger star."[17]

Far from the playing fields of Van Tech was a world of conflict that would soon come close to home for Wilson and his school friends. His high school years were overshadowed by the growing likelihood of war. Wilson was fourteen, in his second year at high school, when war was declared in Europe, and he was sixteen when the Japanese carried out their devastating attack on Pearl Harbor in December of 1941. The coming of war was evident at school in a number of ways. The technical training that Van Tech offered was valuable to the armed forces, so several classrooms were turned over to them, and there were soldiers and airmen around the school. The military cadet system for school students was also being ramped up, and Wilson participated fully. In his second year he led squad drills as a cadet major in the first Vancouver Technical High School Army Cadet battalion. But it was the air force, and particularly the heroics of the Royal Air Force during the battle of Britain, that really captured the imagination of Tech boys. In the fall of 1941 the pupils voted to become part of the Air Cadet League of Canada. When Fifty-Seven Air Cadet Wing was set up for Vancouver high schools, Van Tech had the first eight squadrons. The Air Cadets were designed to be feeder units to the Royal Canadian Air Force. Wilson joined immediately. They were allotted two times a week for drilling and, for some reason known only to the military mind, musketry. The cadets also visited local airfields, and there was great excitement when some went up in an aircraft for the first time.[18] Wilson would have been attracted to the Air Cadets by the more academic side of the training: elementary navigation, the theory of flight, air force mathematics, map reading, aircraft recognition and drawing—all subjects that he would later return to in much greater detail. In his annual message in the school yearbook, the principal stressed the obligation to serve one's country in the war effort. He noted that several Van Tech boys had already joined the Royal Canadian Air Force and reflected upon the "infinitely sad...news of the passing of a boy who only recently was carefree and joyous around the school."[19] Other former students who were now airmen returned to speak to the school assembly and reinforced the message of the value, importance and excitement of serving in the air force. Twice during Wilson's time at Van Tech the yearbook carried a story about the principal's son, also named James Sinclair, who was a Van Tech graduate, a flight lieutenant in the RCAF and a recently elected member of Parliament. Neither he nor the Van Tech students knew that the younger James Sinclair would one day be father-in-law to one Canadian prime minister and grandfather of another,[20] but he was already a figure who could appeal to boys imagining their future in the context of wartime. Wilson would have listened carefully to, and later thought about, the words of all the former students who were now serving in the armed forces and came back to speak at their old school. The class photo taken in his grade twelve year shows Wilson as one of three students proudly wearing their Air Cadet uniforms.

The demands of the Canadian war effort had another major impact on the Vancouver Technical High School. With so many men away in the armed forces, there was a growing demand for women with technical skills in the workforce. Responding to this need, rather than its cultural inclination, Van Tech admitted girls to its halls for the first time in December of 1941. There was a fair amount of fluttering among the boys as the girls arrived on the scene. The editor of the yearbook welcomed them, but he also made comments about the boys' serenity being disturbed "by a ceaseless cacophony of girlish giggles."[21] Oddly perhaps, the principal did not mention the arrival of the girls in his message for that year. Whatever might have been the reservations among boys and teachers, the school came to have a very different atmosphere once it became coed. Wilson, for one, would have watched the appearance of three hundred girls at his school with great interest.

By the time that he was sixteen going on seventeen and in grade twelve, Wilson, according to his graduation write-up in the school yearbook, "Seems to have some strange attraction for the weaker sex across the way (is it his good looks?)."[22] Certainly he was a good-looking teenager, physically fit and active, with luminous blue eyes that were looking brightly at the future. He had become, as the old fortune-telling rhyme describes it, "Monday's child" who "is fair of face," successful in all that he was doing at school. Yet he did not have the arrogance that often went with accomplishment in the young. On the contrary, Wilson was shy and diffident, which only made him more attractive to many young women. The attraction must have been mutual: one of his boyish ambitions as he graduated from school was to be able to drive a truck and shift gears with one hand so, presumably, the other arm could be around a girlfriend.[23] Initially, as the girls arrived and moved into their own wing on the east side of the school, there was supposed to be no mixing of the sexes during school hours. It was a naive notion that could not last. Boys and girls met each other after school, of course, and both took part in official school athletics. Then one of the physical education teachers started a square dancing club after school. Wilson was recognized as a leading athlete and soon he became an avid dancer. It was through these activities that he met Marion Barber.

Only a few months younger than Wilson but a grade behind him at school, Marion Jane Barber came from a family of Irish and English background but with greater means than the Duffs. Her grandfather Francis Henry Barber came to Vancouver with his family at the end of the nineteenth century and founded what would become the Restmore Manufacturing Company, which produced mattresses, beds and furniture. Over time, the family business survived the Depression and became very successful. Early in the development of his business, Francis Barber travelled up the Fraser Valley into the Hope area in search of good lumber. He particularly loved the lie of the land around where Hunter Creek runs into the Fraser River, so in the 1920s he built a lodge close to the St. Elmo railway station so that people, including the Barber family, could spend a relaxing weekend out of Vancouver. Over the years he acquired other properties and developed other interests, including a farm, a sawmill and a fishing camp, in the area between Hope and Laidlaw. A record of his involvement in the area survives in the form of the FH Barber Provincial Park, on the banks of the Fraser near Laidlaw. Francis Barber's eldest son,

Thomas, Marion's father, was brought into the business and would eventually take it over. Marion was born, on October 26, 1925, into a family that operated a successful business in Vancouver and often went out to the Hope area, where they mixed business and pleasure. Marion grew up on East Broadway close to Commercial Drive. She started her high schooling at Britannia High School, but at the end of 1941 she was part of the first cohort of girls to be admitted to Vancouver Technical High School, located closer to the family home, about seven blocks east on Broadway. There she met Wilson.

In some ways, but not all, Wilson and Marion were well matched. She, too, was accomplished and involved at school. She took the same academic subjects as Wilson, along with a number of practical subjects, like typing, clothing and retail. Like Wilson's sister, Win, Marion was probably heading for secretarial or retail work, but she got particularly strong grades in subjects that reflected her interests: especially art, design and music.[24] She also took part in student life at the school. Marion was president of a student club that organized events to encourage the appreciation of fine arts and music.[25] She was also an accomplished school athlete who in her final year was, as Wilson was, Van Tech's junior champion, having accumulated exactly the same number of points as Wilson did the year before. Marion and Wilson shared some interests, yet at the same time they had different personalities. Marion was gregarious and outgoing and liked to socialize, while Wilson was much more inward-looking and reserved. When Wilson left Van Tech, it was Ron who went square dancing and walked home with Marion, and in this way she kept in contact with Wilson and his family. Ron later recalled that it was Marion who set her cap for Wilson, and Wilson, in his way, responded. But even as a teenager, Wilson's studies and training with the air force in mind were his priorities.[26] Though there was a growing understanding that Marion was Wilson's girl, neither of them imagined what twists and turns lay along their future pathways.

And on the theme of the unpredictable, even Raven, that mythic rascal of the Northwest Coast, intruded his inquisitive beak into Wilson's

34

high school years. Growing up in South Vancouver, Wilson would have had very little contact with Indigenous people, except perhaps for the occasional Musqueam woman coming to the back door on Lanark Street to sell woven baskets. Raven's manifestation came through a story featured at the beginning of the school yearbook, *The Vantech*, in each of Wilson's final two years at school. One was a version, one of the many, of the story of Raven releasing daylight into the world.[27] The Northwest Coast "legends" were adapted from a collection compiled by a vice-principal at nearby Lord Selkirk Elementary School. *The Vantech* also sometimes carried Māori legends from the yearbook of the Auckland Technical College in New Zealand. An accompanying editorial comment reflected the prejudices of the era: the Māori resembled the Indians of the Northwest Coast, noted the editor, as both "are credulous to a degree" and "both express a child-like faith in the legends handed down through countless generations."[28] As an avid reader, Wilson would have seen this simple-minded stuff that was typical of the day, but what he made of it we cannot say. What we can safely say is that Raven's presence in Wilson's boyhood consciousness was only fleeting.

*

When he finished high school in the spring of 1942, Wilson had his sights set on the Royal Canadian Air Force and could have signed up at seventeen and a half in September. Some boys slipped in underage, but Wilson did not push the issue and decided on doing a year at the University of British Columbia first. With his father having found better-paying, stable employment in the shipyards of Vancouver, the family could contemplate the financial side of Wilson going to university. This contribution to his future was very significant in a community where many could not afford higher education for their children, even the boys. In the summer between high school and university he had a job as a timber cruiser for the HR MacMillan forestry company that would become part of the merger that created MacMillan Bloedel a decade later. The forestry company provided Wilson with a scholarship for his first year at the University of British Columbia. He registered in the Faculty of Arts and Science and took science courses along with English and psychology, though his intention was to go into forestry. That choice probably reflected the degree to which his father, who would have approved of a practical subject since it would likely lead to a secure career, still had some influence. As he had been at school, Wilson was serious and focused on his university course work, achieving high grades in all his subjects. He took a mathematics course from Walter Gage, who was ten years into building his legendary reputation as a teacher who could pack the halls with students. Wilson later strongly advised brother Ron when he started at the university to take a course from Gage, writing that "he is a prince."[29] Great teaching produced great learning, and Wilson's highest grades were in mathematics. The ease with which he took to mathematics would serve him well in the next phase of his life.[30] At the same time, a large part of him was just biding his time. As soon as final exams were over in the spring semester, Wilson, along with nearly fifty other University of British Columbia students, signed up for the Royal Canadian Air Force. In the group photo taken to mark the occasion he can be seen shyly peeking out between two other faces.[31] That day must have been one of both excitement and trepidation. If it is possible for one day to change a life, Wilson's Vancouver boyhood ended then, on March 26, 1943, three days after his eighteenth birthday.

It is a moment, perhaps, at which to ask, How much is the man to be found in the boy? A simple response would be that, while much there was, much was yet to come. The child of an overbearing father and a nurturing mother, Wilson was brilliant, sensitive and insecure. His self-doubts would have made little sense to those who did not know him well, because striving for perfection he had excelled in all that he tackled at school. Those school years held many portents for the future. Wilson and Marion had met and become friends, but there would be many diversions along the path of love. The principal of Van Tech was fond of reminding graduating students that "the race is not always to the strong," to which he might well have added, completing the thought from Ecclesiastes, because time and chance happen to us all.[32] And we should hold that thought, for Raven, trickster and creator, would make further appearances within the life cycle of Wilson Duff.

2. I, the Navigator

In many of the First Nations cultures that Wilson Duff would learn to know so well, young men were often sent away from the accustomed home culture to another place, particularly if they were destined for greater things that required deeper spiritual understanding. They sought solitude in a quest to find a stronger sense of themselves that would better prepare them for their life to come. Wilson also went through a rite of passage that took him from adolescence to adulthood. He left the family home and went far away to a very different place and a very different life. His was not a solitary experience, although he did find times and places for thought and contemplation. As an airman, he mastered the science, and the magic, of navigating a heavy bomber to a distant target and back again in one piece. Aircraft navigation in wartime was both exacting and complex, and the lives of others depended on it. Wilson, though he was too modest to say it to anyone but his mother, excelled at it. As a flyer in combat, he lived with danger and fear and looked death in the face. Through all this experience he gained some mastery over himself; he returned to Vancouver with the confidence to proclaim to his family that he would no longer be called Junior: he was Wilson Duff.

After signing up to join the Royal Canadian Air Force in March 1943, Wilson had to wait to receive word of his assignment before he began the lengthy training process. In early 1943 there was a large backlog of young men who had signed up but not yet started their training, so the wait could have been even longer than it turned out to be. In early May he was called up to report to Manning Depot Three in Edmonton for the first phase of his education as an airman. For Wilson, as for most young men leaving home to join the armed services, saying goodbye to family and to a sweetheart was a difficult moment because the future was so uncertain.

*

For many airmen, home remained their anchor and letters from home were their lifelines. Throughout his service in the RCAF, Wilson always wrote first to his mother, and the letters were usually sent to "the best mother in the world" and signed "Your loving son."[1] Wilson was not alone among flyers in being particularly close to his mother and ambivalent about his father.[2] He may have assumed that his father would also read the letters, but he rarely wrote specifically to him. He did write on occasion to other members of the family, particularly his sister, Win, in letters that had a much more familiar and breezy tone than those to his mother. Like his fellow airmen, Wilson craved letters from home as his link to normal life, so his mother, Nan, heard about it when there were gaps in the flow of letters from her. After writing regularly to his mother throughout the war, Wilson thought that perhaps she knew him better now than if he had stayed at home "because I think I write more and better than I talk."[3] Wilson told his mother as much as he could or wanted to about his experience; but his letters were limited by air force censorship, by what an eighteen-year-old would not want to tell his mother, and by the very real concern that family members were worrying about the dangers that he was facing. Flyers were often close to their mothers and tended to be casual rather than committed in their romantic relationships. Wilson also wrote to Marion and complained when replies seemed slow, but he clearly understood that the uncertainties of wartime made long-term planning for any future seem pointless, even if an eighteen-year-old were inclined that way. And furthermore, for the next three years in the air force, Wilson would be living largely in the company and comradeship of men.

The sorrow of leaving home was partly relieved, once he was on his way, by excitement and anticipation. Arriving at the Edmonton Exhibition grounds, where Manning Depot Three was located, Wilson became one of the more than 130,000 aircrew trained in Canada during the Second World War.[4] Certainly other young men joining the air force had not the slightest concern about what lay ahead. Like them, Wilson was consumed by what he believed was the beginning of a great adventure.[5] It would, however, be another eighteen months of intensive learning, interspersed with periods of waiting and boredom, before he began combat flying.

The British Commonwealth Air Training Plan, established by an agreement in 1939 between Canada and Britain, and also involving Australia and New Zealand, was a vital part of Canada's contribution to the Allied war effort. Canada was chosen as the location for this training program because many parts of the country offered good flying conditions removed from the theatres of war in Europe and later the Pacific. Negotiating the agreement to establish the program was challenging because Canada insisted that it had to be in command of the training, even though most graduates served in British Royal Air Force squadrons rather than Canadian ones. It was a huge logistical challenge to set up the program to train thousands of aircrew: it eventually involved 105 flight training schools, 184 support units and a staff of 104,000.[6] It cost something like $30,000 to train each pilot or navigator. The initial agreement was to run it until March 1943, the month that Wilson enlisted, but an extension had already been renegotiated in 1942 to improve the quality of instruction and to give Canada more say in the assignment of graduates to the various commands and squadrons. The aircrew training program was such a massive national undertaking that it prompted the president of the United States to call Canada the "aerodrome of democracy."[7]

*

Wilson's air training experience was a mixture of chaos and order. The chaos arose from over a thousand young men, aged seventeen to twenty-five and mostly unknown to each other, being thrown together for the first time. They slept in dormitories with two rows of double bunks accommodating about sixty. There were hijinks and banter and, after lights out at ten o'clock, farting and, eventually, snoring. They showered in a communal facility with a dozen others. One trainee, who was at Manning Depot Two in Brandon at the same time that Wilson was in Edmonton, wondered why he had left his safe and gentle Saskatchewan home "for this barn full of rude, nude raucous strangers."[8] Some were very lonely in this rambunctious male culture. Many who recalled Manning Depot in later years remembered the total lack of privacy, which hardly would have suited Wilson. Two of the main recreations at Manning Depot, which were also part of training for the air force, were drinking beer and singing. Flyers were legendary for their drinking, although Wilson claimed, at least in writing to his mother, that he had not yet had his first beer. Air force men had a robust repertoire of songs about the foibles of military life and disrespectful senior officers, and raunchy ditties about women and sex.

A third recreation of flyers, which Wilson certainly did participate in, was chasing girls. The trainees came from homes and a society where sex and talk about sex were repressed. Now they were in the company of mostly adolescent boys with sex on their minds and the freedom to talk about it, "incessantly," it was said. Some, in later life, admitted the sex was more talked about than realized, yet claimed that they joined the air force just to meet girls. Certainly there was an aura of glamour and romance around flyers and flying. The air force was the newest of the armed services, and it made a virtue of its youthful spirit. The flyboys, reaching for the skies in their ashy blue uniforms with Brylcreemed hair, attracted women.[9] Wilson and the guys would flirt with the girls who came to visit the zoo across the road from Manning Depot. Wilson went out with Dolly, the friend of a cousin, while he was in Edmonton, and there is a photograph of the two of them smiling at the camera in the RCAF scrapbook that he later compiled. He wrote to his mother about how, when he took her home at 1:30 Sunday morning, it was only half dark in the middle of the northern summer night but, just the same, it was dark enough. Wilson knew, however, that nothing was lasting, for tomorrow he would be in another place. In the next letter he asked his mother to tell Marion to hurry up and write.[10]

Those at Manning Depot always found some entertainment and there were lots of invitations to parties. An avid ballroom dancer ever since high school, Wilson revelled in that aspect of air force culture. Like most airmen, Wilson loved to go to Saturday-night dances. As well as being a very social activity, dancing is a ritual in which, through repetition and rhythm, we establish patterns and order where there may otherwise be chaos.[11] We can safely assume that Wilson had other things on his mind as an eighteen-year-old heading out to the Rainbow Ballroom on Whyte Avenue on a Saturday evening, but it was an idea that he entertained in later life.

During the three or four weeks that recruits spent at Manning Depot, the undisputed source for establishing order over adolescent chaos was the imposed discipline of air force rules and regulations. The bible was the *Manual of RCAF Drill and Ceremonial* and it was to be followed like holy writ.[12] On page one, the manual asserted that the "foundation of successful training is discipline." RCAF recruits had to take pride in themselves and their appearance, keep fit and co-operate with their fellows; this was how esprit de corps was built up. The following pages gave detailed instructions on matters such as drill and discipline, saluting, rifle exercises and ceremonial occasions. New recruits were given a number, Wilson's was K22196, and summer and winter uniforms that were often ill-fitting. They wore a white flash in the front of their wedge cap to indicate that they were aircrew trainees. The white flash was a source of pride, although some wags among the ground crews said it indicated that they had a venereal disease. Once in uniform, recruits spent much of their day—up at six and in bed by ten—polishing buttons, getting ready for kit inspections, making their beds with tightly mitered corners, doing physical exercises and, out on the parade ground, being yelled at by loud, sometimes foul-mouthed sergeants. There were endless and often undignified medical inspections and many inoculations. They even had their wisdom teeth removed because they were thought to be a risk at high altitude. There were also interviews, lectures and tests. During those few weeks, many of Wilson's contemporaries felt that they were the lowest form of human life. They were Aircraftsmen Second Class, AC2s, acey-deucys, or, according to air force slang, erks. Manning Depot was meant to eradicate any civilian notions of individualism and to discipline boys into being potential airmen. As one of them colourfully put it, the air force had them "by the short hairs."[13]

Yet, by his own account, Wilson seemed to thrive on the experience. Parts of it were demeaning, but he was driven by ambition, the pride of being in the air force, and his constant competition against himself and others. He made light of the hardships, writing about the six o'clock wake-up call "as we gaily arise to our daily round of fun and play." He reacted to the endless drilling on the parade ground by saying, "Who said education ends in the classroom?" He wrote that all the fellows got on well together, were having a great time and were "really living in high gear." There was a good library at Manning Depot and, though he could hardly have found much time for reading, he reminded his mother, "You know how I am when I get started on a good book." He also had her send his University of British Columbia grades when they came out; they were first-class and "caused quite a sensation among the boys." All this was perhaps putting a bright face on things for the benefit of the family, but he also told them when there were hiccups in his progress. After the first few weeks of training there was a delay before his move to Disposal Wing and the next phase of his training. Wilson was, as always, anxious to get on and, in his frustration, he wondered if the "old Duff luck has faltered, and wavered a bit." But then he further reflected that he had "no doubt...been endowed through heredity with the gift of tolerance."[14] In any event, his patience was not tested for too long and his belief in his luck was restored.

Toward the end of the training at Manning Depot the men were interviewed to determine their suitability for further training and the direction that it would take. When Wilson went for his interview he drew a "swell" officer who turned out to be an old-time dance enthusiast, so they got on well. "Same old luck," he thought. He emerged with an A-level designation, the highest category going forward to Initial Training School, the next level of preparation for aircrew. He was one of only six in his group to earn an A. Suddenly Manning was over and he was heading to Saskatoon for the next phase and, as he took the train across the Prairies that summer, he was sure that he was set on a clear course to his pilot's wings.

*

Wilson knew that the two months at Initial Training School would be intense and rigorous, so he warned the folks back home to expect fewer letters. This phase of training was largely on-the-ground work with occasional flying. He wrote with boyish excitement when he was issued flying gear: "It's really beautiful stuff, warm as Hell." It included an inner suit and an outer one about half an inch thick and covered with "miles and miles of zippers. Then there's helmet and goggles, lovely fur-lined boots and fur-lined gloves. It's the kind of stuff you see in pictures but never dream of wearing. (By the way I got a helmet 5 sizes larger than my head.)"[15] So it felt like he was heading in the right direction and would soon be up in the air. But there was still a lot of routine drilling and physical exercise, and even more thorough medical examinations, with particular attention to eyesight. Above all, there was the relentless classroom work, with homework at the end of each day and many tests to follow. The subjects covered were largely related to flying and so it all seemed more to the point. He learned about the theory of flight, aircraft recognition, meteorology, signals, Morse code and mathematics. Most challenging of all for most trainees, but not for Wilson, was navigation. After three weeks in the Link trainer that simulated the conditions of flying, he went up in an aircraft for the first time. It was a bumpy ride and he got slightly airsick, a reaction he would have to overcome because chronic airsickness would result in being "washed out" of the program. As at Manning Depot, Wilson thrived on it all. He was soon seen as a leader among the trainees and nominated as a "flight senior." He wrote that it was an honour to be nominated, and that he did not expect to get it but he did. He wrote to his mother a month in to say "I think my estimation of myself has increased about 100% since I came here" because he felt that he was doing so well in the program.[16] In that he was not mistaken.

The point of the Initial Training School program was, first, to establish whether the trainees were suitable for aircrew. The RCAF did not want borderline cases to continue and usually about 12 per cent did not make it through initial training.[17] The second objective of the program was to decide what role the trainees would play in an aircrew. About halfway through initial training Wilson started to think that he would raise his sights from pilot to navigator. Only two men were selected from each course to be navigators, but he thought that it was something to aim for. It may have been that he saw the writing on the wall and wanted to make it his choice rather than the selection board's decision. There was a real sense in the RCAF that the most demanding position in a bomber crew was not the pilot but the navigator. Most young men who volunteered for the air force wanted to be pilots, so they were surprised to be told right up front by the recruiting officers that flying an aircraft was as easy as driving a car; the more demanding position was navigator because he told the pilot what course to follow.[18] A bit of an exaggeration, perhaps, but navigators certainly had to absorb and interpret a large amount and variety of information, and Wilson was so strong in mathematics that it probably was a forgone conclusion that he would end up as a navigator. So the new target was selected and the course was set.

With his sights set higher, the initial training course became even more demanding. There was lots of material to cover in a short time and many exams. Wilson found it tougher than university. Midway through he had a forty-eight hour leave, but rather than going out on the town he stayed in the barracks because he was worn out. He had acquired a radio and caught up on music and the news. When the course was over he rested up and reported that "we are as lazy as dogs," though he immediately started to worry that he might get "rusty." To avoid that, he spent time studying in the base library, reasoning that "reading is not really wasting time, is it?" In fact he quickly had an idea about how the base library could be completely rearranged, "as I get a big kick out of doing things like that."[19] He got another big kick out of being highly successful and achieving his goal in the training program. He proudly telegraphed his mother that he had passed the aircrew selection board as a Navigator B, a bomber navigator, and he was congratulated by the commanding officer for having the highest average grade in the class of seventy. In the photo of the graduating class Wilson stands in front of the group with the officers who ran the program.[20]

When he left Saskatoon in mid-September 1943, he knew that his training as an air force navigator would continue over the winter: two months in Bombing and Gunnery School at Mountain View, near Belleville, Ontario, followed by five months in Air Observers School in Chatham, New Brunswick. The name change from Air Observer to Navigator was made when the role of bomb aimer and navigator was split up for many bomber crews, but a navigator still had to be able to do both. In the meantime he had a few days leave at home in Vancouver. Someone took a photograph of him with his arm around Marion: she is wearing his full flying kit and he displays the propeller insignia on the sleeve of his uniform, indicating that he had moved up from aircraftsman second class to leading aircraftsman. As he told his sister, Win, "I am no longer the lowest form of air force life in captivity."[21]

The respite in Vancouver was short, and soon he was on an eastbound train. The long train ride was made more pleasant by the presence of two generous young women with a good supply of grapes and chocolate. Once at Mountain View, and perhaps because of his growing confidence in himself, Wilson found Bombing and Gunnery School to be a bit of a lark compared to the intensity of Initial Training School. It was exciting to be on a real flying station though, and he was looking forward to a lot of fun bombing and shooting machine guns. The shine was only slightly taken off by having to do physical training in an unheated gymnasium. For the first two weeks he spent eight hours a day in the classroom working on theory. After that he was in the air every day practising what he had learned. He loved getting some real flying in, "above the clouds in the blue and the sun."[22] It was an experience that he wished to store away and retain and he hoped that it would not become routine.

There was also the new sensation of looking out of the open hatch and watching the practice bombs drop down. Not always accurately: one trainee dropped a bomb on a farmer's barn. Wilson wrote to his mother that the Americans claimed that they could drop a bomb in a pickle barrel from thirty thousand feet: "That is just eyewash, absolutely impossible." Earlier in the war some leaders in the American Air Force believed that the latest bomb-aiming technology would make precision bombing a reality. Others soon realized, as Wilson did, that such precision was not possible. That realization led to the emphasis on saturation bombing of large targets and the destruction of whole cities.

While he enjoyed the flying part of the training, Wilson also knew that it was not risk-free. The number of training accidents was reduced through the war years but they still happened, and too often instructors and students were killed in serious crashes.[23] Wilson was, however, not thinking much about those risks as he enjoyed the pleasures of flying.

He also found time for some R and R. Belleville, he thought, was not much of a town, so he went to Montreal on a weekend leave to visit relatives. He went out nightclubbing and drinking, "modestly" he told his mother, with a girl that he met, and they ended up at Rockhead's Paradise, Montreal's Black jazz club.[24] Wilson appreciated the downtime because the next phase of training was much more intense. He also knew that he would not get enough leave to get home to Vancouver that Christmas. Shopping opportunities were limited near Mountain View, so he asked Win to buy a Christmas present for his mother. "I figger," he wrote, "if I send you the required mazoola, which is enclosed, you, with your refined taste and superior judgment will be able to buy something…What I want is something for mom that Ron and Dad can't eat or use." Win's husband, Bill, was away at sea in the Canadian Navy and, so that she would not worry too much about her brother as well, Wilson continued to keep the tone of his letters to her lighthearted: "I will write again when I get to Chatham-on-Atlantic. Meanwhile bye, bye, buy bonds etc."[25] As it turned out, three more years would pass before he was back in Vancouver for a Christmas with his family.

Wilson joined a class of twenty-six, from all over the British Commonwealth, at the Number Ten Air Observers School in Chatham, New Brunswick, on November 13, 1943, and was there until early April 1944. The RCAF manual stated on page one that the duties of air force personnel are "fundamentally technical," and this was true times ten for navigators. Wilson's training was designed to give him a high standard of knowledge and skill, but his value to the air force depended on the manner in which he applied that training.[26] As he moved through the RCAF training programs there would be less emphasis on drills and discipline and more on becoming a master of navigation. At Air Observers School he would spend five months immersed in the theory and practice of navigation, and it was demanding work.

At its simplest, aircraft navigation was the means of getting the aeroplane from point A to point B by the most direct and safest route. The most elementary method was based on careful map-reading and following what could be seen on the ground: geographic features, towns, roads and railway lines. Of course, that only worked in daylight and clear weather. The simplest process of navigation by calculation was dead reckoning. Some reckoned that it was so-called because if you made a mistake, you were dead! This process involved first plotting a direct line between point A and point B and calculating the distance. The navigator then established the actual course by measuring the flight path's angle compared to a meridian and therefore true north. This measure enabled him to work out the compass heading to be followed on a magnetic compass. In establishing this heading, information about weather conditions, wind, drift and deviation had to be taken into account. Navigator trainees spent a lot of time studying meteorology and, on the ground and in the air, they had to keep a constant eye on the weather. Having set the heading, the actual flying distance between A and B, the flight time, the required airspeed and the amount of fuel required were also calculated. Dead reckoning was the navigator's basic skill, and while other methods of plotting locations were also available, they were supplements but not substitutes for the basics. Astro-navigation was another means of establishing the location of the aircraft, using a sextant to calculate the angle of the sun, moon or stars and, by taking three readings and triangulating them, fix a current position. This method obviously depended on stars being visible. Increasingly throughout the war, navigation could also be done through radio waves sent out from ground locations. When available, they made calculations much easier for navigators, but they did not always work and were not located in all parts of the world. During cross-country flights, the navigator had to take new readings and make new calculations every time something changed. These computations had to be done quickly, in five minutes maximum, or else they would be irrelevant as conditions changed. As Wilson himself put it, "If you don't work fast, the plane will get away ahead of you, and you're lost, which is very un-navigator like."[27] Air force slang for information was *gen*, and a contemporary of Wilson's described his navigation training as "learning the gen trade."[28] Wilson's name could have been the source of ribbing among the guys because inaccurate information was known in air force parlance as *duff gen*. Needless to say, very little of that originated with Wilson.

A brief description of the methods used is misleading if it makes aircraft navigation in the Second World War appear simple. It was not. It was a complicated process based on detailed information and careful calculation and, even then, it was not foolproof. On the ground, trainees absorbed a barrage of information: maps and charts, meteorological books, an air almanac containing massive amounts of astronomical data and mathematical tables. They made increasingly difficult calculations using devices such as dividers, a straight edge, parallel ruler, and sextant, a flight computer that was like a circular slide rule, and a chronometer watch that had its accuracy checked every day. Calculations that were challenging in the classroom were a lot more difficult in the air and on the fly. Trainees split their days between the ground and, weather permitting, the air, starting with short hops and progressing to longer cross-country flights. Navigators boarded their aircraft loaded down with all their information and gear. They flew in an Avro Anson, a twin-engine reconnaissance bomber, past its prime for warfare and adapted for training. The Anson was drafty, so through the Maritime winter they wore cold-weather flying kit. Even so, readings or photos taken through the open hatches meant an icy blast and frozen hands. The Anson's advantage was that it was a reliable aircraft—as Wilson reassured his mother, "the safest plane in the air."[29] Yet accidents still happened because of foul weather or human error.

Wilson thrived on the challenge of Air Observers School. "I'm having the adventure of my life here," he wrote. "I get a huge kick out of navigation." The work suited his ability to focus on detail and absorb vast amounts of information accurately. He pushed himself by looking at learning navigation as a competition. "I guess that I'm still kid enough to regard it as a complete game of skill," he explained to his mother. "If you learn the rules and play quickly and accurately enough, and use every subtle means you can possibly think of to win, you may land up right over the place at the right time." As the course went on the rules got tougher and it was harder to win, "but that's where the skill comes in." Skill, as is so often the case, was developed through long hours of hard work. Other trainees, recalling their experience, wrote that few students in civilian life worked as hard as student navigators during the war.[30] Sometimes, when Wilson was concentrating "on some tricky problems involving time, compass swinging and meteorology," he worked through the night. There were moments when he felt overwhelmed by it all. When he got tired and the work piled up over his head, "then I get cheesed off and write despondent letters home." In spite of these feelings, though, it was quickly clear that Wilson was becoming a very accomplished navigator. After three weeks in the course, he volunteered to navigate a flight over land and water from Chatham to Summerside, Prince Edward Island. Unbeknownst to the pilot, it was his first time navigating on his own. He hit the Summerside airport "right on the nose" and the same going back to Chatham. It was, he thought, "a tidy bit of navigating for a beginner."[31]

Since learning navigation was so demanding, it is not surprising that Wilson welcomed opportunities to relieve the stress. On the second day there, he went into Chatham "and exhausted its possibilities in an hour." He often went to dances in the area, even though he found the dancing was different in the Maritimes. Usually the girls far outnumbered the boys at these dances. He went to Montreal to visit distant cousins for Christmas and, while he did not want to impose, he was overwhelmed by their hospitality. He also went out on the town with a girl in the family.

Sometime around Christmas, perhaps feeling lonely, he sent Marion a ring; but his commitment to their relationship, amidst the uncertainties of wartime, was still half-hearted. He wrote to his mother not to make too much of what was merely a gift; it was "not officially (or unofficially) an engagement ring." At the same time he was glad that Marion and his mother got on so well together. Wilson and Marion wrote to each other regularly through the war, but they also went out with others during the war years while they were apart. Many years later, one of Marion's admirers, whom she met in Nova Scotia, recalled that she "was a lovely, lovely lady with a beautiful smile and a very devilish sense of humour." A photo shows the two of them looking absolutely radiant. Was he more smitten than Wilson, or just better able to express himself? Marion sent Wilson a picture of just herself while he was in Chatham and he commented in a letter to his mother that "it's a darned good picture" and Marion was a "nice looking girl ... don't you think."[32] The uncertainties of war also came home to Wilson and his family in other ways. He learned while he was in Chatham that his cousin Mervyn, who was also a navigator and flying on a bomber crew, was shot down over Germany and there was no word about whether he had survived.

Wilson's progress toward becoming an air force navigator was tested in a series of exams, both midway and toward the end of the program. He worried, worked hard and did well in the mid-terms. He was still concerned that the final round of exams in March would "puncture my inflated ego a bit," though he felt better after the first one. It "was a lead-pipe cinch, and I think I made a killing on it." And indeed he did throughout the exams. He graduated top of the class with 198 out of 200 for navigational theory and second in the class overall, just seven points out of two thousand behind the leader. He was also the youngest in the class, having just turned nineteen. He did so well that he was invited to be an instructor in the British Commonwealth Air Training Plan, but he declined the offer as he wanted to serve in action, preferably overseas.[33]

Graduation was marked by a wings parade, which was the exciting high-light of every trainee's experience. It was the realization of ambition, the recognition that they had made it through, as they were presented with the coveted air force wings identifying their future role in an aircrew. Wilson received the traditional half wing with an *O* for observer rather than the newer *N* designation for navigator. Air force jokers referred to the *O* wing as the flying arsehole, but Wilson was immensely proud of it. Following the formal wings parade, there was a graduation dinner in the pilots' mess with high spirits in full force, and then Wilson went dancing until three in the morning. He enjoyed and savoured the moment, and his achievement, but he was also thinking about what would come next.

His outstanding success as a trainee navigator was rewarded upon graduation with a commission as a pilot officer. Commissions more frequently went to pilots, but Wilson's placement at or near the top of all his navigation classes ensured that he would be in line for a commission too. Being an officer meant that he would double his pay, live under better conditions and have access to the officers' mess on the bases where he served. Many in the air force resented these hierarchical distinctions, particularly among aircrew, where men of different ranks were doing the same job. Wilson was pleased to be commissioned because of the recognition for achievement that it represented, but he downplayed his new status by calling himself a "sprog" pilot officer.[34] What he was rather more interested in, after earning his navigator's wings, was a rendezvous with "a nice shiny Liberator and then overseas—maybe. But we shall see what we shall see."[35]

*

The final phase of training for aircrew involved assembling a crew and having them fly together in the aircraft that they would be flying in combat. Wilson initially thought that he would be sent to either Nassau, in the Bahamas, or Summerside, on Prince Edward Island, but fortuitously the new Number Five Operational Training Unit was being set up at the Boundary Bay airfield in British Columbia. Being posted to Boundary Bay was perfect for Wilson. Over the three months there he could spend time with his family and with Marion. After a day of flying, he could go home and tell his mother all about it, so of course there is a gap in the flow of letters. He could also enjoy the family beach cottage that was very close at hand on Point Roberts. Just before he arrived back in British Columbia, he learned that cousin Mervyn had survived and was in a prisoner of war camp in Germany. His nose had been almost torn off his face by shrapnel as his plane went down, but a German doctor had patched him up. It was a relief to the family, but also a lesson in the uncertainties that bomber crews faced as Wilson was in the last stages of becoming part of one. It cannot have lessened a mother's worry about her son. The Number Five Operational Training Unit was set up to prepare crews to operate Liberator bombers before being sent to India, so Wilson now knew where he was likely to be heading.

He also quickly found out who the members of his crew would be. Bomber crews were usually put together mostly by self-selection out of a larger group. A fully manned Liberator bomber crew was normally nine or ten. The crew that Wilson served with was assembled soon after they arrived at Boundary Bay. As one Liberator flyer recalled, advice on starting a new crew began with finding two pilots and "one mastermind as navigator."[36] The first pilot and captain was Squadron Leader J.M. (Murray) Stroud. He had enlisted in the RCAF in 1940 and, before coming to Boundary Bay, was flying out of Tofino, on the west coast of Vancouver Island, on anti-submarine duty for Coastal Command. Stroud was an experienced pilot and older than most in Bomber Command. For the kids who made up most of an aircrew, a twenty-eight-year-old like Stroud seemed really old: a father figure of whom Wilson was, initially, very afraid.[37] However, that fear passed as they worked together and recognized each other's skill. It was a compliment to Wilson that he was chosen to fly in a squadron leader's crew because, in due course, being in the lead aircraft, he would be navigating for a whole squadron when they flew missions in formation. The co-pilot, Art Skirrow, came off a farm in the Barrhead area of Alberta. He, too, was impressed with Wilson's ability and later recalled that he was the smartest person he had ever met.[38] In addition to the two pilots and the navigator, a crew included a radio operator, five to man the gun stations and, if the navigator was not filling that role, a bomb aimer. Wilson was most friendly with Bill Kay, the rear gunner, who was also from Vancouver. In the Allied air forces of the Second World War, fighter pilots tended to be glamour-boy individualists, whereas a bomber crew had to be a team, and that required some humility. They were trained for careful, steady precision flying, and they avoided theatrics. Each had to rely on the skill of the others because a mistake by one could be fatal for them all. The captain was the leader and the navigator set the direction, but it was important that the entire crew gel as a team. For the Stroud crew at Boundary Bay, this process began with fifty hours flying in a Mitchell B-25, a twin-engine medium bomber, before they moved up to the Liberator B-24 heavy bomber.

The first Liberator was developed and built by the Consolidated Aircraft Company of San Diego in 1939. For its day, it was a huge aircraft. It was the biggest, fastest, most powerful bomber of the time, capable of flying the longest distances with the largest bomb load. The Allies believed that the war could be won through air power and saturation bombing, and the Liberator could help to achieve that objective. American industry geared up, particularly the Ford Motor Company at its Willow Run plant, and more Liberators came off the assembly lines than any other aircraft during the war. To start with, it did not have a good reputation for safety, as more were lost in accidents than in combat. It was refined through the war as successive models were produced, and by the time Wilson was flying in one over the British Columbia coast in 1944, the Liberator was more reliable. Even so, about the time that Wilson was at Boundary Bay, a Liberator on a training flight crashed near Maple Ridge, killing all the crew. Yet many wartime flyers overlooked the faults of their aircraft and remained deeply, even emotionally, committed to the particular plane that they flew. One member of the crew that Wilson was on, comparing the Liberator to the legendary British Lancaster bomber, described the latter as "a bucket of bolts."[39]

The sense that you got of a Liberator bomber depended on the perspective from which you looked at it. Side on, it was stunted and chunky, with its large vertical tail fins. That aspect earned it the nickname of the Flying Boxcar. From the front, the first impression was of the power of the four massive engines. Then, also from the front, but even more from above, you appreciated its huge, sleek 110-foot wingspan. It was built like an albatross, ungainly on land perhaps, but strong and reliable in the air during long-distance flights. The wings were on the shoulder of the aircraft and the fuselage hung below, which made it hazardous to ditch on water or belly land on the ground. Access to the aeroplane was mostly gained through the bomb bay doors that retracted up inside the body of the aircraft. A short ladder got you onto a catwalk that ran the length of the plane with a rope to hold onto on one side. As Wilson got up into the plane, he saw the huge amount of wire, tubes and piping, four thousand feet of it, that lined the walls. It looked like there was a lot that could go wrong. The navigator's table was located at the nose of the aircraft, a level down from the cockpit. It was reached by crawling along a catwalk that went around the huge front wheel that retracted up into the body of the plane during flight. The wheel hatches would not hold anything that fell on them, so if you slipped off the catwalk, there was nothing between you and eternity. Like most of the crew spaces, the navigator's was confined and claustrophobic, though it was located just behind the Perspex nose cone, which gave the navigator a panoramic view in the direction they were heading. Perhaps the cramped space reminded Wilson of the desk that he had set up for himself in the basement at home as a schoolboy. There he enjoyed the solitude of being alone at his table, doing his calculations.

Yet he was a crucial member of a team as they learned to fly this massive piece of complicated machinery. Operational training at Boundary Bay largely involved flying, navigation exercises and bombing practice, with increasingly longer flights over land and sea. Flights began with equipment checks and then the complicated procedure of firing up each of the powerful engines one by one. As the throttles were opened up, the aircraft strained against the brakes, vibrating alarmingly. The noise was deafening; it was even louder when the brakes were released and the plane began to surge down the runway. It gathered speed until it reached about 120 miles per hour, when the Liberator began lifting off the ground and into the air, only gradually gaining height, particularly when weighted down with a full bomb load. The engine noise was several decibels lower in flight, but it was still a slow assault on the nerves.[40] A Liberator required some physical strength to fly but, at least in calm weather, it felt steady and reliable. As Wilson and the crew practised their flying skills and learned to work together, they appreciated more and more keenly the reason for it all: going overseas and serving in combat. They probably did not think much about the fact that they were training to be killers and destroyers from above. That summer on the West Coast they mostly just enjoyed the flying—in spite of the noise and the risk.

Meanwhile, in Europe, the course of the war was changing. In early June came news of the D-Day landings. There were still months of fighting ahead, but people dared to think that it was the beginning of the end. Certainly Wilson's mother did. She wrote to her son about her hope for the conflict to be over so perhaps he would not have to go overseas. Wilson was more ambiguous about it: he hoped for an end to the war but at the same time wrote, "I would like to see India."[41] After the crew completed the Operational Training course, in late July 1944, they learned the meaning of the military adage "hurry up and wait." The disadvantage of the Boundary Bay location for Wilson was that he would have to go through all the parting moments again—and this time, he missed saying goodbye to his mother. She was out of the house and he was worried about missing his bus.

As he travelled, Wilson started to be more vague about where he was, because they had been told by the censors not to divulge their location. By August he was travelling east across Canada again, presumably heading overseas, although "the powers-that-are-supposed-to-be can't tell us much, because they don't know much," he wrote. He thought that the delay was because of a shortage of Liberators, in spite of huge aircraft production runs. It was more likely the result of the federal government's reluctance to assign Canadian aircrew to Southeast Asian operations, particularly if they were to serve, as Wilson would, in an RAF rather than an RCAF squadron.[42] Eventually he sailed from Halifax to Britain, a voyage that was a lot safer than it was earlier in the war, when German submarines were sinking many more Allied vessels. By early September, he was in Bournemouth, on the south coast of England.

For flight crews waiting for their assignments, Bournemouth represented a holding pattern. The old resort town had been appropriated to accommodate Number Three Personnel Reception Centre for the hundreds of aircrew who touched down there over the course of the war. Wilson spent nearly two months having a "pretty soft time of it." He was billeted in a "hoyty-toyty hotel" and learned to speak the King's English ("wah-tuh, raw-thuh, etc."). They did a couple of hours of air force work every day and then had a lot of time on their hands. He went to pubs, met girls and went dancing—the standard air force forms of recreation. A country that seemed so different from home fascinated him, and he "just sat and looked for hours." But this was not what he had spent more than a year training for, and the Bournemouth waiting room quickly became frustrating. He wrote, after a few days: "We'r [sic] still where we were and there is no sign of our going to where we are supposed to be yet."[43]

Like many Canadian servicemen in Britain during the war, he used his leaves to visit relatives. He went to London, saw the sights and was stunned by the damage done by German bombing, and then he continued on to Edinburgh to visit several relatives on his mother's side of the family. He was apprehensive about meeting new people, but that quickly passed. Aunt Jean looked and talked just like Nan, so he "fell for her right away." He made a phone call to another Jean, who lived in Rothesay, on the west coast of Scotland, and "(as is my habit when speaking to young girls on the phone) I made a date to go dancing with her that night."[44] He travelled across Scotland and took the ferry to the Isle of Bute to go dancing, presumably at the recently opened Rothesay Pavilion.

Leaving Scotland, he travelled to Belfast, where his father had worked in the shipyards, and then to Islandmagee to visit the Irish side of the family. He was particularly looking forward to meeting his grandmother's brother, Wilson Dick. He met another relative who took him along the road to his great-uncle Wilson's cottage, which he could identify from family photos. His great-uncle was out in the yard feeding his chickens. Wilson arrived unannounced and his great-uncle did not know who he was at first, though he certainly saw the family resemblance. They went into the parlour and chatted as they looked at Duff family photos. It was only a two-hour visit but it left a big impression on Wilson. Somehow his great-uncle became a role model. His mother always told him that he would like Uncle Wilson, and after meeting him he could not quite find the words to describe him. "I think that he is the grandest old man I've ever met…If I can be a man like him, I'll be satisfied."[45] What attracted Wilson? Was it the simplicity and stability of his great-uncle's life, so unlike Wilson's present world of turbulence and uncertainty? Or was he a male relative who was very different from his father? Whatever the connection, it was instant, profound and caused him to reflect upon himself.

Still waiting for the air force to decide his future, he took a one-week course at a navy training school in Cardiff, enjoying "the first exercise our wee brains have had for a long time," and went dancing every night.[46] But it all felt like he was filling in time and he wanted to get on with the next move. He was concerned that his navigation skills were getting rusty for lack of practice. Observing that people in Britain were becoming more optimistic about the war coming to an end, he wondered if it would be over before he saw any service. Or had his crew simply been forgotten? Then suddenly, without warning, they were on the move. Knowing that he was heading for active service, he wrote a long letter to Marion and told his mother, "It looks as though we will get where we started out to go."[47] He could not say so, but he was finally on the last leg of his long passage to India.

Wilson and the crew travelled up to Gourock, near Glasgow, and boarded a military transport vessel bound for Bombay (now Mumbai).

Wilson and his fellow officers found their ship, a former P&O passenger liner, the *Strathaird*, to be very like their hotel in Bournemouth. They had cabins, Wilson shared with two others from his crew, and they ate excellent meals in the first-class dining room, served by dozens of deferential Indian waiters. Although they could see that it was not a luxury trip for those in the ranks and did not "agree with the principle of class distinction as we see it here," they still enjoyed being treated like kings and addressed as "gentlemen."[48]

*

They passed by the gateway to India and, when the ship docked at Bombay, they walked down the gangplank into an altogether other culture. If England were different from home, India, as Wilson walked the streets of Bombay, was an assault on the senses. The throngs of people, the tumult, the disparities of wealth and poverty, the smells, the colours—it was like nothing that he had seen before. First impressions hit with a force in this land of extremes, even though it was not a full immersion because large parts of the city were out-of-bounds to them. They stayed at the Worli transit facility for Royal Air Force aircrew and went to exclusive clubs by day, including swimming every afternoon at the prestigious Willingdon Sports Club.

Then the Stroud crew was given its posting and they travelled by train nearly a thousand miles to the other side of India. For a few days in a cramped compartment, they watched the vast Indian landscape slide by and marvelled at the sunsets in the evening. They arrived at the Howrah railway station in Calcutta (now Kolkata) to another Indian scene that, for some, was beyond description: a bedlam of travellers, the homeless who lived on the platforms, and the often horribly disfigured beggars.[49] Did they know that three million people had died of starvation in the Calcutta area during the famine of the previous year? In any event, the scene was both appalling and fascinating. They realized that they had come a long way in a short time. Bournemouth was already a distant memory.

They were transported sixty miles north of Calcutta to Dubalia Air Force Station, where they joined RAF Ninety-Nine Squadron. As they settled into their quarters, they were anxious to get on with the job.

By the time Wilson began his tour of duty out of Dubalia, the Japanese were beginning to be rolled back from Burma (now Myanmar). In 1942 the Japanese had overrun and occupied Burma in order to gain access to its natural resources and to drive a wedge between Allied forces in India and China. It was a disheartening defeat for the Allies, and their initial counterattacks were thwarted. The Allies established South East Asia Command under the hopeful insignia of the phoenix, and its leaders prepared for the expected Japanese advance into India. The invading forces crossed the northwestern border of Burma into India in an effort to capture the city of Imphal in the spring of 1944. But the attack proved that Japan's reach had extended beyond its grasp. It was facing a growing number of defeats in the Pacific and China, and at Imphal the Japanese army faltered and then was turned back over the Burmese border. By the fall of 1944, the Fourteenth Army, under Sir William Slim, was launching offensives into Burma with the objective of moving the Japanese over the Irrawaddy River and recapturing Rangoon (now Yangon), Burma's port of entry in the south. The role of the Stroud crew and the bombers of Ninety-Nine Squadron was to support the ground campaign by destroying Japanese military and transportation targets. To that end, they flew more than fifty bombing sorties over Burma and Siam (now Thailand) during the next nine months.

Before they took to the air, they spent a few days acclimatizing in Dubalia and getting established on the ground. For Wilson the really interesting part of his time in India was that which he could not write about: flying. That just left life on the ground, which he described but did not think was very interesting. Living conditions were very basic. They lived in adjoining huts with thatched roofs, bamboo mats for walls, open doors and windows, and a veranda where they could sit in the shade. Wilson shared a room with Bill Kay, and they also shared an Indian bearer who called them *sahib* and took care of many of their daily needs: polished their shoes, laid out their clothes, drew bathwater and found them things to eat on the side. They ate their regular meals in the officers' mess, where the food was noted for its monotony. There was a village close by where they could buy fruit, though they were warned not to eat the local food. Canadian officials were concerned that living conditions for RCAF personnel in RAF squadrons in India were not up to par, but Wilson did not complain—at least not right away.[50] Throughout his life, though he was fastidious about dress and grooming, he did not mind roughing it. The Canadians on the base had forms of recreation that mystified those from Britain and other parts of the Commonwealth. Craps and baseball were two favourites. An Australian in the next hut had a gramophone and a great selection of good music that they shared. Wilson wrote, "It sure is a treat to hear real music again." He was not in Dubalia for long before he signed up for a course in English literature taught by a Canadian university officer on the base. There were other aspects of India that were less appealing. Stroud was down with dysentery before they had been there a week. Wilson arrived in India during a cooler part of the year, but a few months later the heat became almost unbearable for a Canadian. Still, in the beginning, Wilson wanted to reassure his family that he was fine, so he did not complain in the letters that he wrote each evening to the sound of jackals howling outside.[51] Life on the ground was so different that it had some fascination for Wilson at first, and then, with time, it became monotonous.

Flying the bombing missions, on the other hand, was never boring. After taking their assigned Liberator, named *R for Robert*, for a couple of test flights, the Stroud crew flew their first bombing operation against a Japanese target in Burma on December 11, 1944. Their objective was to destroy as much Japanese infrastructure as possible. They bombed railways and bridges, transportation and military installations around the larger cities, and the occasional vessel out on the ocean. Initially their targets were mostly in northern Burma, with some concentration around Mandalay. Then, as the ground campaign moved farther south, they attacked Rangoon and later Bangkok. Much of the bombing by the Liberators involved long flights at night. The flight out culminated with a low-level approach at less than a thousand feet over the target and then, as much as skill and technology permitted, precision bombing. As the lead plane in the squadron on nighttime raids, the Stroud crew would make a pass over the target to drop flares, go around and then pass over the target again to drop their bomb load. The Liberator would leap twenty feet in the air when the bombs were released, and then they would turn and climb for the long flight back to base.

The bombing missions were, of course, not that simple as there were many hazards that could lead to disaster. They were fortunate that Japanese air power was at a low ebb by the end of 1944, and the few fighter planes that they had in Burma were held back around the major centres. Anti-aircraft installations were not so thick on the ground as they were in Germany, and they were confined to the main centres. Yet there was nothing wrong with the Japanese aim, so flak was a hazard over some targets and very frightening. During the fixed path of a bombing run they were helpless to avoid it. Flak made Rangoon and Bangkok particularly "hot" targets that bombing crews dreaded when it was announced that one or other was their objective. Once, *R for Robert* was coned by searchlights and made a target for anti-aircraft fire while they were at altitude five hundred feet en route to drop flares over railway marshalling yards at Bangkok. Wilson reported that they managed to worm their way out without being hit, and the bombers that followed plastered the target so that "the whole place was on fire when we left."[52] The Japanese were retreating in Burma but they were still a tenacious enemy. The risks of crashing on either sea or land were very scary. If they went down in the Burma jungle, particularly behind Japanese lines, their chances of getting out alive were virtually nil, and they knew it. The rudimentary survival kits that they carried, with a compass, map, identification document and a small amount of money to pay locals for help, only emphasized what little chance they had. And the structure of the Liberator meant that if they ditched in the sea, *R for Robert* would likely break up and survival would be very much in doubt.

Weather could also be an enemy. Flying conditions were fine during the first few months that Wilson was at Dubalia, but that changed when the annual monsoon set in around May and persisted through to October. During the monsoon, the Bay of Bengal south of Calcutta could be a cauldron that stirred up some of the worst cyclones in the world. The clouds, wind and teeming rain reduced flying to a minimum. Towering cumulus clouds and thunderstorms were absolutely terrifying if aircraft had to fly through them. The Liberator was a huge aircraft for its day and usually steady in the air, but in cumulus cloud and high winds it could be tossed around like a feather. Downdrafts could drive it down into the sea or the jungle, which would likely mean that a crew of ten was "gone for a Burton." It was better to prolong a flight and make it home to base by going around cumulus clouds and storms. The Liberator was tricky to fly in close formation, and in bad weather the formations could break up and planes and their crews could vanish forever. Once, while Wilson was at Dubalia, two Liberators collided over the ocean and disintegrated in a rain of debris. Twenty-two men disappeared into the sea without a ripple: their presence gone in an instant from the community of comrades.[53]

All of these risks, and particularly those of weather, made the role of the navigator absolutely crucial to the success and survival of the crew. Once the target of an operation was announced, and before takeoff, Wilson would work with other navigators in the squadron, pouring over maps and weather reports, synchronizing watches and checking instruments. They had to calculate the bomb load and the length of the trip against the fuel requirement to make sure that they had enough to get there and back. During the flight there was little downtime for a navigator. Wilson would be at his fold-out navigator's table near the nose of the plane, calculating and recalculating. Navigation was mostly by dead reckoning since sextant readings and radio signals were unreliable. The work of the navigator in combat suited Wilson because it involved disciplined focus, command of detail and, more than anything, precision. The partnership between the navigator and the pilots required perfection. When *R for Robert* got into heavy weather and severe turbulence, Art Skirrow, the co-pilot, later recalled that Wilson's voice would come through the intercom, clear, calm and certain, with the flying directions that they needed to follow. Art thought that it was magic, the way they always got there and back in one piece.[54] Unusually, the Stroud crew remained intact during their entire tour of duty, as not one of them was killed or injured. Wilson played a large part in that outcome.

They could not predict their future, of course, so fear was a major factor in their lives, and the dread was debilitating if not kept under control. There was initial excitement about finally flying in combat, then a realization of the risks and the dawning of fear. Men new to combat flying feared the unknown, while experienced aircrew feared what they knew. Another flyer, who was at Dubalia at the same time as Wilson, recalled that fear was like "a dark shroud hanging over the place." It rose and fell, but was "always lurking in the corners."[55] Fear was worst just before a mission, between the briefing and getting into the plane to start the takeoff procedure. Getting the dread of death under control was particularly crucial for a navigator, who, if consumed by fear, was liable to make mistakes in his calculations that could have disastrous consequences. Working at his navigator's station in the nose of the bomber, Wilson was calm and capable because he knew that his crewmates relied on him. The underlying fear remained, but he kept it under control.

There were various ways of coping with fear. For some, the simple "it will not happen to me" response was a line of defence. Developing emotional detachment was another: with deaths, and the risk of death, all around you, some found it better to build an emotional wall to help keep the fear at bay. Still others overcame what one flyer called "the last enemy," that is the fear of death.[56] Fear was more intensely felt by those, like Wilson, who tended to be apprehensive and had vivid imaginations. They shared the prevailing expectation of death but they went further. Many flyers imagined, and foretold in detail, the circumstances of their death; some even to the extent that they regarded themselves as already dead. And some flyers also speculated about the possibility of spiritual continuity after death. In this way, the fear of death, as a constraint in their lives, was diminished by wartime experience.[57] While emotional detachment and reducing one's fear of death could be effective mental tactics when faced with daily danger, these became less healthy qualities when the war was over.

Another antidote for fear was superstition. Flyers often had superstitious rituals that they went through before they took off in an effort to boost their sense of control over their fate as they flew to the edge of oblivion. As a graduate student after the war, Wilson wrote an essay on the traditional navigation techniques of Pacific islanders who sailed unerringly thousands of miles between islands that were just pinpoints on a vast ocean. He compared his experience with theirs when the unforeseen arose and they reached the limits of science. The last resort was magic. The Pacific islanders had chants and incantations, while bomber crews used many magical practices and charms. "If a pilot didn't wear his old beat-up flying boots, if the crew didn't urinate on the undercarriage before take off, if a member of the crew was left behind, or if the bomb-aimer didn't have his rabbit's foot, or girl-friend's picture, with him, some wartime crews would have been pretty apprehensive about the trip." He concluded that the line between science and magic was drawn at about the same place in each case. For both groups, scientific techniques were sophisticated but not always enough to ensure success, so the slack was taken up by magic.[58]

Fortified by all these strategies, the flyers' fears began to calm down as they went through the pre-flight routines. There was comfort in these predetermined patterns, like the surety of a dance step. Then on takeoff, they felt the lift and relief of flying. Gaining height south of Calcutta, they flew over the Sundarbans, a shifting tangle of mangrove swamps where several rivers, including the sacred Ganges, flow out to the sea to form the largest delta in the world. Then, still gaining height, they rose up and out into the vivid blue yonder of the Bay of Bengal. Flying has long been associated with aspiration and freedom from the restrictions of the earth. There is something supernatural about the achievement of flying. In flight, particularly in wartime, some tested the limits of mortality and found it exhilarating for that reason.[59] When there were downtimes in the routine of a bombing mission, many crewmembers, flying high above their anxieties on the ground, found themselves reflecting upon ethereal things. For some, it was simply that at twenty thousand feet they felt closer to heaven. Sometimes they would marvel at some spectacular, radiant band of light hovering between sea and sky, and one crew member would nudge another and ask: "Do you ever wonder what it's all about?" Some described the serenity of flying at night, suspended in the darkness. It could make a flyer think that he was out of this world and close to his maker.[60]

So did Wilson feel, as they soared into the heavens, "where never... even eagle flew," that he had "slipped the surly bounds of earth / And danced the skies" in "the high untrespassed sanctity of space," as another RCAF flyer so famously expressed it in his poem "High Flight."[61] It is hard to imagine that he did not. It has been noted that much less poetry came out of the Second World War than the First, partly because there was less agonizing over the justice of the conflict.[62] Though still only nineteen when he arrived in Dubalia, Wilson was possessed of sensitivity and imagination. He also had poetry within him, though it would not emerge until later in life, and he was studying English literature in his spare time. Sitting alone at his navigator's station as the Liberator bored through the sky, surely then his powerful mind would rise above the mundane and he would take the "High Flight" of fancy and imagination, even if he did not write to his mother about it.

Reflective moments brought some relief, but more often reality was relentless, both in the air and on the ground. The Stroud crew was flying several missions a week throughout December of 1944 and into the early months of the new year. By the spring of 1945 the Allied objective was to retake Rangoon from the Japanese and cut off their supply lines to Burma before the monsoon season began in May. To keep ahead of the ground forces as they moved south, the flights became longer and longer, sometimes up to thirteen or fourteen hours in the air. These flights would involve six or seven hours of, by now familiar, flying each way, punctuated by ten minutes of sheer terror over the heavily defended targets. On the bombing runs over Rangoon and Bangkok, as they faced searchlights, tracer fire and, worst of all, flak that sent up puffs of black smoke filled with shrapnel, it was like a traversing a lethal fireworks display, with everything going off at once. The trick was to stay calm enough to carry out the run at low level, during which defensive manoeuvres were secondary to aiming the bombs and hitting the target. As the number of missions piled up, stress increased and nerves began to fray. Wilson had a mantra about his navigational calculations: "all things being equal and ignoring friction."[63] The trouble was, the friction was becoming more difficult to ignore.

By March, the heat was building up toward the coming monsoon and becoming almost unbearable for those who were not used to it. Inside the Liberator on the ground, it was really oppressive, particularly just behind the Perspex nose cone or the rear gunner's bubble. Then, above about five thousand feet, they had to put on their padded flying suits as the temperature dropped below zero. The heat and humidity also led to health problems. Few escaped a bout of dysentery, whatever the temperature. In really hot weather they were soaked in sweat and a real scourge was prickly heat, an irritating skin rash that turned septic if not kept under control. Wilson reported that most of the men on the base had the rash causing both skin and tempers to become irritated: "Mad dogs and Englishmen," he observed.[64] The best cure for prickly heat was a couple of weeks' leave up in the cooler hill towns of northern India.

Flyers were also taking other remedies for a variety of conditions. There were bowls of salt tablets on the tables in the mess to help with dehydration and cramping, and they were given caffeine tablets or Benzedrine to stay awake on long flights which, in addition to the heat and the nightmares, would have made sleep difficult. There were also drugs to help them sleep. Whether drug-induced or not, airmen in India went through a series of highs and lows. They were far from home and, unlike aircrew in Britain, had no contact with family or social interaction with their own community. Wilson confessed that the place was getting on his nerves: it "grows on you like a fungus, so I've been a bit niggly lately—even more so than usual." He was starting to comment on the repulsive side of India, like the sight of crowds of vultures feeding on dead dogs. He wished that he could go to "an ordinary dance where there are lots of pretty colourfully dressed girls to look at," but such things were only "memories in India." By the end of April, he and the crew had been flying constantly, seven days a week for five months, with only the occasional forty-eight-hour break. The constant bombing missions were getting to him and, though he realized that "I shouldn't bind about India so superior like," it was not looking like "the Jewel of the Empire" at this stage. He and his crewmates needed a respite.[65]

Unfortunately, they had a change that was not as good as a holiday. In April 1945 they moved to Digri, west of Calcutta, where they joined 159 Squadron. It was a move, in the words of another Canadian flyer, from "Dusty Dubalia" to "Delectable Digri," and Wilson also thought that there was little difference between the two stations. Digri did have better ground facilities for the Liberators, and 159 Squadron was thought to be an elite group. Wilson was promoted to flying officer, requiring a long night in the officers' mess, where the custom was that he "should stand at the bar and everybody comes and congratulates me by letting me buy them a drink."[66] Wilson bought a gramophone, borrowed a collection of classical music, and spent many hours enjoying listening. With a few exceptions, however, the change of scene did not make any difference to the monotony of daily life on the ground or to the stress of frequent flying.

Contained in the enclaves of their stations, the air force men were sealed off from the real India. They had to get away to really experience much of it, but Wilson did not get out very often in the first five months. When he did, any fascination with the mysterious east soon faded into a darker reality. Like most air force men, he went to Calcutta on weekend leaves but, on the whole, did not like the city; he found it to be "dirty, noisy and expensive." Once he went to a restaurant with a dance floor, but only a few chaps were dancing, for lack of partners. It only reminded him of how much he missed it. "You know," he wrote his mother, "I haven't spoken to a girl (socially) since I got off the boat." Any relations with Indian women were severely frowned upon by the air force, and the prohibition was reinforced with stern lectures about the risks of sexually transmitted diseases. Wilson described a local village that he visited close to Dubalia, where he admired ornate stone buildings that spoke of past prosperity. He also came across a painted clay statue and listened to a local who explained that it represented Saraswati, the goddess of learning.[67] But during his first months in India he did not write in much detail about the local cultures. As Wilson flew above, below him in the jungle of Burma the British social anthropologist Edmund Leach was in the British army and working with the Kachin people of northern Burma, absorbing their culture and learning their language. There was little sign, however, of Wilson Duff the future ethnographer.

*

By the beginning of May, to Wilson's relief, the pressure was easing. Allied forces had retaken Rangoon, in the end without resistance from the Japanese, by the end of April. The coming monsoon would mean a lot fewer bombing missions, as the weather became the biggest enemy. After Akyab (now Sittwe) on the coast of Burma was retaken by the Allies, the Stroud crew moved to the airfield there for a short period so that they could fly to targets even farther south, including the port city of Singora (now Songkhla) near Siam's border with Malaysia. They enjoyed swimming in the ocean when they were not flying, and their spirits became more buoyant. But they were not as joyful as people at home, who celebrated the end of the war in Europe on VE day, May 8, 1945. Although there was a party in the officers' mess at Digri, the merriment was muted because their war was not over; soldiers and airmen were still being killed. The war might have ended in Europe, but in Southeast Asia, Japan was down but not out. The excitement of VE day in the rest of the world led them to the feeling that theirs was a forgotten war. Wilson felt that events in Europe had "overshadowed some amazing military feats out here...I guess brilliant things like the advance on Rangoon lose some of their shine when viewed from 10,000 miles away."[68]

A real respite from the humidity, torrential rain, sweat and prickly heat came for Wilson and the crew in early June, when they had two weeks' leave in Darjeeling. As it had been for the British in India from the beginning of the Raj, Darjeeling was a favourite for air force crews seeking a reprieve from the heat of the plains. Due north of Calcutta and nearly seven thousand feet above sea level, nestled among the famous tea plantations, it was cool and relaxing. They got there on the marvelous narrow-gauge Darjeeling railway that winds and loops its way up to the town. Once there, you are close to the Tibet border, with a view of the Himalayas. On a clear day there is a breathtaking view of the great face of Kangchenjunga, the world's third-highest mountain, forty miles away, and in the far distance the then unclimbed peak of Everest could sometimes be seen. Wilson and Art Skirrow stayed in the home of Canadians Major and Mrs. John Brebner, who provided welcome hospitality to RCAF flyers. The Canadian prints on the living room walls were a reminder of home. There were lots of servants, so Wilson could call up breakfast in bed "and 'James, draw my bawth' sort of thing." They went roller skating, which was "wizard fun," and rode horses along the trails behind the town, stopping to look at an ornately coloured Buddhist monastery. They watched the Indian women working the tea plantations and carrying huge loads secured by a strap over their foreheads. And Darjeeling was blissfully cool; so much so that they had to dig out their "blues," a uniform they never wore at Digri. Darjeeling gave Wilson a new lease on life. India felt like a much more tolerable place, and he returned to Digri "bubbling over."[69]

Wilson was undoubtedly more upbeat because of his growing sense that the war with Japan was nearing an end and he was also getting close to the end of his own tour of duty. One way or another, his war would soon be over. The last few missions of a tour made some bombers very nervous because they did not want a mishap with their duty nearly done. Some were very unlucky, as aircraft and crews "bought it" even in the closing weeks of the war. The Stroud crew was still flying bombing sorties: they were in the air nine times during July. Their last bombing mission was on August 7, 1945, to destroy a railway bridge just east of Mergui (now Myeik),

on the Burmese coast far south of Rangoon. They were in the air for thirteen hours. The day before, the first atomic bomb had been dropped on
Japan and another would follow three days later. On the base at Digri, they
were all talking about the bomb. Wilson was not quite sure what to make
of it, but he knew immediately that something really significant had happened—not only for him personally, but also for the entire world. Japan
announced its surrender on August 15, and Wilson's squadron was stood
down. Still the crews waited "like a boxer in his corner, to see if his oppon-
ent will be counted out or if he will get up and ask for more."[70]

Japan did not ask for more, so quite suddenly the war was finally
finished for Wilson. At "a reasonable facsimile of a formal mess dinner,"
Squadron Leader Stroud spoke about their success and how tremendous
it was that men from many parts of the British Commonwealth could
work so well together. He concluded by saying what all squadron leaders
said: that theirs was the best squadron ever. There were lots of other, wil-
der parties going on, though Wilson made the unlikely claim that he only
went to one and was living exceedingly virtuously "in the midst of all this
dissipation." The Liberator bomber crews were certainly entitled to sav-
our the moment. As William Slim, the commander of the ground army,
acknowledged, the defeat of the Japanese in Burma would not have been
possible without Allied supremacy in the air and the strategic bombing of
the Liberator squadrons.[71] But now the Liberators were immobilized and
the aircrews were quickly relieved of their firearms to "remove all chances
of any wild or dangerous sport."[72]

Wilson was thinking about home and reunions with family and Marion. The longer he was away, the more precious the memory of home
became. The family cottage at Point Roberts became the site of happy
memories—so much so "that I've sort of dreamt it up into a heavenly
place." He was looking forward to spending time there again soon, even
"if only to prove that it's not as heavenly [a] place as it looks from here,
half-way round the world."[73] While anxious to get going, he also knew that
his journey home would not begin right away. With time on his hands, he
suggested to some of his mates that they visit another part of India.

Puri, a city on India's east coast facing the Bay of Bengal, was another favourite destination for airmen stationed in the Calcutta area. It was noted for two things: its beaches, which were the initial attraction for airmen on leave, and that it was a Hindu sacred site, which Wilson became interested in once he got there. He wrote some long letters to his parents describing his impressions in considerable, one might even say ethnographic, detail. Wilson and his friends cavorted on the beach and, although the surf was dangerous, they each hired a local boy as a personal lifeguard and went swimming. Wilson wrote a rare letter to his father describing going out beyond the surf in a makeshift Indian craft that was the same as had been used for a thousand years for fishing. He warned his dad that, when he got home, they would go fishing together and he would give him a few pointers. He learned that Puri was a very holy place where Hindu believers came on pilgrimages, largely because of its sacred temple built in the twelfth century and dedicated to the deity Jagannatha. As Wilson rather irreverently put it, if Hindus get into the temple "all their sins past and present are forgiven, and they are a cinch for Heaven." They visited the temple and, although they were not allowed to enter, they hired a local guide who took them to the roof of a building across the road so that they could look down into it. As the guide talked to them about the temples, Wilson thought that he learned a little about Hinduism. They also visited other temples in Puri: "We were not impressed by them as centres of the religion of 280 million souls," Wilson concluded, "but as objects of ancient art and centres of an ancient faith, they are very impressive." Wilson does not mention it in his letters to family, but other airmen visiting Puri were fascinated by the eroticism of Indian art for sale around the religious sites.[74] Along with temples, Wilson described street scenes and markets where he saw more diseased and starving people than he hoped to see for the rest of his life. The visit to Puri was Wilson's first observation and detailed description of another culture. He did not write free of judgment, particularly about the "eternal and ever-present" demand for "buckshis," or payment, for every little service. But his account of Puri was a first indication of a skill that he would refine throughout his life.[75]

Returning to Digri with his war over, he was more relaxed and positive about India and thinking about getting back to Vancouver and his post-war future. He and the other Canadians were scurrying around, packing their belongings and "excited as kids off to a picnic" as they prepared to head for home. But Wilson knew he would not be home soon. Priority was given to those who had been in Japanese prisoner of war camps, and there was also some sense that he would have been moved more quickly if he were in an RCAF squadron rather than an RAF one. Some air force men expressed open discontent at the slowness with which things moved, but Wilson took things as they came. By mid-September he was packed, cleared and saying his last farewells to those in 159 Squadron. He was getting that "unstable transient feeling" that he normally hated—but it was easier this time because he knew where he was going and thought he knew what was waiting for him, even if the journey were to be a long one. It was still the rainy season in India, so it "rained when we left the squadron, and it was raining when we hit Calcutta. It rained quite a lot in Calcutta" so the water ran ankle-deep down the main street. "It rained when we left Calcutta, and it rained most of the way across India, even in the compartment, which leaked. The result was that we didn't see much of India, and we got wet. This is known as the monsoon."[76] Now that he was heading home, challenges like the weather, which once got on his nerves, were now described with philosophical good humour.

He was soon back in Bombay where he had been ten months ago. After seeing some of the rest of India, he appreciated Bombay more and preferred it to Calcutta. Two weeks later he was again on board the *Strathaird*, the same ship that he come out on, for the seventeen-day voyage back to England. He did not say if his cabin was the coveted port out and starboard home, or "posh" side, but he was much more at ease on this trip than his first on the luxury liner. Enjoying the passage through the Red Sea he noted that the "Red Sea isn't red. Like all other seas, it takes on the colour of the sky it reflects, which at the moment is pale, cloudless blue." With little to do and anxieties falling away, he became absorbed in the water "always beautiful to gaze at, as changeable and fascinating as an open fire." As always with Wilson, though, inactivity led to boredom, particularly after the first few days, when he had "exhausted the meager resources of the ship's library."[77] Eventually, by the end of October, he was back in Bournemouth, staying in the same hotel as before—and waiting.

Wilson knew as he arrived back in Bournemouth that he was unlikely to get a passage across the Atlantic right away. After a while, he realized that he would not be home for Christmas either. Once again he had time on his hands. Crewmembers reacted in different ways to this period of post-combat downtime. Drinking was a release for some. Squadron Leader Stroud was spending most of his waking hours in various pubs in an almost constant state of mellowness. Wilson claimed that he and his closest friend, Bill Kay, were being abstemious, and perhaps, indeed, they were.[78] With Wilson, time was seldom wasting. He spent four hours a day on a six-week senior matriculation algebra course "to get the old brain working again," and there was a hobby shop in Bournemouth where he took some lessons in photography. He even went off to take a one-week course at Cardiff University. At one point he signed up for another six months of flying in Britain and Europe, but that did not eventuate. As he had on the way out, he visited his relatives again. He went to Islandmagee, where he spent a couple of days with his great-uncle Wilson. Again he was very impressed with his elderly relative and namesake. He had his suitcase stolen at King's Cross Station in London, and his great-uncle sent him five pounds to cover some of the loss. Wilson wrote to his family that it was "the type of spirit that makes me love your people." Then he went to Edinburgh for a second time to spend Christmas with his mother's relatives and friends there and visited parts of the city that she would have known well. His visit in Edinburgh made him realize how much he was ready to get back home and back to normal: "It won't be too soon for me," he wrote. At the same time, as he thought about his return home, he determined that back to normal would not mean exactly the same. He told family in Edinburgh that when he got home, he was going to insist on being called Wilson and put an end to Junior.[79]

In his letters to his family, he described his excitement about seeing them again. On the face of it, however, he was low-key about reuniting with Marion. He knew that Marion was in Newfoundland in the Women's Royal Naval Service, discharging returning sailors, so she would not be in Vancouver when he arrived. He had hung her picture on the wall of his sleeping quarters in India and wrote to her regularly throughout his time in the RCAF. Yet he remained somewhat offhand about their relationship—at least until he did not hear from her for a while, when he complained bitterly. The uncertainty of wartime was undoubtedly a factor, but Wilson also seemed insecure in himself. Marion and Wilson's mother were friends and he, more than once, checked with Nan about what she thought of Marion. After he received a parcel from Marion in India that he described as a "work of art," he wrote to his mother that his distant girlfriend was a "a darned good type, that kid. What do you think of her?" This does not sound like head-over-heels love. And, of course, he was socializing with other girls along the way. In Scotland he went dancing on several evenings and "fell in love with the Edinburgh girls in a big way." One young lady, whom he met on his last night there, asked him to stay for a few days longer. Wilson's reluctant response was that "duty called." He did not get across to Rothesay to go dancing as he had during his last trip to Scotland, but he did get a "long letter" from Jean, his dance partner there, after he left. Around Christmas he received cards from girls he had met in Halifax, Cardiff and Winnipeg.[80]

He was back in Bournemouth by the end of December and, early in the new year, Wilson learned that he should get ready to leave for Canada. He packed and labelled his belongings for 3707 Lanark Street, Vancouver, and headed all his letters and packages "Mr Wilson Duff." He wrote that it was "a good feeling to know definitely when, how and where you'r [sic] going at last." He caught the *Queen Elizabeth* at Southhampton, the liner operating as a troop ship and sailing to New York. He heard that Winston Churchill would be aboard and hoped that he might have a chance to see him. From New York he would travel to Montreal, visit relatives there, and then take the train across Canada with a stop in Winnipeg to see friends. As he headed home, Wilson thought, "Boy the nights I've laid and dreamed of that moment when the train pulls into Vancouver, and my travels are over!" He asked his mother to tell "the mayor and the Kitsilano Boys Band not to bother, I'd prefer to be met just by my folks."[81] And so it was that, without fanfare, the blue-eyed boy returned to his family, still with eyes of blue but no longer a boy.

*

It was common for flyers, and those who wrote about flyers, to say that the war turned boys into men, and that they returned strengthened from the challenges that they had faced. That was certainly a part of Wilson's story: he had mastered the art and science of aircraft navigation and very successfully put into practice what he had learned under the most trying and dangerous conditions. And for Wilson there was more: he returned from India intent on being his own man and not junior to his father. He had plotted and followed his own course through the war and was reckoning to do the same in the next phase of his life. Now, back in Vancouver, he was confident, accomplished and stronger in spirit. In many ways, though it always remained a part of him, he tried to lay the air force experience to rest behind him. The saturation bombing of cities in Germany was criticized and disparaged both during and after the war because of the enormous loss of civilian life. Many thought that it was both inhumane and ineffective in the defeat of Germany. In Southeast Asia, the bombing was more precise and focused on strategic targets, though not without collateral casualties. What made it all easier to forget was that the Burma campaign was the forgotten campaign and the Liberator bombers became the forgotten air force. The Burma Liberators get short shrift in the official history of the Royal Canadian Air Force.[82] Perhaps pushing it all out of mind suited Wilson because he wanted to put it behind him and move on. He did assemble a scrapbook of photos and clippings of his three years in the RCAF, but he did little else to cultivate his memories of the experience. He did not keep in touch with his *R for Robert* crewmates and when, after several years, RCAF reunions began to be arranged, he turned down invitations to attend. Like many returned veterans, Wilson seldom spoke about his wartime experience, and then only with people with whom he was particularly comfortable. In fact, in later life, he had close colleagues who worked with him on a day-to-day basis but had no idea that he had been in the Royal Canadian Air Force.

Trying to put the war out of mental sight did not mean, however, that it had no impact on him or that it was out of mind. The war had shaped Wilson's rite of passage from boy to manhood and, therefore, the rest of his life. There were more minor effects: in later life he disliked very hot summer weather and became increasingly intolerant of loud noises. Other more significant effects were psychological rather than physical and therefore, at least at first, less obvious. He had confronted, and to some extent overcome, his fear of death. Many flyers coped with the constant threat of losing friends by shutting off emotionally in an effort to lessen the impact of loss. They could, therefore, appear to be casual about the possibility of dying themselves and the deaths of others. Wilson returned from the war more contained emotionally and, as with many flyers, that reserve limited his ability to fully commit to romantic relations. And for the rest of his life, sometimes when lying in bed at night, Wilson would relive the exhilaration and the terror of those bombing runs over Rangoon and Bangkok in vivid visual detail.

3. Learning Anthropology

In the First Nations cultures of the northern British Columbia coast, men other than their father prepared young men for positions of responsibility and influence. Wilson would come to know, and have strong affiliations with, Haida culture, whose young men were groomed by their mothers' brothers for their future responsibilities. Wilson did not have an uncle who played that role so, given his rather fraught relationship with his own father, he was fortunate to have other father figures in his life. Squadron Leader Stroud assumed that role while Wilson was flying in India, but they lost touch once the war was over. In the next phase of Wilson's life another man would step in and assume the position of mentor.

In the spring of 1946, six hundred thousand men and women from the Canadian armed forces arrived back in Canada to resume their lives. Wilson arrived in Vancouver in February, raring to go. In March he turned twenty-one, the traditional milestone of adulthood, and he was anxious to get on with life and work. Or, in Wilson's case, it would be more accurate to say work and life. The great majority of veterans would successfully reintegrate into civilian life, some even feeling that, having lived through the war, they owed it to the fallen to achieve something worthwhile. A minority of others, however, came home with troubled minds. Their challenges promoted a growing sense of the importance of psychiatry and an expansion in the size of that profession in the decade after the end of the war.[1]

As he returned from his war, Wilson showed no sign that it had affected his ability to cope with life; on the contrary, he was feeling, for him, fairly positive about his future. While still in India, he had plotted the course that he wanted to take when he landed back in Vancouver. He had thought from time to time about his postwar future since he first joined the air force, and his planning became top of mind as the war ended. He felt he had an advantage over many others who had interrupted careers, because he could start where he left off. He looked forward to talking to his cousin Mervyn to see what his plans were and what he could learn from him. Wilson was determined to return to the University of British Columbia and get as much education as he could. When his father told him that UBC was being flooded with students, Wilson was concerned that he might not get in. He made enquiries and learned that the university was working to take as many students as possible, so he sent in his application while he was in England waiting to come home. The fact that he had already done a successful first year at UBC would have contributed to his acceptance. The next question was what direction his studies would take: Would he continue along the path toward a forestry degree? He had consulted an air force career-counselling officer as he passed through Bombay in September 1945. The officer first had him write some kind of intelligence test. Wilson's score of seventy-six out of eighty "shook the old boy, as it's the highest he's seen for some time." From various tests to determine his interests, they found that they "run something like this: mechanical first, then literary, then scientific, with a smattering musical and social thrown in." The counsellor consulted charts and diagrams and came up with something like "writer of highly technical articles in scientific periodicals." In the end, they settled on "some sort of engineering," so Wilson planned to go back to UBC, and engineering it would be.[2] At the same time, we can safely say that his Scottish heritage and study of English literature meant that he would know the line about "The best-laid schemes o' Mice an' Men."[3] Still, by reducing the guesswork, perhaps he was also reducing his anxiety about the future.

As a veteran, Wilson was eligible for financial support to return to university. Indeed, the president of UBC, Norman MacKenzie, had been instrumental in convincing the federal government to provide a kind of assistance to veterans that had not been available to him after the First World War. As chair of the Committee on Post-War Problems for the National Conference of Canadian Universities, MacKenzie wrote a persuasive report advocating for veterans. The Department of Veterans Affairs was established in 1944, and the federal government decided to provide financial support for qualified veterans to attend university.[4]

Wilson understood that when he got home he would be on a month's leave before he was discharged, and when he started university he would be eligible for an initial gratuity of $746 and then $60 a month for thirty months. These amounts were a good deal less than the $3,360 a year he had earned as a flying officer by the end of the war, but the air force had arranged for him to save half of his earnings. He calculated that, if he lived at home, he had the resources to complete a degree and start a career.

Women and men coming home after the war were usually eager to resume or begin romantic relationships and to find domestic happiness. The war had been tough on relationships. Absence did not always make the heart grow fonder. Relationships often fell apart, and many of Wilson and Marion's contemporaries simply did not return. Air force men tended not to commit to relationships while they were away, though many married as soon as they got back. During the war it seemed better not to plan ahead. Wilson and Marion had perhaps agreed that they would see others for the duration, but they also stayed in touch. For his part, Wilson kept his heart contained within him. At one point, when Marion and his mother got together to knit him a sweater, Wilson wondered whether Marion was getting Nan's consent to do "something drastic" like "go after me come Sadie Hawkins day," the day when women are allowed to pursue men.[5] Unlike many others, upon coming home, Wilson and Marion did not rush into anything. Certainly, when Marion returned to Vancouver from Newfoundland a few months after Wilson got home, they started seeing each other again. As ever, though, Wilson was more focused on his studies and future career than romance.

Wilson was one of a wave of men and women who were returning to Canada to resume their interrupted lives, and he rode that wave into his future. He returned to UBC in the fall of 1946, intending to complete a degree in engineering and, like most veterans, he was in a hurry. He returned to a campus that was gearing up to accommodate a flood of students returning from the war. President MacKenzie, a veteran of the First World War, believed in an open door for returned service people. Veteran enrolment hit its peak in the fall of 1946 with about five thousand registered. Student numbers had more than tripled since 1944, and the percentage increase at UBC was greater than at any other Canadian university. The veteran students tended to be older and more likely to be married with a family than the students just out of high school. They had typically been away for several years, but the training and discipline that they had received in the armed forces, along with their own determination to succeed, served them well. The university had hired many new faculty members, and new buildings were going up on campus to provide enough classroom, laboratory and other spaces to meet student demand. The university even made concessions to enable veterans to complete courses and programs faster: for example, allowing them to complete a seven-month course in four by increasing the number of weekly lectures.[6]

Wilson resumed his studies on a campus where there were many other students like him and a university staff that understood his interest in completing his degree without delays. Over the next two academic years, Wilson took a mix of courses in the sciences and in forestry rather than engineering. After his second winter back at UBC, he took two summer courses, one each in English and history. With two exceptions, over the two years he achieved first-class grades in all his courses.[7] Everything was going according to plan. Then, sometime in the second-to-last year of his degree program, Wilson encountered Professor Harry Hawthorn. With one year to go, everything changed.

*

Harry Hawthorn came to UBC in 1947 to lead the development of a new anthropology program. When he arrived he was the only faculty member in anthropology, which was embedded in the omnibus Department of Economics, Political Science and Sociology. The department head was the economist Henry Angus, and he and President Norman Mac-Kenzie invited Hawthorn to UBC. They had tried to attract the American anthropologist H.G. Barnett, who studied Indian cultures and culture change on the West Coast, to the position, but Barnett had other plans.

On the suggestion of the Canadian historian John Brebner, who taught at Columbia University, they wrote to Hawthorn, who accepted the offer. MacKenzie indicated to Hawthorn that he would be coming to a growing institution in a growing community with promise for the future but would be taking the usual gamble that all of us take with a new position.[8] As an experienced anthropologist who had moved around the world, Hawthorn would have understood the point.

Hawthorn was from New Zealand, and it was there that he developed his approach to anthropology. Through the 1930s he completed three degrees, two in mathematics and one in history. He then spent four years living in small, remote Māori communities, teaching school and studying the culture. One result of this experience was a monograph on acculturation in what he took to be a typical Māori village. The book was, he wrote, a descriptive ethnography in a historical context.[9] He studied Māori culture in a country where Māori were leaders in the anthropological examination of their own culture, something that would not happen in Canada for many years to come. In one of the Māori villages where Hawthorn worked, he heard about a man named Te Rangi Hiroa (Peter Buck), who was legendary for his earlier community work. Te Rangi Hiroa was then head of the Bishop Museum in Honolulu and also held a chair in anthropology at Yale University. Te Rangi Hiroa and his friend the Māori cultural and political leader Apirana Ngata believed that their Māori ancestry gave them an "inside angle" on the study of Māori culture. They were also committed to the idea that anthropology should serve to improve the social and economic conditions of Māori people.[10] Te Rangi Hiroa was the pre-eminent ethnographer of the Pacific Islands, and was particularly well known for his detailed studies of the material culture of Samoa and the Cook Islands. According to Hawthorn, Te Rangi Hiroa believed that "it is astonishing how detailed work opens one's eye to big problems."[11] It was a mantra that Hawthorn learned and then passed on to his own students. Te Rangi Hiroa was the connection that took Hawthorn first to the Bishop Museum for a year and then to Yale University to complete a PhD in 1941. At Yale he studied under Bronislaw Malinowski, one of the most influential anthropologists of the day and one of the first to argue that the discipline should align itself with "living social interests" and develop more practical applications.[12] The year before coming to UBC, at an academic conference in Montreal, Hawthorn met T.F. McIlwraith, the head of the first, and at the time the only, department of anthropology in Canada, at the University of Toronto, and learned something of the state of the discipline in the country. Hawthorn came to UBC after teaching for five years at Sarah Lawrence, an innovative teaching-focused college for women in Yonkers, near New York City.

Hawthorn built what became the anthropology department at UBC in an era when strong individuals could build effective disciplinary groups by making many decisions themselves. At the same time, Hawthorn was an assiduous networker. He brought to UBC, and then extended, an amazing set of connections with people that would benefit the growing anthropology group. At that stage, UBC was open and flexible, rather than rule governed, and much could be achieved through personal relations with the right people or, as the more skeptical academics put it, "toadying."[13] Whatever word is appropriate, Hawthorn was a natural. He immediately got to know the university administration. President MacKenzie was a member of the Department of Economics, Political Science and Sociology and soon became a member of the Harry Hawthorn fishing club, along with other administrators. According to non-members, the group made university decisions while fishing on the lakes of Vancouver Island. As well, Hawthorn quickly made contacts with senior bureaucrats in Ottawa and British Columbia. He wrote to Hugh Keenleyside, the federal deputy minister responsible for Indian Affairs, to inform him of his appointment to UBC, and he connected with W.S. Arneil, the British Columbia Indian commissioner.[14] He parlayed his contacts at the Carnegie Foundation into a $75,000 grant that enabled him to initiate a research program and hire some faculty. He brought connections with several New Zealanders who were big names in the international world of anthropology: in addition to Te Rangi Hiroa, he knew and corresponded with Diamond Jenness at the National Museum of Canada; Raymond Firth, who was professor of social anthropology at the London School of Economics; Felix Keesing, who was head of the Department of Anthropology at Stanford University and who Hawthorn addressed as "Dear Fee"; and Ernest Beaglehole at Victoria University in Wellington, New Zealand. Over the years, Hawthorn also brought a succession of New Zealanders, or anthropologists working on New Zealand topics, to UBC. Several, like the first, Diamond Jenness, came on limited-term appointments, but one stayed. Hawthorn was acquainted with the New Zealand economist Horace Belshaw, who was also known to UBC President MacKenzie. Raymond Firth had been a student of Horace Belshaw, and Belshaw's son Cyril was in turn a graduate student of Firth's in London. Cyril Belshaw was teaching at the Australian National University when he contacted Hawthorn about coming to UBC. Thus, the connections played out.[15] Cyril Belshaw came to UBC in 1953 and became a prominent and productive member of the department. Belshaw had served as a colonial administrator in the South Pacific and so had a practical, antipodean bent. He had also been exposed to British social anthropology and was much more interested in theory than Hawthorn. All the same, the two were close colleagues with some shared interests. Like Hawthorn, Belshaw's interest in anthropology was sparked during visits to Māori communities, in his case as a schoolboy accompanying his father. Hawthorn and Belshaw sometimes published together: once, for example, they entered a debate, through the *Journal of the Polynesian Society*, with some of the big guns in American cultural anthropology on whether the peoples of the Pacific had experienced cultural evolution or cultural change.[16] Hawthorn also quickly made two other contacts who would become very important to Wilson Duff. Soon after arriving at UBC he met with Erna Gunther, the chair of the closest anthropology department with a graduate program, at the University of Washington in Seattle, and with Clifford Carl, who was the director of the British Columbia Provincial Museum of Natural History and Anthropology in Victoria.

Hawthorn had worldwide connections, and he was one anthropologist in an omnibus department that included several disciplines. All this context was crucial, but he also needed a way to focus the development of anthropology at UBC. The university had built a small collection of artifacts over the years and, in 1947, the Museum of Anthropology was opened in the basement of the library building. Harry Hawthorn installed his wife, Audrey, as the curator of the museum. Audrey Hawthorn had a master's degree from Columbia University and had met Harry when she was in the graduate program in anthropology at Yale. She developed the collection and, under her leadership, the Museum of Anthropology became a successful centre of research and teaching. The Hawthorns founded and fostered that strong connection between the academic discipline of anthropology and the anthropology museum that endures today. For Harry, the museum was also a base from which to build an anthropology program. In his early years at UBC, much of his correspondence on the academic program went out on Museum of Anthropology letterhead.

Like some of his mentors, Harry Hawthorn was not much of an anthropological theorist. Rather, he left theory to others, like Belshaw. Though it was not his field when he arrived at UBC, he planned to focus on the Indigenous cultures of British Columbia and to develop a program of teaching and research that, he wrote, "I expected to be in the service of Indian needs."[17] He believed, that is to say, in "useful" anthropology, directed toward improving the lives of Indian people and informing public policy. He began by immersing himself in the literature about Indian cultures in British Columbia. In his first two years he also travelled widely through British Columbia to listen to Indian people in their communities, an unusual initiative since listening to First Nations people did not happen much in British Columbia in the 1940s. Hawthorn was committed to initiating an intercultural conversation. At the end of his first academic year at UBC, in April 1948, he organized a conference on what he called "Native Indian affairs," which featured sessions on Indian health, welfare and education as well as arts and crafts. The conference was innovative because it featured First Nations speakers, including some who were prepared to contradict the anthropologists. When Erna Gunther suggested that Indian artists could make supplementary income in the winter when they were not out fishing, Leslie John, a carver from Nanaimo, responded that he was not able to make much of an income from either pursuit. Ellen Neel, an artist from Alert Bay, who as a woman was unique among Northwest Coast totem pole carvers, asserted that the Indigenous art of British Columbia was not dead and that universities and museums needed to play a role in keeping it alive. Summing up the conference, Hawthorn thanked the Indian speakers, who held everyone's attention by their "ability, restraint and dramatic power." He went on to say, "We have heard the facts and conditions of their life, not from someone who has studied those facts, but from those who have lived them. Their speeches can never be forgotten by those who heard them."[18] Hawthorn continued to try to explain the colonial predicament of First Nations people in British Columbia and Canada to an ever-wider audience. Norman MacKenzie was a member of the Royal Commission on National Development in the Arts, Letters and Sciences (the Massey Commission), and he arranged for Harry and Audrey Hawthorn to write a section for its report on Indigenous arts and crafts. The Hawthorns wrote of the need to increase the knowledge and appreciation of Indigenous art among the public and to establish programs that would foster the growth of arts and crafts in Indian communities.[19]

Through his contacts in the federal government, Hawthorn was also the organizer and author of two major reports on the status and social conditions of Indian people: the first, on British Columbia Indians, in the 1950s, and the second, covering all of Canada, in the 1960s. Hawthorn worked on these reports to demonstrate that anthropologists could inform governments with evidence-based policy advice and that anthropology could thereby serve a useful function. Nowadays, these reports can be easily taken out of context and inaccurately criticized as advocating for the assimilation of Indian culture. In fact, the first recommendation in the report on Canada was that neither integration nor assimilation should be objectives. Rather, the report raised the idea of "citizens plus": that is, Indians had the rights of any other Canadian citizens plus Aboriginal rights.[20] In their day, Hawthorn's reports were an effort to speak to newcomers about the challenges faced by the First Nations people in their midst, and about how Indian cultures might be preserved as they adjusted to change in a mid-twentieth-century colonialist environment. Few of the recommendations in the reports, it has to be said, were implemented by governments. Cyril Belshaw, who worked with Hawthorn on the first report on British Columbia, continued to think and write about the fraught relationship between anthropologists and public policy.[21]

Hawthorn was aided in all this collaborative work by the fact that many people related to his charm and social grace. Indeed, he could not have built a successful anthropology department and led it for more than twenty years without persuasive people skills. Many students and colleagues remember how much he encouraged them and fostered the development of their careers. In 1956, now the head of the Department of Anthropology, Sociology and Criminology, he was courted for position at Otago University back in New Zealand. He took a trip south to explore the possibility, but Cyril Belshaw hoped that he would decide against making a move "for I don't know of any Department of this structure which works so smoothly, and I doubt if I could handle things the way he does."[22]

While gregarious and congenial, Hawthorn, along with Belshaw, also had an antipodean edge and directness that was distinct from the usually milder-mannered Canadian academic discourse. Like Wilson's father, he had definite views that he did not mind expressing strongly. Hawthorn could look down a rather long nose of disapprobation at people with ideas that did not meet with his approval. For example, he was absolutely dismissive of physical anthropology, believing that it was a branch of anatomy with no place in an anthropology program. Asked to reflect back on his career, he began by observing that "modesty is at best a wishy-washy virtue."[23] A colleague at the University of Auckland, who had been offhand with Hawthorn after he had delivered a guest lecture there, was dismissed as "an anthropological nincompoop." On the other hand, someone he recommended for a position in the New Zealand Department of Education was described as having "that slight degree of illiteracy which characterizes so many North Americans," though, he added, it had "no implications for capacity…" As new anthropology departments were being founded across Canada, Hawthorn was frequently asked for recommendations on potential faculty members. He responded to one such request by sug-gesting that the inquirer also contact senior anthropologists Edmund Leach at Cambridge University and Raymond Firth at the London School of Economics, because neither has ever been known "to describe a duck as a swan."[24] There were definitely two sides to Hawthorn's personality, and through his long association with him Wilson would experience both.

*

Harry Hawthorn and Wilson Duff would have met sometime in the first half of 1948. Hawthorn was on the lookout for bright, promising students to bring into anthropology. Years later, Hawthorn would recall that, above all things that he had done, he was most proud of the many students whose progress he had encouraged.[25] Seeing Wilson as an ideal prospect, Hawthorn would have been persuasive and enthusiastic. Not totally com-mitted to either forestry or engineering, Wilson was open to Hawthorn's proselytizing and attracted to the study of anthropology because it inte-grated the life of the mind with practical skills. It was unlikely that anthro-pology was practical enough, or a sure enough path to a job and security, to meet with his father's approval, but Wilson had long since stopped fol-lowing his father's advice. More importantly, in Harry Hawthorn, Wilson found a male mentor who, for the time being, was much more compatible and supportive and, unlike his father, recognized his ability and intelli-gence. Wilson had found his element and he took to anthropology, not so much like a duck as a swan to water.

When Wilson Duff became a student of anthropology in the fall of 1948, the program at UBC mostly involved three people. Hawthorn was developing the curriculum and teaching almost all the courses. There were four anthropology courses in the calendar for that year and Wilson took two, both taught by Hawthorn: Anthropology 300, Social Anthro-pology, and Anthropology 402, Indians of British Columbia. Hawthorn reported, in the gendered language of the day, that Wilson "emerged top man in four courses this December."[26] Audrey Hawthorn at the Museum of Anthropology would teach Wilson about museums and museum practice. He would spend lots of time in the museum in the basement of the university library, working with Audrey as she developed the collection in a restricted space.

The third person that was a huge influence on Wilson was Charles Borden. He was a faculty member in the German department, but his real interest was archaeology. He was both earnest and enthusiastic about unearthing British Columbia's Indigenous past. Rigorous and exacting in the practice of archaeology, Borden could be at once intimidating and generous; he did not suffer fools gladly, but he immediately saw the potential in Wilson. There had been earlier pioneers in British Columbia archaeology, but no one played a greater role in establishing it on a professional and scientific basis than Borden. For a couple of years he had been exploring midden sites in the Fraser River delta with a view to establishing, for the first time, a chronology of cultures. Then, in the fall of 1948, Hawthorn's Indians of British Columbia course required each student to carry out a field study. Hawthorn had Borden organize lectures and fieldwork around a dig that he was conducting at a site in Marpole, in South Vancouver. Several students took part; Borden later recalled that they were a mix from very good to poor, but Wilson was a standout. He was, Borden remembered, enthusiastic, perceptive, meticulous and always willing to help others, with a cheerful sense of humour that was uplifting even when terrible weather made the work unpleasant. Wilson's aptitude for, and application to, his first experience in archaeology while still an undergraduate were factors in the success of this trial project. The archaeology course was added to the anthropology curriculum the following year.[27] Wilson's student essay reporting on the work at Marpole revealed the characteristics that would define his scholarly writing throughout his career: clear description and clear ideas expressed in clear language.[28]

Wilson's life changed in another way in September 1948 when he and Marion were married. In their wedding photos outside the church they are caught in the moment surrounded by family and friends and smiling brightly at the camera. Yet that moment in time could not be separated from past and future. They were still quite different people: Wilson was shy, somewhat introverted and already intensely dedicated to his new field of study, while Marion was vivacious and sociable. Postwar marriages often involved challenges around gender roles as well, as the expectation of the fifties was that men went out to work and women took care of home and children. Though Wilson did not marry as soon as he returned from overseas, he was, like many veterans after the disruptions of war, wanting to establish a stable and happy domestic life as a home base for a successful career. Marion's wartime experience working in the Women's Royal Naval Service in different parts of Canada had given her a sense of autonomy. The prospect of settling down to a marriage and raising a family would have required real adjustment on her part. For Marion, that change could not have been easy, particularly when Wilson's image of a wife and mother was the nurturing and supporting role that his own mother epitomized.[29] Yet marriage and children were expected of young people, both by their wider family and by society. After the war, marriage and family were valued as ways to establish social stability. There was pressure to conform to those expectations. At the same time, there were elements of doubt about marriage because of the extended periods that women and men had spent apart had strained relationships. Divorce rates were also high after the war.[30] Marion and Wilson began married life by setting up house on East Broadway, near Commercial Drive, in Vancouver, on the same block as Marion's parents. Marion took a secretarial job while Wilson threw himself into the anthropology program at UBC.

He quickly developed a close association with Harry Hawthorn. They travelled together to meet with members of reserve communities while Wilson was still an undergraduate. One excursion was to visit Stalo (now Stó:lō) people, who were hop-picking in the Mount Vernon area of Washington State. Hop-picking was a time of gathering of people from many Salish communities and an opportunity for a fledgling anthropologist to meet and talk to potential sources of cultural knowledge. Then, in the spring of 1949, Hawthorn arranged with Erna Gunther for the University of Washington to set up a course in archaeology based on a dig at the Whalen

Farm site on the east shore of Point Roberts facing Boundary Bay. Charles Borden supervised the excavation, while Hawthorn arranged with the Department of Veterans Affairs and UBC Department Head Henry Angus for Wilson to take the course. It would, wrote Hawthorn, be "a course in archeological method and in the archeology of the southern coast."[31]

Borden recalled that Wilson's contribution was important to the success of the archaeological training school. This creative inter-university partnership also gave Wilson the final six credits that he needed to complete his bachelor's degree. As he was working at Whalen Farm he would surely have occasionally paused and, looking up from the dig and across Boundary Bay to the airport, reflected on where he had been and how far he had come in the five years since he first took off in a Liberator over the bay. His past was with him, but his focus was the future. The Point Roberts and Boundary Bay area presented a rich archaeological record of centuries of Indigenous life, but Wilson was also thinking about the wider Salish cultural area and other approaches to understanding those cultures. During that summer he would slip away from Whalen Farm on weekends to conduct a survey of pit house sites in the Hope–Chilliwack area of the Upper Fraser Valley. This investigation, amounting to a total of three and a half weeks, involved talking to Stalo elders to find the location of house and other sites, then digging test pits to see if they warranted further study.[32] It was a brief foray into an area that, Wilson concluded, certainly deserved closer examination.

Wilson's initial contact and subsequent work with the Stalo people of the Upper Fraser were facilitated by Marion's family connections with the area. When her grandfather Francis Barber separated from his second wife, Mira Barber, he bought her a piece of land at Haig Station, just across the Fraser River from the town of Hope. Mira lived in a log building at Haig and, for more than twenty years, reached out to and interacted with the Stalo people of the area. She also collected and displayed in her home examples of their arts and crafts. In fact, Mira's house at Haig became a small museum of Stalo artifacts and a centre for the encouragement and understanding of Indigenous culture and art. Mira hosted Wilson and introduced him to the people of the area. She also knew the location of many of the Stalo sites and showed some of them to Wilson. She took him to see caves near the Barbers' Restmore lodge, a few miles down the Fraser River from Haig, and showed him the Stalo artifacts that she had collected there. In the summer of 1949, Marion accompanied Wilson on the field trip. She was always very attached to the area and the family connections there, and Mira was a role model of an independent woman. That same summer, Mira Barber made a gift of her museum to the Fraser Canyon Indian Arts and Crafts Society, established to continue her work by making the museum open to the public, and, in collaboration with the Stalo people, fostering an understanding and appreciation of Indigenous art. Established on this new footing, the museum was opened twice in 1949: first in July by Stalo chiefs Peter Pete from Hope and Peter Emery of Yale, and then again in November when Premier Byron Johnson came to redo the honours. On his first, and later, visits to the Upper Fraser, Wilson stayed with Mira Barber and she provided him with an entree to the people and cultures of the area.[33]

Wilson Duff graduated from UBC with a first-class bachelor of arts at the spring convocation of 1949. On graduation day, Wilson was photographed with two other graduates, both of whom had been navigators on bomber crews. His cousin Mervyn graduated with a social work degree and went on to a career working with inmates in British Columbia's prisons and eventually with the John Howard Society. Percy Gladstone, a Haida, would go on to be the first First Nations person to receive a graduate degree from UBC. Gladstone had a nephew who would soon become important to Wilson as he developed his career in anthropology. The nephew's name was Bill Reid. Having earned their degrees, the veterans were now moving on to the next phase of their lives.

That summer Wilson worked as a temporary field assistant in anthropology at the Provincial Museum in Victoria. Under the aegis of the museum he and Hawthorn travelled north to the Nass and Skeena Rivers to visit Indian communities. Hawthorn thought that it would be a "useful piece of training" for Wilson. The excursion was an opportunity to learn first-hand about the communities of the northern coast and experience the hardships of fieldwork. They gathered ethnographic information from informants in the four Nisga'a villages along the Nass River. In New Aiyansh (now Gitlaxt'aamiks) Wilson asked young men about marriage customs. As an anthropologist in training, he needed to learn about kinship and marriage patterns, though perhaps he was interested because he himself was recently married. He was told that they resented the old clan exogamy rules that limited their choice of marriage partners. Nevertheless, they still followed the old rules to avoid shocking the old people and losing respect in the community. Wilson noted that they could still dance with any girl!

In the Gitksan (now Gitxsan) villages on or near the Skeena—Kitwanga (now Gitwangak), Kitwancool (now Gitanyow) and Kispiox—they saw impressive totem poles but found the elders that they spoke to were very reserved and unwilling to talk freely. Wilson did learn enough to know that he wanted to learn more. Between the Nass and the Skeena Rivers they walked from New Aiyansh to Kitsumkalum Lake, losing their way and getting very sore feet, before taking a boat down the lake to Terrace, where they limped around the town "like a couple of lame old men."[34]

Fortunately, Hawthorn had laid out a clearer, if not easier, path toward Wilson's career as an anthropologist. In the fall of 1949, Wilson registered as a graduate student in anthropology at the University of Washington in Seattle, and began a year of coursework toward a master's degree. Hawthorn had arranged for him to work with Erna Gunther, who, as head, had developed the anthropology department, and was also the director of the Washington State Museum. Marion went with Wilson to Seattle and worked as a secretary for Gunther over the academic year, so they both came to know her well. Outgoing, generous and caring, Erna Gunther was referred to affectionately by the graduate students as "the great white mother."[35]

Erna Gunther had been a student of Franz Boas, the formative figure of North American anthropology and the source of its emphasis on the cultures of the Northwest. The Boasian agenda was to salvage as much information as possible about the culture and language of peoples who he believed were disappearing. At the time of his first field trip to British Columbia, in 1886, and over the years that followed, there was every reason to believe that Indian cultures and languages would disappear as the population continued to decline. By the time Wilson was a student at the University of Washington, the population had passed its lowest point and was slowly increasing. But it was still only a fraction of what it had been at first contact with Europeans. Through the rest of his career, Boas made many trips to the west and collected and published an enormous amount of material on the cultures of the coast and, to a lesser extent, the interior. Much of his work was made possible by the collaboration of colleagues at the local level, most notably George Hunt among the Kwakiutl (now Kwakwaka'wakw) and James Teit, who lived at Spence's Bridge and worked for Boas among the Thompson (Nlaka'pamux) and their neighbours over a wide area. Boas also developed the idea of cultural relativism that held that cultures should not be compared with each other in ways that lead to any kind of ranking or value-laden judgements. He believed that cultures developed from within rather than in response to the forces of nature or by evolution toward a higher western level. Thus each culture should be studied for its own sake and understood on its own terms. It was logical that he should also argue against grouping artifacts in museum displays by artifact type, as was common practice, and insist that, rather, they should be arranged according to the culture that they came from. Boas tried to understand the minds of the people he studied in order to describe the meaning of their culture as they saw it. An account of a culture should therefore cover all its elements in great detail and be acquired directly from the people themselves. Generalizations, he believed, particularly if they were made about more than one culture, or if they suggested universal human patterns, were likely to arise from our own culture and not the one being studied.

Between then and now, Boas's legacy has been assessed and reassessed. He did much to establish the credibility of anthropology as an academic discipline and the value of detailed ethnographic descriptions of other cultures. As a public intellectual he vigorously challenged ideas of the day about the inferiority of cultures and peoples that were based on racism and evolution. Critics, on the other hand, have drawn attention to his obsession with detailed on-the-ground descriptions of cultures and his reluctance to entertain bigger ideas, suggesting that he did not recognize Indigenous people as individuals as he described cultures in cold, scientific detail. His descriptions took too little account of post-contact change and he did little to address the contemporary issues that First Nations people faced as a consequence of newcomer settlement. He was personally uncomfortable when he was in the field in the Northwest and so relied to a great extent on the work of colleagues in local communities, most notably, but not only, George Hunt and James Teit. Then he subsumed their work into his own without giving them appropriate credit for the vital role that they played. More recently he has been criticized for epitomizing the omniscient anthropologist, deciding what's what about Indigenous cultures. For all of the subsequent questioning of Boas and his contribution, there can be no doubt as to his formative role in the development of anthropology as an academic discipline devoted to the study of other cultures.[36] As the first professor of anthropology at Columbia University, Boas bestowed his approach and ideas upon his many graduate students, who then continued his legacy in anthropology departments and museums all over North America. And his students, in turn, handed the torch to the next generation. Wilson learned and practised the Boasian approach to ethnography early in his career and later on went far beyond it.

As befitted a Boas student, Erna Gunther's interests were in descriptive ethnography, material culture and the development of museums that displayed the artifacts of Northwest Coast Indian cultures. Throughout her academic career she developed a detailed knowledge of the culture and history of the people of the Northwest Coast rather than pursuing broader cultural theory or innovative interpretation. Just like Audrey Hawthorn after her, Gunther was appointed to a university position through her partner when she and Leslie Spier came to the anthropology department at the University of Washington. Spier later departed, but Gunther stayed on to become department head. As she developed the anthropology department, Gunther tended to hire other faculty of like mind, and two would have a great influence on Wilson. Viola Garfield, who had also taken courses from Franz Boas, had just published a study of the totem poles of southeast Alaska and was studying Tsimshian culture. Verne Ray was a traditional ethnographer who had published on the Indian cultures of the interior plateau in an effort to show that those cultures were distinctive in their own right rather than merely derivative of their neighbours. Wilson was also one of a group of graduate students in the department, many of whom would go on to contribute to the anthropological literature on the Northwest Coast. Wilson met Wayne Suttles, with whom he shared an interest in Salish cultures, and they became close friends and colleagues. Suttles was the first student to complete a PhD in anthropology at the University of Washington. Bill Holm was another Gunther student at the time who studied Northwest Coast Indian art. Holm does not recall meeting Wilson at that stage, but they too would become colleagues.[37] Gunther had built a strong academic department but, in the judgment of some, it reflected where anthropology had been rather than where it was going. Nevertheless, it was the logical place to go for a UBC graduate wanting to learn more about how to approach the study of Indigenous cultures of the Northwest Coast.[38]

In this intellectual context, Wilson learned the practice of traditional descriptive ethnography. He wrote a number of essays that reflected his growing breadth of interests. In November of the first semester, he submitted a long essay on "The Northwest Coast Village," in which he described the factors that determined the location, layout and size of villages, house types, the makeup of the communities, and social organization. The essay demonstrated a command of the current literature on the Northwest Coast, clarity of ethnographic detail and, within limits, a willingness to speculate. He wrote other essays on subjects such as Arctic pottery, Kwakiutl woodworking, "Primitive" stoneworking, and the sashes worn by the Igorot people of the Philippines. His essays typically earned A grades. In the spring semester he wrote on "Polynesian and Micronesian Navigation" and drew on his own experience as a navigator. That one was an A+ effort.[39]

The course that probably had the most immediate influence on Wilson was Verne Ray's Anthropology 250: Ethnographic Field Techniques. Ethnographic fieldwork is a process by which the anthropologist observes, records and engages in the daily life of another culture in order to write a detailed descriptive account of that culture. It was fundamental to the discipline at the time and had antecedents going back to the great founding figures in anthropology: Bronislaw Malinowski in Britain and Franz Boas in North America. Not surprisingly, Verne Ray's course advocated the traditional Boasian approach to ethnographic fieldwork. Drawing on his own experience and that of other anthropologists, Ray gave a thorough and practical seminar on how to go about doing ethnography. He covered topics such as how to choose your area of study, preparing to go into the field, how to contact and get the best information out of informants, the pros and cons of using an interpreter, and collecting specimens for museums. He was clear that the university-trained ethnographer was the expert who needed to discriminate between reliable and unreliable information, but at the same time the informant should be encouraged to engage with the information: "Make him an ethnographer and your friend," Ray advised his students. He cited the partnership between Franz Boas and his Kwakiutl partner, George Hunt, as an example to emulate. Ray advised against using an interpreter unless absolutely necessary, which meant there would usually be a language barrier between the ethnographer and the individual consulted. In his course, Ray also covered the "culture element distribution" approach that originated with Boas and was practised on the Northwest Coast, particularly by anthropologists from the University of California. This approach involved breaking a culture down into its component parts, compiling lists of the traits, and thereby establishing the distinctions and boundaries between cultures. It was not a foolproof methodology, and Ray was not convinced that it was the right approach, although he had tried it in the Thompson River area of British Columbia. On a more practical level, Ray promoted the use of photography in the field and discussed the merits of various cameras, film, lenses and filters. Indeed, some students thought that Anthropology 250 should be renamed Cameras 250.[40]

One class exercise in Verne Ray's course required every student to produce a proposal for an ethnographic project at short notice. The proposal had to include the name of the group to be studied, a bibliography, a schedule of the time required for the fieldwork and to write the ethnography, and an indication of which granting agencies would be approached for funding. Wilson wrote up a proposal for an ethnographic study of the Nisga'a and Gitksan communities that he had visited along the Nass and Skeena Rivers that summer. He proposed a three-stage process to gather information from local people. The first was to develop a rapport with the people and gain respect for himself. The second would be to work with selected individuals whom he felt that he could trust to obtain reliable cultural information. He presented a long list of cultural topics to be covered, based largely on George Murdock's *Outline of Cultural Materials*, a standard text at the time.[41] The third stage would be to elicit information that might be culturally sensitive from an even smaller group of informants. "Such aspects," he suggested, "may be highly personal, or may have to do with activities or beliefs which are strongly discredited by our culture." He realized that an important issue among the Nisga'a and Gitksan was the fact that they had never signed a treaty and so still had legal claims to the land. "The legal issue is not yet dead," he noted prophetically, and that issue would demand "exact information on the aboriginal system of land ownership."

The class exercise also called for an outline of a particular topic that the ethnographer would consider. Wilson suggested a comparison of the Nisga'a village of New Aiyansh and the Gitksan community of Kitwancool. The difference between the two communities was that New Aiyansh had a strong and continuous missionary presence, whereas Kitwancool had only sporadic missionary and other contacts. His research question was: What were the consequences of these two different experiences of outside contact? Wilson was learning how to approach gathering ethno-graphic detail on another culture, and, at the same time, putting his mind to bigger issues. Establishing detail as a foundation for thinking about more expansive ideas was a pattern that would characterize his life's work as an anthropologist. He always began with the detail. Verne Ray pro-nounced his proposal, which represented the initial steps down that path, to be "very good."[42]

When he wrote that proposal, Wilson seemed to be thinking of doing more ethnographic work among the Nisga'a and Gitksan for his master's thesis, the next phase of his graduate program. Certainly his thesis would be an ethnographic study of a particular culture and would be supervised by Erna Gunther. In the end, he decided to do more work in the Upper Fraser Valley with the Stalo, whom he had also visited the previous sum-mer. The decision about which culture to study may have been partly determined by Gunther's interest in the neighbouring Coast Salish groups of western Washington State. She had published on the ethnography of the Klallam and, more recently, one of her most popular works was on the ethnobotany of Western Washington.[43] Wilson respected Gunther and took in her advice, yet in the end he made his own decisions, even as a graduate student. He had already worked among the Stalo, and the Barber family connections and hospitality were really helpful. Whenever Wilson passed through Vancouver, heading out to the field, he would call in on his parents on Lanark Street, but he usually stayed with the Barbers. In the summer of 1950 Wilson spent nine weeks living and working with Stalo informants in the area between Chilliwack and Yale.

*

While he was completing his first degree at UBC, Wilson already knew that there was a position as a professional anthropologist waiting for him at the British Columbia Provincial Museum in Victoria. Harry Hawthorn had arranged it. The previous anthropologist at the museum, A.E. Pick-ford, was not a trained anthropologist and he was, at least once, on the receiving end of a Hawthorn critique. Pickford's writing about Indian cultures for museum displays and booklets could politely be described as representing the prejudices of the day. Once, Hawthorn read something that Pickford had written on Haida culture that was critical of slavery and so-called Haida avarice. He wrote to Pickford suggesting a "more charitable approach" since "No society, even our own, looks very good when judged without a fair amount of sympathy and affection for it."[44] Clifford Carl, the director of the museum, had been writing to anthropologists across North America looking for a more qualified candidate than Pickford when he retired in 1946. The position involved a range of responsibilities, the salary was not generous, and there were few anthropologists in Canada, so Carl had not found the right person. When Hawthorn suggested Wilson for the position once he had completed his coursework year at the University of Washington, Carl immediately took him up on it. Wilson Duff became a permanent employee of the British Columbia Provincial Museum in June of 1950. His title was assistant in anthropology, but, since he was the only anthropologist at the museum, he was effectively the provincial anthropologist.

Part of the arrangement with the Provincial Museum was that he would do the fieldwork for his thesis on the Stalo over the summer. While he was a graduate student at the University of Washington, his MA research in the Upper Fraser Valley was "done under the auspices of the Provincial Museum of British Columbia." Wilson had learned archaeology at UBC from Charles Borden and now ethnography from Erna Gunther and Verne Ray at the University of Washington. His research in the area the previous summer had been archaeological, whereas this summer it would be ethnographic.[45] The gentle side of Wilson's personality enabled him to move easily in reserve communities. He approached people with grace and humility, was a careful listener, and could absorb and retain vast amounts of detail. It nevertheless took him a few weeks to get the hang of doing ethnography. He started his fieldwork not knowing what to expect and with a rather vague idea of looking at the question of group mobility within the area. In the first few weeks he concentrated on collecting place names, ownership of fishing locations, traditions of population movements, and subsistence activities. He supplemented information on material culture by examining the artifacts from the area held in the Provincial Museum. He also shot movies of Stalo fishing in the Fraser Canyon above Yale and hop-picking around Agassiz. Yet, with all this work, he was still not satisfied that he had found the right way to focus all the cultural information that he was collecting, so he took a month out of the field to reflect.

When he returned to the area, he began to gather more sensitive information on "social organization, shamanism, the acquisition of power, healing with power, and other concepts of the supernatural." He moved in with a couple who he had met at the end of his last trip: Edmond Lorenzetto and his wife, who lived at Katz, just below Hope on the Fraser River. The couple became his most important informants of the seven that he interviewed. Of the other five, Patrick Charlie of Yale was the most interesting. He talked to Wilson "with obvious sincerity" and claimed "that he was born a second time...and retained memories of a previous life." At this early stage in his career, Wilson was skeptical about this individual's belief in rebirth, as, he believed, were others in the Stalo community. He came away happier from his last stint in the field for that summer, and he wrote to Erna Gunther that he had a much better handle on how to approach writing the ethnographic information for a thesis. In fact, he thought that he had enough information for "a sort of introductory ethnography of the part of the River between Chilliwack and Yale." He proposed to make available all of the data that he had gathered, rather than focusing on specialized aspects of it. "Harry agrees with me on this," he added, and so "with your permission, that's what I'll do."[46]

Wilson's nine weeks of ethnographic collecting among the Stalo provided rich material for his master's thesis. As many graduate students learn after the fact, it was the last time in his life that he could single-mindedly focus on one piece of work. He returned to Victoria with a good sense of how to move forward on his thesis, but he also knew that he would be writing it in the midst of many other responsibilities. Two weeks after he wrote to Erna Gunther about his planned approach, he wrote again to point out that "as you know one cannot count on much uninterrupted time with museum work."[47] Fortunately, in addition to his strong commitment to hard work and long hours, he also had the energy of youth on his side. When Wilson took up his position as anthropologist for the province of British Columbia, he was only twenty-five—young in years but mature in experience.

4. Provincial Anthropologist

When Wilson Duff became the British Columbia Provincial Museum's anthropologist in 1950, the Indigenous people of British Columbia were still suffering from the traumatic effects of a century of settler colonization. Those effects were both endemic and intensely local. While they had voted for the first time in a provincial election in 1949, and one of their number, Frank Calder, was elected to the provincial legislature, registered Indians would still wait another ten years before they were able to vote in a federal election. The province of British Columbia dismissed their ownership of the land as irrelevant, and because Indians had been relegated to a tiny land base on allocated reserves, there were still huge constraints on economic and community development. Starting in the 1860s, the reserves that had been originally laid out were systematically whittled away by provincial and federal governments over the following decades. In 1950 it was still illegal to organize or raise money to protest against the historical misappropriation of Indian land, and it was still illegal to hold a potlatch, the ceremony that was fundamental to many of the cultures of British Columbia. Some children, like many of their parents, were still being sent to residential schools, still with devastating results. In 1946 a First Nations man, a decorated veteran, was sent several times to Oakalla Prison Farm for trying to eat in a Vanderhoof cafe that refused to serve Indian people. It was still illegal to drink alcohol if you were an Indian. Initially Indians could not drink anywhere, then the law was updated so that they could drink in beer parlours but not in their homes. Living conditions and health care were still appalling in many communities. In short, settler society in British Columbia had a dreadful record of treatment of the province's First Peoples.

While First Nations people endured the effects of the drastic changes of the last one hundred years, many elements of the traditional cultures had, against the odds, survived. With only a few exceptions, however, newcomer British Columbians turned a deaf ear to complaints about the conditions in which First Nations people lived, their struggle to improve their lives, and their efforts to retain some of their culture. In 1950, most British Columbians knew little, and cared less, about the Indigenous cultures of the province. There was very little appreciation, let alone understanding, of Northwest Coast art and the skill and imagination that created it. Even the iconic totem pole was described in the *Vancouver Sun* in 1952 as "unspeakably hideous."[1] Wilson's role at the Provincial Museum was to do what he could to preserve the Indigenous cultures of British Columbia and interpret them to this largely uncomprehending audience of people who had inherited, benefitted from and perpetuated their colonial past. He was to be a bridge between two cultural islands separated by a sea of ignorance.

*

British Columbia's Provincial Museum was established by an act of the legislature in 1886, in response to pressure from community leaders and interest groups to do something to preserve the province's heritage. In 1898 the museum moved into the east wing of the newly constructed legislature building and was still housed there when Wilson joined the staff more than fifty years later. Over the years the museum would play a major role in the collection and preservation of the art and artifacts of the province's Indigenous cultures, but the anthropology section faced significant challenges in fulfilling its mandate. There was growing concern among the few who knew what was happening that Indian artifacts were being siphoned off by collectors from other countries and lost to British Columbia. The museum did not collect or display material from other parts of the world, prompting Wilson to observe that: "I am afraid that ours is a Provincial Museum in more than one sense."[2] Although, throughout its history, the Provincial Museum never seemed to have enough money or space, it slowly became the leading repository for the province's past that it then interpreted to the present.

In 1940 Clifford Carl was appointed director of the Provincial Museum and led its development for nearly thirty years. Carl was a marine biologist with a PhD from the University of Toronto, yet he also championed the museum's mandate to represent the Indigenous cultures of the province. The Provincial Museum of Natural History was renamed the Provincial Museum of Natural History and Anthropology soon after Carl was appointed director, to reflect its twin interests. In his role as director, Carl was very personable with his staff, so the tension between the natural science and human history divisions that existed in many museums was largely absent. Another stress line in some museums is the relative weight placed on original research versus the need to appeal to the public. Under Carl fieldwork and research continued, yet he clearly understood that for the museum to thrive it needed to attract an increasing number of visitors. The best way to increase the numbers coming through the door, both tourists and locals, was constant communication with people and communities. Carl enthusiastically promoted public lectures, programs for schools and the publication of reports and handbooks. Another of Carl's initiatives was to increase the professional level of the museum staff. In that context, on the advice of Harry Hawthorn, he appointed Wilson Duff.

As he searched for a trained anthropologist, Carl was clear that, since the museum was still a small institution, the position would require someone who could multitask. He needed an anthropologist who could carry out research and also speak to the public. They would also have to take care of the displayed and stored material in the museum, deal with written requests and other correspondence and prepare materials for schools. A certain amount of fieldwork would also be permitted. Unfortunately the salary was not great, less than $2,000 a year, though there might be some room for negotiation. Wilson was appointed on the understanding that he would finish his master's thesis at the University of Washington. The museum now had a staff of eight: Carl and two assistants in Natural History, Wilson the only anthropologist, and four support staff.

There was a sense among anthropologists that Wilson's appointment at the Provincial Museum marked the arrival of a more qualified and

professional approach to anthropology "after these many years of amateur good intentions."[3] That impression was warranted in comparison
with what went before, yet Wilson had not taken many university courses
in anthropology, and he had spent limited time in the field. He took
four undergraduate anthropology courses at UBC and a year of graduate
courses at the University of Washington—his university course work did
not add up to comprehensive conditioning in the discipline. That relative
lack of formal training may well have contributed to his independent and
creative thinking, particularly in later life.

In 1950, at the age of twenty-five, Wilson was keen to get on with his
new career and he did so with a fervour. On his second day as provincial anthropologist, he wrote to a friend at the University of Washington,
"I must say it is exciting and a bit hectic getting straightened around."[4]
Within two weeks he was off for a month of ethnographic fieldwork
among the Upper Stalo of the Fraser Valley. In addition to the work on his
master's thesis, in his first few months at the Provincial Museum Wilson
was immersed in a range of responsibilities, just as Carl had predicted. He
quickly established a close working relationship with Carl, got to know the
rest of the staff at the museum, and started to make contacts with people
in other areas of government. He familiarized himself with the museum's
displays and reorganized the material in storage. A large number of new
artifacts were also acquired in his first year, including a significant collection of Kwakiutl (Kwakwaka'wakw) and Nootkan (Nuu-chah-nulth)
items purchased from William Halliday, the Indian agent who had led the
legal attack on the potlatch following Dan Cranmer's potlatch on Village
Island in 1922. Wilson gave numerous presentations to groups, particularly school children who came to the museum, and to meetings of other
groups by request. He began a long and close association with the Songhees (ləkʷəŋən) in the Victoria area by visiting their reserve to gather
ethnographic information. He did a little archaeology in the local area
when people discovered human remains. It was enough for him to realize
that archaeological sites in the province were seriously threatened. Sites
were being destroyed before they could be investigated, so there was an

urgent need for legislation to protect them. He quickly made plans for an archaeological survey of the province to establish the location and condition of all sites. The information gathered would be shared by the museum and UBC. He made plans for a publication series, to be called Anthropology in British Columbia, as a way get the work done by anthropologists out to a wider public.[5] Wilson continued to be involved in all these things, along with many others, throughout his time at the Provincial Museum. The pace of his work never let up. Wilson threw himself into his duties at the museum with an intensity that left little time for family life.

*

Wilson and Marion arrived in Victoria in the summer of 1950. They moved into an apartment while they looked for the right house, as they were about to become a family. Their first child was on the way and Wilson thought that Marion was looking like "a million dollars," even if she was losing her girlish figure. Marilyn, who would be known as Marnie, was born in January 1951. Wilson was congratulated on becoming a father by Erna Gunther, and he responded that the Duff household had, needless to say, not yet settled down into a fixed routine. The new arrival was tiny except in voice, Wilson explained, and her "little timing mechanism seems to want to operate on a two-hour, rather than a four-hour schedule."[6] The following year they moved into a larger house on Richmond Avenue, not far from Gonzales Bay, that gave the family more room to live and Wilson to work. As people often do when they first move to Victoria, the Duffs had a steady stream of friends and relatives come to stay with them. "Odds are good," Wilson wrote to Harry Hawthorn, "that I'll never live alone with my wife again." Hawthorn, ever the source of clear if not always good advice, replied, "If I were married to a girl like Marion, & I think I am, I would kick the lousy relatives out, & I have as often as necessary."[7] Can we assume that friends were spared the boot at the Hawthorn residence? In any event, Marion had a rather different sense of the reason that she and Wilson had so little time together. She put it down to the amount of work that Wilson was doing. "Every once in awhile I have to lay down the law," she wrote to her family, "because he has to devote some time to his family."[8] Indeed, when he was not out of town in the field or at meetings, Wilson worked day and night, usually retreating to his desk at home in the evening after dinner. He also worked a good deal on the weekends. For a resigned Marion, Saturday and Sunday were not much different from weekdays. Marion's frustration at Wilson's intense focus on his work and its consequences for the family would have been all the more keenly felt because she must have known that these were patterns that Wilson had developed since high school. They were not likely to change much now.

The first priority, though for Wilson not the only one, was to complete his graduate program at the University of Washington by writing his master's thesis and getting it approved. It was his ticket into his chosen profession, and he was also committed to writing up what he had learned from his Upper Stalo informants. Writing a thesis while starting a new job that, in terms of demands and hours, was more than full-time was challenge enough. What was more, he was a careful, meticulous writer who pondered over words with a delicate precision. It was a characteristic that became more ingrained with time and practice. He was also writing his thesis with a clear eye on its publication. By February 1951 he had submitted some chapters to Erna Gunther, who felt that he had made a good start but pushed him to add more comparative material based on other literature on the Salish. Wilson had read and taken detailed notes on earlier authors, such as Franz Boas, James Teit, Marion Smith, Charles Hill-Tout, H.G. Barnett and, we can safely assume, Erna Gunther, but he wanted to write a clear, descriptive ethnography rather than an interpretive piece. Anthropological literature tends to devote a lot of space to the ancestors: to discussing the ideas of anthropologists who went before. For example, there is probably more written *about* Franz Boas than *by* Franz Boas, despite his substantial body of scholarship. Wilson was never strongly committed to that approach. He had an independent mind, even as a graduate student, and he believed that the first need in British Columbia anthropology was to lay a foundation in basic description of the

Indigenous cultures. That, ironically, was a Boasian approach. He did try to reassure Gunther that he would pursue the implications of his introductory ethnography in further papers, but he despaired of even getting the descriptive part done. It would take another year. He made some slight concessions to his supervisor's suggestions, but when his thesis was finally completed, it was a largely descriptive account of Upper Stalo culture with some comparative notes on a few elements such as spirit dancing and the curing of ailments. At its heart, his thesis comprised the stories told by the Upper Stalo people about their culture, related through the filter of the ethnographer and the English language. It was grounded in the detail of what Wilson had learned about the culture, rather than engaging with the work of other anthropologists. Wilson believed, as he sought to explain his approach, that "ethnography was the description of native cultures based on observation and native testimony," while ethnology was "the study and interpretation of ethnography." His master's thesis was presented, as he intended it to be, as "an ethnography, not an ethnology."[9]

When he submitted the thesis he wrote to Viola Garfield, one of his thesis committee members: "I hope and beseech that the committee will not require further changes before they approve it." Indeed, it was approved within days of it being submitted. Wilson was already more interested in any "evaluations, reflections and suggested revisions to guide in preparing it for publication." In particular, he wanted ideas about what could be deleted to bring the manuscript down to a more manageable size.[10] He worked fast on the revisions, and the published version appeared in the same year as his thesis.[11] He had set up the Anthropology in British Columbia series to provide a listing of current research in the field and a place to publish papers coming out of the research. The first in the series was Wilson's *The Upper Stalo Indians*. Like Harry Hawthorn, he wanted to get serious professional anthropology going in British Columbia. Both the series and his Stalo piece drew positive comments from Victoria, Vancouver and London, England. Alice Ravenhill, the long-time advocate for Indian culture and art, congratulated him on launching Anthropology in British Columbia. Writing in the *Vancouver Province*, Bruce McKelvie praised Wilson's work in presenting "the Natives' views of their own culture..." Raymond Firth, at the London School of Economics, wrote that while there was a flood of publications from the United States, it was a good reminder of the important work being done in Canada.[12] The positive responses were gratifying, but Wilson's mind was already moving on to other areas of scholarship, and in the next few years he wrote on several topics. Some of his work was published and much of it was not.

Taking a similar approach as he did with his Stalo ethnography, he next wrote a detailed study of Kwakiutl culture. He began by visiting a number of Kwakiutl communities. He was particularly captivated by his first visit to Alert Bay, where he had arranged to stay at the Cranmers' house. The father, Dan Cranmer, was away fishing, but he met the rest of the family, including one of the daughters, Gloria Cranmer. Gloria had vacated her bedroom so that Wilson could use it. She helped him up the stairs with his luggage, prompting her sister to ask if she was going to sleep with him. Wilson turned bright red with embarrassment and hurried off to drink beer with the great Kwakiutl artist Willie Seaweed. He was impressed with the "wonderful Cranmer family," particularly Gloria, whom he thought to be "pretty, smart, straight thinking." She was the first Indigenous woman to attend UBC, and they would be colleagues at various points in their later careers.

Wilson also absorbed the atmosphere at Alert Bay: the morning fog, the chatter of radio phones rising and falling over the water from the boats, the racket of crows and seagulls, kids playing on the water all day, and girls walking by, harmonizing on popular songs at night. He recognized that the artistic tradition of the Kwakiutl was still alive, if not well. He also saw the totem poles in the community and worried, from his newcomer point of view, about the condition of many of them.[13] Willie Seaweed told Wilson that he was the best carver on the coast, and Wilson thought that he might be right but wished that his talents could be appreciated more fully in a wider context. Two years later, Wilson was back in Kwakiutl territory and visiting the village of Ba'a's in Blunden Harbour, where Seaweed grew up. The village was now deserted, but Wilson saw fine examples of Sea-weed's art: a totem pole in the graveyard and a large feast dish among the undergrowth. At Alert Bay again, he admired more recent Seaweed work. The artist showed him coppers, rattles, headdresses and masks that were "beautifully carved and painted." He photographed Seaweed dressed in traditional regalia and holding two of his coppers. Wilson, the museum collector, also understood on this visit how much Seaweed "values these old things and won't part with them."[14]

Wilson gathered information from people at Alert Bay and other communities and had many conversations with Mungo Martin, a Kwaki-utl community member from Fort Rupert who was now working at the Provincial Museum carving totem poles. Wilson's consultants provided the basis for a detailed account of the southern Kwakiutl in the area from Smith Inlet in the north to Cape Mudge in the south. The study describes all of the groups, their history, the names and locations of villages and estimates of population, including population decline and any movement of population that had occurred. It was a groundbreaking study that had the Wilson Duff hallmark of meticulous attention to detail. Once again, Wilson was providing basic information where it was lacking. It was never published, though even now some think that it should be. It did, as Wilson would have hoped, provide a foundation for further work by others.[15] One part of Kwakiutl history that particularly interested him was the his-toric southward movement of the Lekwiltok into the Campbell River–Cape Mudge area. This aggressive expansion by Kwakiutl groups involved the displacement or extinction of the Coast Salish who had lived in the area. That small piece of the larger puzzle was published. There was an amazing amount of detailed research behind the ten-page article, which challenged the view that cultural boundaries on the coast were static.[16]

At the same time as he was working on the southern Kwakiutl pro-ject, Wilson became increasingly interested in Indian artifacts crafted in stone—or, as he began to refer to them, *stone sculptures*. He first came across stone artifacts when he was doing fieldwork among the Upper Stalo, and then he noticed pieces from the surrounding areas. He compiled an inventory of examples large and small, from seated human figure bowls to little objects worked in soapstone and of unknown use, and originating over a wide area, from the Gulf Islands to Shuswap Lake. He published a preliminary piece on "Unique Stone Artifacts from the Gulf Islands" in the museum's annual report for 1955 and, the following year, a much longer examination of *Prehistoric Stone Sculpture of the Fraser River and Gulf of Georgia* in the Anthropology in British Columbia series. His primary purpose was again descriptive: to provide a full listing and a detailed written depiction, along with photographs or drawings, of all the stone pieces that he had located. By now he was also prepared to venture into some interpretation. He wondered about the function of many of the pieces, particularly the seated human figure bowls. He was suitably cautious but thought, based on ethnographic evidence, that they could have been used in the rituals carried out by shamans who could see into the future by putting water into the bowls. He conferred with Wayne Suttles on the bowls, and he also believed that they were used by shamans and associated with spells and visions.[17] Because they were made of stone, these artifacts were usually much older than most Northwest Coast art that is fashioned in wood so does not survive for long. Wilson contemplated the question of whether the stone sculpture was "the ancestral form of Northwest Coast art as we know it." He concluded, again cautiously, that in some respects it was.[18] Wilson maintained his interest in stone art and a few years later wrote about stone clubs from the Skeena River area based on a cache that was unearthed at Hagwilget, on the Bulkley River Canyon near Hazelton, and others that were found at Metlakatla, near Prince Rupert. This report was also largely descriptive, though he did look at them as an art form and decided that these clubs represented a distinct local style that was not strongly connected to the later classic northern coast style.[19] His writing on stone sculpture attracted attention and positive comments from anthropologists. Some appreciated the way he was assembling and presenting the basic information on a neglected area, since what was required in anthropological research was "more fact, less fancy." Hawthorn, who did not give praise lightly, thought it "a masterful treatment of this fascinating subject."[20] Twenty years later, Wilson would revisit this ancient stone art and think about it in an entirely different way that would attract both attention and controversy.

*

Wilson accomplished these, and other, research projects in the midst of the variety of duties and activities required of the anthropologist at the Provincial Museum. Much of his writing was done at home in the evening, away from the routine of the office. Encouraged by Hawthorn, he toyed with the idea of enrolling in a PhD program in anthropology, but museum work constantly intervened and it did not happen. Wilson was always very clear about the limits of his expertise: after only six months at the Provincial Museum, in January 1951, he was appointed to the Indian Studies Committee of the Canadian Social Science Research Council, but he repeatedly reminded the chair of the committee, T.F. McIlwraith, that he did not feel qualified to judge research proposals on eastern subjects.[21]

Within the limits of his time and expertise Wilson continued to engage in research, because he clearly understood that museum collections are only as good as the knowledge that we have of them. His biggest obligation as curator was not simply to display the objects but also to "tell the stories they have to tell." Wilson strongly believed that, as an educational institution, an anthropology museum "displays ideas, not things."[22] Translating that ideal into practice would be a challenge.

The anthropology exhibits at the Provincial Museum, in the east wing of the legislature building, were cramped for space when Wilson arrived in 1950 and it only got worse with time. The space and the displays had not changed fundamentally since the museum moved into the building in 1898. There was an emphasis on natural history, symbolized by the live reptiles at the public entrance to the museum. Wilson valued the natural history exhibits because they set the stage for the arrival of human cultures; however, human culture was displayed in a very traditional way in confined quarters. Much of the anthropology display was in the basement, either in rows of glass cases or mounted on the wall and unprotected. The artifacts were largely arranged by cultural area, along with some thematic displays on subjects such as Nootkan whaling or totem poles. The space was packed to the gills, and there was very little room to work. There was no running water except in the washrooms. Valuable artifacts were stored in nooks and crannies all over the legislative precinct, some accessed by underground tunnels and all without temperature control. The collection continued to grow through acquisitions while the display space remained much the same, so more and more went into storage. Though there was plenty of scope for improvement, Wilson soon realized that he was not going to make a lot of rapid progress updating the presentation of material at the museum. His many other duties, the fact that he was the only staff member on the anthropology side and a lack of new funding were all limitations. After only a few months on the job he was "certainly not breaking any world records in getting up new displays, in fact, I qualify for the world booby-prize."[23] Help did not arrive until Michael Kew joined Wilson as an assistant in anthropology in 1956. Kew, like Wilson, was a Hawthorn student from UBC. He and Wilson would be colleagues and good friends over the years. Kew worked on refurbishing the displays and, as part of that project, Wilson asked him to locate and identify every item in an old handwritten catalogue of the anthropology collection. It was a long-term task and Wilson was not a directive supervisor, so Michael Kew was left to do the work on his own.[24] Over the next couple of years the two of them slowly upgraded the displays and brought the province's Indigenous cultures to greater prominence in the public galleries. A visitor now arrived in the entry hall to the dramatic impression created by totem poles rather than a live rattlesnake and a guestbook.

Wilson and his anthropology assistant shared an office on the second floor of the east wing building that opened onto the natural history collection. There was no admission fee and people could walk in at will. Privacy may have been an issue sometimes, but it was a pretty informal workplace with very little emphasis on security. Being open and available to the public was a major mandate of the museum, so Wilson regularly interacted with visitors. People who came into his office were welcomed. He enjoyed talking about the Indian cultures of British Columbia, and his quiet humility attracted visitors. He struck up conversations with individuals who were out among the collections. He enjoyed talking to school groups, particularly if they were from the Indian residential schools. He brought out items for them to handle and reminded the children that their parents and family back home had much to teach them about their cultures.[25] He continued to give talks, delivered with enthusiasm and illustrated with films and slides, to service and interest groups in Victoria and up Vancouver Island. He often taught Introduction to Anthropology as an evening course at Victoria College, as the University of Victoria was then known. Some contacts were with groups and some with individuals, some were fleeting and some had lifelong effects.

On one occasion he noticed a teenager taking his time looking at the anthropology collection. Wilson recognized that he had seen him in the museum more than once before, so he went over and began a conversation. He learned that the young man was born in Greenville (now Laxgalts'ap), near the mouth of the Nass River, though his home community was the Tsimshian village of Kitkatla, on the coast near the Skeena River, and that part of his ancestry was Haida. His family had moved to Victoria and he was attending Oak Bay High School, where for the first time he learned the meaning of the word *discrimination*. He was taking a course at school on European art but could not really relate to it. His art teacher, Bill West, suggested that he go to the museum and study the Northwest Coast Indian art there and report back to the class. The schoolboy found the Provincial Museum, with the art of his own people, a much more congenial place than his school. He loved to sit in the trapper's cabin that was one of the exhibits. Wilson talked with him about some of the art and artifacts and then they went up to his office on the second floor. He opened his filing cabinet, took out a photo and showed the young man a picture of his grandfather, Amos Collinson. He conveyed knowledge of the boy's ancestors on his father's side and his enthusiasm for their art. It was clear that Wilson loved the art of the coast: "He thought it, he slept it, he dreamt it," the student later recalled. Wilson became the boy's mentor, guiding him through the collections in the museum, and in the process lighting a fire in the young man that never went out. The two remained connected, and Roy Henry Vickers gives Wilson much of the credit for the fact that he became a celebrated artist.[26]

Another encounter, equally auspicious for those involved, took place outside the museum. Wilson was walking along the beach on Ten Mile Point, near Victoria, one day when he came across two boys fossicking in a shell midden. He approached and asked them if they knew what they were doing. Their response was that they at least knew what they were looking for: any artifacts that they could find. Wilson then asked them if they would be interested in learning how to do archaeology properly. John Sendey and Richard Cox liked the idea, so Wilson put them in contact with Charles Borden. They worked on Borden digs at Marpole and later at Yale, and on a dig that Wilson organized in Victoria. Both of them took to the work, both had careers in archaeology, and John Sendey was later employed at the Provincial Museum.[27]

Such stories are not isolated cases. Beth Hill lived near a midden on Salt Spring Island and had found some artifacts that she took to the museum to get information. She was flattered to be warmly received by Wilson. On his advice she did further research and was stunned when he invited her to give a presentation to the local archaeological society. He then suggested that she take courses and, eventually, that she should go to Cambridge University. For Beth Hill, meeting Wilson was a turning point in her life as he saw the potential in her. She went on to publish comprehensive studies of Indian petroglyphs along the coast.[28] Many other people have memories of Wilson's sensitivity to their interests and his warm encouragement for them to pursue them.

Wilson also provided help and advice in a more routine way through the flow of correspondence that came into the museum. After only a few months at the museum, he wrote a detailed two-page letter on Nootka whaling in response to a request for information. It may have been the work on that letter that led him, later, to think about the form of the Nootka canoe. He advanced the theory that the lines of the canoes and wolf-like shapes of the prows meant that Nootka canoes had northern origins in Eskimo (Inuit) culture. His "Thoughts on the Nootka Canoe" was one of his entries into the debate over the cultural origins of the Northwest Coast Indians, which, put simply, was about whether the peoples and cultures of the Northwest Coast had their origins in Asia or Alaska.[29] It was an ideal academic debate because it was not really resolved one way or the other and, in the end, perhaps the answer was neither. He responded in a similar way when people suggested a stone sculpture had Asian origins, asking, "Why go searching around the world for the roots of this stone art?" To the writer from the Okanagan who wondered if some pictographs were "pre-Indian," he responded that for him there was no such thing as "pre-Indian": "That word is in bad repute among archaeologists, because it usually comes with the weird implication of wandering Welshmen, Chinese, lost tribes of Israel etc. ... All the earlier inhabitants of this area were, by definition, Indians." A member of the Campbell River District Historical Society prefaced a question with the assertion that it was "the age of the amateur" so Wilson should be tolerant of "what might be loosely termed our ideas." Reading a history of China, the letter writer had come across a couple of words in Chinese that looked similar to Haida words. He wondered if this was evidence of a cultural connection. Wilson replied, "I rather think, old chap, that it is going too far to draw any conclusion on the basis of a superficial similarity between two 2-syllable words in Chinese and Haida." Moreover, the English rendition of Haida words was not very close to the Haida pronunciation. "Let's put the whole thing down to coincidence," he concluded.[30] In all these exchanges Wilson was giving patient lessons in basic anthropology to members of the public who were looking for information.

With other anthropologists he could be more forthright. He indicated that he was in two minds when asked for advice by two anthropologists who had worked in other areas and now planned to undertake fieldwork in Gitksan communities for the first time. "In answering such letters I am always torn between my desire to encourage projects which may result in constructive contributions to knowledge and my obligation to protect my Indian friends from bothersome and sometimes disruptive activities of inept outside investigators." In this case he was willing to assume that his correspondents would do more good than harm. He was right, at least in terms of anthropology, as the research trip resulted in a book on the Gitksan potlatch.[31] He corresponded with Joyce Wike at the University of Nebraska, who had submitted a manuscript to him for possible publication. Wike had developed the argument that the maritime fur trade on the Northwest Coast had operated along pre-existing Indian trading lines and the trade with Europeans did not, therefore, cause a significant reorientation for the Indians. She was developing the so-called "enrichment thesis." According to the argument, new wealth and metal tools brought by the fur trade also led to a florescence in Northwest Coast art. It was an interpretation of early European contact that Wilson would also develop in his own writing.[32] But he was having trouble with Wike's manuscript and wrote to her: "Joyce, dear Joyce, you are a lovable person but your blasted manuscript is giving me ulcers." Wilson was frustrated because he thought that she was not making the argument strongly enough and was not sufficiently focused on saying what she wanted to say. At the same time, he was impressed with how she had marshalled the factual data. He offered to revise and retype it for her, but she seems not to have taken him up on the offer. When the article appeared in *American Anthropologist*, her conclusion was that the research was incomplete and more study was needed.[33]

While he might have been blunt with colleagues, with the public Wilson generally responded politely no matter how bizarre the request. For example, he responded to several requests for information about the existence, or not, of the sasquatch. He knew that Stalo people believed in the presence of the sasquatch and had seen them, but Wilson was not convinced. He believed that an explanation for sasquatch sightings could be found in understanding the role of the imagination and the extent to which people see what they expect to see. It was probably more in the provenance of a psychologist to explain "how it happens that a person can look at a bear, or stump or a shadow on a moonlit night and see a hairy giant." He did allow that "some day (or night) I may see one too, but I won't believe it until I touch it or it touches me."[34] Later in life, Wilson would come to give much more credence to the power of the imagination. He presumably responded with a polite "none available" to the request from a Victoria resident that if he had any smaller totem poles to spare, he should not burn them, as the letter writer would like to have some to put up on the rocks in front of his new house. His friend Willard Ireland, the provincial archivist, passed on a letter from the owner of a cattery for Burmese cats who wanted recommendations of Indian names that he could give them. Ireland made light of the request, writing that "I could not have my conscience clogged by Burmese cats bearing Indian names," but Wilson responded respectfully with a list of names of Indian groups and personalities. He did, on the other hand, reject a request from the Victoria College Alma Mater Society to hold a totem-pole-sitting contest at Thunderbird Park. It would, he wrote, "show a complete lack of consideration and respect" for Indian people and their cultures.[35]

*

Thunderbird Park, located a block away from the museum building on the corner of Douglas and Belleville Streets, was perhaps the most successful exhibit that Wilson developed while he was provincial anthropologist. It had been established ten years before Wilson arrived at the museum. Thunderbird Park was seen as a way to get the museum's totem poles out of storage and set up, along with some house fronts, so that people could appreciate them. The idea was also that it would become a tourist attraction. Beyond that, not much thought went into the development of the display and, even worse, there was no consultation with any anthropologist, let alone the people of the cultures from whence the totem poles came.[36] The Thunderbird Park display did attract tourists, some of them very high profile. In October 1951, Princess Elizabeth and the Duke of Edinburgh visited, and at Thunderbird Park they watched George Clutesi and his dancers from Port Alberni perform. Wilson was on the stand next to the premier and was introduced to the royal visitors. He chatted with them about the dancers and Thunderbird Park's totem poles and houses. Marion wrote to her family, "Wilson does not get excited about very many things, but he was certainly a proud and excited boy this day."[37] He would have cast Thunderbird Park in the best light for the princess and the duke, but he knew that the totem poles were deteriorating and the house fronts were not authentic. The poles needed to be brought inside if they were to survive and replicas made, along with a new house built, on the outside site. Thunderbird Park needed some new thinking and a lot of work. Wilson needed an experienced carver to work with him on the project, and he found that person in Mungo Martin, the Kwakiutl artist and elder.

Mungo Martin was born in Fort Rupert, probably about 1880. While of mixed parentage, he grew up totally immersed in Kwakiutl culture and learned to carve from his stepfather, the famous artist Charlie James. He lived his life as an artist, carving poles and masks, and as a commercial fisherman. In 1947 he came to UBC to work at Totem Park carving totem poles, some restored and some original, and working on smaller pieces in the evening. He got to know Harry and Audrey Hawthorn particularly well. Audrey Hawthorn wrote about his skill as a carver, noting that "he makes no mistakes. His blade is sure and precise, the length of his stroke exact and controlled."[38] In 1952 the funding for the UBC project ran out, so Wilson stepped in and, with funding support from the provincial government, brought Mungo Martin over to work at Thunderbird Park. Wilson arranged for him, his wife, Abaya'a, and other family members to live in a house on Michigan Street, near the park, at government expense. Wilson and Mungo developed a close friendship based on mutual respect. They visited each other's houses, where they drank beer and danced with each other's partner. Wilson joined the wild parties at the carvers' house on payday.[39] Mungo made Wilson a set of carving tools and taught him to carve. Wilson set up a carving area in his garage and carved some very creditable generic-image masks, although he did not presume to carve anything that might represent a crest owned by an Indian group or individual. Nor could there be any doubt about who was the master and who was the student. After a few years of working together, Wilson described Mungo as "Carver of the Century."[40]

As Mungo and Wilson began work on the restoration of Thunderbird Park, it quickly became the largest single project at the museum. They set up a carving shed and Mungo Martin made both replicas of some of the old totem poles in the park and also some originals. It soon became apparent that there was more work than one carver could handle, so David Martin, Mungo's son, sometimes worked with his father. They carved replicas of Kwakiutl totem poles as well as poles from other Northwest Coast cultures. In the case of Haida totem poles, for example, they aimed to remain true to Haida forms while including their own artistic details. The carving work was certainly a success as a tourist attraction. Progress on Thunderbird Park was reported in the Victoria newspapers and other papers south of the border. Mungo Martin, at work in his carving shed, even appeared in *Reader's Digest*. Wilson was described as an evangelist on a crusade to preserve totem poles and was quoted in the Victoria *Colonist* as saying: "Nothing makes tourists with cameras so delirious with joy, so click-happy, as totem poles." The *Times* claimed that Mungo Martin was the most photographed man in Victoria. More important in the long run, the Martins also kept the traditional art form going. Gloria Cranmer Webster, who was related to Mungo Martin and was later a driving force behind the establishment of the U'mista Cultural Centre and museum in Alert Bay, believed that Wilson and Mungo kept the carving tradition alive by a slender thread when others did not.[41]

Since Mungo Martin was a repository of Kwakiutl culture, he and Wilson worked together in many ways to create a record of that culture. The two spent hours talking about the Kwakiutl past and present ways of life: Mungo told his stories and sang his songs, and Wilson recorded them on tape and film. Mungo carved and painted masks and other smaller items for the museum collection. Abaya'a Martin wove baskets and Chilkat blankets, which were also added to the museum's collection. The partnership between Wilson and the Martins contributed to the Provincial Museum in a variety of ways. Besides the totem poles, perhaps the most spectacular was the house that Mungo built, and the potlatch that announced its opening.

After working for several months at Thunderbird Park, Mungo decided to begin work on a new Kwakiutl house in the traditional style. Wilson got permission from the provincial government and arranged for the logs and lumber to be provided by British Columbia forest companies. Mungo and his carvers set to work, and the house was built over long hours throughout the summer of 1953. It was built according to the traditional pattern, with the huge roof beams, hand hewn and running lengthwise, supported by posts. Two interior posts at the back of the house were elaborately carved replicas of earlier Kwakiutl house posts. The spectacular painted house front represented a supernatural sea monster shaped like a sculpin. Mungo carved a large, heraldic totem pole to stand in front of the house, representing all the Kwakiutl groups. In designing the house, Mungo drew on several examples of houses that he was connected to by family and lineage. It was to some extent a composite, but it was also Mungo's. As Wilson said, "This new house is more than just an authentic Kwakiutl house. It is Mungo Martin's house, and bears on its house-posts hereditary crests of his family." Mungo named his house Wa'waditla meaning "he orders them to come inside."[42] And many were ordered to come inside when Mungo's house was opened with Mungo's potlatch.

Wilson was adamant that the first potlatch in Wa'waditla would be done the way that Mungo Martin wanted, according to his knowledge of Kwakiutl traditions. After several rehearsals, the ceremonies took place over three days in mid-December. The first day was for First Nations guests only and not, Wilson wrote, "a show for outsiders." In addition to the Kwakiutl, other Indian guests and leaders from up and down the coast were invited. Wilson did press Mungo to allow some anthropologists from Victoria, UBC and the University of Washington to be "classified as Indians" to attend and witness the proceedings. The reclassification did not work flawlessly in all cases. One of them, Cyril Belshaw, arrived late and opened the door of the house at the wrong moment during a cedar-bark dance, much to the annoyance of Mungo, who thought that the public was being admitted. Apart from that glitch in protocol, the potlatch on day one was the most traditional of the three days. It began with mourning songs for those who had passed, followed by a ceremony to open the winter dance season. Cedar-bark headbands were handed out and worn by the guests, feast songs followed and there were masked dances through the evening. Days two and three presented similar programs in the afternoon and evening. Provincial officials, donors and the media were invited on day two, and the public on the third day, when the house was packed with about three hundred people and another estimated 1,500 had to be turned away. On each day Mungo Martin gave speeches of welcome and conclusion that were interpreted by Dan Cranmer from Alert Bay. There was a cradle ceremony that was the property of the Martin family and Mungo's son, David, was the Hamatsa (the wild spirit from the woods) dancer.[43] Throughout the three days, Wilson acted as the usher, directing guests to their seats.

If the newspaper commentary is any guide, non-Indigenous British Columbians reacted in a variety of ways to this potlatch taking place in the midst of iconic Victoria, down the street from the provincial legislature and across from the Empress Hotel. A writer in Victoria's *Colonist* hoped that its citizens would hang the welcome sign out for the Indian visitors and that the event would be an opportunity for greater goodwill and friendship. The Hamatsa was described as a "weird dance performed in the old days" in the Victoria *Times*, though the writer did at least understand that, at a potlatch, the more that is given away the higher the prestige of the giver. Some Vancouver writers were more scathing. Day one was described in the *Vancouver Sun* under the headline "White Men Barred" and went on about drums beating wildly and "masked medicine men" plying the "tricks of their dying trade." The *Vancouver News-Herald* was more perplexed: it reported that Victoria had finally got some nightlife as Mungo Martin "opened the new joint with everything on the house." Apparently the "floor show was a fantasia of masks, exotic dances and speeches" that went on while Victorians gathered on the sidewalks "and listened aghast at such gaiety."[44]

Fortunately, instant disparagement is often no measure of long-term significance. Thunderbird Park, the house named Wa'waditla, and the potlatch to open it were all examples of involving First Nations people in the representation of their cultures and engaging the wider community in that endeavour. These initiatives were also a partnership between two individuals and two institutions from two cultures. At the end of the third day, Mungo bestowed upon Wilson a name, Xi'tilelak^w, "as I don't consider us to be two men (rather, as one or related)." The name had belonged to Mungo Martin's father and was the last name bestowed at the ceremony.[45] Though not in an Indian community and, in some respects, innovative as well as traditional, the "house-warming" potlatch was the first to be held after the clause banning the ritual was dropped from the Indian Act. Wilson wondered at the time whether it might also be the last, but fortunately he was mistaken. It is a part of First Nations cultures in British Columbia that has continued to thrive. Wilson's work with Mungo Martin was an early example of an anthropologist working in partnership with First Nations people on a museum presentation. Decades later, that approach would be unwittingly emulated, and touted as a bold new initiative in museum practice.

The opening of Mungo's house was a high point, but the carving program continued. It never became the school for young apprentice carvers that Wilson had hoped, but other carvers worked with Mungo. In addition to his son, David, his relatives Henry Hunt, Tony Hunt and Douglas Cranmer all joined Mungo at different times. Bill Reid came over to work with Mungo for a couple of weeks in 1956. At that stage he was crafting jewellery and working as a radio announcer for the Canadian Broadcasting Corporation. Reid accepted an offer from Wilson, describing it as a "two week fellowship to study under Professor M. Martin at your distinguished institution." He returned to Vancouver and wrote to Wilson that the two weeks "in your little hand made never never land has just about spoiled me completely. Returning to working in a practical world and even trying to make jewelry seems quite ridiculous."[46] He was hoping for carving work at UBC, and three years later he started work at Totem Park, sculpting totem poles and building houses in the Haida style. The playful tone of his letters to Wilson was an expression of their close friendship; the two would collaborate on other projects throughout Wilson's life.

While the totem pole carving and restoration continued at Thunderbird Park, Wilson struggled to maintain a steady level of funding from the provincial government. Some years he employed three carvers, although the budget supported only two. From the mid-1950s on, the budget was supplemented by taking commissions for totem poles. They also resorted to gimmicks like carving the world's tallest totem pole, financed by selling shares to the public. Wilson thought that the idea might seem "slightly corny to some," but the carvers had fun with it, it attracted tourists, and it bailed Wilson out of a budget bind. When it was completed, the pole was erected in Beacon Hill Park, where, after major restorations, it still stands today. Commissions came in from other museums and private individuals for smaller poles and masks. There were other public projects, too, such as the pole carved as a gift to Queen Elizabeth and set up in Windsor Great Park to mark British Columbia's centennial in 1958. Such projects rejuvenated the totem pole carving program and enabled it to continue through the uncertainties of government funding. As Wilson wrote to Harry Hawthorn at UBC, "The chips are flying as never before and public interest is at a new high."[47]

*

Throughout his early years at the Provincial Museum, Wilson also continued to work with Charles Borden, his archaeological mentor. Now colleagues rather than teacher and student, the two had a warm and respectful, if sometimes edgy, relationship. They stayed in each other's houses when they travelled back and forth between Victoria and Vancouver. Their letters concluded with best wishes for each other's family, and when Marnie was born, Borden's wife sent the Duffs a copy Dr. Spock's much-read book on baby and child care. On the professional level, Wilson told Borden soon after he started at the museum that his primary focus was to be ethnography rather than archaeology: "No matter how critical the archaeological situation may be, the ethnographic situation is even more critical." He also found ethnography more rewarding. As for archaeology, at this stage of his career Wilson did not feel qualified to supervise a dig, though he would not mind tackling an archaeological survey.[48] This announcement would not have made Borden happy, as he tended to want those who he saw as his students to focus on archaeology. Wilson published Borden's proposed archaeological site designation scheme based on Canadian topographical maps in Anthropology in British Columbia. Borden, in turn, acknowledged Wilson's help with developing the scheme.[49] Borden's pattern was soon adopted across Canada.

While a system to identify and locate archaeological sites was one thing, protecting those sites was quite another. Within six months of starting at the museum, Wilson was quoted in the press on the need for stricter supervision of archaeological sites and to protect them from souvenir hunters and industrial development.[50] He also wrote to successive ministers of education, to whom the Provincial Museum reported, about the issue. He was clear in a letter to W.T. Straith, for example, that archaeological sites, "which are the only records we have of man's prehistoric past in the Province," were being destroyed and needed to be protected.[51] Two things were needed: legislation to protect archaeological sites and funding to excavate them. The legislation would take a decade to get passed. In the meantime Wilson was gathering information, and he set up a printed site description form as a first step in developing an archaeological survey of the province.[52]

Both Wilson and Borden became acutely aware of how vulnerable these sites were when they did a survey on the Nechako River system. In 1950 there were rumours of Alcan's plans to develop a massive aluminum smelter at Kitimat—the smelter would be powered by hydroelectricity, which would be produced by damming the Nechako River. The project would lead to the flooding of more than nine hundred square kilometres of land and the brutal displacement of Cheslatta communities. Horrified by this development, Wilson and Borden managed to get funding to do a survey of archaeological sites in the area. The following summer Wilson carried out an ethnographic survey of Carrier (now Dakelh) communities. Then he and Borden surveyed archaeological sites. Their survey nearly ended in disaster when, two days out, their boat was swamped near the mouth of the Tahtsa River and they lost all their equipment. They had to re-equip and start out again, as Borden wrote, "much the wiser." In the end they identified 130 significant archaeological sites, many of which would be lost to the flooding.[53] When they were done, Wilson urged Borden to write a report for the minister of education as soon as possible and advised him, "Shuck off some of your cold scientific hyper-caution and make it good—you have exciting material to do it with." He also urged sending press releases to the newspapers to attract public support for their work.[54] Their advocacy did not slow down the Alcan project or the removal of the Cheslatta people.

Borden excavated some sites starting at Chinlac, a Carrier site on the Stuart River near where it joins the Nechako and below the proposed flood area. Chinlac was an uninhabited site that, according to tradition, had been attacked and destroyed two hundred years earlier. Wilson was passing through the area in the summer of 1952 and dropped by to visit the site and to film the work. He played a trick on Borden by planting an artifact from the coast on the site that, when found, prompted Borden to expound on it as evidence of connections between the coast and the interior. When Wilson admitted to his prank, Borden was not amused. He did not approve of any hijinks around his archaeological sites. Other archaeologists would probably not have found Wilson's little caper all that funny either.[55] Perhaps Wilson presumed too much on his friendship, for Charles Borden was deadly serious when it came to digging up the past. He and Wilson would clash more publicly later on over the question of possible interior sources of coastal cultures, when Wilson was developing his ideas about Alaskan origins. Borden was skeptical of those who pushed ethnographic evidence further than was warranted—then presumed to write prehistory on the basis of such evidence—as did those who argued for the Far North as the wellspring of Northwest Coast cultures.[56] Nevertheless, the two continued to work together to find better ways to protect the archaeological remains of the province's Indian cultures.

*

Another of Wilson's interests as an ethnographer, right from the start at the Provincial Museum, was Coast Salish spirit dancing. He first learned about winter spirit dancing, which he described as "the most prominent and satisfying phase of Stalo religious and ceremonial life," from his Upper Stalo informants. Soon after he arrived in Victoria, he began working with a Songhees (lək̓ʷəŋən) informant, Jimmy Fraser. Though Fraser was hesitant at first, he was soon visiting the museum, and he and Wilson developed a close relationship. Wilson also had a close bond with Sophie Misheal, who took him to spirit dances. He both cared about and cared for his Indigenous consultants. Years later, a professional colleague was concerned about Sophie Misheal's welfare and brought her groceries. Most people in the museum community were critical of getting too involved in this way, but Wilson's response was quite different. He approved of providing help and said that he would do the same thing.[57] Wilson cared for his consultants as human beings and they responded in kind.

Out of these connections with people, Wilson began to get invitations to spirit dances. He attended many dances throughout the winter season, particularly in the Victoria to Duncan area, but sometimes further afield in Coast Salish territory, from Nanaimo in the north to La Conner in Washington State. Often he had permission to take others along. Marion and Marnie sometimes went with him, or Abaya'a Martin, and he also invited anthropological colleagues such as Harry Hawthorn and Wayne Suttles.[58] He described spirit dancing among the Upper Stalo in his master's thesis and made notes on the dances that he attended after that, but he did not publish more on the subject partly because he understood that they were very private experiences. It was dangerous for spirit dancers to risk offending their spirit by revealing too much detail about it. The regular invitations that Wilson received to the dances were a measure of the respect with which he was held in First Nations communities.

The spirit dance cycle took place in most Salish communities through the mid-winter months. Typically, they began in the late afternoon and continued until dawn. Some dances were small and took place in family homes. At larger dances, the whole community was invited, or even a number of villages. They usually involved three phases: hospitality and welcoming of the guests, including a meal; the "work," comprised of speeches that called upon the guests to witness changes in the status of the living or the dead and the conferring of names; then the spirit dancing itself. A dancer who could no longer contain their spirit might interrupt the proceedings with their dance during either of the first two phases. While not potlatches as such, spirit dances included gift-giving to guests and helpers, with all of its implications about status.[59]

Most Salish adults acquired a guardian spirit or spiritual helper that often came to them in the form of an animal. Some took the quest further and were initiated as spirit dancers who expressed the power of their spirit through costume, song, drumming and dance. One person danced at a time, going around the floor in a clockwise direction, while everyone supported the dancer with singing and drumming. Possessed by their spirit, the dancer entered a trancelike state as they connected with the supernatural. Some have said that an initiate's first dance, and even later dances, involved a passage from life through death, to be reborn as a new person. Certainly dancers were exhilarated and felt renewed and healed, both in body and mind, by the experience.[60] Dancers were of all ages, and Wilson's impression was that there was a revival of spirit dances in the 1950s as younger Indians were initiated as dancers and, through their dancing and songs, kept a hold on that part of traditional culture. It was, wrote Wilson, "a rich and exclusive way of being Indian."[61] Winter spirit dancing culture was maintained amidst the sea of change brought by newcomers.

Wilson connected with the dancing on many levels. He was excited by spirit dancing as an element of Indian cultural survival. He saw it as part of his work as a museum ethnographer to understand, participate in and create a record of spirit dancing ceremonies. Before he went to many dances, he absorbed as much understanding as he could about them from his Songhees community consultant Jimmy Fraser, who then took him to his first dances. When he started attending dances, Wilson sat among the guests, taking it all in and recording the proceedings in his mind so that he could later write descriptions of the dances. Being a dancer in his own culture, Wilson was captivated by the rhythm and movement. He could not be a dancer in this cultural context, but he sometimes participated in the drumming by the assembly of guests. Marnie remembers going to a spirit dance with her father, falling asleep on one of the benches and waking up to see Wilson drumming.[62] Rhythm and dance is often the route to spiritual experience. "The only truth," Wilson once wrote, "is rhythm."[63] He had been schooled in the tradition of objective ethnography and taught to maintain boundaries between anthropologist and so-called informant, but spirit dancing took him into another world—to the realm of the spirit beyond reality. The spirit dance was the bridge over which dancers met those from the spirit world. Today, anthropologists have become more open to these extraordinary experiences, but in Wilson's day just talking, let alone writing, about them as an ethnographic observer would have invited ridicule.[64] Wilson was not just an observer, and he participated in a more profound way than was normally meant by that ethnographic formula. Experiencing rituals that take one into contact with the supernatural was bound to change the observer if he were as sensitive as Wilson. The spirit and the deep spirituality of Salish winter dancing had touched him.

Wilson's diverse work during his early years at the Provincial Museum involved three areas: archaeology, ethnography and museum practice. His preference was for ethnography, so he gathered, and published when he could, descriptions of Indian cultures. He responded to the desperate need to protect the surviving material record of the cultures by getting archaeology operating in a more systematic and professional way. And he was constantly working with new acquisitions to the museum's collection and improving the public displays. Yet another project that engaged much of his time and interest during this same period was the salvage, restoration and preservation of totem poles from a number of Indian villages on the coast. Wilson was engrossed in the preservation of totem poles partly because it engaged all three areas of his expertise.

5. Restoring Totem Poles

Standing in place and through time, grounded in the land and facing the water, totem poles were proclamations of social power and artistic imagination. They expressed the authority and the prestige of the owner of the pole and the skill and creativity of the artist who carved it. They were standing along the edges of the coast when the first newcomers anchored in the coves and set foot on the beaches. During the early years of European contact, the fur trade brought new wealth and iron tools that enabled a florescence of Northwest Coast art, so totem poles became larger and more numerous. By the late nineteenth century, visitors who photographed northern Indian villages described them as a forest of totem poles. And yet, no sooner did they flourish than they began to disappear. The combined efforts of missionaries, governments, museum collectors and weather led to a winnowing of the poles. Missionaries believed that totem poles were heathen symbols and persuaded Indians to take them down and even burn them. The federal government decreed in the Indian Act of 1886 that the potlatches that accompanied the raising of totem poles were illegal. Collectors representing museums in other countries took many totem poles away from British Columbia. Sculptured in wood rather than stone, totem poles suffered from the ravages of winter storms. Even without the influence of the newcomers, they did not last forever. Nor did the people who carved them: the Indigenous population was drastically reduced and many villages abandoned between 1850 and 1950. At the same time, the power and imagination that totem poles represented was diminished by the impact of colonization, as the strong voice of culture was muted to a whisper. Some poles still stood against time and leaned into the future, decaying away in desolate, deserted villages.

Very few new poles were carved in the first half of the twentieth century. Wilson would often point out that in most museums, if you wanted to find a totem pole, you had to go to the stairwell. It was the only place with enough ceiling height to display them. When he became provincial anthropologist in 1950, there were many totem poles in the stairwells of museums in America and Europe, but precious few anywhere in British Columbia.

In their heyday, and now again, totem poles, or "monumental sculptures," as they are sometimes called, were a feature of Northwest coastal villages among the Nootka (Nuu-chah-nulth) and Kwakiutl (Kwakwaka'wakw) on Vancouver Island, and groups as far north as the Tlingit in Alaska. The Coast Salish are carving totem poles in their distinctive style today, although at the time of contact their villages only featured carved house posts. Among most groups, totem poles are of three main types: interior house posts that support the roof beams running lengthwise in a plank house; free-standing poles or poles attached to the fronts of houses, including the entryways, and mortuary poles that often have a flat frontal board and contain the remains of a deceased person of rank. Totem poles were carved according to different styles and patterns in different groups. Designs ranged from the colourful exuberance of Kwakiutl poles to the more austere, controlled compositions of the Haida. For the Indigenous people the mostly animal and bird figures on the totem poles represented crests and stories, while for the newcomers they represented Northwest Coast Indian culture itself. That was why they attracted so much attention from museums and their collectors.

By 1950 there was a long history of removing totem poles from the villages on the coast of British Columbia. Serious collecting of Northwest Coast cultural material began in the 1870s when Port Townsend resident James G. Swan was commissioned by the United States government to gather artifacts for American institutions. The following decade, United States naval officer George Emmons became the pre-eminent collector. He was particularly active in Alaska, but he was secretive about the locations and methods of his acquisitions. Ironically, from a Canadian point of view, Americans were becoming concerned about Europeans, such as J.A. Jacobsen, who collected for a Berlin museum, taking cultural material out of North America. Canadians came late to collecting on the coast. Charles

F. Newcombe collected for the Provincial Museum after it was established in 1886, but he was also active on behalf of American institutions, and he was especially interested in totem poles. Marius Barbeau, from what was then the Victoria Memorial Museum in Ottawa, first came to the coast in 1914, and throughout his long career with Canada's national museum he was an avid collector. He also published extensive and detailed, though not always accurate, studies of totem poles.[1] He became particularly interested in the preservation of the remaining totem poles in the Gitksan villages of the Skeena Valley. In 1947 he was engaged by UBC to collect poles for its developing program that would lead to the establishment of Totem Park. All of these individuals, and the many museums that they represented, are less important than their cumulative effect.[2] Today, if you visit museums, particularly in the United States, like the Field Museum in Chicago, the American Museum of Natural History in New York, or the Smithsonian Museum of the American Indian in Washington, DC, you might well get the feeling that a giant vacuum cleaner has sucked away the material culture of the Northwest Coast and deposited it in out-of-province places.

Little wonder, then, that when Wilson became provincial anthropologist he was very clear that the few totem poles that remained should be preserved in British Columbia. As he wrote to a representative of a German museum who asked about the availability of totem poles for salvage in coastal villages: "We in British Columbia feel that we were late in our efforts to preserve our Indian art, and are extremely reluctant to see any more of it leave the Province."[3]

*

Both UBC and the Provincial Museum had carving programs in the 1950s to restore the old poles already collected and to carve new ones. For both Wilson and Harry Hawthorn, however, that was not enough. They were very concerned about the survival of the few totem poles still standing in the Indian villages and wanted to preserve at least some of them. Early in his time at the Provincial Museum, Wilson visited many of the villages and was shocked at what he saw, particularly in the deserted locations. He counted and assessed surviving poles in Kwakiutl villages on the inlets and islands around northern Vancouver Island and in the Gitksan communities along the Skeena River. But it was when he got to the old village sites on Haida Gwaii that he was most deeply affected. "As a museum man accustomed to handling every object of Haida art with care and respect, I was appalled at what I saw." The totem poles that he knew from photographs taken seventy years earlier "lay broken and disintegrating on the ground. House timbers lay askew, covered with a lush, wet growth of moss, grass and vegetation. A spruce forest had overrun each village, masking the ruins and partially shielding the few poles that still stood."[4] As he visited the deserted Haida villages, with names that resonated from the past and the lives that were lived there, Wilson's writing in his field notebooks took on a lyrical tone as he felt the melancholy of these places, once vibrant with life, now silent. He spent a day at Cumshewa, near the entrance to Cumshewa Inlet. It was once a major Haida village and, in historic times, the scene of an active trading relationship with traders who came by ship from many parts of the world. Even fifty years ago, when collector Charles Newcombe visited Cumshewa, there were still some totem poles standing. "But what a desolate place" it was now, Wilson wrote. He shot some film with the idea of providing a "portrait of a dead village... with the bits of fine old carving you can see betraying the life and vitality of old."[5] But there was nothing that could be salvaged.

Across the inlet, he stumbled upon the site of a tiny village called Clew. Sometimes the name was spelled "Clue," and it was a clue in the English sense of the word: a microcosm of Haida history in the late nineteenth century. The site was close to the mouth of a large creek named Mathers Creek on Wilson's map, but the boat crew he was with called it Church Creek. He asked about the discrepancy and was told that there had been a Haida church there many years ago. There was also an old graveyard, they said, that he might be interested in looking at. Wilson was intrigued. He could find no sign of the church or of any houses. The graveyard was there, with European-style headstones that recorded deaths between 1887 and 1897. Wilson took down the details from the gravestones. His notes on the site are an illustration of his curiosity and attention to detail. Later, in Skidegate, he talked to some of the older people about Clew. He learned a small group had moved there from Tanu (T'anuu) in the 1880s at the behest of the Methodist missionary Thomas Crosby. They built a row of houses in a new style, "just like Victoria," with a church in the middle. Led by a Native preacher, they tried to live a Christian life. Bill Reid's grandparents lived there, attending the school and the church as committed Christians.[6] The population of the village was never more than one hundred and it declined over the next few years. In 1897 the remaining sixty-eight people moved to Skidegate, which was then known as Skidegate Mission. Wilson wrote with feeling about the haunting place with the sad story, where the only glimpse into the past was a small graveyard from another culture and an unofficial place name: Church Creek.[7]

Located near the entrance to Cumshewa Inlet was Skedans (sometimes known as K'una): the village that had it both ways. Like all Haida villages, the houses faced a beach, but it was unique in that, behind the houses, over a narrow neck of land, there was another beach facing the opposite direction. Wilson camped there on his own for three days, during which there was a raging storm, so he stayed in his tent. He wondered why the inhabitants had not chosen the lee beach for the village, since it was much more sheltered than the one facing south. He was uneasy when two bears came down to visit the village site. He made sure to sleep in his pup tent, where he also kept his food and clothes, hoping that a shout would scare the bears away—otherwise the tent would soon have holes from his .22 pistol. Wilson took notes on the remaining house frames and totem poles. Most of the frontal poles of the houses had fallen, but some of the stubbier mortuary columns still stood upright on their rotting bases. The carvings that were out in the open had weathered almost beyond recognition. Skedans, he thought, was a "classic little village site. Wonderful." He held its image in his mind. Years later, when he was writing poetry, he recalled it with these lines:

Skedans is a paradox site
South beach
Mirrored by north beach
Whatever way the wind blows
You got it made
Reversible beach
Self-reversing beach
All-purpose beach[8]

The south-facing aspect of the one Skedans beach meant that it had a view toward Tanu, where he also camped alone for several days. At Tanu he experienced the loneliness of isolation and, in his imagination, saw a village once alive with people. While he was there, he did not see a single boat pass by, whereas "In old days I'd see several canoes slipping out to fish or seek out cedar, or voyaging by, and the chant and beat of the paddles would come over the water." Now the "solitary daily airliner boring north to Anchorage & Tokio [sic] only accentuates the loneliness." There were a few totem poles still standing or leaning at Tanu, poles that were "grey-silver when dry and shining in the sunlight, almost black when wet." At the same time, Wilson realized how close they were to falling. A few more winter storms and they "will be one with the earth and the strange beauty and strength of the figures carved by the sure strong hand of a long dead artist will be obliterated forever."[9] Wilson came away from Skedans and Tanu resolved to preserve some of the artistic heritage and, for that matter, the magic of those places.

On his visits to Haida Gwaii he also spent time in Skidegate, which, along with Masset in the north, comprised the only remaining centres of the Haida population. The older people in Skidegate were surprised that he would camp alone in the deserted villages. They would not have done so, Wilson reported, because of the spirits of the departed, while Wilson was more concerned with the bears.[10] In Skidegate he talked to Haida elder Solomon Wilson, who, as was often the case, was initially hesitant to talk freely lest he make mistakes or misrepresent others. But within a day they got comfortable with each other, and Wilson listened closely to the careful cadences of Solomon's voice as he talked about Haida culture and tradition. They talked about many things, and Solomon would become Wilson's chief source of understanding about the Haida. He recounted a "story of the first white ship seen by a west coast village" and how the people "sang songs asking the power to make it go away." The ship did not leave, so braver ones paddled out to go aboard, he said. Solomon also told Wilson some of the Raven stories. Raven was the Haida culture's hero and the protagonist in a cycle of myths in which he appears as creator, transformer and inveterate reprobate. Solomon told Wilson one story, from the Raven Travelling series, in which Raven creates Haida Gwaii by spitting out pieces of pebbles taken from a fifth box contained within four others. That story would set Wilson thinking for the rest of his life. Later, when he got to know Raven much better, he would call him Mr. Paradox. They also talked about why the Haida believed in reincarnation. Wilson knew something about these beliefs from reading the ethnologist and linguist John Swanton. A Boas protege who worked at the Bureau of American Ethnology of the Smithsonian Institution, Swanton spent a winter at the turn of the nineteenth century recording Haida stories. But hearing about Haida beliefs from Solomon took Wilson into deeper levels of understanding.[11] On matters more immediately at hand, they talked about the ownership of the poles in Skedans and Tanu. Who owned the poles at deserted villages was sometimes going to be difficult to determine, so they agreed that it required a discussion with the Band Council.

Wilson spent time with others at Skidegate. He met Henry Young, an argillite carver who also had stories to tell. Once he got started, Young's mind filled with things faster than he could translate them into English and express them. He spoke in long tangents of traditional stories that would take days to tell. He lamented the impact of colonization, referring to the boats coming to the Queen Charlotte Islands to pick up girls for prostitution in Victoria. Many did not return, he said. Wilson also met Bill Reid's grandfather Charles Gladstone, who told him about the Slatechuck Creek that was the source of the black slate that the Haida used for argillite carving. Talking to Gladstone and others in Skidigate about totem poles and stories, Wilson started to hear more about the village that was called Ninstints. The name was that of the chief of the village during the nineteenth century and meant "one who is two." The village, Wilson learned, was "more properly called sgun qway ilangai 'red cod village.'" It is now known as SGang Gwaay.[12]

Ninstints is located on Anthony Island, near the southern tip of the Queen Charlotte Islands, as Haida Gwaii was then known. Like many Haida villages, it had been deserted since the 1880s. Other collectors, such as Newcombe and Barbeau, had been there, but few totem poles had been taken out. Its remoteness had protected its poles. Ninstints was reputed to have the largest number of Haida totem poles still standing. Wilson was intrigued by the place, and he returned from his visits to Haida Gwaii fascinated by the possibilities at Ninstints. He determined to salvage some totem poles for the Provincial Museum.

He worked closely with Harry Hawthorn to turn these possibilities into reality. Together they established the British Columbia Totem Pole Preservation Committee, involving UBC and the Provincial Museum along with the federal Department of Indian Affairs. Under a revision of the Indian Act in 1926, anyone removing a totem pole from an Indian reserve had to have the permission of Indian Affairs. In the 1950s, that provision was still the only protection against the wholesale removal of poles. Hawthorn was the chair of the Totem Pole Preservation Committee and Wilson was director of the restoration program, reflecting the fact that, while others were involved, he would be doing much of the organizing. Hawthorn's contacts through UBC President Norman MacKenzie brought the project financial support from H.R. MacMillan and W.C. Koerner, two leaders of British Columbia's forestry industry. Some of the forestry companies, particularly the Powell River Company, provided logistical and material assistance as well. Wilson met with the politicians and lined up government support through the Provincial Museum.[13] He also wrote articles for magazines, gave newspaper interviews in Victoria and spoke to interested groups, such as the British Columbia Indian Arts and Welfare Society, to promote public support for the work of preserving totem poles.

Both Hawthorn and Duff realized that there was nothing like universal support in settler society for the work that they were doing, either in the province or the country. The columnist Harold Weir was writing in the *Vancouver Sun*, under headlines like "Hideous Totems" and "More Totem Nonsense," that he could not believe that the provincial government would provide funding for carving "these monstrosities." He was unrepentant when several people responded with outrage on the pages of the *Native Voice*, the newspaper of the Native Brotherhood. He is quoted as describing advocates for the preservation of totem poles as "preposterous fanatics." Apparently Weir had heard "that even the legends connected with these things are fakes and have no legitimate place in ancient Indian lore." Bill Reid castigated Weir in the pages of the *Sun* because he could not "let such a slur as he cast upon our most outstanding west coast art form pass unchallenged."[14] Weir continued undeterred. Totem pole restoration was also dismissed from a perhaps more substantial source. Hawthorn applied for a grant from the Canada Council to repair and preserve the totem poles being collected. He clearly noted in the application that after several years' experience working with the ancient massive carvings, he knew they needed to be stored indoors in controlled conditions if they were to have a chance of surviving. The Canada Council turned down the application "on the grounds that the unnatural, or artificial, perpetuation of a dying art does not make sense." The advice was that, if the request were recast "on historical and anthropological lines," rather than the value of the art itself, it would have more chance of success.[15] Audrey and Harry Hawthorn had advised the Massey Commission a few years earlier on the critical need to preserve and nurture Indian art. Apparently the Canada Council had not yet taken in their advice. A year later, however, a revised application was approved, enabling Bill Reid to work at UBC, carving and restoring poles and building houses at Totem Park.

Both Wilson and Hawthorn were aware that there were questions in First Nations communities about appropriation around totem pole preservation. Worry about the appropriation of cultural material by one culture from another is much more keenly felt today than it was in the 1950s, but Wilson understood that by taking totem poles from Indian villages they were capturing the art, moving it to a very different cultural context and then playing a role in determining its significance and meaning. At the same time, for Wilson, any concern about appropriation was overwhelmed by his passion to save a few of the monumental sculptures in British Columbia before it was too late. Many anthropologists and some Indigenous people, including Bill Reid, believed that the art form was dead and those totem poles still standing would be the last. For them, therefore, it was an urgent matter to save a few examples of the art. While we now know that the art form has survived, it was at a very low ebb in Wilson's day, when it was not at all clear that it would rise again. Wilson also knew that many of the Indigenous people of the coast believed that the fate of a totem pole should be to fall to the ground and become part of the earth again. That expectation was, in part, based on the assumption that new poles would replace those that fell. Very few new totem poles were erected in the first half of the twentieth century, and by the 1950s, with few exceptions, the only ones being carved were coming out of the restoration programs at UBC and the Provincial Museum. Wilson was aware of the sometimes murky history of totem pole collecting on the Northwest Coast. In the past, cultural material was often taken from the coast, without the permission of the owners, in ways that amounted to theft. People without authorization were still going into deserted villages and either removing or defacing totem poles. For Wilson, all of these factors added up to two things in his mind. First, it was an urgent matter to preserve some of the few remaining poles and, second, he wanted to be scrupulous about consulting with Indian people before any poles were removed.

Wilson recognized both the importance and the difficulty of establishing the ownership of totem poles, particularly those in villages that had been deserted for a generation or more. He spoke many times to elders and Band Council members to establish, where possible, the ownership. He wrote an article in the *Native Voice*, the newspaper directed at Indigenous communities, under a headline asking, "Have We the Vision to Save Haida Totems?" He emphasized that it was necessary to find the "owners" of poles, that the ownership and sale needed to be approved by the Band Council and that there should be a payment for the sale. He indicated that he wanted to develop a program to save the totems and ended by inviting "support and suggestions from all who may be interested."[16] At the same time he worked with W.S. Arneil, the Indian commissioner for British Columbia, who in turn consulted the Band Councils, to make the case to the federal minister of citizenship and immigration, who was responsible for Indian affairs, for permission to remove totem poles. Following this process, Wilson, accompanied by Bill Reid and others, salvaged six poles from Skedans and Tanu in 1954. Three went to the Provincial Museum and three to UBC. The following year Wilson and Wayne Suttles, now a faculty member in anthropology at UBC, conducted a survey of Kwakiutl village sites. They negotiated with the owners and arranged the salvage of some poles, house frames and posts. Again the two partners in the reclamation program shared the artifacts equally. These poles were valued additions to the collections at UBC and the Provincial Museum. And yet, for Wilson, Ninstints, with its long row of totem poles still standing but being steadily engulfed by the forest, silently beckoned.

The first step was to visit Ninstints to see the site and examine the totem poles. Because of its relative remoteness, getting there was not easy. After trying for three years, he had his opportunity in October of 1956. The Canadian navy took a party from the Provincial Museum up to the Queen Charlotte Islands on HMCS *Brockville*. With Wilson were Clifford Carl, Michael Kew and the curator of birds and animals, Charles Guiguet. Between two very sharp Pacific storms with winds of 85 miles per hour, heading north from Cape Saint James through rolling Pacific swells, they approached the lee side of Anthony Island. Ninstints is tucked away in a tiny, secluded cove masked by a small islet across from the village site. The cove and the channel into it are shallow and at low tide both are dry land. When you approach from the sea you may catch glimpses of the old poles peeking out from the forest, silver grey against the green. The museum party was not sure that they would be able to land. A small whaler boat was lowered into the rise and fall of the swell. They scrambled aboard and were able to row into the calm water of the cove and step ashore. Wilson was excited every time he visited Ninstints, but never more so than the first time. "For me, and my fellow anthropologist Michael Kew, the landing was something of a personal triumph" after waiting so long to get there. Even today, SGang Gwaay is a powerful, haunting place. Wilson felt its spirit and it spoke to him:

> As the whaler pulled through the narrow entrance into the curving, sheltered bay, the sight before us far exceeded my expectations. Three dozen weather-bleached totems, crowded close together around the rim of the bay, faced us as we entered. In a way it was a depressing scene. Here were the bleached bones of a proud way of life that was dead. Many of the carvings were decayed beyond recognition, the frames of the old houses had fallen askew and lay rotting on the ground, moist vegetation had overrun the village. But it was also an awesome and stirring scene. There was a strength and a strange beauty in the boldly carved figures of Grizzlies, Beavers and Whales staring from the poles. This art had been developed on this rugged tempestuous coast, by a hardy and vigorous people attuned to its rhythms, and like all great art, it reflected the spirit of its time and its makers. At any rate, I was awed by the sight, and so were the others who came ashore.

He could imagine the village when it was alive with people before smallpox brought north from Victoria had depopulated it until, finally, the few survivors moved to Skidegate. After assessing the totem poles, he thought that sixteen were salvageable, either wholly or in part. More than he had dared hope to find and more than remained in all the other Haida villages put together.[17]

While Ninstints had the most poles on Haida Gwaii, it also presented Wilson with the biggest challenge when arranging salvage. With the help of the Skidegate Band Council, he was able to establish the owners of the Skedans and Tanu poles, but for Ninstints it was much more difficult as there were few people left with a direct connection to the village. In his discussions with the Band Council at Skidegate about Ninstints, Wilson had taken along Peter Kelly for support. Born in Skidegate, Kelly was a United Church minister and a prominent advocate for Indian rights over several decades. He had been the founding chair of the steering committee of the Allied Tribes of British Columbia and was later the chair of the legislative committee of the Native Brotherhood of British Columbia. Both organizations pressed governments for a recognition of Indian claims to their land and for a revision of the paternalism of the Indian Act. Kelly's support for preserving totem poles also made sense in the particular case of Ninstints because his mother's second marriage was to Tom Price, a prominent Haida artist and the last chief named Ninstints to live in the village. Yet, in spite of all Wilson's due diligence, there were setbacks.

The reconnaissance trip to Ninstints attracted a good deal of media attention. In the midst of that publicity, a Victoria newspaper conveyed the impression that the museum party had already taken out some poles before they had the approval of the Skidegate Band Council. Understandably, this report distressed individual Haida and angered the Skidegate councillors, who passed a resolution calling for a halt to the removal of any material from Haida villages. Having read in the newspaper that some totem poles had already been removed from Ninstints, Molly Stewart wrote from Ketchikan to the Indian agent in Prince Rupert claiming ownership of some Ninstints poles through her grandfather. At the same time, she expressed a willingness to work with the Provincial Museum to reach a "mutual satisfactory agreement whereby the Museum can retain the property."[18] Stewart had written to the Indian agent on the mistaken assumption that Ninstints was an Indian reserve. Though he was not convinced that she had a very strong claim to the Ninstints poles,

Wilson wrote a polite and reassuring reply to Molly Stewart asking her for help with any information that she could give him about the village of Ninstints and the families that came from there. He noted, "Since we are trying to help them preserve their history, the Haida people have given us their full co-operation in the past." Wilson also wrote immediately to the Band Council to reassure them that they had not removed any poles, and that none would be taken without the permission of the Band Council and any confirmed owners that they could find. He told the Band Council that he was working with Peter Kelly, and now with Molly Stewart, to establish who the owners were. He also asked the councillors for any help that they could provide in tracing the descendants of Ninstints. Wilson suggested to the Band Council that he come up to Skidegate in the spring to work with them to resolve these misunderstandings.[19]

He was back in Skidegate in April of 1957, following another Band Council resolution that it was willing to work with the museum representatives. He was not surprised that the Ninstints poles were the subject of much discussion in the village, but it was still not clear who were the owners. He worked with Peter Martin, the chief band councillor, to find a way though the issue, since they were agreed on the urgency of saving the poles. The Band Council wanted all claimants to have an opportunity to establish their rights, but they wanted claims to apply to specific poles and not just a relationship to the village. It helped that Martin thought that the fact that Tom Price was the last man to hold the name Ninstints was an important connection, and he wanted Wilson to pass this on to Peter Kelly. In the end, the Band Council decided to hold an open meeting so that everyone could be heard, and then the council would, if it were possible, determine the ownership of the Ninstints poles. In the meantime, the salvage operation could go ahead and payment for the poles would be made to the Band Council, who would then decide on the dispersal of the money. Wilson was pleased with the council's action, thinking, "It is proper that the decision on ownership should be decided in the village without any pressure one way or another from me."[20] He also hoped that he would be able to arrange the salvage operation that summer.

Then, at the eleventh hour, Indian Affairs threatened to throw a spanner in the works. Indian Commissioner Arneil wrote to Wilson wondering how, since Ninstints was not an Indian reserve, the Skidegate Band Council could assume jurisdiction and take responsibility for these arrangements? Arneil suggested that Wilson check with the attorney general's office. Although he got legal advice, Wilson was not going to be governed by the outcome. He was convinced that the approach the Skidegate Band Council was taking was the right thing to do, even if the legalities were a bit obscure. As soon as he had returned from the reconnaissance to Ninstints the previous fall, he had arranged with the provincial forest service to have the village declared a class A provincial park to give it some degree of protection given that, strictly speaking, the Indian Act did not apply. Wilson responded to Arneil that, while there may not be a strict legal obligation to establish ownership of the Ninstints poles, there was a more powerful moral imperative to recognize Haida rights and ownership of the poles. The best body to judge the validity of the various claims to ownership was the Skidegate Band acting through its council. "I feel," he concluded, "that this procedure gives full recognition of the Indians' rights despite the fact that Anthony Island in not an Indian Reserve."[21] With the negotiations completed and matters resolved as best he could, Wilson turned his mind to a return visit to the totem poles of Ninstints.

First were the logistical arrangements. Wilson contacted Roy Jones in Skidegate to arrange to be taken to Anthony Island in his seine boat. The salvage party arrived at Sandspit over two days and walked over to the dock, where *Seiner II*'s decks were littered with equipment and food supplies for a ten-day expedition. Roy Jones was the boat's captain and his two brothers, Clarence and Frank (Molly Stewart's grandson), were mate and cook. The party was something of a who's who of British Columbia anthropology at the time: accompanying Wilson were Harry Hawthorn, Michael Kew and Wayne Suttles. Bill Reid, along with a photographer, were there to record proceedings for the CBC, and John Smyly, the carpenter, also kept a diary of the trip.[22] Wilson was the operational leader of the expedition. They sailed south, made brief landings at Skedans and Tanu, and approached Anthony Island from the east through Houston Stewart Channel. Several trips in a small boat brought them and their gear ashore, and they set up camp on a piece of low-lying ground at the north end of the village. That turned out to be a mistake because their camp was flooded out in the teeming rain in the middle of their stay. Wilson later referred to his Ninstints experience as "ruins in the rain."[23] Once they were set up, they began the process of assessing the totem poles and taking some of them down.

Wilson's reverence for the totem poles at Ninstints is clear from his writing about them and the way that he can be seen approaching them in the staged movies that were made of the expedition.[24] At the same time, the operation of taking them down was not pretty. With ropes and pulleys, block and tackle and crosscut saws, they cut the poles at the base and lowered them onto a bed of spruce boughs on the ground, where some were cut into sections. Some had to be disentangled from trees and the vegetation growing around—and sometimes inside—them. Once the poles were on the ground, crates were built around them so that they would be protected as they were transported out. The poles were then rolled down to the beach on pieces of driftwood, ready to leave their home. While they were on Anthony Island, members of the party also spent time exploring. They found a few artifacts other than totem poles and they carried out brief archaeological probes. When the work was completed, the poles were lashed together in a single row, pulled out through the channel behind a small boat and secured behind the *Seiner II*. They spent a night in the sheltered waters of Louscoone Inlet, just north of Anthony Island. Next morning the poles were transferred to a Canadian navy vessel and taken to Victoria and Vancouver, to be shared equally by the Provincial Museum and UBC, where most are still standing today.

Leaving Ninstints in June of 1957, Wilson reflected upon, and later wrote about, his sadness at the world that was lost:

What was destroyed here was not just a few hundred individual human lives. Human beings must die anyway. It was something even more complex and even more human—a vigorous and functioning society, the product of just as long an evolution as our own, well suited to its environment and vital enough to participate in human cultural achievements not duplicated anywhere else. What was destroyed was one more bright tile in the complicated and wonderful mosaic of man's achievement on earth. Mankind is the loser. We are the losers.[25]

While he mourned a village that was emptied of human life, he did not regret saving a few examples of its monumental art so that it would endure to speak to others, even if "with only silent whispers."[26]

When the news got out about the arrival of the Ninstints totem poles in Victoria and Vancouver, Wilson had to respond to a little flurry of correspondence from people who thought that they would like to have one of them. He was forwarded one request that came through the Powell River Company from someone in Boston who had heard about the totem poles salvaged from "Nimsinks" and would like to have one. Could Wilson please send along some photographs of the poles so that he could select one? The word had not reached many in America that original totem poles were no longer available to carry off from British Columbia. It takes little imagination to know how Wilson responded to these naive requests. He patiently explained that, with so few poles left, the province had to retain as many samples of the art of its Native people as it could. Furthermore, the Ninstints poles could no longer stand outdoors and survive. There was, in short, "no possibility of obtaining an original pole."[27]

The removal of totem poles from Northwest Coast villages was not particularly controversial at the time, except in the minds of those who thought that it was a waste of time and money. Since then, however, it has become more contentious. At the time, some people in Skidegate may have had concerns about the removal of the totem poles, but it appears that most did not. The Haida elder Captain Gold recalls chief Band Councillor Peter Martin saying that there was unhappiness within the Band Council and some members wanted to take legal action.[28] There is no mention of this happening in the documentary record, but the absence of a record does not mean that it was not contemplated. Molly Stewart did mention the possibility of taking legal advice in her letter about the Ninstints poles, but was apparently happy with Wilson's response. The thought of legal action may have occurred to others over the winter of 1956–57, during the time between the Victoria newspaper reports that poles had already been taken and Wilson's reassurance of the Band Council that he would follow the same procedure as he had with the Skedans and Tanu poles. After he returned from Ninstints, Roy Jones, the seiner skipper, "never heard a word" of controversy about the removal of the poles.[29] More recently some scholars have found it easy in retrospect to find fault with the process that Wilson and his colleagues followed to acquire the SGang Gwaay poles. To suggest, more than forty years later, that Wilson and the Totem Pole Preservation Committee "slipped out of assuming responsibility for deciding validity of title claims" by agreeing that the Band Council should make the decisions on ownership is a remarkable example of seeing the past from the perspective of the present.[30] What would the optics have been, as we like to say today, if Wilson had presumed to adjudicate on the ownership of the SGang Gwaay totem poles? After the Ninstints poles had arrived in Victoria and Vancouver, the agreed-upon payment of $800 was made to Peter Martin and the Skidegate Band Council. They continued to try to establish the ownership of the poles, but without success, so in the end the council decided that the money would go to the Skidegate Church.

Wilson was in no way *persona non grata* on Haida Gwaii after the removal of the totem poles. It has been argued that Bill Reid's visits to Haida Gwaii with Wilson to salvage totem poles shaped Reid's growing Haida identity. After one visit to Skidegate, in a letter cheekily addressed to "Dr Mr Duff," Reid wrote that the people told him that Wilson "had made the best impression of any visitor for years. Everybody spoke very highly of you, and is still amazed by your ability to pronounce Haida words."[31] It is true that the two were becoming close friends, but Bill Reid still did not convey compliments lightly. Even more significant, Wilson was given a Haida name by Mrs. Watson Tulip of Skidegate. She was a descendant of the great Haida artist Albert Edward Edenshaw, to whom the name had belonged. Her family owned one of the Tanu poles that Wilson had salvaged. Florence Davidson, the daughter of Charles Edenshaw, was also involved in giving Wilson his Haida name.[32] Wilson loved having tea with the elderly women on Haida Gwaii. His given name was *gwaaygu7anhlan*, meaning "his head is resting on an island." That name was a powerful one for Wilson, as he was becoming increasingly interested in both Albert Edward Edenshaw and his nephew Charles Edenshaw as artists. He discussed them and their art often with Bill Reid, describing his excitement when he saw the Edenshaw carving tools on a visit to Haida Gwaii: "they are beautiful," he wrote.[33] The Edenshaws' contributions to Haida art were a fascination for Wilson that only grew in intensity over time. After the totem pole salvage work, Wilson maintained his close connections with people from Haida Gwaii. He learned from the relationships that he had developed there and applied that experience to other situations.

*

Wilson had been interested in the totem poles in the Gitksan (Gitxsan) communities along the Skeena River ever since he visited them with Harry Hawthorn in 1949. He went to the area again in the summer of 1952 and, after stopping in Hazelton, revisited the Gitksan villages, the four *K*s, as they were then known: Kispiox, Kitsegukla (now Gitsegukla), Kitwanga (now Gitwangak) and Kitwancool (now Gitanyow). On this trip, he conducted a detailed examination of all the totem poles in these villages and published an inventory of them in Anthropology in British Columbia. He described and mapped the location of the poles in each village and established the individual and clan owners of each pole. Marius Barbeau had been through the Skeena Valley nearly thirty years previously and published a detailed study of the totem poles.[34] Wilson was interested in how the number and the condition of the totem poles had changed in the three decades. He found that the total number had not changed much, but their condition had definitely deteriorated. Wilson counted more than a hundred poles in the Gitksan villages and eighty-two were still standing. But several had fallen, most were suffering from the effects of weathering and many were at risk of rotting away. While he was concerned about the future of the poles on the Skeena, the prospects for the survival of the art were not as bleak as they appeared to be on Haida Gwaii. A difference from the Haida was that, among the Gitksan, some new poles had been raised and others restored, although Wilson thought that the quality of carving had declined. He was especially impressed with the totem poles at Kitwancool, where there was the largest number of standing poles of all the Gitksan villages; he judged them to "rank with the finest poles ever carved."[35] Among them was the marvelous "hole in the sky" pole. Another pole includes, near its base, a little human figure with its hand in its mouth. A warning to Wilson, perhaps, that he should be careful what he said.

Wilson opened up the discussion of removing some totem poles and taking them to the Provincial Museum but came away with a clear sense of the depth of opposition to the idea, particularly in Kitwancool. The Gitksan people had a strong history of resisting the encroachment of settler society and asserting their ownership of their territory. In 1927, for example, five Kitwancool leaders were convicted and sentenced to three-month jail terms in Oakalla Prison Farm for obstructing a survey party. Some of them were still alive when Wilson went to Kitwancool to talk about removing totem poles. At one level, the totem poles were affirmation of the people's place on the land. They were also, Wilson learned, deeply embedded in the social system of the Gitksan. Their primary purpose, he wrote, was "as certificates of social standing."[36] These functions meant that a pole could not be raised or taken down, or even restored, without a ceremonial feast that involved payment to the witnesses. Most leaders could no longer afford the multiple feasts that the prestige of their ancestors required. For all these reasons, no totem poles had ever been removed from Kitwancool.

Albert Douse, a Kitwancool leader, explained to Wilson that a totem pole was "a symbol of all the privileges, power, territory, traditions and prestige of the owning clan." Wilson, on the other hand, was trying to explain the importance of the totem poles as art, and the need to preserve some examples of that art before they rotted away. Those that he talked to in Kitwancool were initially very guarded but, as they developed, discussions became "friendly, serious, dignified." Still, Albert Douse and Wilson Duff were poles apart. Wilson later described the Kitwancool people as "the proudest, most aloof, and most conservative of Indians (and I think the most admirable)."[37] He left Kitwancool in 1952 with the clear understanding that no poles would be relinquished, and that further requests would only harden the determination not to let any go.

For the next few years, Wilson salvaged totem poles from Kwakiutl and Haida villages. After the Ninstints expedition, in the fall of 1957, he went back to the Skeena and Kitwancool to see if the leaders there had changed their minds. They had not. To avoid giving offence, Wilson did not press the matter immediately. He pursued other interests in the area. He went to Port Edward, at the mouth of the Skeena, to visit William Beynon, the Tsimshian ethnographer who worked with both Marius Barbeau and Franz Boas for many years. Beynon was seventy and suffering from a recent stroke, but he was still a mine of information on Tsimshian culture. He told Wilson he was skeptical of some of Barbeau's ideas, including his notion of recent migrations of Indigenous people from China to the Northwest Coast, and the idea that the Nass Valley was the promised land for the new arrivals.[38] The meeting was fortuitous as Beynon passed away the following year. Wilson did not forget Beynon or the conversation that they had about Barbeau.

On another visit, Wilson was in Kitwanga filming and taking photos. There had been a totem pole restoration program there in the 1920s. Here Wilson felt the bite of conscience that a museum collector will experience if they are at all sensitive. He met a Kitwanga woman who had a moon mask and a rattle in her possession that he had his eye on for the Provincial Museum collection. She did not want to sell them at first, but then agreed to take $100 for them. Wilson knew "It hurt her to sell them and I felt like a heel," but he also wanted to see them on display in the museum.[39] Meeting Beynon and buying the rattle and mask were, in different ways, important learning moments for Wilson, but they were also diversions from his primary interest.

From Kitwanga, the back road led north to Kitwancool, and Wilson knew that he had to take that road again. In late October, as he headed north, winter was coming and it was starting to snow. He stopped to take some film of Battle Hill, the former site of a spectacular and impregnable fortified village on the banks of the Kitwanga River. Farther up the road he ran into Albert Douse's brother, Walter, who was driving in the other direction, and had stopped on the side of the road with a flat tire. Wilson helped him to change the tire and they decided to postpone their planned interview for a few days, until they would both be in Hazelton. There are few better ways to build rapport with someone than to help them out on a northern road as the snow flies. The encounter would prove to be auspicious, but not immediately. When he got to Kitwancool Wilson found that six more poles had fallen since he was there five years before. That left fifteen standing. "It won't be long now," Wilson wrote. Their imminent fall only intensified his belief in the artistic value of the Kitwancool totem poles and the importance, from his perspective, of saving some of them. His conversations in Kitwancool quickly established, however, that the elders had not changed their minds. He was told that the "white man has taken everything else that was theirs, and they are not going to take the totem poles."[40]

Sometimes the toughest challenge will lead to the most creative thinking. Wilson suggested that they bring out only a few totem poles from Kitwancool to the Provincial Museum so that the carving program could make replicas that could be returned to the village. The originals would go to either the Provincial Museum or to UBC, where they would be preserved under cover. The idea did not take hold immediately, but Wilson continued to hold conversations with the Douse brothers and other elders and owners from the community. He was clear that, in order for the plan to go ahead, the owners would have to approve of the plan and then an agreement would have to be reached with the Kitwancool Band Council. He also talked to Walter Derrick, the chief councillor, and Peter Williams, the president of Kitwancool. Gradually people began to see some merit in Wilson's idea. He was also working with Walter Douse on the history of his family and Kitwancool culture, and out of those conversations emerged the idea of recording and publishing the history of Kitwancool as told by its people.[41] That idea was very appealing. When Wilson left the Skeena in the fall of 1957 he had a verbal agreement for the removal of three totem poles, providing he could make the necessary arrangements in the south. He arranged for the museum's carving program to make exact replicas of the Kitwancool poles, informed Hawthorn and others at UBC of the plan, solicited funding for parts of the project from Walter Koerner and lined up the Canadian navy to transport the poles. By the following spring everything was in place.

Wilson returned to Kitwancool and signed a legal contract with the Band Council leaders confirming the arrangement to remove and make replicas of three totem poles, then return the copies and erect them in the community. There was also a provision to have a mutually agreed upon person come to Kitwancool to "write down the authentic stories of the totem poles and the history and laws of the Kitwancool people as dictated by them."[42] It was further specified that the publication of these stories would be made available and used for teaching in universities. Both the agreement itself and the written communication during its implementation involved a degree of formality and legality on the part of the Kitwancool, particularly Peter Williams, who remained anxious that Wilson and the museum would honour all aspects of the arrangement. That concern was justified given Kitwancool's history, and Wilson remained committed to this new way of doing things. Once signed, the agreement was implemented without a hitch, at least at the Kitwancool end.

Three totem poles were taken to Victoria and copies made. They were the first poles ever to be taken out of Kitwancool, and they were not sold but rather ownership remained in the community. Three years later a fourth pole was removed under the same arrangement at the request of the Kitwancool, and then in 1965 the community leaders asked Wilson to remove and restore all remaining poles in the village and make copies "without prejudice to the right of every owner..."[43] When copies were returned to Kitwancool, there was some controversy because they were erected along the road into the village rather than facing the river where they had traditionally stood, but that was a decision made within the community. Later Wilson had other copies made for Thunderbird Park, where they still stand today. The originals eventually went to the museums in Victoria and Vancouver. Wilson did have a spat with Walter Koerner, who wrote in stentorian tones that, based on his funding of a part of the project, all three poles were to go to UBC. Wilson's initial understanding was that Koerner wanted the third pole to go to UBC, not all three. He was willing to send one or more to the university, but only when they had better facilities to house them and ensure their preservation. Other poles that he was involved in collecting were now in a storage shed at UBC that Wilson called the "pole vault."[44] Until UBC had a better place to keep the poles, Wilson preferred that they stay in Victoria, where the storage was better, if not perfect. All this back and forth went on outside the agreement with the Kitwancool.

The work with the Kitwancool, by contrast, went relatively smoothly. Wilson arranged for Constance Cox, who had lived in Hazelton for most of her life, spoke the Gitksan language and was known and trusted in the community, to go to Kitwancool and write down the stories. He was clear throughout that process that the Kitwancool must determine the content. Wilson did not intend to intervene in any way as they presented their stories. He wrote to Peter Williams, "I regard it as extremely important that what is written down is what you people regard as the important facts, and that it be said as you people want it said." He advised that they decide what stories they wanted to tell. Presumably, he suggested, the stories of the totem poles, the histories of each clan, and Kitwancool history, laws and customs. A representative of each clan or family should be appointed to sit down with Cox to tell the stories. "This is your history, to be told in your way," he reiterated.[45] Cox spent two weeks listening to and writing down what the spokespeople had to say. She sent the manuscript to the Provincial Museum, where it was prepared for publication. There was some editing to make it easier to read in places, but all changes were sent to Peter Williams, who consulted with the community before anything became final. *The Histories, Territories, and Laws of the Kitwancool* was published in 1959 as a memoir in Wilson's Anthropology in British Columbia series. The first sentence declared: "The authors of this book are the Kitwancool themselves."[46] Constance Cox thought that "Kitwancool is the first Indian village that has willingly given up their History to the Gov: and for the use of schools."[47] This was an exaggeration, discounting decades of ethnographic work by various people from government agencies, and yet there was something in what she said. Wilson's agreement with the Kitwancool, which provided for the removal and return of totem poles along with the publication of their history, was an innovative way for a government museum representative to work with a First Nations community on the preservation of their heritage.

Many acknowledged the significance of the Kitwancool agreement, some at the time and others in retrospect. Once the Kitwancool publication appeared, other First Nations groups along the Skeena wanted to have their histories and land claims written up in a similar way. Harry Hawthorn was impressed with Wilson's achievements on behalf of the Totem Pole Preservation Committee. Even Walter Koerner was "very thankful for the nice inscription" in the copy of *The Histories, Territories, and Laws of the Kitwancool* that Wilson sent to him. Peter Macnair, who was the curator of ethnology at the Provincial Museum for thirty years, and who did not agree with Wilson on all things, thought that the Kitwancool arrangement was a "brilliant move." The last word went to Peter Williams, president of Kitwancool, who, two decades later, recalled how Wilson had approached the people of Kitwancool to talk about their totem poles: "His voice was soft and gentle, but firm in truth and honour." Wilson had earned respect because, when "he dealt with the Indian histories and rights of this land, he did it resolutely, profoundly and with intense care."[48] The poles that still stand, both in Kitwancool and in the museums, are the clearest testament to what was generally true of Wilson's approach to totem pole reclamation: he took some poles down so that many could rise again.

Taking down totem poles and bringing them to the Provincial Museum was, for Wilson, a way to preserve and recognize the art that he believed was disappearing. The poles and their stories also testified that the Indian cultures of the coast were viable, even if threatened. This had been their place for thousands of years, and they had valid cultural and territorial claims that needed to be recognized. Such was Wilson's thinking and motivation. And yet, of all his work at the Provincial Museum, totem pole restoration would, in the future, raise the biggest questions about museums as curators of culture.

6. Museums and Beyond

Even after Wilson had taken some totem poles, others remained in Ninstints and Kitwancool. In the Ninstints cove, many still lined the beach, leaning, falling and decaying into the ground as the forest encroached. Though diminished, some endured for decades, along with the spirits of the people who had lived there, silent testimony to past power. In Kitwancool the people passed by the poles every day, both the originals and those that Wilson had copied, as they were lined up along the road into the heart of the village. There they stood, representing the social power and prestige that still lived in the community and the assertion of rights that had not been relinquished. But what of the totem poles that were now in the museums? What meaning did they have there? What function did they serve?

As he was restoring totem poles from Ninstints and Kitwancool, Wilson was seven and eight years into his career at the Provincial Museum and thinking more and more about the role of museums in British Columbia and beyond. He understood that salvaging the poles meant taking them out of their Indigenous context and incorporating them into a different culture. That much was obvious. He also recognized that he was the representative of a settler society that continued to colonize Indian cultures. Taking down the poles, however, was neither theft nor even simple appropriation. It would be easy to say that it was the outcome of an unequal power relationship because there would be some truth to that. Yet was Wilson in a position of power when he was on his own in Kitwancool, a community that had resisted settlers and their government for decades? Totem pole restoration was the outcome of negotiations in which the Indigenous people had interests and agency. Wilson did not take the poles without permission. He saw, first-hand, the impact of settlers and governments when he visited Indian communities and talked to the people. Increasingly, he worked to mitigate the impact of newcomer settlement and advocate for Indigenous rights, particularly to the land. Nevertheless, he was still a government employee working for a government agency—he knew he was implicated in the repercussions of colonization and collecting on Indian cultures. As he once remarked, mindful of future generations and speaking about Haida art in distant museums, "New York kids can see it, Masset kids can't."[1] Amidst all this ambiguity, Wilson needed to articulate clearly the value of the museums that had captured so much of Indian culture.

For Wilson, a museum should, first and foremost, be a public educational institution that taught ideas to the people. He held that this role was unique to museums. "No other institution in our society is concerned with preserving and propounding truths in the same way." Libraries and archives were repositories but not actively engaged in teaching; universities were teaching institutions but only to a limited audience; and churches dealt with faith rather than science. Museums instructed whoever walked through the door. They could, therefore, no longer be musty mausoleums full of unremembered relics and artifacts under anaesthetic. To be sure, museums displayed objects and "objects do have great appeal, being the real thing." But displaying the objects was just the first step. It was what the objects had to teach that really mattered. The role of the museum anthropologist was to display the meaning of the objects. As Wilson put it, the "objects should be pushed as hard as possible to tell the stories that are built into them."[2] An anthropological museum should, for example, show how material culture represents a whole culture. Bringing out the meaning of objects demanded research, and Wilson was a strong advocate of the research function of the museum. He became a fan of A.E. Parr, the director of the American Museum of Natural History, who shared his belief that museums should be both archives for preservation and centres of active research. Wilson discussed these ideas with Parr when he visited Victoria to give a talk to the Canadian Museum Association Annual Meeting in 1963. A copy of Parr's book, *Mostly About Museums*, is inscribed to Wilson and full of his penciled notes and underlining.[3] Based on objects, ideas and research, museums were ultimately repositories of truths: truths about the past and truths about the present. In a world of false advertising and political dissembling, in which things are not what they seem to be on the surface, Wilson believed that "there is a hunger for the real truths" that museums could provide. Museums should teach about the value of different cultures—then, by comparison, encourage people to think about what is right and, more importantly for Wilson, what is wrong, with their own ways of life. While people came to museums to look at the things, Wilson was convinced that they also came to learn about other cultures and thereby about themselves. They came, that is to say, to think about ideas and truths from the past made relevant to today.[4] In his own gentle way, Wilson was passionate about the role of a museum. Of course, there was cultural assumption, and perhaps presumption, in Wilson's vision of an anthropology museum. His approach of using "anthropological insights to the hilt" meant that the museum anthropologist was deciding what was important about other cultures and interpreting them to the public.[5] Wilson was aware of that. That awareness is not surprising, since he developed his thinking about museums in the time and place in which he worked. Even so, being Wilson, he was ahead of that time and place. At a time when Indian people were not encouraged to speak and were seldom heard by settler society, Wilson was listening. For him, anthropology to the hilt meant hearing Indigenous voices tell their stories about their artifacts.

Wilson also saw value in the particular configuration of British Columbia's Provincial Museum of Natural History and Anthropology. Its twin mandate made for two halves of a compelling whole. It enabled the museum to tell citizens the story of the province that results from the meeting of two things, "the natural environment, and our human cultures." The unifying theme of the Provincial Museum's entire approach was "the interaction of man and nature in British Columbia; that is the interaction of Indian and White cultures and this natural environment."[6] There was a purity and idealism about Wilson's vision for museums generally and the Provincial Museum in particular. But that vision proved to be difficult to implement in the real world of limited government funding and inadequate space in the basement of the legislature.

Wilson got an even stronger dose of reality when he took these ideas about the role of museums on visits to small local museums in the interior of the province. The Provincial Museum decided that it should be offering support to the small museums that were proliferating outside Victoria and the Lower Mainland. The Anthropology Museum at UBC also participated in the initiative by putting on a short course in museum management in September 1957, which Wilson attended, representing the Provincial Museum. Wilson then began visiting local museums around the province, beginning in October 1957. He quickly saw that there was a good deal of variety among them. He drove to Penticton and then up the Okanagan Valley. He arrived in Kamloops in time to attend the official opening of a new museum. At a luncheon he was invited to give a speech and "praised the museum highly. Played the role of the visiting museum expert from the coast who was really impressed." Obviously uneasy in that role, he felt that he was more effective giving advice to individuals like the local architect, to whom he thought that he "got some ideas across." He had a rather more delicate conversation with the mayor of Kamloops, who wanted to have either an original or a restored totem pole erected in his city. Wilson managed to disabuse him of the idea.

Wilson went on to Cache Creek and Clinton. When he was shown the Clinton museum, his reaction, as recorded in his notebook, was simple and direct: "What a clutter!" He continued north through Vanderhoof and Hazelton, ending in Prince Rupert, where he spent a day "talking shop, seeing museum, identifying objects." Many of the local museums relied on enthusiastic community volunteers and many needed real help, more than could be given during a quick visit.[7] Some more sustained form of advice was required. One step in that direction was Wilson's suggestion to Wayne Suttles at UBC that a little book by Carl Guthe titled *So You Want a Good Museum* be sent around the province. The book provided a guide to developing small museums based on the author's visits to more than one hundred such museums in the United States. It gave basic practical advice starting with the first point: to establish a clear focus for your museum and have the discipline to stick to it.[8] An initiative coming out of the UBC course led to the establishment of the British Columbia Museums Association in 1959. At the annual meeting the following year, Clifford Carl was elected president and Wilson vice-president.[9] Three years later Wilson became the president. With this additional role he continued to visit local museums and offer advice when he could.

*

In the midst of this work with small museums in British Columbia, Wilson was also working on an opportunity to spend some time at a much larger museum in the nation's capital. He wanted to spend a year at the National Museum in Ottawa studying and organizing the huge collection of ethnographic material on the Tsimshian that Marius Barbeau and William Beynon had generated. Marius Barbeau was seen as the grand old man of Canadian anthropology. Throughout a long career at the National Museum, beginning in 1914, he made many field trips to the Northwest Coast and published extensively in academic journals. He was known to the public for his more popular books, which were loosely based on his ethnographic notes. He supported Wilson's interest in working on his ethnographic records because he thought that it was critical for a younger generation to understand his field notes while he was still there to help.[10] Although retired, Barbeau still came into the museum, so the idea was that Wilson could consult with him while he was going through the Tsimshian material. Wilson got a leave of absence from the Provincial Museum on half salary and support from the Canada Council and the Guggenheim Foundation. He had a few qualms on intellectual grounds. Barbeau's ideas were fixed fifty years ago and no one was going to change them now. Other anthropologists had doubts about the accuracy of Barbeau's research and the validity of some of his ideas. Hawthorn warned him that some of Barbeau's ideas about migration to the Northwest Coast from Asia could require "a fairly rugged self-discipline" to resist. Yet he was a major figure in the field and the Tsimshian files were impressive, with their potential yet to be realized. Wilson wrote to Barbeau to be clear that he was aware that some of his interpretations had been questioned, but he would come to Ottawa with an open mind, ready to learn and make his own decisions. "I will want to have the right to reach and express my own interpretations if they should differ from yours," he wrote. He concluded that these were "small matters which we can soon work out easily enough."[11] As it turned out, these things were not worked out either easily or soon. In the meantime, though, all the plans and understandings seemed to be in place.

So Wilson packed up the family and they headed for Ottawa. The Duffs were now a family of four. A son, Thomas (Tom) Wilson, who was born in May 1956, would turn three in Ottawa, and Marnie was seven. The Marion and Wilson marriage was intact but not idyllic. Wilson was consumed by work and by now his letters to colleagues included fewer comments about the family. Marion was expected to take care of everything in the home, much as Wilson's mother had done. Their lives were lived fairly separately, but Marion tried to engage with Wilson's work. She took up painting, and her subjects were often totem poles, including those from Kitwancool that Wilson had recovered. For his part, Wilson did not make much effort to include Marion in his work and thinking. Marion no longer went with him on field trips. She and the children would often go to Vancouver in the summer and stay with her parents when Wilson was away.

Marnie recalls a strained home life from an early age. Evening meals were often perfunctory, then Wilson would quickly head off to his study, where he did not want to be interrupted. Still, Marnie has some fond memories of moments with her father. She sometimes went with him to his office in the Provincial Museum and played on the floor while he worked. She also remembers sitting with him in front of the TV watching the Smothers Brothers singing "my old man's an anthropologist." But Wilson was an absent father when he was at work, in the field or even in his study at home. In addition, Marion tended to be regimented as a mother, an approach that was stressful for Marnie, who increasingly withdrew into her own interests.

The trip to Ottawa in the fall of 1958 was actually made separately. Wilson drove and visited museums in Canada and the United States on the way. Once he had found a place to live in Ottawa, Marion and children flew out to join him. In Ottawa, Marion took lessons from the painter Henri Masson and learned new styles of painting. But the children did not have fond memories of Ottawa; the cold winters were a shock, and they both got whooping cough during the year. Marnie was definitely happier when they returned to the warmth and familiarity of their house and neighbourhood in Victoria the following spring. Wilson, of course, threw himself into his work on the Tsimshian material at the National Museum.

He had intended that the year's work on the Tsimshian files at the National Museum would serve two purposes: to prepare some of the Barbeau material for publication and to make a start on a PhD program. He had arranged to do a PhD at UBC and for Harry Hawthorn to be his supervisor. The idea was that the work in Ottawa would constitute the first year of his PhD program. Hawthorn started to make arrangements for Wilson to take a French test to cover the language requirement for the degree. They had joked that maybe Wilson's second language could be Tsimshian; they thought that it would not fly with the language department, even though Wilson reckoned that his Tsimshian was better than his French and would only improve while he was working on the files in Ottawa. They did not test that aspect of university regulations, but they did push the university administration on another rule. Wilson was admitted to the PhD program, but everything came to an abrupt halt when he wrote to the registrar with a cheque to cover his fees and asked that the registration forms be sent to him by mail, as he would be working on his program in Ottawa. University regulations demanded that a PhD candidate spend the first year in residence, and that meant on campus. There were exceptions in the biological sciences that involved off-campus research, but not in anthropology. Hawthorn tried his best to get a dispensation for Wilson by appealing to Gordon Shrum, the dean of graduate studies. In spite of his considerable influence around the university, he was not able to persuade Shrum. There was not much scope for ethnographic research on the UBC campus so, while they thought that the ruling was arbitrary, Hawthorn and Wilson agreed not to pursue it any further.[12] Wilson would have been the first PhD candidate in anthropology at UBC. It was the last time that he would attempt to register in a PhD program.

The PhD was off the table, but an undaunted Wilson started working on the Tsimshian files. The huge collection was made up of Barbeau's original field notes, written over several seasons, and a large number of narratives collected by Beynon over forty years. Wilson "plunged directly into the material on social organisation," thinking that he would arrange it for publication. He was immediately impressed with the volume and the quality of the material. It was, he thought, "the most complete body of information on the social organization of any Indian nation." Reviewing Barbeau's early field notes beginning in 1915 he realized that, whatever the reservations about Barbeau's scholarship since, "he was a pretty darned good field ethnographer then." His work was thorough and well organized, and his transcriptions were very good, if not quite as precise as those of the linguist Edward Sapir, the first head of the anthropology division at the museum and Barbeau's colleague early in his career. Some of the information was written out in Barbeau's personal shorthand, which had to be "translated," then scattered field notes needed to be brought together in a systematic way. The files included information on the three groups broadly defined by Barbeau as Tsimshian: the coastal Tsimshian, the Gitksan (Gitxsan) up the Skeena River, and the Nishga (Nisga'a) of the Nass River. Wilson began to organize the material on social organization by tribe, starting with the nine Tsimshian tribes of Port Simpson. He created files for names, crests, origins, relationships and territories for each tribe. He also identified appropriate myths that should be included. It was the kind of work, making order out of chaos, that Wilson particularly enjoyed. By working on social organization, he hoped to avoid conflict with Barbeau, who, working mostly at home, was concentrating on the huge mass of Tsimshian myths and narratives. As it turned out, though, the misgivings that Wilson had about "working with the old gentleman" were quickly dispelled and "replaced by affection and respect." Barbeau turned over the material on social organization to Wilson, who worked with a free hand. Barbeau did not try to direct his work or his thinking. At the same time, Wilson quickly realized that the daunting task of organiz-ing the vast body of material for publication would take more than a year.[13]

The year at the National Museum was a learning experience in other unexpected ways. The museum, and especially the Human History Branch, was in turmoil. Initially observing from the sidelines, then increasingly involved, Wilson described the "sorry shambles" with growing alarm. Hawthorn was still his advisor, now on museum matters rather than a PhD program. After five months, Wilson wrote to him that, in effect, he was taking "an advanced seminar and workshop on museum problems, with the National Museum supplying the topics for discussion." Soon after he started work at the museum, he realized that the staff were either absent or not talking to each other much. They were certainly not talk-ing to the director of the Human History Branch, Jacques Rousseau, who, according to Wilson, was hated by all the scientific staff. The breakdown in human relations had a long history at the museum and was a symptom of more fundamental problems. Two years earlier the museum had been divided into two: a Natural History Branch and a Human History Branch. The Human History Branch was a disaster in the making.

Since he was taking a "seminar" in museum practice, it followed that Wilson would write a paper analyzing the issues at the museum. His first contention was that the branch had not defined its role and was trying to be too broad in scope, to the detriment of fundamental subjects like Canadian ethnography. The National Museum of Canada did not have the resources to be a museum for the world, like other national museums. The Massey Commission had recommended that the museum expand its coverage of Canadian history, but Wilson thought that could only happen to the detriment of existing interests if no more resources were forthcom-ing. The Human History Branch was slated to move into a larger space but, according to Wilson, it was not well prepared to mount the new dis-plays. He thought that the staff was made up of scientists, experts in their field, but not museologists with expertise in the design of displays. The museum had gone to outside consultants for the designs, but there was "no firm hand in overall control" of the implementation of the plans. "To ward off this great debacle," Wilson suggested that they scour the world for a strong-willed museologist to whip the plans into shape. In consultation with Hawthorn, he also put forward the idea of "working fellowships" for students who were training in museum practice and could work under a knowledgeable leader to develop the displays and their own expertise. Hawthorn thought that it was a great idea and immediately had candidates in mind. These ideas did not get any traction and the chaos continued. Wilson wrote to Hawthorn that "the clash of personalities and policies is so fierce that something's gotta give before long."[14]

By the beginning of 1959 there was some change, but not the fundamental change in organization and attitude that Wilson had hoped for. Rousseau was gone, replaced by Loris Russell, the former head of the Natural History Branch who now led both branches. Other staff members had departed, leaving vacancies, including the position of senior ethnologist. Wilson toyed with the idea of applying for the position, as some at the National Museum suggested. It would have been a big change in direction for him, and his family would not have been very happy with the idea. Perhaps more importantly for Wilson, Hawthorn warned him "to take no job which is not set up at a satisfactory level. By that I mean … making sure that anything you accepted had enough status and power to enable you to do what you wanted." Hawthorn believed that the troubles at the National Museum were too great to be solved by a change in leadership.[15]

When he arrived at the museum, Wilson had vowed to "refrain from rocking the boat," but later he circulated his paper describing the problems at the museum to its leaders, the assistant deputy minister and the Canada Council.[16] If those who ran the museum were looking for a new staff member with a scathing critique of the status quo and forthright ideas about what had to change, Wilson would be their man. With the issues around display design in mind, he attended the first museum training course sponsored by the Canadian Museums Association, held at the Redpath Museum at McGill University in Montreal. The course was entitled "Display in Museums" and the idea was that the thirty-five attendees would hear about display design and take what they learned back to their museums. The course was experimental and not completely successful, but for Wilson it was still instructive. Often the advice over the two weeks was high level and esoteric, coming from people whose interests were modern art and design, and Wilson thought that much of it had limited application "to the day-to-day work of our grubby little museums." He came away with greater sympathy for the small local museums that he had visited in British Columbia. Based on the seminar, he wrote a paper that he presented in British Columbia entitled "Ten Steps in the Development of Effective Museum Exhibits," in which he gave more down-to-earth advice for smaller museums with limited resources. In the end, he decided not to apply for the ethnography position at the National Museum. He wrote to Hawthorn that there was no single reason; it just did not feel right.[17] So the Duff family returned home to Victoria in June of 1959, and Wilson returned to his office in the Provincial Museum.

*

Wilson returned, having learned so much from developments in other museums, to find that things were changing at his own museum. Michael Kew, who had held the fort while Wilson was away, was moving on. The two of them would work together as friends and colleagues again, but in the meantime, Kew left for Saskatchewan to do community development work. Diane MacEachern, a graduate in anthropology from UBC, replaced him and stayed for a year. Donald Abbott was then appointed to the position of assistant in anthropology. He was also a graduate of UBC and had been doing postgraduate work in archaeology at the University of London. When he arrived in Victoria, and before he started work, Abbott went over to Wilson's house to make himself known. Wilson was in the driveway washing his car. They chatted and Wilson took Don and Maria Abbott over to Clifford Carl's house, where they had arranged to stay while they got settled.[18] It suited Wilson that there continued to be an informal, friendly collegiality among the twelve or thirteen staff members at the Provincial Museum. At the same time, all was not well.

TOP: Growing up in the depression of the 1930s, Wilson and his brother Ron shared a bicycle. *Courtesy of Marnie Duff*

LEFT: Wilson in his teens. *Courtesy of Marnie Duff*

A mother and her sons: Nan Duff with Ron, left, and Wilson.

Courtesy of Marnie Duff

TOP: Wilson and Marion during a break in his training in front of the Duff home on Lanark Street, she in his flying gear and he in the uniform of Leading Aircraftsman. *Courtesy of Marnie Duff*

LEFT: Wilson in the Indian heat in tropical kit. *Courtesy of Marnie Duff*

A Liberator bomber is prepared for takeoff in India. *Courtesy of Marnie Duff*

Wilson and some of the *R for Robert* aircrew, left to right: L. Barnes, Ken Welch, squadron leader Murray Stroud and Wilson. *Courtesy of Marnie Duff*

The navigators synchronize their watches prior to takeoff on a bombing mission.
Wilson is second from the right. *Courtesy of Marnie Duff*

Storage issues in the Provincial Museum as it acquires the large C.F. Newcombe
collection. *Image PN 13417-0 courtesy of the Royal BC Museum*

TOP: Wilson Duff in his office at the Provincial Museum. *Courtesy of Marnie Duff*

LEFT: Wilson in his thirties when he was provincial anthropologist. *Courtesy of Marnie Duff*

Archaeology in a white shirt. Wilson the student archaeologist in 1949. *Courtesy of UBC Museum of Anthropology, Archives image a060242, Herb Watson fonds*

The opening of Wa'waditla, Mungo Martin's house in Thunderbird Park. Mungo Martin is third from the left in the middle row, Wilson fifth from the left and Marion Duff at the far right. They are surrounded by members of the Cranmer, Hunt and Neel families. *Image* PN *13871 courtesy of the Royal* BC *Museum and included with the permission of David Mungo Knox*

LEFT: Mask carved by Wilson Duff after being taught by Mungo Martin. *Robin Fisher photo*

BOTTOM: Among the totem poles, left to right, Michael Kew, Bill Reid, Harry Hawthorn behind Reid and Wilson Duff at Ninstints (SGang Gwaay) in 1957. *Courtesy of UBC Museum of Anthropology, Archives image a040031, William McLennan fonds*

Looking up to the totem poles, left to right, Michael Kew, Bill Reid, Harry Hawthorn and Wilson Duff at Ninstints (SGang Gwaay) in 1957. *Courtesy of UBC Museum of Anthropology, Archives image a040038, William McLennan fonds*

Wilson assessing a decaying totem pole during a survey of village sites in Southwest Alaska. *Courtesy of UBC Museum of Anthropology, Archives image a035046c, Wilson Duff fonds*

TOP: Wilson on the road, taken near Topley, British Columbia. The jacket was a gift from a First Nations community. *Courtesy of UBC Museum of Anthropology, Archives image a060241, Wilson Duff fonds*

LEFT: Raising Robert Davidson's totem pole in Masset in 1969. *Courtesy of UBC Museum of Anthropology, Archives image a060244, Wilson Duff fonds*

LEFT: Solomon Wilson was Wilson Duff's Haida colleague. *Courtesy of UBC Museum of Anthropology, Archives image a060243, Wilson Duff fonds*

BOTTOM: Wilson Duff and Richard Cox examine a bone fragment from a dig on Kitty Islet. *Image PN 20484 courtesy of the Royal BC Museum*

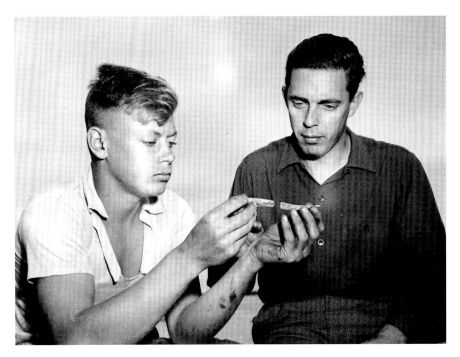

Charles Edenshaw's Raven compote. *Courtesy of UBC Museum of Anthropology, Object A47047, Kyla Bailey photograph*

Bill Reid with the Final Exam and the screens that he painted to replicate the design for the *Arts of the Raven* exhibition. *Photo by Ross Kenward of* The Province *(E91-5, 25-179) and courtesy of the Bill Reid estate*

As well as reproducing the images from the Final Exam on panels for *Arts of the Raven*, Bill Reid also reproduced the four ravens from the Raven Screens in the Denver Art Gallery. This image is of one of those ravens. *Courtesy of UBC Museum of Anthropology, Archives image a060240, Wilson Duff fonds*

The twin masks, inward looking and outward looking, from *images stone b.c.,* photographed by Wilson Duff. *Courtesy of UBC Museum of Anthropology, Archives image a060239, Wilson Duff fonds*

Wilson in his backyard on Tolmie Street. Probably the last photo of Wilson. *Courtesy of Marnie Duff*

Government funding and display space were still seriously insufficient for the Provincial Museum to realize its potential. Wilson struggled to maintain a multitude of responsibilities, as he was pulled in many directions in both ethnography and archaeology. It was touch and go whether Michael Kew would be replaced with a permanent staff member. With Abbott's arrival, Wilson had a close colleague who complemented him in many ways, but there were still only two anthropologists for a vast amount of work. Most disquieting for Wilson were the warning signs that creeping bureaucracy was closing in.

In 1961 the museum began reporting to a different ministry in the provincial government. Since Wilson had been there, the Provincial Museum had been under the Ministry of Education, and that suited him, at least philosophically. If it were Wilson's choice, the museum would be under the aegis of the provincial secretary, Lawrie Wallace, who had worked closely with Wilson and with Willard Ireland, the provincial archivist. The three had developed initiatives together. The decision, however, was to move the archives under the provincial secretary and the museum to the Department of Recreation and Conservation. The rationale given in the museum's *Annual Report*, that the move would bring "closer contact with branches working in related fields," was true for the natural history side but much less so for the anthropology division.[19] The move to Recreation and Conservation brought with it new rules and regulations, some of them merely irritating, others insulting. There was a series of instructions to the museum from David Turner, the deputy minister, about the routing of letters, contact with the minister, and around vacation leave, travel and expenses. A trip to Vancouver on the ferry now required the written approval of the deputy minister.[20] There was even a moment when Wilson wrote to a colleague in Ottawa, "I rather miss the fun and games around the old National Museum of Canada."[21] He was not very serious, as he was ensconced back in Victoria. These irritants could be endured because they applied to everyone at the museum, but Wilson was enraged at the treatment he personally received. For ten years Wilson's title had been assistant anthropologist. It was not a particularly exalted designation, but when the new ministry changed it to "research assistant grade 3" it felt really demeaning. While Wilson was not hung up on status, he did believe that he was owed some respect. He wrote an angry letter to Carl demanding that, given his many responsibilities, his title be changed to curator or museum anthropologist. I "reject and resent," he wrote, the comparisons with more junior positions in other provinces that do not include administrative and other responsibilities.[22] Carl supported Wilson's request, sent it up to Deputy Minister Turner, and Wilson was quickly reclassified as curator of anthropology. Yet the incident still rankled. It was a textbook example of how to undermine a valued employee's loyalty to an institution through a change that was only cosmetic. Wilson was never as settled at the Provincial Museum after this incident, and he kept his eye out for other possibilities.

With these constraints encircling the Provincial Museum, Wilson's response was to broaden the scope of his work according to his own interests. Some initiatives expanded on work that he was already doing and some were new. They all related to his role at the museum, if it were broadly defined. For Wilson, a museum's educational mandate involved three abiding responsibilities—research, collections and displays—and of these three, the greatest was research.[23] During the five years after he returned from Ottawa, he researched a variety of topics and wrote on them extensively, though only some of that writing was published. Most of his research and writing was done at home in the evening as he sat at his desk, which was always stacked with files.

He brought copies of the Barbeau material on Tsimshian social organization to Victoria and continued to work on those files with a view to publication, but that work was never completed as other interests came to the top of his mind. He did feel impelled to write a commentary arising from his misgivings about Barbeau's broader interpretations of Northwest Coast culture and history based on the myths and narratives. He wrote a paper criticizing Barbeau's work, gave it at a conference in Vancouver, and circulated it to several academic colleagues, including Barbeau, for commentary. He refined and expanded the initial drafts of the paper before it was published in 1964. It was entitled "Contributions of Marius Barbeau to West Coast Ethnology."[24] It began by outlining Barbeau's positive contributions, such as the volume and, in some cases, the value of his publications; but the burden of the article was much less positive than the title might suggest. It was a sharp critique of some of Barbeau's fundamental ideas. He took issue with the notion that significant traits of Tsimshian culture were established through recent migration from Asia southward via the Aleutian Islands. Wilson believed that Barbeau had reached this conclusion through the comparison of a very limited number of cultural elements, such as the supposed similarity between Chinese dirge songs and some Northwest Coast songs. Wilson also strongly disagreed with Barbeau's corollary conclusions that major aspects of Northwest Coast culture, such as secret societies, clan exogamy and the crest system, were recent imports from Asia. His most detailed demolition job was on Barbeau's view that the totem pole was a post-contact innovation rather than embedded in centuries of traditional Indigenous culture. The cumulative effect of these individual disagreements about particular cultural traits added up to a fundamental difference of opinion about the origins of Northwest Coast culture. Were some of the basic traits of the coastal cultures a result of recent imports from Asia and responses to European contact, or were they "an indigenous and aboriginal accomplishment"? It was a basic question with important implications.

Wilson would have been selective about who he asked for feedback on the draft article, as he was sensitive about how colleagues would react. He knew that others shared his views about Barbeau's work but were not willing express them in print. He sent it to Hawthorn with the comment: "If it stimulates any perceptible reactions in your head, heart or tummy, I'd be happy to hear about them."[25] Some responded along the lines of "how politely you anthropologists knife each other in the back," but most colleagues were supportive, and Viola Garfield commended him for not softening the critique. Such responses, Wilson wrote, "brought much aid and comfort."[26] Barbeau himself was gracious in response to receiving the article from Wilson, writing back that while they will be arguing about interpretation "the truth will take care of itself." He sent Wilson a list of other people to whom the article should be sent.[27] It was a very gentlemanly response since Barbeau would have known that Wilson had also sent the article to others, including the director at the National Museum. The museum was planning to publish more of Barbeau's books that would perpetuate his interpretations, and Wilson thought they should have his views before they committed to publishing.[28] There was some discussion with people at the National Museum about whether, when Wilson published his article, Barbeau should have the right of response. Wilson was not keen on the idea because he wanted his argument to stand on its own and he thought Barbeau could go through the normal channels of publication with a response if he wished. "Why not let him (and anybody else who chooses to) simply dismiss the article as a juvenile attack on an old proven authority, and preserve the fiction of Barbeau the great ethnologist...?"[29] Other anthropologists claimed in retrospect that Barbeau was devastated by the critique and that it was disrespectful of Wilson to publish the article. For Wilson it was certainly difficult to critique a senior figure in that way. Yet, after careful thought, he decided that the honest expression of different views was more important than hurt feelings.[30] Barbeau's manipulation of evidence is more clearly understood today than it was in 1964, so Wilson was ahead of his time. The publication of "Contributions of Marius Barbeau" was a clear signal that Wilson's strength of mind and intellectual independence had led to a disposition to challenge the anthropological establishment.

*

Another research project that he gave more sustained attention to from 1960 on was one that had been percolating in his mind for some time. He sometimes called it a handbook, though that was a rather modest description. He wanted to write an account, a balance sheet even, of the changes brought to the lives of First Nations people since the arrival of newcomers. At the time, very little history, as distinct from anthropology, had been published about the Indigenous people of British Columbia. Wilson's writing was a mixture of both. He also wanted to publish something that was more credible than were some earlier Provincial Museum publications on Indian people. He believed that if he could make some basic information about the Indigenous role in the history of the province readily available, it would lead to better understanding by settler society and greater respect for Indians and their rights. He wrote over a few years, and in 1964 he published *The Indian History of British Columbia, Volume 1: The Impact of the White Man.*[31] It began with a listing of ethnic groups according to language and the names of tribes and bands. Wilson had done a great deal of careful, detailed research over the years on the population of individual groups. He provided those numbers, followed by an estimate of the total Indian population of the province, its precipitous decline through to its low point around 1929 and then its recent resurgence. He described the positive and negative effects of the fur trade, followed by the disruptive impact of the advance of settlers. The dismissal of Indian rights to their territories that led to the repeated dispossession of land and livelihood was covered in some detail. He noted, for the information of settler society, that the matter of Indian claims to the land was still "unfinished business." The book concludes with some information on religion among Indian people and the development of Indian political organizations. On a personal note, at the end of the introduction, he acknowledges that writing a book like this "involves the theft of time from family activities." He thanks Marion, Marilyn (Marnie) and Tom for their understanding. The book is largely descriptive because Wilson wanted to get some basic information in front of British Columbians. In a thoughtful review in a local newspaper, the columnist Art Stott wrote that the book tells us "a lot of things we ought to know" so now we are armed with "facts to take the place of suppositions."[32]

If *The Indian History of British Columbia* is an accounting of the past to inform the future, then the bottom line was that Indians "should always retain the right to find their own identity and develop their own lives as they wish within the framework of Canadian society." Indigenous people in the province had endured through drastic changes imposed upon them by colonization. Yet they had preserved a distinct history and culture. They should now "gain complete control over their own affairs" along with equality within Canadian society.[33] These were not widely held views in British Columbia in 1964. They were, therefore, messages that Wilson believed settler society needed to hear.

The book was intended to be the first volume of a series of publications, and reviewers wrote that they looked forward to further volumes. Volume two was to be on prehistory, followed by a series of handbooks on the histories of individual language groups to replace earlier, and for Wilson unsatisfactory, museum publications. Alas, none of these volumes was ever published, though Wilson made considerable progress on the prehistory volume. He developed a chapter outline for the book and wrote a lengthy first chapter that dealt largely with methodology. Once again, he wanted to get some basic information across to the reading public, though he did include more interpretation of other scholars' ideas than in *The Indian History of British Columbia*. In his draft preface, he acknowledged his intellectual debt to other scholars in the field, such as Philip Drucker, Erna Gunther, Wayne Suttles and, above all, Charles Borden, from whom, over sixteen years, he had learned most of what he knew about archaeology.[34] But he was not writing for them. "This volume is not written to impress my professional colleagues, it is written for students and interested laymen who want to know what the professionals are doing," he wrote.

Writing with his usual precision and clarity, Wilson began by reminding the reader that the history of Indigenous people in British Columbia "is unbroken from the past, and is still being made." At the same time, he wrote, it can be divided into the two phases of prehistory and history. He defined prehistory as the period prior to European contact and the availability of written records. This distinction was largely because prehistory relied on different sources in the absence of written documents. Prehistory was different from post-contact history in that it could not follow the fortunes of individual people or groups but rather "must trace generalised developments of language, culture and physical type." Approaches to prehistory came through talking to people to ask what they know about their pasts, analyzing myths and family histories and looking at recent patterns of culture, language and physical type to try to understand the developments that brought them into being. None of these sources was necessarily a direct line into the past and each one needed to be carefully evaluated. Myths, for example, were not historical documents in the European sense, yet they provided insights into the past. Perhaps the best, and certainly the best-known, source for knowledge of prehistory was archaeology. Yet archaeology had a deceptive certainty about it. On one hand, it seemed conclusive by providing real objects that could be analyzed in different ways, and by revealing chronological sequences fixed by accurate dates. As Wilson was writing this chapter, archaeologists knew that the Indigenous people of British Columbia had been here for at least ten thousand years. On the other hand, only a tiny fraction of a material culture survived, and even that survival was select-ive, depending on the composition of the artifact and the environment where it was located. Moreover, the further back in time, the smaller the fragment of culture which archaeology reveals. Sometimes archaeologists found remains of the people themselves that disclosed something about them but, as Wilson put it, "the old bones are always distressingly mute as to the ideas that they lived by." Inferences based on archaeology about "such non-material aspects of life as social structure, religion, ceremonies, music, folklore" are very tenuous. Nevertheless, despite the limitations of the source, "the archaeologist assumes the role of prehistory's spokes-man," Wilson observed. Prehistory and history are similar in that they have to take into account the fact that cultures are constantly changing. In prehistoric times, change came through diffusion from one culture to another, as a result of the migrations of people, or through internal elab-oration. Which of these sources of change was paramount at a particular time and place was a question that prompted fundamental disagreements among anthropologists. Wilson was clear about which was the primary factor among Northwest Coast cultures. While he conceded that, in the very distant past, the ancestors of the American Indians may have come from Asia, the development of Indigenous cultures in British Columbia, he asserted, "is essentially a local story. 'Where did the Indians come from?' They didn't come from anywhere else, they developed here."[35]

Wilson pointed out that while history and prehistory were two parts of a continuous story, they were usually approached in different ways. The historian writing about Indigenous cultures usually starts with European contact and works forward, whereas the pre-historian starts with contact (the end product of prehistory) and works backwards into an unknown past. Indeed, he observed, trying to understand prehistory "is rather like following a winding road in the fog."[36] While the sources for prehistory may lack the immediacy of an explorer's journal, there was no "reason to assume that prehistoric people lacked the qualities found in the great men of history." After all, Wilson concluded, over a hundred centuries, Indigenous men and women built unique and complex cultures and the most distinctive ways of life to be found anywhere in the world.[37]

*

Because archaeology could provide glimpses of certainty in the fog of prehistory, Wilson was determined to do all that he could to preserve that record of the past. Even before he was officially appointed provincial anthropologist at the museum, Wilson had urged the government to pass legislation to protect archaeological sites and an advisory board to implement the regulations. He continued to lobby politicians, right up to the premier, to act on the matter. It took ten years for such legislation to come to pass. Over that decade, Wilson and Charles Borden worked constantly to protect the province's at-risk archaeological sites. They worked in the belief, or at least the hope, that "some day, those that escape the heedless bulldozers of advancing civilisation and the insensitive shovels of relic hunters will yield their long and complex records to archaeologists."[38] Wilson believed that it was time for archaeology to get beyond gathering and identifying artifacts and become more analytical. His work on prehistory led him to see that archaeology could answer a number of questions about specific areas. He told the senior archaeologist at the National Museum that there would be "archaeological plums, real beauts. If we ever can get a problem-oriented programme as distinct from a salvage-oriented one, we have some real dandy little problems to investigate."[39]

During those ten years, Wilson did not do a lot of hands-on digging in the dirt, but he did visit and inspect numerous archaeological sites, whether or not there were active excavations in progress. These surveys meant that he was on the ground and talking to the local people who owned the sites. He developed a clear and detailed understanding of the state of archaeological play in the province. As ever, Wilson was at ease when he visited Indian communities, as they were with him. Donald Mitchell, who worked closely with Wilson on archaeological projects, remembers going with him to look at a site on Dionisio Point, at the north end of Galiano Island. They were walking out when they passed an old man going the other way, and Wilson casually greeted him in Halkomelem (now Hul'q'umi'num). The old man did a double take, as if to say, Who is this white man who speaks my language? Even Mitchell did not know that Wilson could speak some of the language. It was, Mitchell said, "a perfect Wilson moment."[40]

Wilson did supervise, and take a greater part in, one archaeological dig, on a site very close to the Provincial Museum. Along Beach Drive on the eastern end of McNeill Bay is a little promontory called Kitty Islet, a neck of land with a beach on either side that leads to a low, rocky point that was a popular picnicking site. A midden there indicated an Indigenous presence in the past. It was only a small site, probably not of huge significance, that was gradually being eroded by the tides. Wilson set up and supervised an archaeological dig there. The objective of this dig was not to find major new insights into a past culture, but rather to educate the public of the day about the value of archaeology.

Michael Kew worked with him, and he also employed John Sendey and Richard Cox, the two boys that he had encountered fossicking in a midden at Ten Mile Point a couple of years earlier, who would work with Charles Borden. Some school children also took part in the dig. As well as taking the work seriously, the young people had fun with it, as students do at archaeological sites. They put up a sign indicating that it was "Duffy's trench." Some members of the public also joined in, working under careful supervision. As the dig attracted public attention, more and more people came to watch the proceedings, and an American film crew even recorded the work.

The McNeill Bay dig enabled Wilson to educate the public on everything from the minutiae of an archaeological dig to the big questions of the origins of Northwest Coast Indigenous culture. Wilson kept up a running commentary during the two weeks of excavation in a series of articles published in the Victoria *Times*. He described how to plan and set up an archaeological project, how to dig the trench, and "the pure detective work of archaeology." He gave advice to amateur archaeologists who might try their hand in other places, and he told potential volunteers on the site why, given the delicacy of archaeological unearthing, they needed some training before they got their hands dirty. He explained that the time depth of the McNeill Bay site was probably not huge in archaeological terms: maybe four thousand years based on what they knew about the rise and fall of sea levels in the area. The opportunity for an accurate dating came when they found a hearth made of charred wood that could be radiocarbon dated. The oldest radiocarbon date established so far in British Columbia was of an object from a dig that Borden conducted near Yale a year earlier. It was 8,150 years old. At Kitty Islet, each cultural item uncovered was put in a separate numbered bag, a written description recorded, along with the exact location on the site where it was found. Then it was taken to the lab to be washed. This detailed work was important because another way to establish timelines was to compare what they found with items from other sites.

In one article Wilson used the "highly non-technical archaeological term...whatsit." He was asked several times "What's a whatsit?" He explained that it was a word that he used to describe small items, usually made of soapstone, with a smooth, satisfying shape and form but of undetermined function. He did not expect to find any whatsits on Kitty

Islet because they were usually older than four thousand years. He wondered if they indicated a cultural connection with the far northern coast. As he continued to think about them, whatsits would fascinate him for years to come. In one of the newspaper articles about the dig, Wilson took the opportunity to raise one of his "pet peeves" that the usual maps of ancient migration routes to the Northwest Coast showed a broad arrow coming across the Bering Strait and curving down into British Columbia, suggesting that the first inhabitants of the coast were recently transplanted Siberians. That interpretation was "probably quite false," he wrote.

A final article about the dig was written by a *Times* reporter who had observed the process and got the point: "If the McNeill Bay dig has served to arouse some public interest in our ancient history it will have achieved a purpose far beyond the immediate finds made here." Surely it is time, the article concluded, to give more serious thought to protecting this record.[41] The dig was a clever and effective public relations tactic.

Whether or not there was direct cause and effect is hard to say, but the following year the British Columbia government finally passed an Act for the Protection of Archaeological and Historic Sites and Objects. After they had both worked for so long to make it happen, Wilson was excited to send copies of the legislation to Borden, who also thought that it was wonderful, but that it was "still hard to believe that it is actually law now." He also sent copies to the senior archaeologist at the National Museum and advised him that it was "to be known as Duff's Third Law," an allusion to Newton's third law that declares that for every action there is a reaction. Wilson told his colleague in Ottawa, "Borden and I think it is the best Act of its kind," to which claim he added the zinger "if we can make it work."[42] Wilson was right to be concerned as implementation of the act would prove to be a challenge. The act established an Archaeological Sites Advisory Board with Wilson as the first chair. Other members were people with whom he had worked closely: Lawrie Wallace, Willard Ireland, Charles Borden and the anthropologist Robert Lane. At the first meeting, A.C. Milliken from Yale, who would have a major archaeological site named after him, was added to the board to represent amateur archaeologists. Those wanting to carry out archaeological investigations were now required to apply to the advisory board for an evaluation and a permit. The act also provided for the archaeological examination of land slated for major development. Neither Wilson, nor the act, intended to discourage amateur archaeologists, but he wanted them to make a contribution rather than doing damage, so they needed to follow what he called "the ground rules..." He wrote, and widely circulated, a pamphlet called *Preserving British Columbia's Prehistory* to provide advice to amateur archaeologists. He explained the fundamental principle behind the new law: that it was in the public interest to protect the archaeological record, so the public interest overrode that of any individual. Because "each site is like a book which can only be opened once, because opening it destroys it," he recommended that amateurs stick to searching the surface rather than excavating. He outlined standards for systematic procedures and careful record keeping. He was also emphatic that the consent of the community was mandatory before entering an Indian reserve, and that written permission of the band was required before any excavating was started.[43]

While all this was a promising start, setting up the rules was one thing and implementing them on the ground entirely another. The act and the advisory board required a lot of work and travel for Wilson as he supervised and inspected operating and potential archaeological sites. The act would not be effective without some administrative staff and ways to police adherence to the provisions of the legislation. The government was slow to provide support funding, so it was a couple of years before any staff was appointed. They started by hiring Donald Mitchell to direct the work for a summer. On more than one occasion, Wilson had to remind ministries that archaeological surveys were now required by law before major economic development projects went ahead. So, while progress was slower than Wilson would have wanted, the archaeological record in British Columbia was better protected in the 1960s than it had been in previous decades. Wilson also knew that archaeological evidence had much wider implications in British Columbia than simply knowledge of the past for its own sake.

*

Archaeology is one source of evidence that Indigenous people have lived in British Columbia for tens of thousands of years. Myths and stories speak of a past that is still present. Totem poles testified to Indian possession of their lands. Wilson was immersed in all these sources of knowledge about the Indigenous past and had played a significant role in preserving and restoring these records. For him, this evidence naturally led to the conclusion that, having owned and occupied the land for centuries, Indians should be entitled to retain it. They had established social order and governance, they had built houses and villages, they had harvested the resources of the land and the sea, and they understood territories, boundaries and rights to living and gathering places. All this evidence, Wilson thought, added up to Aboriginal title to the land. That was not, however, the view of newcomers and their governments. British Columbia had always taken the position that the province's First People had no valid claim to the land, or if they did, that their claim had been extinguished by the actions of colonial governments that simply acted as if there were no land rights. The provincial position was that if you ignored these rights, then they did not exist. Ever since he was a graduate student, Wilson had "always hoped my knowledge would be used by Indians."[44] Now he was about to have the opportunity to play a significant part in an effort that, in the long run, would reverse the province of British Columbia's historic position on Indian title.

In July 1963 two Snuneymuxw men, Clifford White and David Bob, were hunting for food to feed their families on the slopes of Mount Benson, behind Nanaimo. They had shot some deer and were heading home when they were apprehended by a game warden, who charged them with hunting out of season. They were convicted in a magistrate's court, and White was sent to Oakalla Prison Farm because he could not afford to pay the fine. Maisie Hurley, the redoubtable editor of the *Native Voice*, got wind of the situation and brought the lawyer-politician Thomas Berger into the case. White and Bob told Berger that they believed they were not subject to British Columbia's game regulations because of a treaty that was signed with the governor of the Colony of Vancouver Island, James Douglas. Berger's investigation into the case took him to Willard Ireland, the provincial archivist, who found the original Douglas Treaties in the archives. The treaty for the Nanaimo area, the last of the Douglas Treaties, was signed with a mark by 159 members of the Saalequun (now Snuneymuxw) band, but the text of the treaty had not been added. It was assumed that the wording would be the same as the other treaties, including the provision that Indians were "at liberty to hunt over the unoccupied lands…"[45] Having found the treaty, they needed to establish that the people who signed it owned the territory that included Mount Benson. The next question was: Were White and Bob descendants of those who had signed the Douglas Treaty? At that point, Berger and Ireland came to see Wilson to draw on his knowledge of the Indigenous culture and history of the Nanaimo area. Wilson was delighted to be involved. He would introduce Berger to an even bigger question than those raised by the Douglas Treaties in Nanaimo. He knew that anthropologists south of the border, in Washington and Oregon, had been working on land claim cases and providing statements to the courts. He gave Berger copies of judgments in the United States that spoke to the more fundamental matter of Aboriginal title to the land that had existed prior to any treaties. He felt that Berger's conception of Aboriginal title was "based on usufruct and the right to use the products of the land. My conception is that native title is based on more than use, it is based on clear-cut Indian concepts of ownership of the land." He thought that the United States court had made this case well and that it could apply to all of the coastal groups in British Columbia.[46] While this more far-reaching question hovered in the background, the White and Bob case turned on the legal validity of the Douglas Treaty and whether it applied to the two plaintiffs.

The case was appealed in a new trial in the county court of Nanaimo, and Wilson and Ireland were called as expert witnesses. Berger and Ireland made the case for the treaty being an authentic and binding treaty, not just a conveyance of land. Wilson testified that there were five bands in the Nanaimo area and that Douglas had used the name Saalequun to apply to all of them. He described the extent of each band's territory, the way that they used the lands and the waters in their territory and how that territory would be recognized as belonging to them. A remaining question was whether Mount Benson lay within the territory of the Saalequun. When Berger asked Wilson that question during his testimony, he replied that Mount Benson could be seen through a window in the courthouse. Before the trial he had pointed it out to Berger: "That's Mount Benson, right there."[47] For Berger, that really wrapped up the story. It was their territory. He recalled that Wilson was a capable and convincing witness and believed that he was the first anthropologist to present evidence in a land claims case in Canada. The Nanaimo court found in favour of White and Bob and their conviction was overturned. As would be ever thus in land claims cases, however, that was not the end of the story.

The Province appealed the Nanaimo decision to the British Columbia Court of Appeal. That was a mistake, because the appeal court upheld the lower court's ruling on the specifics of *White and Bob* and, at the same time, raised the much bigger question of Aboriginal title. In his presentation in Nanaimo, after he had made the case based on the Douglas Treaty, Berger had gone on to advance an alternative argument: if the document was not a treaty then Aboriginal title to the land had not been extinguished and, incidentally, nor had the right to hunt. The inference that, in the absence of a treaty, Aboriginal title still existed, was a Pandora's box in British Columbia. The judge in the Nanaimo court agreed with Berger. At the Court of Appeal, Chief Justice Thomas Norris wrote a concurring judgement that took up Berger's alternative argument and concluded that Aboriginal rights still existed in British Columbia for the simple reason that, in most of the province, they had never been extinguished. Those rights included the right to the land. Dismayed at these developments, the British Columbia government appealed the *White and Bob* case to the Supreme Court of Canada—and lost again. More significantly, though, Justice Norris had got others thinking about the implications. Frank Calder, the Nisga'a leader and member of the Legislative Assembly of British

Columbia, brought a case to the courts asking the Province to declare that the Aboriginal rights of his people, and by implication most other Indigenous groups, had never been extinguished.

In *Calder v. Attorney-General of British Columbia*, Berger was the lawyer for the Nisga'a and again Wilson was an expert witness, testifying to the Nisga'a ownership and use of the lands in their entire territory. Before the case went to court, Wilson did get an earful from Calder because some of his earlier maps of Kitwancool territory overlapped with Nisga'a claims. Wilson's response was that the Nisga'a case was to test the question of Aboriginal title, not to settle tribal boundary disputes. In the courtroom, Wilson was, once again, an effective witness, completely assured and on top of the details. He was cross-examined, but there was no real challenge to his evidence.[48] The Calder case went to the Supreme Court and the judgment in 1973 was inconclusive. Of the seven judges, three found for the Nisga'a and three against with one abstaining on a technicality. It was a legal draw, and yet it seemed like something of a victory in that three Canadian Supreme Court judges had agreed that, in law, there was such a thing as Aboriginal title to the land.

More recent writers have expressed the view that museum anthropologists such as Wilson Duff distracted attention from Indian land claims by exhibiting artifacts and restoring totem poles. They call it "displacement by display." Their argument is: by removing cultural items from the land, anthropologists were removing evidence of prior possession and therefore were complicit in the dispossession of Indigenous people.[49] That conclusion could only be reached by looking at only some aspects of Wilson's museum career rather than the full scope of his work. Those making the argument are, perhaps, the Marius Barbeaus of our own age: they have got their story and they are sticking to it, never mind the evidence. For Wilson, the artifacts and the totem poles absolutely confirmed Indigenous ownership of the land in British Columbia, and that knowledge prompted him to contribute to court cases that sought to establish that point in law.

For First Nations people in British Columbia, the *White and Bob* and *Calder* cases were the first steps in what became a long dance with law and politics before it was acknowledged that their Aboriginal title existed and had not been extinguished. It was a pas de deux that lasted beyond Wilson's lifetime and into the next century. But he was there when it all began and played an important role in pivotal cases. His knowledge was certainly useful to Indigenous people, just as he had hoped. Berger delivered his summation of *White and Bob* in the Nanaimo courtroom, with its carved wood panelling, heavy dark beams in the high ceiling and five leaded-glass windows high above the judge's bench. It was meant to be an imposing house of colonial law, heavy with the weight of authority. Along the side, the large public gallery was full of First Nations people, excited that their land claims were being discussed in such a court of law.[50] It was an exquisite historical moment, and, as Wilson knew, the province of British Columbia would never be the same.

Heady moments like that one came amidst so much more mundane, day-to-day work at the Provincial Museum. There were also significant changes, which were not mundane, through the early 1960s, at the same time as Wilson was assessing his situation there. In 1960 the museum acquired the Newcombe Collection. When Charles Newcombe's son, W.A. Newcombe, passed away, he left a "treasure trove" in his father's house.[51] It was a huge collection of botanical specimens, art and Indigenous artifacts that represented a lifetime of collecting, particularly on the part of the elder Newcombe. The ethnographic material comprised about half of the collection. The government found the money to purchase the collection for the Provincial Museum, where there was a special exhibition of some items. The arrival of the Newcombe Collection at the museum attracted attention in the local press and excitement in the anthropology community. Hawthorn wrote to Wilson to say that securing the collection was "a tremendous thing to have done."[52] The problem was there was no spare display space. They had to close the anthropology exhibit area in the basement to be able to receive and store the material. Unless they got more space, they would not be able to reopen.[53] Much of the collection ended up in storage. Acquiring the Newcombe Collection only highlighted the inadequacy of the museum's physical plant.

*

A death two years later affected Wilson in a different way. In August 1962, after a brief period in hospital, Mungo Martin passed away. Mungo's death hit Wilson hard. The two were not merely colleagues but also close friends. Wilson heard the news while he was on a field trip in northern British Columbia, and he hurried back to Victoria. Mungo was laid out in the house that he had built in Thunderbird Park and, once again, as he had done at the potlatch in 1953, Wilson screened people at the door to turn away curious sightseers. Mungo Martin was then taken to Alert Bay for burial.

Mungo had already donated his masks and ceremonial regalia to the Provincial Museum. Three years earlier his son, David, had drowned off a fishing boat in the Salish Sea, and Mungo had been devastated. Having lost his successor, he handed over his "carved song-leader's baton, symbol of authority over the masked dances," to the minister of education, who received it for the museum in a ceremony in the house named Wa'wadit-la.[54] Henry Hunt, Mungo's son-in-law, and his son, Tony Hunt, continued the carving program. The Hunts would carve a memorial pole at Thunder-bird Park for Mungo Martin, and it would be raised in Alert Bay. Wilson arranged for Mungo to receive a Canada Council medal posthumously. He was only the second person to be given the award. In his letter to the Canada Council, Wilson wrote that, for him, Mungo Martin "was one of the truly great men I have had the privilege of knowing."[55]

Wilson was away from the museum and from Victoria more and more frequently. There were field trips, travel as chair of the Archaeological Sites Advisory Board to inspect sites and digs in progress, as well as conferen-ces and meetings out of town. He enjoyed being away from the office and perhaps even from home. The Duffs moved to a larger house on Beach Drive in September 1963. If the move were made to make life better for the family—beyond their physical surroundings—it was not successful. Wilson and Marion were living increasingly separate lives, and Marnie felt a lot of tension in the home. Wilson enjoyed the company of women, and Marion enjoyed the company of men, but they seldom enjoyed being together. In fact, Wilson looked for reasons to be away. In the same year they moved house, he attended a summer museum training institute at the University of Arizona in Tucson. According to his former graduate supervisor, Wilson was the star of the show. Erna Gunther wrote to Clifford Carl to tell him that Wilson's presentation on totem pole preservation was by far the best student presentation of the course. He developed great rapport with the other students and became a leader among them as they waited for him to respond to questions first. It was as if the student were the teacher. Gunther wrote to Carl to remind him of what a great asset Wilson was to the Provincial Museum, but Wilson was not so sure that he was viewed that way in his workplace. "After less than four weeks back at the old stone pile," he wrote to someone he met at the course, the "pleasant memories" of Tucson seemed pretty far away. He could not say that he had fully adjusted to the "cold hard life of the real world."[56] It seemed as though Wilson was looking for challenges and enjoyment outside of his home and his office.

*

Ever since he started at the Provincial Museum, Wilson had frequently taught evening classes at Victoria College. After getting the mandatory approval of the deputy minister, in the fall of 1964 he began teaching a regular course that involved three lectures a week. Teaching at what had now become the University of Victoria was another thing that took him away from the office. His students remember him as a gifted teacher who drew them into the fold of interest in, and love of, Indian cultures. He brought a great depth of knowledge to the classroom while, as one of them put it, "he spoke less than he knew." He used his extensive contacts to bring in interesting guest lecturers from First Nations communities, government and the academic world. There was also an opportunity to push against gender boundaries. He asked if any students were interested in volunteering to work at a dig that the Archaeological Sites Advisory

Board was sponsoring on the Gulf Islands. When one of the female students expressed interest, Wilson was nonplussed: apparently it had not occurred to him that women would go on digs. But he promptly said that, if Donald Mitchell, who was supervising the dig, agreed, it was fine with him. The student had to press the matter but did go to work at the dig. Wilson invited female students to dances, but in this case spirit dances. He took two students, who were working on class projects on the dancing, to spirit dances in the Victoria area and in Duncan. The students were "wide-eyed" and recognized that it was a privilege to attend the dances. They saw how close Wilson's relationship was with his community of friends who came with them to the spirit dances, the respect with which he was held in the communities, and the way in which he was moved by the dances. The students recall that there was nothing flirtatious about going to these dances. Wilson was a teacher introducing them to another world. He enjoyed teaching and the interaction with students, particularly his female students. Male students, on the other hand, felt that Wilson preferred to take women to the spirit dances. Students of both genders clearly remember Wilson as a formative teacher, and some of them went on to careers in anthropology and at museums.[57] For Wilson, teaching that course at the University of Victoria was a pleasure at a time when his own sense of his work at the museum was more mixed.

*

Wilson was wearing thin at the Provincial Museum, even though he should have felt at least some excitement that they were working on the plans for a new building. Clifford Carl had called for a new museum building as far back as 1944.[58] When Wilson arrived in 1950, the space and the facilities were inadequate and neither changed in more than a decade as the collections grew. The east wing of the legislature building was not designed as a museum. Wilson commented fairly mildly in the Victoria *Colonist* in 1954 that the Provincial Museum was "like a frail old lady of Victorian age." People had a soft "spot in their hearts for her," but she "is long overdue for retirement...the fine old lady tried, but she just isn't a real museum."[59] As time went on, the descriptions of the Provincial Museum became more strident. In 1959 a Victoria *Times* columnist likened it to a "continental public lavatory." The visiting American museums expert Carl Guthe was only slightly more measured when he pronounced, "conditions are terrible."[60] Finally, in 1959, the premier, W.A.C. Bennett, announced that a new museum would be built. Some planning was done but no money allocated, so the premier announced the project again three years later, and this time it seemed more serious. The building program was being developed by the Department of Public Works, not an agency that one would necessarily think of as the fountainhead of inspirational architecture. Certainly no one in Public Works had experience planning a museum. Wilson was on a planning committee, along with Clifford Carl, Willard Ireland, Public Works architect J.A. Cochrane and some technical people. They travelled around Canada and the United States looking at museums, art galleries and other public buildings. They visited seventeen institutions in all and learned a good deal about what not to do.[61] Construction started in May 1965, not with the traditional shovel in the ground, but with Premier Bennett pushing down on a plunger to set off an explosion. By the time construction began, Wilson, although too contained to explode, had worked up a good head of frustration.

Because he knew more about museum design than anyone else involved, it was not surprising that he also had strong ideas about the new Provincial Museum building. Nor was he shy about expressing those views. He had at least two areas of concern. The first was the size of the new building. He thought that Carl had in mind a one-storey building that would be too small for the collections already in hand, let alone new acquisitions. He convinced Carl that a much larger two-storey building, with higher ceilings, was required. Some at the museum credited Wilson for pushing for, and getting, a building that was larger than originally planned. Yet he was still not convinced that it would be large enough to accommodate the museum's current mandate. As well, at a time of rising construction costs, there were the inevitable compromises on the size and configuration of the building. Wilson was pleased with the large glassed-in area adjacent to Thunderbird Park for the totem poles—at least the poles would not be in the stairwell. But he was alarmed when Carl told the deputy minister that he planned to expand the scope of human history to include British Columbia history in its entirety, and not "just Indian history."[62]

For Wilson, his second issue was more important than the first, and that was the way in which the programs inside the building were to be arranged. He wrote a position paper to express his ideas about how the new Provincial Museum should be configured. He began by reminding the building planners of the educational function of a museum. With that in mind, he went on to contend that they had before them an opportunity to write "a new version of the history of British Columbia." By drawing upon the two divisions of the museum, natural history and human history, they could present the province's history from "the ecological point of view" by showing "the interaction between human culture and the natural environment." He thought that the lobby of the new museum should feature a large relief map of the province, because that was the starting point, the stage upon which British Columbia history was played out. He then presented a plan for the organization of the exhibits in the two areas. He saw the Human History Division, which for Wilson meant anthropology, in a close relationship with the other two areas: Natural History because they shared museum practice, and the Provincial Archives because they shared subject matter. The Archives was the "working library" for historians and anthropologists doing research and preparing displays. Human History, he argued, would therefore suffer most from a divided administration.

As the spokesperson for Human History, Wilson considered it his "duty to make the strongest possible plea for a single administrative framework for the entire building." He also believed that there were many staff positions and facilities that all three divisions could share. This logic brought him to a final point that, being based in principle rather than politics, was vulnerable. Given the many common interests of the three divisions, he concluded that they should come under one administration reporting to one government department: the Department of the Provincial Secretary.[63] Wilson's ideas—about presenting a view of history founded in ecology, and about the joint administration of the museum and archives—both have a very modern ring to them. In 1964, however, they were dismissed. The museum and archives ended up in two separate buildings under two different ministries.

As Wilson's frustrations were mounting at the Provincial Museum, there were changes afoot in anthropology at UBC. Hawthorn had founded the discipline with an emphasis on the cultures, history and current challenges facing Indigenous people in British Columbia. He had built a strong academic group in many ways, but by 1965 it lacked a permanent strength in the anthropology of local cultures. Hawthorn himself was a busy administrator, and working on his surveys of the contemporary Indian issues and publishing the volumes on British Columbia in the 1950s, and Canada in the 1960s. In the past he had hired some Northwest Coast specialists on one-year contracts, and Helen Codere, who published on the Kwakiutl potlatch, was a faculty member in the early 1950s. Wilson's friend Wayne Suttles, with whom he shared a deep interest in Stalo culture, was the Northwest Coast mainstay at UBC after he was appointed in 1951, but he left to take up a position in the United States in 1963. Hawthorn had not yet found a strong replacement for Suttles. Wilson also knew that Hawthorn had ideas about a new building for the anthropology collection. Another new museum, where perhaps he might have more influence, tweaked Wilson's interest. He wrote to Hawthorn, in a letter about other subjects, with a "thinly-veiled attempt to probe your intentions on museum development on campus. If you were ever to have a position offering the opportunity for a bit of teaching, a bit of museum work, and a bit of time for writing, you might find me knocking on your door." Hawthorn immediately jumped on the suggestion and wrote to Wilson to arrange to meet and explore the idea.[64] They had a conversation and, after some due process, Wilson accepted an appointment as associate professor in anthropology at UBC starting in the fall of 1965.

People around the Provincial Museum recall that Wilson did not discuss his decision to leave with any of his colleagues. That would have been Wilson's way—just to make his decision and go. He had grown weary of the political interference and the bureaucracy in Victoria. He may also have grown weary of some of his colleagues who, in his view, were not keeping up with recent developments in museum practice and were stuck in the past. He told the American anthropologist Frederica de Laguna, who had been a referee for him for the UBC position, that "an open and amicable difference of opinion on basic policies at the museum is a factor in my decision to move on."[65] That was Wilson putting it mildly, for his disaffection was deeper seated. One of his university students, who also spent time at the museum, observed a lack of camaraderie among the staff, which was a change from the early days. The same student observed that Wilson was more relaxed when he was in the classroom. He certainly had enjoyed teaching the course at the University of Victoria and the interaction with students.[66] He looked forward to more teaching at UBC and hoped that he would have more time for research and writing. During July 1965, there was a flurry of activity as he cleared off his desk at the museum and packed up home and family for the move to Vancouver. He still found time for a two-week field trip that July.

Clifford Carl knew that Wilson's departure was a "serious loss" to the museum, although not to the province and its Indigenous people. Over fifteen years as provincial anthropologist, Wilson had made many innovative contributions to the museum itself and beyond, throughout the province. He was highly regarded by other anthropologists and museologists. He had a reputation as an anthropologist for the twentieth century; someone who made a difference.[67] He was accepted and respected in Indian communities throughout the province. That respect was not just among the coastal groups whom he knew best. The Shuswap (Secwépemc) leader George Manuel wrote that what distinguished Wilson from other anthropologists was not only his manner and style, but also his willingness to share what he learned from the people, with the people. Along with giving back to communities "was a desire only to go where he was invited, and to draw a line between honest enquiry and prying into other people's lives." Manuel's people honoured Wilson "by giving him an Indian name" because of these qualities.[68] In Victoria, however, he no doubt irritated some people around him with his clearly expressed views about the new building and the organization of the Provincial Museum. It is also not hard to imagine that some of those who moved through the bureaucratic corridors of the legislative precinct took umbrage at the part that he played, in *White and Bob* and *Calder*, in overturning British Columbia's historic position that First Nations people had no valid claim to the land.

After Wilson left the Provincial Museum there were further construction delays before the new building was finally opened in August 1968. It drew mixed reviews, and two things in particular made the staff unhappy. A rain screen was installed inside the museum, which added to the humidity in the building and threatened the preservation of artifacts. The second was one that Wilson had a hand in before he left. He had suggested commissioning a large representation of a Nootka (Nuu-chah-nulth) whaling scene. Wilson wanted Bill Reid to do the work, but he turned it down because he was not of Nootkan descent. The commission fell to Lionel Thomas, a UBC fine arts professor, but when it was installed it attracted much criticism for being ethnographically inaccurate. It no longer stands at the entrance to the museum. Some members of the museum staff were so upset by these two installations that, when their unhappiness became public, they were summoned to the deputy minister's office and told to behave themselves. Wilson wisely stayed out of these debates. He had moved on to another phase of his life. He was now a member, as Bill Reid later put it, "of the strange tribe who inhabit the groves of Academe..."[69]

7. Teaching Anthropology

Wilson's world was changing. In one sense his move in 1965 was a short trip across the Salish Sea, while in another he was moving to a different world. The year before, Bob Dylan had released the song that would become an anthem for the age: "The Times They Are a-Changin'." While Wilson listened to and quoted Dylan, he actually much preferred Joan Baez. Whatever his taste in music, the sixties were upon him. The fifties were a decade during which veterans buckled down to establish their lives and careers. It was a time of domesticity, building wealth and material possessions, and of conformity to existing values. The sense of the sixties developed a few years into the decade as the veterans' children came of age. The baby boomer students had broader interests and enthusiasms than the postwar generation, who simply put their heads down to plot their life's course. It was a period during which affluence enabled a questioning of received values. The boomers made new norms for themselves: different clothes, different music, different drugs, different politics, along with public demonstrations to bear witness to it all for their often uncomprehending parents. University students in particular, and sometimes vociferously, raised questions about how universities were run, about authority and content in the classroom, sometimes even asking what was the point and purpose of higher education anyway?

Not all students were radicals. One area that did not change as fast as some would have wished, despite greater sexual freedom, was gender relations. The engineering undergraduates were still holding Lady Godiva rides on the UBC campus. Romantic and intimate relations between faculty members and students were not uncommon and not officially proscribed nor even unofficially frowned upon. The advocates of the counterculture did, however, admonish people of Wilson's generation about many other things. For fifteen years, living in Victoria and working at the Provincial Museum, Wilson had been in a relatively ordered world. There were plenty of rules and many had become constraints. UBC was not disorderly, but it appeared that the rules were fewer and there was at least a veneer of intellectual independence. So Wilson threw himself into a new career in a different time and place.

*

Compared to nearly twenty years earlier, when Wilson was a student, anthropology at UBC in 1965 was, like the world around it, in the midst of constant change. Anthropology was no longer anonymous within the omnibus Department of Economics, Political Science and Sociology. It was now, by design, named first in the Department of Anthropology and Sociology. Just before Wilson arrived, there was a departmental discussion about dividing the two disciplines up into separate departments. The faculty voted to retain the benefits of interdisciplinary contacts and some cross teaching by staying together. Not that there was complete harmony either between the disciplines or among the faculty. Differences of opinion were partly the product of growth and diversity. UBC, like other Canadian universities, was growing rapidly though the sixties, and Anthropology grew with it. Undergraduate student numbers increased by 40 per cent over two years, in 1964 and 1965, and when Wilson arrived there were nearly sixty graduate students in the department. Over the period 1960 to 1975, thirty-eight new faculty members arrived to ongoing (tenure-track) appointments. In 1965 they had just moved into the Henry Angus building—some called it the anguish building— named after the head of department, who had brought Hawthorn to UBC in 1947.[1]

With more faculty came greater intellectual diversity in the Department of Anthropology and Sociology. Gone were the days when a department could be built around a single professor to reflect his approach to anthropology and regional interests. The transplanted British social anthropology of the early Hawthorn and Belshaw era was being replaced with a variety of views as faculty with degrees from many parts of the world were hired. The standard American four fields of anthropology (cultural anthropology, archaeology, linguistic and physical anthropology) were not evenly represented. Hawthorn maintained his disdain for physical anthropology, thinking that it should be left to the biology department. Later commentators have written that debate and disagreement was more intense in sociology than anthropology, but neither group was immune from the other.[2] There was some debate between those who held firm to science and logic and those who were more interested in symbolic and imaginative interpretations of culture. Wilson was hired because he was of one persuasion, then, over time, he moved to the other. Some continued to espouse the older ideas of functionalism (how the various elements in a culture function together), while others were excited by the newer thinking of structuralism (the underlying structure and ideas behind a culture). During a time of growth, competition for new faculty hires was fierce. Hawthorn was concerned that they had not built enough strength in archaeology and ethnography, while "the biggest current shortage is of museum anthropologists."[3] Wilson brought experience in all three areas, along with his focus on British Columbia, though he would be stretched very thin to cover all of these fields.

As the department was growing rapidly, faculty members demanded a different approach to running it. Hawthorn was still the department head in 1965, but when Wilson arrived the influence of his mentor was beginning to wane. Hawthorn's declining influence was gradual and certainly did not happen fast enough for some of the faculty. Only a few years earlier he had gone through the entire academic year without calling a department meeting. Some colleagues felt that there was not enough communication, and so Hawthorn ran a trial of monthly department meetings held at 10:00 a.m. on Saturday mornings. That kind of response was no longer acceptable, and meetings were now held at more reasonable times. The tone and the outcome of a meeting usually depends on who is running it and, at UBC, the head chaired the department meetings.

During Wilson's first academic year, a colleague, writing on Valentine's Day but not feeling much love, described the lack of agreement on most matters. On any issue "there is one more point of view than there are people discussing it," leaving room for Hawthorn's view to prevail.[4] Disgruntled faculty members complained that he still had too much say in things, such as the appointment of new faculty. Hawthorn did have his supporters in the department. The New Zealand nexus remained and Cyril Belshaw was his right-hand man. Belshaw was a prolific scholar, increasingly involved in international initiatives and frequently invited to accept positions in other places. He stayed at UBC, and he and Hawthorn did a lot of the thinking together about future directions in the department. They wrote to keep each other up with the state of play when either one was out of the country. Belshaw was acting head of department while Hawthorn was away for the 1959–60 academic year. In 1965 Hawthorn took a trip to New Zealand and then, when he returned, he had bout of serious ill health. He recovered, but going by his correspondence outside the department, whatever he was saying to colleagues inside, he was starting to think of retirement. He stepped down as head and Belshaw took over in 1968. Under Belshaw there was much more process around decision making, though faculty still had to push to have real input on sensitive issues like appointment and promotion decisions. Hawthorn stayed on for several more years. During that time his influence in the department diminished, although he remained front and centre in the plans for a new museum on campus.

The transition into his new role in this different context was not an easy one for Wilson. He was full of uncertainties. For those who lack a rampant ego, it is not unusual to feel in the grip of what some now call *imposter syndrome* when taking up a new role in a new place. It is a frame of mind that can come from being a perfectionist and yet not believing in your own accomplishments. As he started at UBC, Wilson was certainly questioning himself. Am I up to this? Am I what people expect, or am I fraud who is in over my head? People could see that he was self-effacing on the surface, but few understood the depth of his anxiety. As was usually the case, Wilson's colleagues thought more highly of him than he thought of himself.

He was welcomed into the Department of Anthropology and Sociology, and most of his colleagues were glad to have him there. His name was known across North America for his museum work and publications on British Columbia Indigenous culture and history. Hawthorn wrote to Belshaw to let him know that "our new men are all here" and "Wilson is so eager to launch he can't wait." Others judged that "Wilson will be a good one..."[5] Michael Kew also began as a faculty member that fall, and so he and Wilson were working together again and were close colleagues during the first few years at UBC. They were the departmental specialists on the cultures of the Northwest Coast. They both lived close to the university gates so often walked in and out to their offices in the Angus Building together. Audrey Hawthorn was pleased to have Wilson, with all his museum experience, to work with her at the Museum of Anthropology. She wrote to a colleague that he "is a great addition to our campus and a pleasant person to work with."[6] He was not alone in his new role—he had support from colleagues—but he was apprehensive. Not having a PhD was one reason for his sense of inferiority. He had reached the stage of having no interest in pursuing one himself. He did advise Michael Kew to complete one, which he did in 1970. Hawthorn thought that an incomplete degree was a "thorough nuisance" and preferred colleagues who did not want a PhD if they did not already have one.[7] David Aberle came to UBC two years after Wilson with a Harvard degree and extensive publications, particularly on the Navajo of the American Southwest. Aberle was exacting, caustic and brilliant. He said that it was "dammed silly" that Wilson should be seen as second-string because he did not have a PhD. Aberle had great respect for Wilson and acknowledged his help with his work on kinship systems. If you got respect from Aberle, "you did not need it from anyone else," one colleague later observed.[8] And yet Wilson's antennae would have picked up and taken on any sense that his lack of a PhD diminished him in the department.

Some colleagues, seeing Wilson as a local ethnographer from a museum background, underestimated him. Moreover, when he arrived in the department, Wilson was not a theorist in a department where anthropological theory was more and more the trend. In the academic world there was an important distinction between theory (knowing what other people were thinking) and ideas (thinking for yourself). When he started at UBC, Wilson was full of ideas, though diffident to express them, and less engaged with theory. The graduate students, who were pumped up on the anthropological theories of functionalism and structuralism, may have felt themselves superior to Wilson. They would soon change their minds when they knew him better. It is also likely that Wilson arrived at UBC expecting that he would shortly be made the director of the Museum of Anthropology.[9] Certainly others in anthropology believed that it was the understanding that he had with Harry Hawthorn, but Audrey Hawthorn continued in that role. There was no rancour between them, as she and Wilson were friends as well as colleagues, but Wilson would have been disappointed if he had been expecting to move into the position.

The challenge of becoming a university professor of anthropology was one reason why Wilson, after only one semester at UBC, applied to return to his former position at the Provincial Museum. His position as curator of anthropology had been advertised but not yet filled. Clifford Carl supported Wilson's reinstatement at the museum in a letter to the deputy minister.[10] The letter disappeared into the bowels of the bureaucracy without a trace. Presumably Wilson had burned too many bridges. Don Abbott, Wilson's colleague at the museum, was made curator of anthropology, and Peter Macnair, a recent UBC graduate, was appointed initially as assistant in anthropology. Wilson maintained connections with the Provincial Museum and was sometimes invited over to give presentations. He did have a squabble with Macnair, who complained that Wilson had taken papers to UBC, most notably the Barbeau Tsimshian files, that Macnair believed should have stayed in the museum. Those papers had come from the National Museum, though Wilson was a provincial employee when he worked on them. Under the rules of the day there was room for interpretation about the provenance of the papers. In a clearer infringement, Wilson had also taken at least one artifact, a rattle, with him—an appropriation that he later regretted.

If the uncertainties of his role at UBC were a factor in his second thoughts about the move to Vancouver, his family was an even bigger consideration. The move was not a happy one for them. In some ways it seemed like a good idea: it was a way to start over. Marion and Wilson were returning to the city where they grew up and had extended family. Wilson's father had passed away of lung cancer in 1960, but his mother, with whom he had always been close, was living in an apartment in South Granville. His sister, Win, the one family member with whom he could talk about his thinking and ideas, was in Vancouver with her family. His brother, Ron, was a high-school teacher in Burnaby. They saw each other at family gatherings at Christmas but were seldom in close contact in the midst of busy lives. Marion was particularly close to her father, and they spent many weekends in Hope together, where he was renovating a house to live in. There were supportive family members who would be needed in difficult times.

Marion and Wilson's son, Tom, seemed to be the only one who sailed through the move to Vancouver initially unscathed. Marnie, now a teenager, found it very difficult as she watched her parents growing further and further apart. For the three of them, the move to Vancouver was not a remedy. They bought a capacious house in west Point Grey, at Thirteenth and Tolmie. The house was light and airy with a good-sized living and dining room, a delightful little den on the main floor where Wilson worked, spacious bedrooms upstairs and a half-finished basement. It was the ideal space for a functional family to function in. Having progressed from the east side of their youth to the west of the city, Wilson and Marion were upwardly mobile in material terms, but that did not lead to a better life. Wilson's insecurities flowed into his relationship with Marion. He felt inadequate as a husband and yet was so self-contained that he could not communicate about his emotions, let alone hers. The growing tension between Wilson and Marion got worse, not better, after the move to Vancouver. They were living in the same house but seldom together. When they were at home there were long silences and arguments, meal times were perfunctory, and both were drinking a fair bit. It was all very stressful for Marnie, who had a miserable first year at Lord Byng Secondary School before she was moved to York House, a private school for girls. She found friends and ways that took her out of the house as much as possible, for it felt like the family was breaking apart.[11] Wilson felt guilty that he could not provide a close and loving family life for his children.

The bright spot for Wilson, though he was also unsure of himself there, was the classroom. As head of the department, Hawthorn faced the challenge of funding that did not keep pace with growth. He managed, nevertheless, to keep the undergraduate teaching responsibilities at a reasonable level in the interests of faculty time for research and graduate supervision. Wilson usually taught two courses a semester, as well as supervising an increasing number of graduate students. In his first semester, and most semesters thereafter, he taught Anthropology 301: Indians of British Columbia, and it quickly became his signature course. As his course became known on campus, it soon attracted large numbers of students. Soon there would be more than three hundred in a large lecture theatre in the Buchanan Building and, by 1970, there were almost four hundred. As a large lecture course there was no opportunity for smaller group discussions. Sometimes colleagues gave guest lectures, and he also had teaching assistants working with him. But it was known as Wilson's course. After a few years, the library was failing to meet the student demand. The shortage of books affected the quality of teaching and learning. Most of the students were not anthropology majors, as his course attracted students from many disciplines across campus.

Looking back, it seems as though a whole generation of students took Wilson's Anthropology 301. Like much of his work at the Provincial Museum, it made a major contribution to spreading greater knowledge, and therefore understanding, of First Nations people at a time when those qualities were sorely needed in newcomer society. The Indians of British Columbia course evolved with Wilson's interests: it was largely ethnographic in the first years, and later there was more content on Northwest Coast art. Throughout, Wilson connected the past with the present by talking to students about the current predicament of British Columbia's Indian people as a result of their encounter with colonialism.

Wilson was not brand new to teaching when he came to UBC. He had taught at the University of Victoria and had always believed that a museum was a place for teaching. Now he was at a large, research-focused university, but he still believed that the highest function of a university professor was teaching. Particularly in the first couple of years, he was not confident in the classroom. As with most things that he did, Wilson read and thought a great deal about the nature of teaching, and the more he thought about it, to all appearances at least, the more confident he became. He read, among other things, Raymond Firth on teaching anthropology. Firth believed that ideas were more important than facts and, therefore, while a masterful lecture is a great thing, seminars are of the greatest value. The ultimate goal was to teach students to think for themselves. Firth also stressed the importance of personal contact with students, which today is still said to be the single most important factor in student success. Because many more students heard them, Wilson is most remembered for his lectures. Most semesters Wilson also taught a seminar course at either the senior undergraduate or graduate level. In these courses he enjoyed sharing ideas with a small group of students who were fully engaged with learning anthropology at a deeper level. Wilson quoted Firth's ideas about teaching at the first seminar that he conducted at UBC, an advanced ethnography of the Northwest Coast. Wilson also asked around the department for advice on teaching, and the general answer was "do it your own way."[12] Wilson certainly took that piece of advice.

Teaching "is like making love," he once told an Anthropology 301 class. He went on to explain, as well he might, that what he meant was that teaching is not about one person doing something to another, nor a matter of the teacher teaching and the student learning; teaching is something that teacher and student do together. They are "creating each other as they are being created." It is a mutual transaction in which students teach and teachers learn. Anthropologists, he said, "should of all people be willing to learn from all people, not just from the tribal 'experts.'" While university teaching is usually predicated on what the professor knows, Wilson believed that everyone should be aware of what they do not know and, therefore, teacher and student alike should embrace the need to learn.

Upon further reflection he did realize that the professor had an advantage over the student. In a course like Anthropology 301, the lecture is an important form of communication and learning, but it is only the surface level of learning. Below that surface, "in the slow, private, but deep give and take of reading, doing research, discussing, a great many dialogues take place." Only the professor has access to all of them, and therefore he or she learns the most. Then, at the end of the semester, three hundred term papers come in to the professor for grading. Many will be indifferent, but among them will be "some of the finest thought and writing in his field."[13] Wilson copied many of those student essays from which he had learned something and kept them in his files for reference. They became part of his of his academic library. The student papers that he saved got a lot of As, or sometimes even a "big A," and are replete with delicate little check marks recognizing good points and brief but affirming comments at the end. "This is the kind of paper that makes the whole thing worthwhile," he wrote on an essay that looked at Haida art as a way of life. On another, he simply wrote, "any mark you want."[14]

Though he gained some confidence after a couple of years in the classroom at UBC, he always found the large lectures stressful. Therefore, a lot of thought and planning went into them. Before he stood in front of Anthropology 301, he had to take some quiet downtime in his office and get mentally prepared. For him lectures were an ordeal; for his students they were a joy. He was so in command of his material that he lectured from short notes. He presented concepts in clear, concise language. There were very few superfluous words floating around in Wilson's lectures, because they were all so carefully chosen. There was an "unconscious eloquence" to his lectures, one student recalled.[15] He gave many of his lectures by talking to projected images. Other times he had a huge piece of chalk in his hand. He often invited guest speakers into the classes, including First Nations leaders. He had a multifaceted approach to lecturing. He used a minimum amount of arcane disciplinary jargon and largely avoided very technical subjects. In his first year of teaching he gave lectures on phonetics and language, but he dropped the subject after that. Nor did he subject students in Anthropology 301 to complex kinship charts of extended Indigenous families. He did not spend time, as one student later put it, on "how many cross cousins could dance on the head of a pin."[16] Not tightly bound to the anthropological literature in the classroom, he believed that there was truth in fiction. He assigned novels such as Christie Harris's *Raven's Cry*, a history of the Haida and the Edenshaws, and Alan Fry's *How a People Die*, a didactic novel about the appalling and intractable conditions in some reserve communities. He believed they had as much to teach as books that expounded the latest theories on the potlatch.[17] He talked about the Indians of British Columbia in a social and political context as he connected the past to current issues. For example, he gave a lecture called "Parable of Civil Disobedience," on the tactics that First Nations people had used over the years to fight the "Establishment." Examples included the Kitwancool and ended with the Nishga case, and he raised the question of whether the tactics were working. That depended on the students. The moral, he said, was "Their protest is aimed at you, can you LISTEN as well as speak?" And he asked, directed at each individual student in the large class, "You—are you learning?"[18] Mostly they were.

They also listened and learned about the biggest unresolved issue between Natives and newcomers in British Columbia: the fact that the Indians still owned title to the land. Wilson described traditional Indian concepts of territory, and their ownership and use of the land and its resources. He was clear that he was talking about ownership and not just the use of the land. He outlined the history of the provincial and federal governments' refusal to recognize, or even discuss, those concepts. He noted the logical inconsistency of the Douglas Treaties on Vancouver Island and the numbered treaties that had been signed by Indians in the northeast corner of the province, which recognized Indigenous rights but apparently could not be models for the rest of the province where there were still no treaties. He was able to bring his own involvement in the current discussion of Indian land question into the classroom. He referred to his work with Tom Berger on *White and Bob* and, later, the Nishga case. He was also giving advice to the recently established Indian Claims Commission, which was set up to look at claims from individual Indian groups. He talked about the need for real negotiations with all of the Indians of British Columbia and not with separate groups. He asked the students to discuss how the issue should be resolved but, at the same time, he was clear that he believed that there needed to be a treaty with all of the Indians. When all was said and done, he thought that Aboriginal title was "the right to make a good living in the land." It would be another thirty years before there were meaningful treaty negotiations between the three levels of government: First Nations, federal and provincial. They might have started sooner if more British Columbians had taken Anthropology 301 from Wilson Duff. He called the Indian land question in British Columbia "the Great Debate." Perhaps the most important point that Wilson made to his students was: "We started on the Great Debate talking about the future of the Indian people then came to realise that what we are really talking about is the future of ourselves."[19]

The students also learned lessons for their own lives. Wilson could turn ideas around before a large class with complete clarity. When he was thinking about the meaning of Northwest Coast art, he liked to play in his mind with the image of the Möbius strip. It is a concept that came out of mathematics: a strip of paper twisted in a half loop with the two ends connected so that it has only one side and a continuous line. It is also a metaphor for things that seem contradictory yet are not. One of the implicit reasons why anthropologists study other cultures is to provide a commentary on their own. Wilson spoke in Anthropology 301 of the way in which Indian culture was becoming a counterculture. Indian culture is being used, he argued, to make up for the deficiencies in our own culture. Thus the "'Resurgence' in Indian culture is answering a great need in our culture." Then he also spoke, conversely, about the extent to which "Indian" culture was being created by anthropologists and settler society. There was no such thing as "Indian" before the white man came, Wilson told his students; there were Stalo, Kwakiutl and Haida. "'Indian' is a script written by the white man to define, first, who he isn't and lately, now, who he (implicitly) is. We are creating Indian because we need it."[20] The cultures were like a Möbius strip: two loops interlinked on a continuum.

As if to emphasize that point, Wilson once took a story from the annals of Northwest Coast mythology and made it a parable for the present. The Bear Mother story tells of a young woman out picking berries when she steps in bear excrement and speaks disparagingly about bears. She sees a young man, who is actually a bear, who offers to help. She goes with him to his den and they live together. They have two children who are both bear and human. In time, the woman's brothers and their dog find the couple in their den, and the bear father allows himself to be killed by his human brother-in-law. The Bear Mother and her children return to the human community, but the children are not at ease among the humans and, in some versions of the story, eventually return to live among the bears. It was a well-known story on the northern coast. Wilson had read one rendition recorded by William Beynon at Kincolith (Gingolx) and published by Marius Barbeau. Another storyteller described it as the "greatest of all the sagas of the Northwest Coast people."[21] In class Wilson projected an image of a Haida sculpture depicting the Bear Mother on the screen. He acknowledged that he was being doubly presumptuous because "here I am a non-Indian talking about Indians, and here I am a male talking about being an Indian woman." He then went on to compare the ambiguous situation of the Bear Mother and her children with that of Indian women who married non-Indian men and thereby lost their status as registered Indians. Under the law at the time, the children of such marriages did not have Indian status. At the same time, Indian men who married out of the community did not lose their status and their wives became registered Indians. It was, Wilson said, "a four part system: Indian/White, male/female." The law had recently been unsuccessfully challenged in the Supreme Court of Canada, and in his lecture Wilson outlined the different points of view in the controversy that followed. At one level, the dispute set the equality provisions of the Canadian Bill of Rights against the Indian Act that decreed who was, and who was not, an Indian. The law was not changed until 1985, when the Bill C-31 revision to the Indian Act provided equality of status for both women and men in such marriages. But Wilson talked more about the human cost of the terrible dilemmas that face people when they are placed in ambiguous roles with limited choices. In the last part of the lecture, Wilson came back to the projected image of the Bear Mother story in the Haida sculpture to explore those dilemmas: the "woman married to a bear...who marries into those others so that she is not sure whether her children are us or they," the role of men who must kill or be killed, and the place of children who are two that are one, both human and bear. As it was throughout the talk, the lecture hall was quiet when Wilson concluded as he began, with a moment of humility, saying "I'm not quite satisfied with the way I put that, but I hope you get the pattern." [22]

*

Wilson drew lessons in class from his own earlier experience. At least once, he came into an Anthropology 301 lecture and started by saying that he was going to cover something that was very personal and emotional for him. He went on to say that if any student really objected to professors laying on personal trips they were welcome to leave. It was an introduction that would have ensured that nearly every student stayed. He then told the story of his experience salvaging and restoring the totem poles from Haida villages nearly twenty years before. He showed a film of the totem pole expedition to Ninstints on Anthony Island. He urged students to read the book *Out of the Silence*, with its text by Bill Reid and his concluding line stating that the poles that are left "return to the forest that gave them birth." He then asked each student to write on the question of whether it was a good idea to salvage some of the poles or if it would have been better to leave them to decay. The essays fell on both sides of the question. Wilson himself thought about the implications of taking a few of the poles, but he did not have serious doubts about what he had done. He did know that it was becoming more of question and therefore students of anthropology in British Columbia should think about it and make up their own minds. Others were less certain. Michael Kew, who was with Wilson at Ninstints in 1957, was having doubts upon reflection. He did not believe he "could wield again a cross-cut saw in such a task." Wilson also asked the students to comment on the question of whether museums should return Indian artifacts to the communities from whence they came. He raised that dilemma out of an interest in the growing debate around museums and Indigenous art that was partly occasioned by the planning for the new Museum of Anthropology on the UBC campus. There was an editorial in *The Native Voice* headed "Great Art Robbery" that welcomed a new anthropology museum but went on question how much Indians had originally received for the pieces that were now in the museum and gathering monetary value. Students were moved by Wilson describing his own experience and then asking them to think now about whether or not he had done the right thing. It was a teaching moment that some never forgot.[23]

It was obvious to students that Wilson brought a great depth of academic knowledge and first-hand experience of Indigenous cultures to the classroom. He prepared with care and attention to detail, he was brimming with ideas, and he had a quick and impish sense of humour. Most of all, students were drawn to Wilson as a teacher because of his humility. He had a shy and diffident manner and did not seek to impress anyone by showing off his knowledge. These qualities made him approachable, rather than intimidating, to students. They flocked around him at the end of lectures to ask individual questions. Humility was not the first characteristic that one would expect among academics of the day, and so Wilson stood out and students were drawn to him. Because of this, he could bring them into his ideas without imposing them, and take them to higher and higher levels of thinking.

Gloria Cranmer Webster was an assistant curator in the Museum of Anthropology at UBC and also gave some lectures in Anthropology 301. She watched Wilson in front of 350 students. She could be sharp, in both senses of the word, and certainly did not agree with all of Wilson's ideas. She does remember that he was a wonderful teacher. "Such a good teacher," she said, who could make topics that did not seem exciting to her, such as Nisga'a land claims, "so interesting and so alive."[24] There were students who would not miss one of his lectures for anything, and some who, in later life, could not remember many of their university teachers but clearly remembered Wilson and the impact that he had on them. One student revelled in Wilson's class because it was the only one where the thinking was going on in front of the students. In other classes everything had already been thought through and the students were just told the final results and not shown the thinking process. Wilson also expected the students to do the thinking. He was in the habit of saying, "think," and then adding, "now think hard." Another student spoke for many when she wrote that she could walk out at the end of his lectures and say to herself, "Gee, I really learned something."[25]

Wilson was nervous in front of large groups, so lectures took a toll on him. He was much more comfortable with small group seminars. He taught a graduate-level course on advanced ethnography of a particular region, usually with six or seven students. The first time he taught the seminar, the special area was the Northwest Coast, then in later versions he narrowed the scope to, say, the southern Kwakiutl. Since the students would be doing ethnography in the library rather than in the field, he chose a culture where there was a reasonable amount of published work already available. He introduced ethnography as taking a broad approach to a culture. Broader than archaeology, for example, which looked at pieces of a culture. Ethnography was an effort to know the whole culture and how it had evolved over time: a goal that was unattainable but nevertheless important to keep in mind. Yet a "seminar in ethnography" was still a bit of a quandary for Wilson because ethnography was largely descriptive information, whereas a seminar should be the discussion of ideas. The seminar ran over two winter semesters, so in the first they concentrated on developing a common ethnographic knowledge, and in the second they discussed approaches and ideas. In the second semester, each student would present a research paper to the seminar for discussion. Throughout the semester, for the discussion of papers, each student was asked to take a particular anthropological perspective—Boasian, material culture, artistic, economic anthropologist, social anthropologist, culture and personality, mythology and so on—and discuss the paper of the day from that point of view.[26] Wilson and the students thereby talked about the play of ideas around ethnographic description. It was a great learning experience for students going on to further graduate work and careers.

One-on-one, Wilson was even more relaxed and calm, as well as helpful and supportive. He soon attracted a large number of graduate students and students writing research papers. One of the first, Susan Davidson, who wrote a BA essay on Charles Edenshaw under Wilson's supervision, recalls that he pushed her hard but accepted her ideas when they were different from his. She felt that, at this early stage as a teacher, Wilson believed that he had something to prove to his colleagues as a supervisor, since he came from a material culture and museum background rather than a theoretical one. Her essay asked the question of whether innovative artistic creativity came from within an individual artist like Edenshaw or arose out of the culture in which he worked. It was a classic historical question to which, in the end, the answer could not be either-or: both could be valid. Her research and thinking led her to the conclusion that the culture was the primary factor, whereas Wilson, who had also thought a lot about Edenshaw, laid more emphasis on the individual. Yet he did not press her to change her interpretation.[27] Wilson also took on students who did not come via a straight line through anthropology, including even the odd refugee from history. Louise Jilek-Aall and Wolfgang Jilek, for example, both had several degrees already, including MDs, and were interested in studying Indigenous culture. The anthropology department was reluctant to take them on, but Wilson advocated for them, and they worked on master's degrees under his supervision. Wolfgang Jilek's research led to a book on the healing role of Salish spirit dancing.[28] A few years later, Martine de Widerspach-Thor came to UBC, planning to do graduate work on Kwakwaka'wakw culture. She spoke little English at that stage and had to learn it, along with the Kwak'wala language, in order to pursue her intended studies. Wilson took her on when others in the department would not, introduced her to the right people, including Bill Reid, and did all he could "to make things possible for her."[29] Most of all, he cultivated ideas in the minds of his many graduate students. He achieved that by pointing the direction, then standing aside and intellectually letting them go.

Sometimes he gave classes at the Museum of Anthropology in the basement of the library. There he could talk about Northwest Coast Indian art and point out the many great examples in the collection. In her characteristically gracious way, Audrey Hawthorn sent him a note of thanks for lectures Wilson gave in her course on museum practice. "It was a marvellous and stimulating series of ideas, slides, concepts and exposition. I myself came away full of new thoughts, and I know the students were impressed, to the point where I think we may have developed some new lines of research."[30] Along with Audrey Hawthorn, Wilson began working as a consultant on the development of the new City of Vancouver Museum in 1967 and reaffirmed his commitment to museums as places for teaching and research. He gave advice based on lessons he had learned in the past, emphasizing the primary educational function of a museum and the need to clearly define and strictly adhere to its focus: in this case the city of Vancouver and its surroundings. Vancouver's Centennial Museum, like all museums, should be an educational resource conveying meaningful ideas but, even more, the relevance of the exhibits to the viewer's community "should always be apparent." He advised that the first exhibit of the new museum should deal with the Indigenous people and cultures of the area and be divided into two areas: first prehistory, drawing on the rich archaeological record of the Vancouver area, and second ethnology, or the way of life and artistic accomplishments of the Indians at and since European contact.[31] As an advisor to the new Centennial Museum, Wilson was able to reiterate his belief in the teaching function of museums, whether or not they were connected with a university. At the same time, there was some discussion of a possible new Museum of Anthropology at UBC, though at this stage it was little more than a gleam in Harry Hawthorn's eye.

Wilson knew that teaching and learning was not confined to the classroom or museum. He continued to take students with him to spirit dances, and they continued to be moved by the experience. When a controversy about the dances arose in the local press, Wilson used it as a public teachable moment. It was reported that a Musqueam man believed that he was about to be kidnapped and initiated as a dancer. Then a *Province* reporter tried to gatecrash a dance and was turned away at the door. Fanciful ideas about spirit dancing began to fly around under headlines like "Secret tom-toms throb of past." Were the dances secret, were they painful, and was forcible abduction involved? Wilson was interviewed and reported in both Vancouver newspapers, the *Sun* and the *Province*, saying that the commentators did not know what they were talking about. While "grabbing" was part of the ritual, it only happened if the initiate were willing and had the power of a guardian spirit. Indeed, becoming a dancer was a great privilege. "I only wish there was a similar dance tradition in my own culture," he added, remembering his younger days when he loved to dance. UBC students who went with Wilson to spirit dances sensed that he wanted to dance but had to appear as the dispassionate anthropologist. Besides, he told the reporters, he did not have the spirit power.[32]

Some of his colleagues in the anthropology department did feel the influence of Wilson's spirit. They remember him as a caring, generous person during times of stress. Robin Ridington recalls Wilson rescuing his career when he was under a deportation order for possession of marijuana. Wilson came to the hearing and spoke glowingly of his colleague as a promising young anthropologist who was going to be an asset to Canada. He was brilliant and persuasive, and Ridington remained at UBC, a grateful colleague. Elvi Whittaker was being considered for tenure and Wilson was made one of her reviewers. Whittaker had seen other faculty members cut dead in the corridor by their colleagues at that nerve-racking time. She ran into Wilson in the supermarket, and he told her how well the consideration of her work had gone and what great things she was doing. It was a gesture he did not have to make, and she remembers that kindness.[33] Wilson, alas, found it difficult to open up to the same kindness from others.

He found teaching and learning opportunities through the boards and committees that he served on. He continued as a member of the Archaeological Sites Advisory Board, though he passed the chairmanship over to Charles Borden about the time that he moved to UBC. He was able to provide opportunities for students—including his son, Tom—to work on archaeological sites. He was also a member of the Provincial Indian Advisory Committee, first established in 1950, then reconstituted under the Indian Advisory Act of 1960. The purpose of the committee was to "advise the Minister on all matters regarding the status and rights of Indians..."[34] Wilson served on the committee with a number of Indian leaders from around the province. In 1966, when there was concern among its members that the advisory committee could be more effective, it was Wilson and George Manuel, the Shuswap elder, who took the concerns to Lawrie Wallace, the deputy provincial secretary, in an effort to improve committee process and communication with government. On more than one occasion Wilson gave presentations to the committee on the status and predicament of Indians in British Columbia. He was also behind a detailed resolution passed at the November 1968 meeting of the advisory committee that, after a long list of "whereases," got to the punchline: "that the Provincial Secretary be asked to declare that it is the view of the Government of the Province of British Columbia that the native title to the lands of the Province has not been extinguished." That, of course, was not going to happen in British Columbia in 1968, and Lawrie Wallace deftly sent the resolution to the Attorney General's Department for a legal opinion since Indian title was a matter to be decided by the courts rather than politics.[35]

The Indian Advisory Committee was a vehicle for Wilson to initiate work in Indian communities, and it also provided support for an anthropology student. Under the aegis of the committee, he arranged for Susanne Storie to spend time in Bella Bella villages collecting stories. Kitty Carpenter, a Heiltsuk elder from Bella Bella, was a committee member, and she paved the way into the communities. There was still some resistance to telling and recording the stories, so it took longer than expected to gain the confidence of the storytellers. Patience prevailed, and Storie recorded 150 stories in four different communities. She and Wilson agreed that they should be transcribed exactly as they were spoken and not rendered into perfect English. Both the tapes and the transcriptions were returned to each narrator for approval and, once validated, they were entrusted to the Provincial Museum. They could not be used without the permission of the storyteller.[36] Wilson was adamant that these protocols be followed to protect the rights of the Indian storytellers. Such obligations to informants would be taken for granted today, but they were not routine in 1968.

*

Wilson realized that things were changing. There were many more anthropologists working in reserve communities than there were twenty years ago, when he started out, and Indian people were becoming more concerned about the capture of their cultures. At a meeting of the Northwest Anthropological Association in 1969, Wilson convened a supplementary session on a Saturday morning to discuss, and perhaps even take some action on, ethics in anthropological fieldwork. He introduced the subject by saying that the main concern was that the work of anthropologists should not do Indian people "any harm, and if possible should do them some good." He pointed out that in British Columbia the Indian population lived in a large number of small communities and so it did not take "very many ethnologists, linguists and archaeologists to make a crowd." He had a representative of each of those subdisciplines speak on ethics in fieldwork followed by a general discussion. The Victoria ethnologist Barbara Lane pointed out that they were there to discuss their relationship with Indian people while there were no Indian people in the room. Someone from the audience responded that this was really not a problem since they were there to discuss "our business." Wilson gently tried to move the meeting in the direction of actually doing something. He suggested the possibility of a registry of research projects and noted that, for archaeology in British Columbia, there was legislation to exercise some control over what happened in the field. But teaching in this context was more difficult than in the classroom. In the discussion period, rather than focusing on the matter at hand, there was a good deal of ponderous academic pontificating on matters such as whether anthropologists were "special" when it came to social responsibility. Wilson did get a show of hands that indicated that most present would be willing to submit their research projects to a central registry. A couple of committees were struck to move the ideas into reality, then a member of the audience suggested that the discussion of next steps be postponed to the business meeting after lunch. There was not much appetite for any measures to regulate fieldwork. One issue was that regulation had to be approached separately in different jurisdictions, especially Canada and the United States.[37] In British Columbia a newsletter was put out with a listing of field research in progress to provide information to both anthropologists and Indian communities, and a short-lived repository for Indian languages and cultures was established at the Provincial Museum. Wilson hoped that more action would come out of the talk. He soon predicted "a shift in the locus of field research from the universities to the people themselves."[38]

While at UBC, Wilson was not able to do as much work in the field as he had done when he was at the Provincial Museum. He did publish a significant piece of work based on his earlier work with consultants in the Victoria area. In his article, "The Fort Victoria Treaties," Wilson looks at Indigenous ownership of the land from two perspectives. The first was ethnographic: to provide a list of Songhees (ləkʷəŋən) place names for the Victoria area gathered from informants over the years. "A place name," Wilson wrote, "is a reminder of history, indelibly stamped on the land." To work with the numerous Indian place names is to "learn something about the Indian versions of what happened in history," as well as the detail and density of their ownership of the land. The second approach was historical: a close examination of the treaties that James Douglas negotiated with the Songhees groups that were the colonial, legal devices for first recognizing, then extinguishing, Indian title to the land. This perspective arose from his work to prepare for testimony in the *White and Bob* trial that confirmed the legal standing of the treaties. The two perspectives are then intertwined. Wilson reflects on what the ethnographic information from Indigenous community members reveals about the process of making the treaties and what the treaties reveal as ethnographic documents.[39] It is a study that appears simple on the surface but is actually very profound. It was a sign that Wilson's thinking and writing would, increasingly, be ahead of its time.

Wilson's most outstanding achievement outside the classroom, during his first few years at UBC, was in the summer of 1967, when he played a crucial role in a groundbreaking exhibition of Northwest Coast art at the Vancouver Art Gallery. *Arts of the Raven* was the outcome of a collaboration between the three leading figures in the study and practice of Northwest Coast Indian art: Wilson Duff, Bill Holm and Bill Reid. Bill Holm was almost an exact contemporary of Wilson—they missed being the same age by one day. They had not met when they were both at the University of Washington at the same time, but they got to know each other when Wilson was at the Provincial Museum and Holm had visited. Holm was now a teacher, and the following year he would become curator at the Burke Museum at the University of Washington. He was a tireless advocate of the importance and value of Indian art and culture and an artist who created his own works in the Northwest Coast style. Two years earlier Bill Holm had published the book that established the vocabulary and grammar for describing Northwest Coast Indian art. His groundbreaking *Northwest Coast Indian Art* is subtitled *An Analysis of Form*. In it, Holm set down the rules that First Nations artists followed for the highly abstract forms of the art. He writes about the three colours used: black the primary, red the secondary and blue-green the tertiary colours. He describes the use of formlines to establish the basic pattern and the shapes—the ovoids and U forms—that make up the repeated designs. There were also forms for eyelids, eyebrows, hands and claws. The "perfection of line was the essence of the style" that was highly refined and conventionalized. In the preface, Holm makes a point of thanking Wilson for his help with the research on examples of the art and Bill Reid for his insights.[40] Artists and scholars alike, including Bill Reid, have used Bill Holm's book ever since to understand the fundamentals of form in Northwest Coast Indian art. By the time that Bill Reid was involved in *Arts of the Raven*, he had built the Haida houses and carved totem poles at UBC's Totem Park. He was creating a wide range of artistic work, from totem poles to jewelry, and was becoming recognized as the pre-eminent Haida artist. Wilson and Bill Reid were close friends, and Wilson had done much to promote his friend's reputation as an artist. Wilson and the two Bills were a team of three and they worked well together. Wilson had great respect for, was even in awe of, his two colleagues, yet they acknowledged that Wilson was the leader.[41]

They began by dividing up the work of visiting museums and art galleries in North America in search of masterpieces to include in the exhibition. Holm went to museums in the west and Reid those in the east. Teaching meant that Wilson was less able to travel through the academic year, so he covered the local museums and collectors. Together they found and selected the great works that would make up the show. Bill Reid visited the American Museum of Natural History, near Central Park in New York City, and, after looking at what was on public display in the Northwest Coast Hall, he was taken into the storage area where much more material was housed. On a dusty shelf he saw a box that he took down to reveal a worn but extraordinary painted design. It was a classic four-sided bentwood box, but because the tops of two sides were concave and two were convex, it was sometimes called a bowl. The American collector George Emmons had acquired it from a Tlingit village in the late nineteenth century. The artwork was identified, probably incorrectly, as representing a seal. Each of the four sides of the box was subdivided into four segments, each containing a stylized representation of a head, an eye, a claw or a wing. The painted images on the box were certainly open to interpretation because they were so highly abstract. It was also an innovative work of art because, on each of the sides, the classic black formlines were expanded to become fields, or the background to the image. It was a fabulous work of art. *Arts of the Raven* was subtitled *Masterworks by the Northwest Coast Indian*, and this box clearly qualified. The painting on the box was somewhat faded, so, when it came to Vancouver, Reid painted a copy of the design on four larger panels to make its pattern crystal clear. The box was displayed in the show, in a space on its own, with Reid's rendition of the artwork in the background: transforming the old, faded box into one of "the objects of bright pride."[42] Wilson and Reid contemplated the meaning of those images through long periods of shared silence, as they thought a lot but said little. The images were so powerful, yet so ambiguous, that figuring them out was the ultimate test. So they called the box the Final Exam. If they could understand this box, they could understand Northwest Coast Indian art. Some say Reid came up with the name, but it sounds much more like Wilson, the university teacher, with his playful sense of humour. Perhaps they arrived at the name together. Wilson would spend the rest of his life thinking about "the box" in an effort to pass that exam.

When *Arts of the Raven* opened, the thousands who came to take it in saw Northwest Coast Indian art displayed as never before. The three curators had chosen items for their aesthetic, rather than ethnological, value. This was an exhibition of fine art, not primitive artifacts. It was a large exhibition, taking up nearly thirteen thousand square feet divided onto several galleries. The masterpieces came from the northern coastal groups, Tlingit, Haida and Tsimshian, as well as farther south, from the Kwakiutl. But the pieces were displayed by type rather than representing the culture that they came from. The first gallery featured representations of faces, the second small sculptures in wood, and so on. There was light and sound. Music played throughout, and creative use was made of light and shadow around individual pieces. There was also a minimum of written information about each individual item, as viewers were invited to appreciate them as works of art, for their own sake, without a lot of context. The spectacular exhibition catalogue provided more information, with essays by each of the three curators: Holm wrote a summary of his book on form, Reid a personal appreciation of the art, and Wilson wrote on the history and nature of Northwest Coast art.

Two galleries were particularly innovative. At Wilson's behest, one gallery was devoted entirely to the artistic work of Charles Edenshaw. Wilson had a growing interest in the extent to which the works of individual Indian artists could be isolated and identified. That thinking was part of the process of seeing the art as the creation of individual imaginations as much as the product of the culture from whence they arose. That is to say: seeing Indian art more like western art in its creative wellsprings. Wilson had an intense interest in the work of the Haida artists Albert Edward Edenshaw and his successor, Charles Edenshaw. Florence Davidson, the daughter of Charles Edenshaw, came to see *Arts of the Raven*, and Wilson spent time with her recording information about her famous father. He believed that he could identify enough pieces by Charles Edenshaw to justify a gallery devoted to his work, to make the point that he was a great individual artist as well as a great Haida artist. Holm and Reid did not agree with all of Wilson's attributions to Edenshaw, but they let him make the choices. Wilson knew that judgments about which artist created a particular piece had to be based on recognizing the patterns of line and form as coming from the hand of an individual. Such recognition was made even harder if the artist was innovative, as Charles Edenshaw certainly was. Judgements about attribution were further based on aesthetic sense and, in the end, intuition. Wilson made it clear that sometimes he might be mistaken. Subsequent scholars have made much ado by pointing out that some of Wilson's attributions to Edenshaw were incorrect, though even these revisions are frequently preceded by the word "probably."[43] For Wilson, it was somewhat beside the point. Seeing Indian artists as individual creative thinkers was far more compelling than the odd error in attribution.

A second avant-garde gallery was the last in the show, titled "The Art Today." It spoke to the future. Anthropologists and museum people of Wilson's generation have been criticized for only being interested in the historic art that was created before the decline in the twentieth century. This gallery, Wilson noted in the catalogue for the show, demonstrated that "the art styles continue on in new and modern contexts."[44] The largest number of works was by Bill Reid. A new generation of artists—Douglas Cranmer, Robert Davidson and Henry and Tony Hunt—were also represented, along with two artists who were not Northwest Coast Indians, Bill Holm and Don Lelooska Smith. Wilson, we can safely assume, was too modest to include any of his own carved masks.

Arts of the Raven was a resounding success at the time and, in retrospect, it is remembered as clear public announcement that the Indigenous art of the Northwest Coast was fine art, as much as anything that could be found in the galleries of Europe. Doris Shadbolt, the director of the Vancouver Art Gallery, put it clearly in the first few words that she wrote in the preface to the *Arts of the Raven* catalogue: "This is an exhibition of art, high art, not ethnology," she declared. The purpose of the show is to "establish its claim to greatness."[45] In Canada's centennial year, the show said to Canadians that the Indigenous art of the West Coast was a national treasure. Some fifty thousand people came to see *Arts of the Raven*, and the show received rave reviews, describing it as a "revelation," from Vancouver to New York.[46] Bill Reid was probably the first person of Indian background to curate a major art show and it did much to enhance his reputation as the pre-eminent Haida artist of the day. Wilson's stature was enhanced in the anthropology department at UBC as more of his academic colleagues could now appreciate the impact of scholarship in the art and museum field. His former co-workers in Victoria would have been less thrilled when, a year later, the Northwest Coast displays in the new Provincial Museum were opened and someone from the Metropolitan Museum of Art in New York, in a letter to the *Colonist*, panned them as dated and lacking in fresh ideas. "After the triumph of the 'Arts of the Raven' show at Vancouver last year, it is hard to see why a neighbour city didn't profit from that fine example." All three of the curators of *Arts of the Raven* were energized by the experience of bringing the show together and the resounding response it received. When it was over, Bill Reid's deep involvement with the art led to new creative inspiration for his own work, while for Wilson, the show had stimulated new lines of thinking about the hidden meanings in the art. They resolved to work together to explore the mysteries of Haida art. Reid and Holm went on to have a conversation about *Form and Freedom* in Northwest Coast Indian art, while Wilson, already thinking at another level, asked them the more fundamental question: "Is it all form and freedom and very little substance?"[47]

*

During the same summer that *Arts of the Raven* was running, Wilson was becoming involved in another totem pole salvage initiative, in Alaska. The Alaska State Museum wanted to carry out totem pole restoration work in Tlingit and Haida villages on the southern Alaska panhandle. As in British Columbia, there were earlier projects to preserve totem poles in Alaska, especially in the 1930s with the help of federal New Deal funding. That work had involved the establishment of totem pole parks in several Alaskan communities. Restoration results were mixed and by the 1960s the poles in the old villages were in an advanced state of decay. While others were involved in this latest initiative, most contacts led to Wilson. Erna Gunther, now at the University of Alaska, had taken a preliminary look at some of the locations and Bill Holm was consulted. Jane Wallen, from the Alaska Museum, was soon in touch with Wilson, who was recognized by all involved for his experience and know-how in this area. He attended a conference in Juneau in July 1967 that brought together expertise from various quarters. It was agreed that a totem pole conservation and protection program would begin with a thorough survey of the old villages and a detailed inventory of the totem poles in each one. Wilson told them that the salvageable poles could not be preserved where they stood but had to be taken down and removed to a protected location. Also, if they were going to carve copies, the success of that work lay in being able "to study the good old pieces as their models." He was also very clear that every effort should be made to establish who owned the totem poles before anything was done to remove or restore them. The totem poles "belonged to family lines" and the legitimate owners had to be treated with integrity. There was a second meeting in November that Wilson could not attend. In his absence there was some drifting around the need to establish ownership. Philip Ward, from the Provincial Museum in Victoria, whose expertise was in conservation practice not relations with Indigenous communities, tried to play down the importance of establishing ownership. He argued that "it was very easy to get involved in protracted negotiations as to who owns them" while the poles continued to deteriorate.[48] Fortunately that advice was not followed, as Wilson's was remembered.

After two years of further planning Wilson returned to Alaska for a month in June 1969 to take part in a detailed survey of the totem pole villages. Bill Holm was asked to join the survey, but he deferred to Wilson's greater knowledge. Wilson had been appointed a research associate with the Smithsonian Institution in order to facilitate funding. Jane Wallen was the organizer, and Joe Clark, a wood pathologist from the United States Forest Service, was on the team. Dennis Demmert, a Tlingit student at Harvard University and member of the Alaska Native Brotherhood, also joined the party. He was initially opposed to removing the poles before he saw that they were in such a bad state of decay and that many were being vandalized. Very important for Wilson was the company of several Tlingit and Haida elders when they visited the villages. He spent the most time with Walter Young, an eighty-two-year-old from Ketchikan who had lived in Old Kasaan as a child. One of the first things he learned was that Young was believed to be the reincarnation of a boy who had passed, whose name Wilson translated as "child of fairy." In earlier generations the people took reincarnation for granted.[49] The belief endures, though it is seldom spoken of to newcomers. The group travelled from Juneau to Ketchikan and then on to Old Kasaan and abandoned village sites such as Howkan, Klinkwan, and Kaigani. Some were occupied and others were deserted. They also visited and assessed the seven totem parks in southeast Alaska. It was Wilson Duff doing fieldwork of old, like he had not done since the early years at the Provincial Museum. He relished the experience. Some of the travel in a small plane brought back vivid wartime memories of viewing the lay of sea and land from the air. At each of the villages he sketched a map with the location of each of the existing or former houses and the placement and condition of the totem poles. He recorded what information he could gather about the families associated with the houses and their histories in the short time he spent in each place.[50] He was as meticulous as ever in his note taking, and the party shot lots of photographs. Wilson came away knowing that the information they were gathering was just a start, as the elders had so much more to tell.

After the survey, Wilson edited a report written by himself, Jane Wallen and Joe Clark that described the work in the field and made recommendations for the future. It was very thorough, including detailed maps of the villages and information on the totem poles. They were distressed at how many of the poles were beyond repair and how few were salvageable: forty-one poles or fragments in all "that still display the strength and beauty of the old sculptural styles." They reiterated that those poles could only be restored if they were removed from the villages to a secure location. There was detailed advice on the removal, preservation and copying of totem poles, and recommendations on steps to protect the old village sites.[51] The report was effective in prompting follow-up. In order to gather more information on history, culture and, where possible, the families that owned the poles, Wilson arranged for his student Andrea Laforet to spend an extended period talking to elders. Her work resulted in an account of conversations that focused on Old Kasaan, its people and its houses.[52] The Alaska organizers worked to publicize the initiative, and it gained widespread support in Indigenous communities. Haida and Tlingit people formed the Southeastern Alaska Indian Arts Council to oversee adherence to Indian practices and assume ownership of individual poles where the traditional owners could not be found. Most of the salvageable poles were removed to Ketchikan for safe storage, repair or replication. A traditional carving training program was started involving, among others, the great Tlingit carver Nathan Jackson. In 1976 the Totem Heritage Centre was opened in Ketchikan with a display of totem poles and a training program for Native artists. It was part of a renewal of Northwest Coast Indigenous art in Alaska. One factor in that renewal was that artists with new ideas could also study the old examples.

Wilson's contribution to these successes was greater than he would ever have acknowledged. Jane Wallen (later Jane Demmert) and Dennis Demmert made it very clear that much of the success of the southeast Alaska totem pole initiative was a result of Wilson's knowledge and personality. Wilson had more experience with totem pole preservation than anyone involved in the project—he was open about sharing that knowledge, and they relied on it. He was very familiar with the technical side of preserving old poles, and he knew his way around the Northwest Coast Indian art community and could introduce them to the key figures. Dennis Demmert remembers that listening to Wilson and Bill Reid talk about art was a real eye-opener. He tried to follow the conversation, but they had ideas that he had never thought of. Wilson's eye for the art and ability to articulate what he saw was an education. When Wilson accompanied Dennis and Jane Demmert on a visit to the Smithsonian, they saw his knowledge of the collections and his intense interest when individual pieces were brought out for viewing. Up in Alaska he was "kind of low key compared to many anthropologists." He did insist on involving the Native communities in the project, and that approach was "not a familiar experience for most of the government types in Alaska." Bringing Indigenous people around to engage with the work required lots of patience and some persuasion. Wilson moved easily among the people in the Indian communities and was humble with the elders at the same time as he had searching questions for them. He was a gentle, easy connector with people. He urged the Alaska organizers to use the opportunity of the totem pole project to get a carving program started so that the art would survive in the minds and hands of new artists.[53]

*

Wilson returned from Alaska at the end of June 1969 to find his family in crisis. Marion had hit a wall. She was depressed in spirit and physically ill. Wilson was an absent husband who had not given her much support. Marnie was very unhappy and rebelling in ways that Marion, who was pretty straightlaced about how young people should behave, found difficult. Tom was the only one who did not seem to be suffering. Marion was afflicted with chronic Crohn's disease, a debilitating illness. She had been in hospital to have it checked out and was due to go back to have an abscess drained. In an effort to end her anguish she had swallowed a bottle of sleeping pills. When they found her, Wilson called the ambulance and Marnie did mouth-to-mouth resuscitation in an effort to revive her. They got her to hospital, and for a few hours it was uncertain whether she would survive. Finally she began to recover, and gradually she regained some strength. When Wilson visited her in the hospital as she was recuperating, she reached out to him, saying, "See, I do need you."[54] Wilson was not responsive. In a letter to a colleague, he rather made light of this near tragedy, writing that Marion was home and "seems to be cured of what ailed her."[55] If that were all he felt, it arose from either optimism or denial.

A few weeks after Marion's illness, Wilson, as he had so often done before when he should have been with his family, took a trip into the field, where he was more at home. He went up to Masset in August for a totem pole raising. He had already seen the talent and encouraged the artistic development of Robert Davidson, a young Haida artist from Masset. Through his grandmother Florence Davidson, Robert was the grandson of Charles Edenshaw. His lineage as a Haida artist was strong. Knowing Florence Davidson, Wilson knew of Robert before he met him at the UBC museum, where he was demonstrating carving. Robert Davidson worked at Bill Reid's studio on Pender Street, and he took courses from Wilson at the university. Through Wilson and Bill Reid, Davidson spent some time instructing at 'Ksan, the museum and training program for carvers that was being set up in Hazelton. In 1969 Davidson decided to make good on his long-held thought of carving a totem pole in his community at Masset. He saw how little of the traditional art remained in Masset and wanted to contribute to its revival. Wilson, Bill Reid and Audrey Hawthorn recommended that he receive a grant from the British Columbia Cultural Fund. Robert's father, Claude Davidson, selected a cedar tree that became a forty-eight-foot log from which to carve the totem. They set up a carving shed, and Robert began the long hours of carving. His younger brother, Reg Davidson, assisted him, along with others who dropped by for brief periods. The pole would depict the Bear Mother story because Davidson thought it was a neutral story, not owned by either eagles or ravens. At first there was little interest in this revival of tradition in Masset, then gradually people began to take notice. When the time came to raise the pole there was great excitement in the community, and Wilson had to be there for the ceremony. He put a few carving strokes on the pole just to connect with it and the joy in its completion.[56] He enjoyed seeing old friends in the Davidson family, and his close informant from Skidegate with whom he shared a name, Solomon Wilson, was there. Robert's grandfather Robert Davidson Sr. and his father, Claude, directed the pole raising according to traditional protocols. A hole was dug to receive the pole, it was rolled into position, and then, with ropes and A-frames, it was gradually levered up to vertical. With the pole in place, firmly in the earth and standing against the sky, there was a potlatch feast in the evening, with regalia, singing and dancing. As part of the celebration, Robert Davidson formally presented the pole to his community. It was a propitious occasion for the Haida and those who were devoted to reviving their art. It was the first new totem pole on Haida Gwaii for more than a generation. No one present could remember a pole being raised. Robert Davidson's Masset pole would be the first of many. Wilson went back to the university to tell his students what a hugely significant moment it had been in a lecture entitled "Resurgence of Haida Culture." He thought that the fact that the pole was raised in front of the church was an ironic switch.[57] It was also an affirmation of Wilson's work on totem pole restoration. Robert Davidson was always very clear that he would not have been able to carve the new pole in Masset had he not been able to see the examples of the old art in the museums and, in particular, how they had weathered over time. "If they were not there then there is no way I would have known the standard."[58] The trip to Masset was much more uplifting for Wilson than his return to Vancouver, where his family was still in turmoil.

Marion was restored to physical health, but the family was broken beyond repair. An attempted suicide is usually a cry for help. After leaving hospital Marion went to stay with friends in Ontario for a few weeks to regain her spirits. Marnie found the whole episode traumatic. In her last year at school, she had to take an exam the day her mother tried to end her life. Neither of her parents was able to attend her graduation. Once the school year was over, she was off falling in love with a man who was very much from the counterculture. He was living in a bread van on a UBC parking lot and was a friend of Jochim Foikis, the official Vancouver town fool who wore jester's garb and provided jocular social commentary in public. Wilson was not impressed. In October Marnie slipped out the basement window to join her boyfriend. She closed the window on the family home, and together she and her boyfriend hitchhiked across Canada to Toronto. Marnie soon returned to British Columbia but had very little to do with her father over the next few years. She always believed that the move to Vancouver, so that Wilson could work at UBC, was the beginning of the end for her family. She felt guilty that she could not do anything to prevent them from flying apart. Wilson also left the family home that fall. He moved into an apartment in Kitsilano. He and Marion were separated, though they never divorced. The emotional side of all this upheaval was not talked about much among the immediate, let alone the wider, family. Marion and Wilson's marriage was of the fifties rather than the sixties: emotions were battened down and appearances kept up as long as possible. When appearances could not be sustained, there was little explanation. It is tempting to say that Wilson simply moved on. It would not be simple, but he did move on.

He was chatting with Michael Kew one day in the corridor outside their offices, in the Henry Angus Building at UBC, when he happened to mention that "if you hear a rumour that I am seeing one of the students—it's true."[59] Probably starting before he left Marion, and certainly after, he had a series of relationships with other women, several of whom were students. Some were romantic and intimate, some were intellectual and some were both. Yet none was completely fulfilling. In all his searching he never found another long-term partner. He was often alone and increasingly lonely. He still loved to dance, but he could not make a complete emotional commitment to another person. There were moments of joy in a new relationship, when it all seemed so right, but they were always mirrored by the sorrow of ending. He could have avoided the pain of separation, but then he would have missed the joy of the dance.

Wilson also continued to dance with other cultures. He was passionate about Haida art and would kindle that passion for the rest of his days. In *Arts of the Raven*, he, Bill Reid and Bill Holm had presented their interpretation of the past and future of Northwest Coast Indian art. Over time, his belief grew stronger that the exhibition was "the threshold over which Northwest Coast art had come into full recognition as 'fine art' as well as 'primitive art.'"[60] Robert Davidson's new pole in Masset was now a standing statement of the future of Haida art. Wilson had a vast knowledge of Indian cultures and art, yet he was not satisfied with the current state of that knowledge. He was still thinking, probing and speculating, as he felt that there was much more that was knowable, and he was particularly intrigued by the austerity and discipline of Haida art. In the next few years his interpretations of the art would soar to what were, for some, dizzying new levels. Having determined, in *Arts of the Raven*, that Northwest Coast Indian art, particularly Haida art, was serious art, Wilson proceeded to take it seriously.

Wilson took this photo of the Final Exam while he and Bill Reid and
Bill Holm were setting up the *Arts of the Raven* exhibition. The box is in
the American Museum of Natural History in New York. *Courtesy of UBC*
Museum of Anthropology, Archives image a060238, Wilson Duff fonds

8. Meaning in Haida Art

Beginning in about 1970, Wilson devoted much of his time, and most of his thinking power, to reflecting upon the meaning that lay within Northwest Coast, and particularly Haida, art. He was completely absorbed by this search for understanding. As only Wilson could be, he was focused and intense—some said obsessed—and his ideas went to places that even he did not expect. He strove to push past the boundaries of existing thought about Haida art: beyond matters of attribution, form and representation to understanding its deeper meaning. It was a quest to get into the minds of artists from another time and another culture. Some would say that is just not possible: that the western intellectual tradition is not capable of taking one into the mind of an artist from another culture. Wilson knew that even to ask, "What does Haida art mean? is an English question asking for an English kind of answer."[1] Yet he wanted to get beyond the limitations of his own culture, so he went where colleagues, never mind angels, feared to tread. He developed new ideas not imagined before, or since. It was a burst of creative thought and writing such as sometimes comes to gifted people in later life.[2]

Because he was searching beyond conscious logic, new ideas arose out of new ways of thinking. Kenelm Burridge, Wilson's colleague in the anthropology department, once wrote that we gain knowledge in two main ways: "by means of deliberate and systematic processes of investigation; and by a variety of phenomena (dreams, visions etc.) or procedures (meditation, trance etc.)" that allow awareness and intuition to lead to ideas.[3] Wilson was well grounded in the first approach. Until now, all of his museum work, writing and publishing were based on careful research and meticulous attention to detail. Since there was a level of exactitude and precision in Haida art, it was even reasonable for Wilson to see it in mathematical terms, a mode of thought that went right back to his time as a navigator. He did not lose these skills as he developed other ways of knowing. Colleagues like Burridge, who had some sense of Wilson's new thinking, knew that he was now flying at a different altitude. Others wondered if his navigational instruments were not working very well. Those who saw themselves as firmly grounded in reality were dismissive of the thinking that came from other levels of the conscious or unconscious mind.

Many of Wilson's ideas about art came to him when he was in a hypnopompic state: that time between sleeping and waking when the mind is free of mundane constraints. Most people have experienced having a great idea just as they wake up in the morning, but for the really creative person this is very fruitful time, especially if they cultivate the practice. Artists and inventors have said that the hypnopompic state in the first moments after waking was the source of their most creative insights. When the mind is free of the clutter of the fully waking day, it is free to make connections between seemingly unrelated ideas. As Wilson wrote, it was a time for developing "uninhibited hunches" when "analogy can work unfettered." He also knew that it was important to accept the perceptions received in this state and not to censor them out. Often the connections involved vivid images. Wilson likened it to the myth of Raven creating the world: "That little bite is the first ray of daylight." It brought new understanding. "This morning I 'understand' the myth (origin myth) better, in hypnopompic state, because it allows the play of opposite tendencies of thought at the same time." He realized that understanding is more than simple reason. He wrote that he had "learned to use the full depth of my mind by trusting the unconscious mind, welcoming intuition and hunches as products of a higher reasoning inside, which has taken account of more factors than the conscious mind can carry at once; as deeper thinking."[4]

Sometimes dreams during sleep will fade into the hypnopompic moment that comes with partial wakefulness. Wilson had an active, vivid dream life and sometimes wrote about his dreams. To him dreams were "a mental process dealing with analogies." For example, he was constantly thinking about the Haida box from *Arts of the Raven*—the Final Exam. After a very real dream about the box, he woke around four in the morning "convinced that I had finally 'seen' the chest design transforming from design into pure meaning, pure power...I could look at it and receive the full 'charge' of its inner force." It was the kind of experience that leads some, including Wilson, to say, "I shut my eyes in order to see." Wilson also experimented with hallucinogenic drugs to take him over the threshold into the realm of the inward eye. When he was contemplating the same box: "Last night, a joint, and fantastic views of the box design spiralling both ways at the same time."[5] Interested in the possibilities offered by LSD, he talked to his cousin, Mervyn Davis, about its effects and he read Stanislav Grof's book on LSD when it appeared in 1975. Grof wanted to elevate knowledge of the drug above the hysteria that drove much of the public discussion at the time. He noted that some users reported unusual aesthetic experiences and insights into the creative process while, for others, there were negative effects such as increased levels of anxiety and depression.[6] Wilson may have experimented with LSD, but he did not use it often. He certainly did seek pathways to understanding the unconscious mind that went beyond rational logic. Occasionally, when he was giving presentations on Northwest Coast Indian art, he would say something fairly speculative then add, "I don't know how I know that, but I know it."[7] He did know how he knew; he just did not want to explain to his audience.

The trick to capturing the thoughts arising from an altered state is to write them down as soon as possible. Wilson wrote with a fervour, in pencil on yellow pads that he purchased for fifty cents at the UBC bookstore. He wrote at home in the morning and evening, in his office on campus when he got a moment, and on flights to Toronto. When his mind was flowing freely with ideas, he wrote legato, fast and fully, page after page in his impeccable hand, with few breaks or corrections. At other times his thinking, and therefore his writing, was more staccato, as he made quick points, jumping from one thing to another. He would worry away at ideas for days and months. Sometimes he would conclude his writing for the day with "(to be continued)." There are occasional references to the books that he was reading and that fed his ideas, but usually he was thinking way beyond footnotes. "Documentation," he noted, "is not a substitute for meaning."[8] On those yellow pads, Wilson was writing for himself in private. They were his notes for thinking, setting his thoughts down on paper so that he could push them further. There are several introductions to, and chapter outlines for, books on meaning in Haida art; there are draft chapters on the Edenshaws; and an endless flow of thinking about particular pieces of art, like the Final Exam, that he thought were seminal. It is all there in his papers in the archives of the Museum of Anthropology at UBC but, unfortunately, with some exceptions, little of it was published.

Wilson's ideas about Haida art did not always come through the usual academic channels. He broached the question of promotion to full professor, the highest rank for a faculty member, and was not successful the first time. Cyril Belshaw was the department head at the time, and he advised Wilson that he should engage more with theory, by which he meant anthropological theory.[9] It was an observation that would not have resonated with Wilson, who was embarking on developing his own ideas rather than replicating those of others. Notwithstanding Belshaw's opinion, he was promoted to full professor in 1971.

At the time he was doing a vast amount of reading, although not much of it from the anthropological canon of received wisdom. He read and gathered ideas eclectically. For example, he read Carl Jung, along with a great deal of neo-Freudian psychoanalysis in books such as Georg Groddeck's *The Book of the It*. His thinking was stimulated by Arthur Koestler's writing on the creative process and particularly his idea of bisociation, by which disparate things can be linked in thought.[10] Wilson also read, annotated and thought deeply about George Kubler, who argued that time can be measured by the evolution of material objects, including works of art. An artist's creation from the past can send a signal through time to be received in the present, thus making a connection between the two. Kubler wrote: "The perception of a signal happens 'now,' but its impulse and its transition happened 'then.'"[11] From the ethnopsychiatrist George Devereux he gleaned the idea that art is a stylized form of communication that expresses thinking on otherwise taboo subjects.[12] *The Crack in the Cosmic Egg*, by Joseph Chilton Pearce, affirmed the value of hypnopompic thinking, reminding Wilson that it was particularly important to ask questions even when he was not sure that he could find the answer, which took him to the thought that "if you can conceive of it, it exists."[13] He was gathering up ideas from diverse sources. And then Claude Lévi-Strauss came to town.

*

Lévi-Strauss was a celebrity anthropologist and the pre-eminent exponent of structuralism. His thinking took off from the premise that people of all cultures have similar mental processes and are capable of sophisticated thought. He believed that behind cultural elements like art and myth there lies a hidden structure of thinking. He searched to find that structure, or rules of the game, that connect apparently distinct cultural ingredients in one culture, or in many cultures. He took apart the components of a particular Tsimshian myth in order to discover the thinking, or hidden codes, that linked them together. He looked at food preparation and eating in a number of cultures through the medium of myth to get at the underlying structures and ideas behind those rituals, which he believed were related across cultures.[14] He wanted to find what was common about different things; the order behind apparent disorder. He thought that it was "absolutely impossible to conceive of meaning without order."[15] His books are packed with ideas, stacked one upon the other. They are complex, difficult and slippery.

Lévi-Strauss operated in high-altitude realms of thought and, to his critics, his theories were not well connected to what happened on the ground. Some commentators observed that he always seemed to be able to find what he was looking for, while others referred to his "breathtaking associative leaps."[16] He roamed around the ethnographies of the world in his mind, picking up details with which to fashion a unified message. Furthermore, his whole attitude to the measure and meaning of language, wrote one commentator, "is poet's country."[17] Wilson shared that quality, as he too had the mind, and the imagination, of a poet. When he came to UBC, Lévi-Strauss was all the rage: his books had been translated from the original French, there had been several symposia and collections of essays about his ideas, and he gave interviews to the highbrow media. None other than Susan Sontag, the American writer and critic, thought that Lévi-Strauss's *Tristes Tropiques*, in which he recounted his one period of sustained ethnographic fieldwork in Brazil, was one of the great books of the century.[18]

Lévi-Strauss came to Vancouver twice at the height of his fame, once in 1973 and again in 1974. At UBC, as in the international anthropological community, he attracted both skepticism and veneration. Empirical anthropologists like Harry Hawthorn, who believed in useful anthropology, did not find Lévi-Strauss much use. He had earlier written to Wilson about Lévi-Strauss and remarked, as pointed as ever, "you know: the social anthropologist whose works on kinship we read and hope we grasp but know we don't." Others wondered what all the fuss was about. Gloria Cranmer Webster, who "did not even know who this guy was," recalled Lévi-Strauss's arrival on campus, saying, "Oh God, it was like the second coming of Christ, everyone was so excited."[19] She was not even referring to the second appearance. By contrast, Wilson's colleague Pierre Maranda was deeply engaged with Lévi-Strauss's structuralist ideas and was instrumental in arranging his visits.

There was great excitement on campus when Lévi-Strauss arrived. At his public lecture, the large lecture hall was overflowing, so his talk was piped into other rooms. Wilson attended the seminars and lectures that Lévi-Strauss gave at the university and had him over to his house with a group of students. And, of course, he read Lévi-Strauss's books. Wilson sometimes described Lévi-Strauss as one among many of his teachers, but we should remember that Wilson believed that teaching was a two-way street. So Wilson was taken, but not taken in, by Lévi-Strauss and structuralism. To describe Wilson as a "structuralist scholar" is an attempt to put his ideas into an academic box.[20] As we will see, in his thinking about Haida art, Wilson was not to be boxed in by four sides, no matter how fashionable the box might be.

Like Lévi-Strauss, Wilson wanted to understand the structure of ideas that was the inspiration for Haida art, and so some of Lévi-Strauss's thinking resonated. The first section of Lévi-Strauss's *The Raw and the Cooked*, for instance, called "Overture," argues for the relationship between myths and music. Both have sound and meaning. In music the sound prevails, whereas in myth it is the meaning that is paramount.[21] That comparison certainly echoed for Wilson; he was also interested in the interplay of apparent opposites that were connected and therefore the same. There were, however, three ways in which Wilson and Lévi-Strauss were opposites and therefore not the same. First, compared to Lévi-Strauss's looping prose, Wilson wrote to be read with exquisite clarity. His ideas were made perfectly clear and therefore became easy targets for his critics. Second, there was nothing superficial about Wilson's deep and detailed ethnographic knowledge of the cultures that he wrote about. It is sometimes said that really creative ideas only come after years of disciplined and meticulous study and empirical observation. Wilson exemplified the concept that it takes ten thousand hours of disciplined practice to achieve the mastery that leads to creativity.[22] Third, in his thinking about Haida art, Wilson was deeply grounded in one culture rather than flitting about the world in search of examples from different cultures to support his ideas. When he took high flights of speculation, he was still grounded in accurate, detailed fact. Lévi-Strauss would later remark that Wilson was on a "desperate quest for infinite mysteries."[23] The comment was pretty rich coming from someone who constantly pushed ideas way beyond any evidence to support them. Lévi-Strauss and structuralism gave Wilson some clues, but they did not solve the mystery of meaning.

*

During the years that Wilson was working at, and thinking about, meaning in Haida art, he was very much living the life of the mind. He was completely immersed in his world of creative thinking, to the increasing exclusion of other people and other parts of his work. Once, when he was on a visit to Victoria, writing in his hotel room, he observed that "the best show in town tonight is the one going on in my head."[24] Wilson, the perfectionist who delighted in precision, was now moving into more intuitive areas of thinking, where perfection was less definable and precision less possible. Obsession and brilliance often go together as a two-edged sword. Wilson was increasingly thinking on that sharp edge.

He became more and more out of step in the academic dance with some of his colleagues, who felt that his thinking was not going anywhere that was verifiable. Academic institutions could be compared to Haida art in that both allowed for creativity within rigidly defined disciplines and constraints. Wilson was fond of comparing meetings in the anthropology department with Haida art, as both being framed by Robert's Rules of Order—literally or metaphorically. The danger in each case was that the form would become more important than content, with the result that, in either context, it was risky to push beyond the proscribed boundaries. If you seemed to break free of tradition as, say, with some of Robert Davidson's later work, commentators may start to wonder if it really were still within the tradition of Haida art. Universities, too, provided the opportunity for creative thinking but were not always receptive when ideas went beyond the pale. Skepticism was a powerful force within limited minds. Or did it run deeper than that? Wilson thought that a "preoccupation with 'proper form' may reflect an anxious society."[25] That suggestion would certainly apply to Haida society through the decades of colonization and, also, perhaps to the anthropology department at UBC in the late 1960s.

While he intended to go beyond them, Wilson acknowledged the contribution of scholars who went before him. In *Primitive Art* and other writing, Franz Boas explored representation; that is, what was being depicted in Northwest Coast art—the animal crests of Raven, eagle, bear, killer whale and so on. Unable to push beyond what the art depicted, Boas was inclined to describe it as decoration, much to Wilson's dismay. After Boas, many others would write about the art in the same vein. While his former graduate supervisor, Erna Gunther, explained the art in its cultural context, Wilson thought that explaining the context did not explain the art.[26] Then Bill Holm, in *Northwest Coast Indian Art*, provided an analysis and a vocabulary that described the form and the shape of the art.[27] Holm's book was an important contribution as far as it went. It was a template for templates that can still be found in carving sheds up and down the coast. Yet, in Wilson's view, he had written "a whole book about 'form' without a hint that it contains meaning." He had delineated the style but not explained it. Wilson "felt massive frustration" that scholarship had not achieved "a satisfactory comprehension of what we know intuitively to be the greatest masterpieces."[28] Why, he wondered, had it taken so long for scholarship on Haida art to get beyond looking at representation and form? For Wilson, it was not enough. He wanted to bring to light other, deeper levels of meaning.

He developed an initial framework for diving deeper into meaning by exploring the distinction between the iconographic and the iconic levels in the art. The iconographic was the surface level, the depiction of what the art was about. The iconic level beneath was what the art was trying to say. The iconographic level was the subject and the iconic the predicate, or all that the art had to say about the subject. The iconographic level appealed to the eye; the iconic level appealed to the mind. The iconographic involved "a restricted vocabulary of subjects without predicates, utterances started but not finished." Naturally it was the iconic level that really interested Wilson. This was the much more difficult level to decipher because the meanings arise as metaphors that invite analogies. Moreover, the art may depict only a small piece of what is being represented. Rather than a full view of Raven, for example, there may only be Raven's wing or claw, yet the part represents the whole. Then the image of Raven may imply much greater meaning than Raven himself: perhaps all of the people of the Raven crest, or any aspect of the Raven mythology, such as Raven creating the world. The iconic meanings "are latent and implicit, lying mutely embedded in the 'style.'" Therefore the "shape of an iconic message, like the 'shape' of a musical phrase, may be isomorphic not with a concept but with a feeling, urge, emotion. It yields meaning to empathy, not analysis." Iconic design could not exist alone, however. It rested on a foundation of iconography, "just as poetry needs a foundation of ordinary speech."[29] The two were like logic and paradox. In Haida art, as in the patterns of Wilson's own thinking, they were interrelated.

This framework, based on the distinction between the iconographic and the iconic, was a starting point that Wilson continued to refine. Wilson found the seeds of his ideas in some of the authors that he was reading. The art historian Erwin Panofsky was a source of the concepts of the iconographic and iconic in art. He learned from the psychiatrist Silvano Arieti about the distinction between wholes and parts, and how the mind understands wholes through logic and parts through *paleologic*, or perception by means other than logic, such as feeling and emotion. Paleologic works through metaphor to connect things that are alike, in part because they share one significant attribute. Wilson was finding ideas that stimulated his own thinking from this wide range of reading. But his understandings were mainly coming from reading the art.[30] He went way beyond his sources as he followed his own pathways of thinking.

*

The next step toward understanding was to know more about individual Haida artists. The great Haida artists were deeply connected to their community while they were also individual talents. Indeed, Wilson's study of meaning in Haida art depended on understanding the styles of individual artists. He knew that there were others, like Tom Price and John Robson, but he became very focused on the two Edenshaws, Albert Edward and his nephew Charles. They were, for Wilson, two outstanding Haida artists. Edenshaw the elder was born in about 1812 and lived in various villages on the northern coast of Haida Gwaii. He took the name Edenshaw in mid-life and Albert Edward, after the Prince of Wales, when he was baptized in 1890. He appears in several accounts by Europeans who visited the Queen Charlotte Islands during his lifetime. He considered himself as Haida royalty and was a great artist. Albert Edward Edenshaw had a mixed reputation both among his own people and among newcomers, but not in Wilson's mind. He saw the elder Edenshaw as the pre-eminent Haida thinker and artist. Charles Edenshaw was born about 1839 and grew up in Skidegate. Among the high-born in Haida society, males often inherit from their mother's brother, so somewhere about 1858 Charles joined his uncle in the village of Kung. Charles learned the skills and thinking of an artist from Albert Edward, and when his uncle passed away in 1894 he inherited the Edenshaw name. The two lived through a period of massive change for their people, beginning with the maritime fur trade and continuing through the impact of colonization. Charles Edenshaw died in Masset in 1920, by which time the Haida population was decimated, and though the culture survived, it was shattered. As artists, they worked in different forms determined partly, Wilson believed, by the fact that they had to make a living in these turbulent times. Albert Edward carved totem poles and made painted bentwood chests, often for other chiefly patrons. Charles created miniature totem poles, platters, compotes and chests from argillite, crafted silver jewellery and even waking sticks with beautiful heads carved of ivory. Much of his work was directed to the market provided by the newcomers.

Artists from the past speak to us through their art, and Wilson was acutely tuned in to the messages he received from the Edenshaws, particularly Albert Edward, with whom he was in regular communication. The fact that he had been given Edenshaw's boyhood name, gwaaygu7an-hlan, was a powerful connection for Wilson. He knew, along with First Nations people, that names were living things and that names find people rather than people finding names. Wilson believed that he was receiving and reading messages from his namesake through his art. "I see what A.E. thought. I share his thoughts. We/I share thought, consciousness, cognition. He and I are the same, in this aspect."[31] In his poem "Messages," Wilson reflects upon these gifts of meaning:

A message is a gift
of meaning.
Communication, part of every message,
is part of every gift.
Communication is the essence of gift.
The purest gift is pure communication:
the gift of sight.
Let me show you how to see
it my way.
Show me how to see
it your way.
A message sent and received
is a mutual gift of meaning.
The least message sent and received
is the whole mutual gift of life.[32]

Wilson often wrote that Haida art was for thinking. Erudite artists made it to encourage deep thought. The Edenshaws were superb craftsmen and makers of visual design that was powerful and pleasing, but they were more than that. Their art "was also as intensely intellectual as a composition by Michelangelo or an equation by Einstein." Both Edenshaws frequently left their home villages and moved around to spend time in other places. They had connections with many of the Haida, Tlingit and Tsimshian communities on the coast. Albert Edward Edenshaw's painted chests or boxes, for example, ended up in many villages on the northern coast. Thus, the distribution of the art was a complication when it came to attribution. A particular Edenshaw work of art did not have to be collected at one of the home villages, such as Kuista or Kung, on Haida Gwaii, where Albert Edward spent most of his time. Wilson thought of him as the leading thinker, teacher and scribe of his generation who travelled like a prophet, proclaiming and painting ideas. When he built a new house in his own village, as Wilson visualized it, he was "recreating his church and his theatre…The fire then became the hearth, footlights and the source of his holy smoke, all in one... His kinfolk were his audience and his congregation." Edenshaw was at once an artist, preacher and thespian. As chief and artist he was "the authority on Haida social things. It was his job to teach these things."[33] And above all, for Wilson, his ideas were expressed through his art.

Haida art was largely composed of lines and a set of forms defined by lines. Wilson found general meanings in those lines and forms. Most of Albert Edward Edenshaw's painted designs were done on bentwood boxes and bowls or on house panels—art, as Wilson noted, for vertical surfaces. It was essentially two-dimensional or flat design. The black formlines were the foundation, delineating the outline and establishing the relationship between forms. They also formed the line between positive and negative spaces. The formline had an outside and an inside edge: the outside edge defined the boundary and the inside edge the field. They can also be called framelines as they frame the images and ideas within. In a great artist's hand, a brush could make a perfect formline to delineate a superb design. Like Chinese calligraphy, there was nothing accidental about a line. "It is mathematics..." at one level, with everything calculated because the artist knows what he wants to convey. Therefore, the line was more than mere decoration—it conveyed messages of analogic meanings. One meaning of a perfect line was perfection. Wilson believed that it was a metaphor for behaviour: of how Haida, and by implication, all those who viewed and thought about the art, should behave. So a perfect line stood for perfect behaviour, something that Wilson wished for yet, like most of us, could never achieve. The underlying message was aspirational; "Haida art," Wilson wrote, "is the shape of behaviour." Formlines were also about discipline and containment. Wilson thought that Haida art tried to contain nature, whereas Kwakiutl art celebrated its exuberance. Formlines imposed control over the images that made up the design just as the artist wanted to control his world: to establish an order out of the chaos that was the Haida experience of the impact of the newcomers.[34]

Formlines delineated all of the other elements in an Edenshaw design. Two of the most common forms were ovoids and salmon-trout heads. The ovoid is like a circle that is under pressure from the inside and has become elongated. The bottom line of an ovoid is usually flatter than the top one, so Wilson thought of an ovoid as half a circle, implying the existence of the other half: its opposite. Much of Haida art involved splitting an image down the middle and laying out the two halves on a flat surface, the one the mirror image of the other. That bilateral symmetry, or split representation, enabled the viewer to see both sides at once. These images pointed both ways at the same time and, therefore, denied time by showing the beginning and the end. The two that is one. As Wilson wrote: "The human mind has two irresistible urges, 1) to see the other half, 2) to put 2 and 2 together: they are really the same."[35] On the other hand, the ovoid as a half circle meant seeing one as two, drawing "something that is two things and one thing at the same time." Wilson likened the halving of an ovoid to cell division, a halving that produces doubling. It was not much of a leap to suggest that an ovoid implies the inside of an egg and so contains meanings associated with emergence, fertilization, life—and death. Or perhaps its elliptical shape had to do with the path that the sun and the moon trace in the firmament as they travel around the earth. Wilson was sure that Edenshaw was thinking of these cosmic things. Ovoids encompassed space, and so, to fill that space, often another ovoid would be drawn within it to make another classic form: the salmon-trout head. Because the salmon-trout head is a fixed and frequent element of Haida design, Wilson asked himself whether it was "conceivable that it did not take on a generalised meaning, as the symbol of some concept?" Was the inner ovoid "like a seed not yet burst" or was it "an embryo in the womb? The generation not yet born?" An "expression of human potential?" The one ovoid within another form often represented an eye, with obvious connotations of clear sight and vision. Since parts suggest wholes, an eye suggests a face, a human and, by further extension, all Haida people. Edenshaw's salmon-trout head was a perfect artistic form that, by analogy for Wilson, represented perfect behaviour. "It is the ideal Haida personality, an entity always inside, contained within a larger ovoid whole."[36] Even though the Haida world was in turmoil, control of individual behaviour endured.

A work of art, Wilson believed, could have many meanings at the same time. The meaning of lines and forms was only one level of meaning. Another level was the meaning of what was depicted by the overall design. Wilson had a broad and detailed knowledge of all the artworks that he identified as created by the Edenshaws. In a draft letter to Erna Gunther, he wrote that "The sheer volume of the Edenshaws' output is utterly astonishing."[37] Yet, when it came to deep thinking about meaning in Haida art, he focused on only a few pieces and two in particular. He regarded these as supreme examples of flat art coming from the hand, and brush, of Albert Edward Edenshaw. He still realized that attributions could be fraught because they were so subjective. He now admitted that some of the pieces attributed to Charles Edenshaw in *Arts of the Raven* were probably incorrect. There were good reasons for attributing these two masterpieces to Albert Edward Edenshaw, but Wilson was the first to admit that there was room for error. But Albert Edward Edenshaw had become, for Wilson, not only the most brilliant but also the representative Haida artist. His ideas about the art took off from the credit given to Edenshaw, but ascended into visions of the Haida worldview. He spent endless hours thinking and writing notes to himself about a set of Raven screens and "the box" that he called the Final Exam. He drafted outlines of books on meaning in Haida art that would have been based on just these two masterpieces.

The Raven screens, now in the Denver Art Museum, consist of two panels of horizontal boards depicting four versions, two pairs facing each other, of the culture hero Raven. They were probably house dividers, and there were some reports that they were about to be cut up to build a fence when they were salvaged. The box was the one that Bill Reid had brought from the American Museum of Natural History for the *Arts of the Raven* show. Both pieces were collected from Tlingit villages in the late nineteenth century, but that in itself did not discount Albert Edward Edenshaw as the artist. He travelled to many villages on the northern coast; his wife came from Klinkwan, in Alaska, where he owned a house. Even the Edenshaw name may have had Tlingit origins. Like a poem with a clear descriptive title, there was no doubt about what the Raven screens were depicting at the iconographic level. It was Raven times four. The images on the box, on the other hand, were like a poem without a title. They were highly abstract and open to interpretation. The box was already known in the anthropological literature. It was labelled as representing a seal when Emmons collected it at Klukwan. Then Franz Boas made drawings of the four sides of the box and took them to show Charles Edenshaw when he saw him in Port Essington in 1897. Decades later, Boas wrote in *Primitive Art* that Edenshaw had told him the box represented Raven, but Boas considered that interpretation to be "entirely fanciful."[38] Wilson, however, preferred to believe Charles Edenshaw, who had been trained by his uncle, the master. He visualized Boas in a hurry, doing ethnography on the fly, covering many subjects and not listening very carefully.[39] Wilson also noted that Boas had apparently not thought to ask the big question: Who was the artist?

So what did Wilson think that the artist, whoever he might be, was saying with each of these great works? The Raven screens are designed with heavy black formlines, which is one reason why Wilson connected the screens and the box to the same artist. He also noted that there are very few perfect circles in Haida graphic art. The Raven screens are an exception, as a circle forms the body of each Raven. At a deeper level, he thought that the circles represented infinite size, or, to put it another way, the wholeness of the world. In each of the four beaks of the Ravens is a tiny ovoid, possibly a seed or a pebble. These images brought to Wilson's mind one of the Raven creation myths. He found more evidence for that interpretation of meaning in the box that he sometimes referred to, along with the four Ravens on the screens, as the fifth Raven. The Raven screens were a prelude that Wilson thought had to be mastered before attempting to understand the much more complicated "fugue" of the box. He saw the Raven screens as instructional training before the Final Exam.

The art on the box was not easy to understand at any level: surface iconographic or deep iconic. Its meaning was a riddle that Wilson had constantly before him. He had photographs of the original, and Bill Reid's newly painted panels of the design from *Arts of the Raven* were in his house. The box was square, so each of the four sides was of equal size. Each of the four sides of the box was subdivided into four quadrants, each with a distinct image, so the four sides could be seen as each also having four sides. Thus Wilson often called the box Edenshaw's 4 × 4. He knew that four was a powerful number among many coastal groups. The mathematics of the box were strong. If Charles Edenshaw and Wilson Duff are correct that the box depicts Raven, then each quarter on each side of the box depicts a piece of Raven. The first and the third sides mirror each other to some extent, as do the second and the fourth sides. On sides one and three, the upper right quarter shows the head of Raven with a large eye to the left of it, while the lower quarters depict a foot and claw on the right and a wing on the left. On sides two and four, the top left image is the head of Raven along with a human hand, perhaps suggesting transformation to human form. The top right beside the head is a shoulder, while underneath is the tail in one quarter and a leg and foot in the other. Unlike the screens, the pieces in each of the four quadrants on each side of the box do not form a readily recognizable image of Raven. For Wilson, reading the box design turned on the idea that a fragment represents the whole. He once likened each fragment on the box to a single frame of a movie: a split-second image from a larger story.[40] Similarly, looking at a tiny fragment of Raven suggested to Wilson the complete Raven and the full range of his mythological activities. It also has to be said that the images on the box are enigmatic, and the box itself is possibly the most ambiguous piece of Northwest Coast art. That ambiguity may have served a ritual function. The powerful chief for whom the artist may have made the box would have displayed it at ceremonies, but it would not reveal its meaning to everyone and therefore limit access to the knowledge and the power that it contained.[41] For Wilson, the creativity and ambiguity of the images lay in the mind of the artist, whose box was also innovative because it broke the rules. In the bottom right quadrant of each side of the box, instead of the usual black formline being used to create an outline, black is expanded to become the field against which the image is painted in red. Because of this feature, the artist who painted the box is some-times called the Master of the Black Field.[42] For Wilson, the black field was the unique signature of an artist who was creative and daring enough to bend the fundamental rules of order in Haida art. Did that black field represent a Haida world that was now out of order? Against the black field the formlines became red rather than black. Wilson wondered if the black field became a heart, with the red lines being blood coursing through its veins. An image of life if ever there was one. The skilled execution and the innovative design, along with the questions that the images raised, con-vinced Wilson that the box was "the supreme masterpiece of Northwest Coast painting."[43]

Beyond the 4 × 4 of painted sides, Wilson was also thinking out of the box. For him there was also a fifth box to contemplate: the box itself, contained by the four sides. Boxes were made to hold possessions and the remains of people after they died, but they were also containers of ideas. The Haida myth of Raven, the trickster and creator, opening a box that was so small and yet contained all the light of the world has been fre-quently retold. Wilson's thinking about the meaning of the fifth box arose from his ideas about one thing relating to its opposite and therefore signi-fying both. The inside of the fifth box was empty, containing nothing but light, and therefore stood for its opposite, the world outside the box that is everything. That image in Wilson's mind led him to think about another myth that told of how Raven created everything, the world of Haida Gwaii, out of nothing. Thinking about this meaning of the box led him to define a third level of meaning, beyond iconographic and iconic, beyond parts representing wholes, that he described as *paradoxic meaning*. This third level of meaning is entirely metaphorical: opposites which share one characteristic that will make them not only comparable, but the same. Art at this level makes statements "that take the form of riddles which are at the same time logical paradoxes." An example might be a shark that has a beak like Raven, and therefore this shark is Raven. At this level, Wilson also saw a strong connection between the artistic statements in a work of flat art, like the box, and Haida mythology. At its most sophisticated level, Haida art "sometimes became a medium for the explicit analysis of paradoxes which are implicit in the myths: that is, a deliberate structural analysis of Haida myths."[44] And while he knew that any piece of art could have several meanings, the meaning that Wilson most often saw in the box was:

> It is about Creation
> How raven created this world
> Not really about how the world was made,
> But about how the world is.
> How things are patterned ... [45]

Since the box is about creation, and the meaning of the box is an examination of mythology, it made sense that Wilson would want to retell a creation story. He did so in his own story, entitled "Nothing Comes Only in Pieces," in which he relates a Raven myth and provides an exegesis on it. He creates a contemporary setting for the story in a schoolroom in Queen Charlotte City, using a classroom setting because: "Myth is teaching. It is a consolidation of knowledge, and is told to teach."[46] A new teacher, fresh out of university, wants to introduce the students to some content on Haida culture. She hands out copies of one of the stories about Raven creating the world of the Haida, a version from the Raven travelling series recorded by the ethnographer John Swanton, as told to him by Skaay, or John Sky, in Skidegate in the winter of 1900–1901. In this version, the crux of the story comes when Raven is invited into a house where an old man sits. He has a box that contains four other boxes inside it. Out of the tiny innermost box, he hands Raven two stones, one speckled and the other black. As he passes them over, he says, "I am you." The old man is giving Raven his knowledge, the key to how things are and how they are to be. He is passing on the means of creation. The old man's phrase will resonate with Wilson forever. Raven is instructed to lay the pebbles in the water and to bite off a piece of the black one first and spit it out. Never good at following instructions, Raven bites the stones in the wrong order, spitting a piece of the speckled one first. When he gets the right order and spits out pieces of both stones, trees and land are formed and supernatural beings swim over to Haida Gwaii.[47]

As the teacher struggles to get the class engaged with the story, she suggests to a Haida boy, Ray Wilson, that he talk to his grandfather Chini Sol (Solomon Wilson) about the meaning of the story and report back to the class. Ray visits his grandfather, whom he greets as "Chini-chin-chin," and they have conversations delving into the meanings of the story: how "emptiness has to be in pieces before we can see it"; how within the last box was "the presence of nothing is the absence of everything"; how "at least that Creation does kind of get things started." They wonder about the old man saying, "I am you," which seems to be an answer to a question that Raven has not even asked. Does it mean that the listener is as much part of the story as the teller? Wilson believed that "'I am you' is absolutely the most meaningful statement that anyone can say to another person. It is the ultimate communication." Perhaps most importantly, Ray and Sol talk about how the myth cannot be understood without perception and imagination. Back at school, Ray finds it difficult to explain things to the class. "Well, it's pretty hard to say," he says, "but those two things can be nothing and everything, or darkness and daylight, or you and me. In a way, they can be everything we want them to be. Or pieces of everything." The teacher is disappointed and there is a ripple of laughter through the class. What made sense in Chini Sol's living room—if nothing is everything, then the whole world is in the tiny box—does not make sense in the classroom.[48]

In "Nothing Comes Only in Pieces," Ray and Chini Sol have, for a schoolboy and his grandfather, a pretty deep philosophical conversation about the meaning of a myth, even though, when their thoughts seem particularly far-fetched, it is punctuated with chuckles and laughter. That is why some reviewers of the story felt that the dialogue did not fit with the context. But Wilson was trying to make the point that the Raven myths, and the art that explained them, contain serious lessons from the past that are relevant in the present if we are receptive to them.

While Wilson was very serious about exploring the meanings in Haida art, he had not lost his sense of humour. He was intrigued by a little figure that he saw on Edenshaw's and other painted chests, often, but not always, in the lower centre of the design. He identified the image by its big all-seeing eyes. Various versions had different combinations of the following features: a mouth with teeth, U form ears above and protuberances below the head. Sometimes it had a big grin, as if it were enjoying a joke. Sometimes the figure is rendered upside down because, Wilson thought, "the opposite (upside down) of seriousness is humour..."[49] Wilson called the figure Mighty Mouse. Robert Davidson shared in the play when Wilson pointed out and named the image. He recalled that Wilson "became my measure of knowledge," and he created his own Mighty Mouse, thinking, "That'll fool Wilson." Later it seemed more appropriate to Davidson to call the image Kuugan Jaad, or mouse woman, a supernatural presence in Haida origin stories.[50] Wilson was also intrigued by the figure of Frog that he saw in the Edenshaw's art as well as in stone sculpture. Frog fascinated him because he was an enigma. Frog often has a mouth large enough to eat himself, so he is beginning and end. Other than his mouth, his back and front shape are similar, so his gender is undefined. Frog was a conundrum. In the poem "Frog's Mirror" Wilson wrote:

> His mirror shows him
> no reflection.
> His beginning and end are the same
> Because he has no story.

He once sent a note to a student saying that he was "On the track of Frog (who leaves no tracks)."[51]

*

Having fun with Haida art led Wilson quite naturally to think about the ambiguities represented in Haida art in argillite. Sometimes called slate, argillite is a black stone that has affinities with coal, though it will not burn. Excavated from Slatechuck Creek, to the west of Skidegate village, it is soft enough to carve when it first comes out of the ground, before it loses its moisture through exposure to the air. It can still be brittle, so it was not used to make functional implements. It is as black as a Raven and can be polished up to a shiny lustre. Argillite art took a variety of forms. There were panel pipes, chests, dishes and compotes. The beautiful miniature totem poles made of argillite became almost as synonymous with Haida art as the totem poles themselves. More than one expert has asserted that argillite art was, until recently, ignored or disparaged by academics because it was, to a large extent, the product of newcomer contact rather than a genuinely traditional Haida art form.[52] This was just another generalization about the anthropologists of his generation that did not apply to Wilson. He was fascinated by argillite art, and he developed a detailed knowledge of the pieces owned by collectors and in museums around the world. He then applied the same power of thinking and imagination to argillite art as he did to painted flat design. While he wrote a good deal about argillite art, unfortunately none of it appeared in print. To be recognized in academe, ideas have to be published, otherwise they scarcely exist.

Wilson was particularly interested in panel pipes. With the decline of the maritime fur trade on Haida Gwaii, Haida artists mostly made the pipes to sell to visitors who came to their shores. Wilson believed that they got the idea by watching sailors smoking pipes on their ships, and the Haida pipes were derived from scrimshaw, the sailors' art engraved in ivory. Function was, however, quickly taken over by form. Early in their development of the pipe form, Haida artists made gestures to them being functional pipes by fashioning bowls and stems, but they quickly became panels of pure art form that could not be smoked. Wilson called them "pipes that won't smoke" made from "coal that won't burn."[53] With the development of argillite carving, Haida artists were doing two-sided sculpture more than they had before. There may have been earlier examples, but they started proliferating in the 1820s. Initially they depicted

Haida crest animals, though the artists rendered them in such a way that they ceased to be crests in order to avoid the faux pas of selling crests to those who did not own them. But before long the images on the panel pipes came to represent the newcomers and their activities. Wilson saw the development of the panel pipes going through two phases. He called the first-phase panel pipes *Haida pipes* and the second-phase examples *whiteman pipes*. By about 1850, the output of panel pipes declined as other forms of argillite art replaced them, though they did not disappear altogether. In terms of design and composition, panel pipes were, for Wilson, "one of the high points of the art." Of course, he wanted to get beyond form and depiction and address the question, "What did they mean?" He concluded that, while they were made for sale to newcomers, panel pipes "were not just products of the transaction, but commentaries on it."[54]

According to Wilson, argillite panel pipes portrayed nonsense that made perfect sense. He prefaced one of his essays on the pipes with the most famous lines of nonsense poetry in the English language, from Lewis Carroll's *Through the Looking-Glass*:

> 'Twas brillig, and the slithy toves
>   Did gyre and gimble in the wabe:
> All mimsy were the borogoves,
>   And the mome raths outgrabe.[55]

Wilson would have first been intrigued by the fact that, in Carroll's story, Alice had to use a mirror to read the Jabberwocky poem, but he also found several analogies between these nonsense lines and Haida panel pipes. If nonsense is to make sense, rather than being read as merely error, it has to be anchored in "precise sense." Thus the grammar, syntax and poetic form of Carroll's poem are perfect English. Even the many nonsense words in the poem are derived from English words, but without English meaning. Similarly, the Haida-type pipes depict Haida crest figures, but the traditional meanings have been removed from them. The creatures have Haida form but not Haida meaning, so they can be presented for sale.

They were "borogoves." The actions of the figures depicted on the pipes were also not traditional activities; some were sexual activities not usually displayed overtly in Haida art. The nonsense had taken a ribald turn. The whiteman panel pipes portrayed the newcomers engaged in strange and curious activities. Either the Haida pipe makers misunderstood what the white men were doing or, much more likely, they were making fun of it.

The coming of newcomers had dire consequences for the Haida. The fur trade brought new wealth, then declining opportunities when it passed them by. Gold miners were the next wave of would-be exploiters to come to Haida Gwaii, but not the last. Missionaries brought new ideas and an assault on the culture. New forms of government were instigated as the Queen Charlotte Islands became part of first the colony, and then the province, of British Columbia. Through it all, the population continued to decline, almost to oblivion. As a consequence of the European presence, Haida life was eroding. Accordingly, much of the art had serious meaning. As Wilson wrote, "Its beauty is a serene, intelligent and serious kind of beauty." Yet he believed that, in the midst of these calamities, Haida artists could still make fun of the white man. He visualized Haida carvers of argillite panel pipes "chuckling amongst themselves at the subtle artistic nonsense they were 'selling' to the white men. What makes the humour the more delicious is that it seems to have taken us a century and a half to catch the point." There was more involved "than just a sly joke on the busy, pipe-puffing sailormen"; they were making "astute and timeless" comments on the newcomers. Again, Wilson believed that Haida artists were thinking through the issues of their day in their art. He concluded: "Like all good nonsense, it was a happy exploration of the ways of making sense... It is, I think, nonsense to be proud of."[56]

Not all work in argillite was nonsense. Other forms of argillite art depicted traditional Haida culture and presented its mythological history. Work in argillite was more Charles Edenshaw's forte than his uncle Albert Edward's. He made compotes and platters that were crafted for the newcomer market. Some had purely European images with, for example, floral designs on them, but more of them were serious explorations of

Haida myths. One of his compotes, a dish with a lid set on a pedestal, is now in the Museum of Anthropology at UBC. The dominant image is of Raven in full flight, heading somewhere with real purpose. The lid of the compote is Raven's back, and standing on it is a small human figure with a Raven headdress. Riding on the back of Raven, the little figure is carrying a small box on his shoulder that appears to be very heavy and has on it an image of Frog, that great enigma. Wilson actually referred to the compote as a "comport," since *comport* comes from the Latin verb "to carry" and because he thought that much of Haida art was about behaviour that is proper "comportment." So, beyond depiction, what do the images on the compote mean? Wilson's interpretation, based on Haida creation mythology, is that Raven is looking for a place to land so the man can put the box down. Raven, along with the artist, is "looking for a world." The two-sided box on the figure's shoulder contains time. The frog on the box is facing both ways, "forward in time and backward in time." The frog box is empty, but the human thinks it is heavy because it contains the whole world. Frog is also an image of the world. The compote itself asks the question, "What is inside?" When you to lift its lid to see what is inside, it is empty. It contains nothing and everything, the "inside of its outside": that is, it contains the light of the world. A compote "is a container for valuables. What is more valuable than the world?" Therefore when, prompted by curiosity, "you lift the lid—you are creating the world ... It is a moment in myth. The first moment."[57]

Charles Edenshaw also made argillite platters that depicted other Raven myths. He crafted, for example, a series of three platters that are now in three different museums. Each one of the three is slightly different, but they all show Raven holding a large spear and heading off in a canoe, with fungus man at the helm, in search of female genitals (*tsaw* in Haida). The image on the platters is a depiction of another story told to John Swanton by John Sky. The tsaw were to be found on a particular reef in what is now Gwaii Haanas. The place had a power that prevented Raven from approaching on earlier attempts. This time he manages to spear two and gives one to his wife and one to his sister.[58] It is another Raven creation story, this time enabling sexual relations and future generations. Wilson was becoming increasingly interested in sexual meanings in Northwest Coast art. Raven, with his large spear within the circle of the platter, had obvious male and female connotations. Just as he had called the box Edenshaw's 4 × 4, he referred to the story shown on these platters, with characteristic directness of language, as "C.Es. cunt hunt."[59] More recent interpretations of the story refer to the power of female sexuality.[60]

Haida art continued to express Haida ideas, but increasingly it was influenced by a non-Haida market. Whereas Albert Edward Edenshaw had painted flat design for Indian chiefly patrons, by Charles Edenshaw's generation much of the art was made for Europeans. Wilson believed that the art played an important mediating role between the Haida and newcomer cultures, creating a point of connection where they could come together. That should not, however, obscure the reality that the demand side of the transaction increasingly determined the nature of the art. Haida art was one thing that the newcomers found acceptable about Indigenous people, and it was a venue for the Haida to approach the colonizers without hostility. It is a place where "the two cultures 'come to terms.'" Yet there was an underlying dominance and submission in the relationship. The power imbalance was always in play. The very word *art* was a newcomer word, not a Haida word, and for the newcomers the "art" was an acceptable part of Indian culture, just as "artist" was an acceptable role for the Indian. And that acceptance had an impact on the art. The form had to be Haida and "authentic" to satisfy the demand, but for the artist it had to be non-traditional in Haida culture but authentic anyway. Newcomer interest in Haida art was a positive mediation between the cultures, a "happy agenda," as Wilson put it, though he hastened to add that it did not help, and probably masked, the real conflicts over land and law.[61]

Wilson was keen to understand meaning in Haida art and "return" those ideas to the Haida. But he knew equally well that such an aspiration only followed from the fact that Haida art had been taken away from the Haida by the newcomers, just as they had taken the land. Wilson knew that his work and thinking had played a role in that process. It was perhaps not as conscious a theft as taking the land—it was more of an unintended consequence—but that did not mitigate the outcome. Today we would call it cultural appropriation. As Wilson admitted, "since acquiring it we have redefined what it is." As it was validated and supported by non-Haida, the art of the Haida was turned from ethnographic specimen into fine art. Meanwhile, what role did it play in Haida life? Certainly it had diminished. Haida art was more visible in Victoria and Vancouver than it was on Haida Gwaii. In 1967, Canada's centennial year, totem poles were carved and erected at ferry terminals and border crossings, and even in other countries, but not in Haida Gwaii. "We took their art and made it ours," Wilson wrote. He observed that his friends Bill Reid and Robert Davidson, pre-eminent artists of the day, both had to leave Haida Gwaii and come to Vancouver to become Haida artists. On a more positive note, he could foresee a giving back to the Haida communities. He saw great hope when Robert Davidson, the great-grandson of Charles Edenshaw, returned to carve and erect a new totem pole in Masset in 1969. The art that "was Haida," Wilson predicted, "will be once again."[62]

As he delved more deeply into meaning in Haida art, Wilson was the first to admit that his ideas were speculative. When analyzing the Final Exam, he wondered, in moments of uncertainty, if he had projected onto the box "only the contents of my own head." And yet he was convinced of at least two things. One was that, thinking along the lines of Lévi-Strauss, "ambiguity is the most important resource of the human mind."[63] Second, he was certain that he was tuned in to the messages that the Edenshaws were sending through their art. Those two frames of mind generated some original ideas about meaning in Haida art. It is unfortunate that, with a few exceptions, so little of his thinking appeared in print. Part of the problem was that he was concerned about the reaction that he might get from academic commentators if he laid his ideas out in the open. After all, he once reminded a colleague, "Readers are perverse bastards who are always reading 'between the lines.'"[64] Needless to say, Wilson himself was pretty good at reading between the lines, whether of print or of Edenshaw's flat designs. And, increasingly, neither his mind, nor his life, was constrained by lines. But there was a price to pay. As he was consumed by a burst of highly creative thinking about meaning in Haida art, Wilson was slipping through the formlines into negative spaces.

9. Negative Spaces

Wilson was very fond of the Haida saying "The world is as sharp as a knife." It comes up frequently in his "Notes for Thinking," often as the conclusion to a line of thought, and it is cited in the conversation between Ray and Sol in Wilson's story "Nothing Comes Only in Pieces." Wilson posted it on his office door at UBC. As he was developing his ideas about meaning in Haida art, we can safely say that the aphorism was never far from the top of his mind. As with the myths that provided the themes for the art, this piece of Haida wisdom came to Wilson through John Swanton, who heard the saying in Masset. It was a reminder of the sharp divide between life and death; if a person were not careful, they could fall off the edge. As Swanton heard it, a father told his son the saying, and the son responded by pointing out that the earth was broad and expansive and there was no danger of falling off. To emphasize his point, the son kicked his foot into the ground, ran a splinter into it and died. Swanton noted that Boas had heard the story from the Tlingit, where it may have originated. For Wilson, the story was Haida. It meant that "the human condition was to balance on the sharp edge."[1] He took it to heart, as well he might, as the intensity of his thinking about Haida art was taking its toll.

For all of his achievements, Wilson was self-deprecating. It was one quality that attracted people to him. Yet he was so mistrustful that he had difficulty accepting praise. Bill Holm enjoyed Wilson's company and recalled that the only time that they got into a "fuss" was when they were in Alaska looking at totem poles and Holm said some complimentary things about Wilson in front of others and was later chastised for it.[2] On the outside Wilson was contained and reserved. He was always impeccably dressed and groomed. He never wore jeans, the uniform of the day for students and many younger faculty. He appeared to have a strong sense of decorum as a university professor. People who met him, before they knew him well, would most often describe him as very shy. He did not readily reveal much of himself. Some colleagues who thought that they knew him fairly well actually knew very little about his private or early life. One faculty member in the Anthropology Department, who often enjoyed a tipple in Wilson's office on Friday afternoons, did not know that Wilson had been a navigator in the RCAF.[3] He was reluctant to open up to other people for, within himself, Wilson was full of uncertainty and fears.

His anxiety arose from his childhood. He believed that he had been rejected by both his parents and still recalled the traumatic moment at two when he was left in the hands of a nurse at the hospital to have his tonsils out and be circumcised. He was at times ambivalent about his mother, while he particularly blamed his father for the fact that he still could not make connections with others. When he was growing up, Wilson felt that he constantly had to please his father and just as constantly failed to do so. Perceiving censure, he withdrew himself from his father and now, as a result of that experience, he withdrew himself from others. As he once put it, "I have to be good but I can't let myself love, because my parents rejected me."[4]

Wilson was possessed of a vivid imagination that was both a blessing and a curse. He believed that imagination was "man's greatest gift" but also a source of insecurity.[5] He was troubled by his many dreams, and sometimes he wrote about them. He had dreams that involved large, threatening male figures that were associated with his father or seemed connected to Harry Hawthorn, another father figure who he felt was not happy with him. He awoke from those dreams with a jolt of fear. Other dreams arose from his flying days when he was young. In one he was on the outside front, like the nose wheel, of a large four-engine aircraft that was flying low over the water of English Bay, he assumed, after takeoff. But then he realized that they were descending rapidly into the water. The feeling of terror "ZAPS me into being awake." He saw a crash landing as meaning death and "(my 'father' is at the controls.)" He also had dreams about unsuccessful sexual encounters with women, as he worried about getting older. These dreams both arose from and contributed to his fears about himself. He had more creative dreams about Edenshaw and the shape and spirit of Haida art. He wondered what they all meant: "Are dreams the deeper wisdom of the unconscious given visible form? Do they tell you something the conscious mind cannot figure out?"[6] Some dreams stimulated his thinking, while others were very troubling.

Wilson's fears and uncertainties about himself translated into anxiety in relations with others. He commented to himself that he did not mean for his aversion to his father to create distance with all men. But it did. He always connected more readily with women. He flirted with women, was guarded with men, and could not form a deep relationship with either. His father demanded high standards, and Wilson believed that he was always found wanting. He also had high expectations of himself that he projected onto others, only to find that they fell short. He continued to form romantic relationships, usually with younger women, but, by his own admission, he could not let go of his anxiety about himself and commit to a lasting partnership with another. Once, when he was in Ottawa, he visited a woman his own age who had been a neighbour when they lived in Victoria. Her husband was out of town and Wilson thought that they were separated, so he suggested that they might get together. The woman was happily married. In his love life he was looking for something that he could not find. His affairs always ended in separation and heartbreak, yet he continued to search. As he often did, he expressed his emotions in poetry.

> Lay down together
> two pieces of wood
> in the fireplace.
> They burn together,
> each beside the other,
> reflecting
> each other's heat
> enough to make a fire,
> A dance of flame,
> Which is the purpose.

In the morning,
two charred shells.
A space between,
just enough space,
a slightly twisting space
which shows the shape of growth
to reach the sun
and gather in the light
and warmth, …
and cold white ash between,
which is the result.
One partner in the dance
Is Time.
The other,
wood's Wish to burn.

The poem is untitled, simply dated November 30, 1974. It has been interpreted in different ways: that it is about life and death, which is possible, or that it is a metaphor "for the relationship between another culture's meaning and our own experience." That is less likely. It is mostly about love and loss. The poem was attached to a letter to Collyne Bunn, his close friend in the Yukon, in which he writes: "Last night my young lover opted for a younger man, and I feel the resonation of death." A year later he wrote to say: "I have a new girlfriend; or at least I think I have. My mind is bubbling over with her." He continued to dance in the flame but, with each ending, there was only "cold white ash."[7]

The intensity of his focus on Northwest Coast art and its meaning was at times debilitating. He had long mood swings, major ups and downs that, over time, became chronic. When he pursued a particular line of thought over days or weeks, he was left mentally exhausted and physically debilitated. "Consumed by the ferment inside my head," he became irritable, apprehensive, tense and often on the edge of tears. His state of mind had physical consequences. Loss of appetite and therefore weight loss, difficulty sleeping, dizziness and weakness of voice were all symptoms. In that mood, he withdrew from people, telling them that he was working on something even when he was not. At these times he was despondent about life in general and his in particular. He wondered if his life just involved playing a variety of roles—anthropologist, professor, thinker, father, lover—none of which, no matter how good he was at them, was the real Wilson. It was, he thought, "the ultimate conundrum. In order to be somebody I have to be somebody else."[8] These down times were assuaged by periods of joy. When he had a big breakthrough of insight, say on the Edenshaws and their thinking, he took a new lease on life. He was euphoric with new understanding and all was well with the world. The things that he learned and the way that he felt was "a massive payoff for all the mental work." Now the emotions were "elation, excitement, self acceptance." During these times he was "one step closer to finding myself and loving others and the world." It was, he told himself, like a Salish person finding his guardian spirit.[9] Unfortunately that spirit was not strong enough to prevent the dark times becoming more common than the moments of radiance.

At one of his low ebbs, when Wilson seemed particularly fragile, his family doctor recommended that he seek psychiatric help. He started seeing James Tyhurst and continued to do so, off and on, over several years. To describe Tyhurst as an interesting character would be to underestimate both his talents and his serious flaws. There was some murkiness around his medical qualifications from McGill University. While in Montreal he also worked for the Allan Institute, a CIA-funded facility where drugs, including LSD, and sensory deprivation techniques were used to repattern people's minds. In crude terms it was brainwashing.[10] In 1957 he returned to British Columbia, where he was born, to be head of the Department of Psychiatry at UBC. By the time Wilson was seeing him, in the 1970s, he had stepped down as department head but was still a professor. At one level Wilson found his psychiatrist very engaging. Tyhurst was intellectually very bright and he revelled in, even demanded, a vigorous to and fro about ideas. Wilson would have had lively conversations with him about books and ideas. Tyhurst introduced Wilson to some of the reading that he was doing on psychological subjects. Tyhurst was friendly with Pierre Maranda in the anthropology department and when Claude Lévi-Strauss visited UBC, Tyhurst had him over to his house on Gabriola Island for the weekend. Tyhurst could be captivating, but there was a dark side to the man. Wilson called him "big daddy." He could be overbearing and peremptory, particularly with patients. He once insisted that Paul Spong, a Greenpeace activist who advocated freeing the whales from the Vancouver Aquarium, be admitted to the UBC psychiatric hospital and then refused to release him when he was ready to go home.[11] As a result of encounters beginning in the 1960s, in 1991 Tyhurst was convicted in the Supreme Court of British Columbia of sexual assault and holding women in bondage in his house.

Tyhurst diagnosed Wilson as suffering from depression. Certainly there were moments in Wilson's life, and they were becoming more frequent, that provided evidence for that conclusion. The trouble was that, in the early 1970s, *depression* was the all-purpose psychiatric diagnosis. Neither the exact nature of the disorder nor its treatment was precise. At that time, there was an inevitability by which psychiatry led to depression and depression led to drugs. Tyhurst prescribed a variety of drugs for Wilson. He was, on and off, taking sleeping pills and antidepressants. The antidepressants of the day produced short-term improvement, at best, at the cost of making the symptoms worse over the longer term. The medication interfered with dopamine, the mood-regulating transmitter in the brain, and over time reduced its effectiveness. The brain determines the way we act, so changes in the chemistry of the brain lead to changes in behaviour.

Along with chemical solutions, Wilson was also subject to psychoanalysis. He would have talked to Tyhurst about his fears, his dreams, his thinking and how his behaviour revealed his underlying unconscious mind.[12] Tyhurst was adamant with advice about strategies that he thought would help. Other UBC professors were also seeing Tyhurst and one of them, sociologist and Dean of Arts Kaspar Naegele, had taken his own life only a few months before Wilson came to the university. Tyhurst was by no means the only psychiatrist with a patient who committed suicide, and other faculty members who were not Tyhurst patients also killed themselves. Even so, some did wonder if Tyhurst either encouraged, or did not discourage, thoughts of suicide. One piece of advice that he certainly did give to male patients, including Kaspar Naegele, was to seek out affairs with women.[13] Wilson sought help from Tyhurst from time to time when things seemed really bad but, in the long run, he admitted that, whatever the therapy and advice, it was not working.

Family relations did not bring much stability to Wilson's life. Sometimes when he spoke to his mother about his work, he was surprised and delighted when she seemed to understand what he was getting at. But Nan Duff passed away in 1973, so, with the loss of his father thirteen years earlier, both parents were gone. The passing of parents often brings a realization of one's own mortality, for then there is no one between you and eternity. After they separated, Marion and Wilson kept in touch, particularly over their children, while they lived their separate lives. Wilson had an apartment on Balsam Street, in Kitsilano, for a few years, and then, in 1974, when Marion moved out, he returned to take over the house near the university. He was excited when he found a big old desk, which he set up in his bedroom. It made for a light moment in a letter to Marnie, as the back and the front of the desk were the same. "Beautiful bilateral symmetry... I'm a gonna to sit at both sides of that old desk at the same time, and write two books at the same time, because that old desk is really one, and those books are really about the same thing. Haven't flipped, really."[14] Having his work in the bedroom meant that, sleeping and waking, it was always there. He often had renters in the basement space. Marnie was living her own life, now with a daughter named Raven. Wilson was very proud of his granddaughter and sometimes babysat so Marnie could go out on a Friday night. Marnie and Raven lived for a short time in the basement, but it was dark and gloomy and Wilson demanded a lot of privacy, so the arrangement did not last long. Tom was growing into a young man. He sometimes lived with Wilson in the house and in the summers worked on archaeological digs, including one with Charles Borden. One summer

Wilson picked Tom up at a dig near Yale and they went on a road trip up to the Hazeltons (Old Hazelton and New Hazelton) together. Then Tom moved into his own apartment. Wilson was not really close to his brother, Ron, though they saw each other from time to time. He was perhaps closest to his older sister, Win, as she was the family member with whom he was most able to share his ideas about Indian cultures and history. She could keep up with him as he explained his most esoteric thinking. Other family members were not very interested, or even skeptical, about his commitment to understanding First Nations people.

*

His colleagues' reactions to his ideas ran the gamut. Wilson was sensitive to negative feedback and therefore limited what he told some people about what was on his mind. Kenelm Burridge, who became the head of anthropology and sociology after Cyril Belshaw, could be on Wilson's wavelength. When Wilson sent him a long memo explaining his ideas about Mr. Ambiguity, otherwise known as Frog, Burridge responded with encouragement, suggesting he publish his ideas right away. On another occasion he wrote to Wilson that there was no such thing as going too far. Another colleague, Elvi Whittaker, loved Wilson's poetry and felt privileged to have read it.[15] Wilson did not share his poems with many. He was not the first anthropologist to conceal their poetry from colleagues. Some of Boas's students did the same, hiding their poetry from their mentor. Wilson knew that several of his colleagues were much more inclined to define boundaries than was Burridge. More empirically inclined anthropologists were concerned about Wilson's creative thinking. His early mentors, Harry Hawthorn and Charles Borden, did not appreciate Wilson's new ideas. Long-time colleague Michael Kew warned him that his "insights had to be validated by a rigid system to strain out 'what exists only in Duff's head.'" For Wilson, of course, that which existed in his head was what it was all about. Kew and Wilson drifted apart, as Wilson was developing ideas that Kew did not think were going anywhere.[16] Some thought that his ideas about the Edenshaws and meaning in Northwest Coast art were just weird. Many thought he went too far.

Wilson's intense interest in Raven rattles also produced a disconcerting response from a colleague. Raven or other bird rattles were used in dances and rituals up and down the coast. The carved wooden rattles were hollow with a pebble inside that made the rattling sound when they were shaken. Wilson was thinking about the images on the rattles and what they meant. Often on the back of the Raven there would be figure lying with legs apart, with another figure, sometimes Frog, between the legs and facing it. The figures had protruding, connected tongues. Wilson saw obvious sexual meaning in the images and their placement, observing that he knew of only one reason for assuming that position. He was also intrigued with the thought that when you took hold of the rattle to shake it, the power of Raven flowed into you through your hand and you partook of his world-creating potential. Through your grasp you became one with Raven as his beak pierced the firmament and brought the light to the world. You experienced Raven's cry at the crack of dawn.

Once, at the Museum of Anthropology, he took a Raven rattle in his hand and said to Gloria Cranmer Webster, "Isn't it beautiful?" They agreed that it was beautiful. Then Wilson asked, "But how do you read this rattle?" Her response was: "Shit, Wilson, I don't read those things, I shake them." She has often retold the story, and others have related it with amusement. It has, more seriously, become part of the anthropological literature, along with academic profundities about the cultural divide between readers and shakers.[17] Even Lévi-Strauss used this little incident to make a big point, without bothering to get the facts right. Giving introductory remarks at one of the many academic conferences organized "in homage to Claude Lévi-Strauss" he began by saying that "I would not want to put wrong ideas in anybody's head." He then related a very garbled version of the exchange between Wilson and Gloria Cranmer Webster and went on to say that the lesson of the story was that communication through the art of Indigenous cultures is not possible because we cannot crack the code of messages that are not meant for us.[18] It was, on the face of it, an odd commentary from an anthropologist who spent most of his intellectual life trying to crack the codes of Indigenous cultures. For Wilson, the exchange at the Museum of Anthropology was a telling moment. Gloria Cranmer Webster was being her playful self and, when they were both younger, Wilson would have played along. In his current frame of mind, he surely found it hurtful, even if it were not intended that way. Applied generally, and particularly to Wilson, the dichotomy between readers and rattlers is a false one. The distinction between art and function is not absolute. Just because a cultural item has function does not mean that it cannot also be art. To take a non-Northwest Coast example that Wilson used: Is a medieval cathedral not a work of art because it also serves social and ritual functions? Few knew the function of things such as Raven rattles better than Wilson. But he wanted to go further and find the meaning of the carved images on the rattles. He was thinking at a different level but found that others, even old friends, were not prepared to go there with him. Even his *Arts of the Raven* colleagues had reservations about his later thinking about meaning in Haida art. Bill Holm thought that there was some basis for Wilson's ideas but that he was "stretching real hard to make more of them," and Bill Reid, in his continuing conversations with Wilson, disagreed, for example, with his overwhelming emphasis on the Edenshaws.[19]

Wilson could handle criticism, but he was rattled when he felt disdain: "My only measure of worth was the immediate approval of others." In that frame of mind, disapproval was hard to bear. He began to think that he should not reveal his more esoteric thinking to students and colleagues. He wondered if his ideas could do harm to some of his graduate students. In his senior seminar, perhaps he should unfold ideas slowly and selectively. In Anthropology 301, perhaps he should stay in a "pre-Edenshaw mode of thought" and focus on Bill Holm's much safer ideas about form and representation. The New Zealand anthropologist Hirini Moko Mead was on a short-term appointment at UBC and giving a seminar on Māori art. Wilson wanted to attend but thought that he should say little and just listen and learn.[20] Universities are supposed to be about the open exchange of ideas, but Wilson was feeling constraints closing in. He responded by being less open about his ideas and also more apt to remind people, and himself, that his thinking did not lead to certainties.

Wilson was thinking more and more about life and death. While only in his late forties, he worried about getting old. He feared the possibility of losing physical, sexual and, particularly, intellectual strength. At one point he recognized that the fear that arose from some of his dreams "was the elemental fear of death." He feared death as the end of thinking, the end of comprehension. "Does a man die when he reaches the limits of comprehension? Does the ovoid burst?" Could he fall off the knife edge, he wondered.[21] For the second time in his life, he grappled with, and overcame, his fear of death. He had diminished his dread of death when he was flying bombing missions out of India by containing his emotions. Now, in middle age, he defeated the demon by envisaging death, not as an end, but as a beginning. Death was part of the design of life. That realization was deeply connected with his thinking about the Edenshaws and Haida mythology and art. He knew about reincarnation among Northwest Coast people, especially the Haida, from studying Swanton and talking to Indigenous people over the years.[22] He had spoken about the subject with Stó:lō, Haida and Tlingit people during the course of his career. They took it for granted that there was communication with the ancestors and that individuals were reborn in the children that followed them. Wilson believed, because Haida art and mythology told him so, that life and death were two parts of the same thing. If the painting on Edenshaw's box, the Final Exam, was about Raven and the moment of creation, then it was equally about both life and death. "The paintings are not only of death, but of life struggling to re-emerge, to get back into focus...Death is life struggling to reorganize itself."[23] When the ovoid bursts it is the moment of birth from death. Or when Raven's beak pierces the sky and brings light to the world, he is bringing life out of death. Wilson's mind was full of images of rebirth.

Those ideas about reincarnation were also closely associated with his identification with Albert Edward Edenshaw. The giving of childhood names, such as Wilson receiving Albert Edward Edenshaw's early life name, is related to the idea of reincarnation.[24] For Wilson, that name was very powerful and he amplified the connection. Edenshaw was a great thinker and artist, and Wilson believed that they were in communication. "Life flowed out of him, through his hands, better organised than it flowed in." Wilson heard Edenshaw through his art, particularly the box, saying to him, like the old man in the myth who gives Raven the stones out of his box, "I am you." Wilson believed that he and Edenshaw were of one mind. "He became my hero, my teacher."[25] Wilson walked into an Anthropology 301 class one day and announced that Professor Duff was unable to make it and that Albert Edward Edenshaw would be giving the lecture in his place. The students were then treated to a discourse on Edenshaw/Duff ideas about Haida art. Some of his colleagues, on a trip to visit the Ozette archaeological site, laughed when they learned that Wilson had excused himself from the excursion because he was spending the week with "the old man" (Albert Edward Edenshaw). Had Wilson, they wondered, "gone too far this time"?[26] In fact, he had found a lifeline in his communication with Edenshaw. He described Edenshaw as becoming like a guardian spirit, adding, significantly, that in "a way he fills part of the role of father."[27] Did Wilson actually believe that he was the reincarnation of Albert Edward Edenshaw, as several have supposed? If not, it was certainly something pretty close to that.

Perhaps Wilson best expressed his collection of thoughts about Edenshaw, life and death, and life again, in his poem called "Death is a Lie." Once again, he plays on the theme of messages from the past.

> If I know
> (as I do know)
> that I have received, in this life
> a message
> sent long ago, during another life;
> a secret message,
> sent only once,
> known only to the sender:

then I know
that the message I have received
must be from myself.
And if the message says
(as it does say)
"Death is inevitable",
then I know
that message I have sent myself
must be a lie.
What is the truth
In the sending and receiving of a message
averring time, averring death,
but refuting time in the sending
and refuting death in the receiving?
I am the truth in the message.
Time is the lie.
Death is the lie.[28]

All of this thinking was heavy and weighed on Wilson's mind. There were moments of levity, though fewer as time went on, when he was frivolous about all these reflections. Since space and time are curved, he thought, if you go far enough, you will come upon yourself again. So, after a complete circuit, "you will see your own backside."[29] While he could be irreverent, mostly he was deadly serious about losing his fear of death. In his mind death became, according to the Haida saying, as effortless as a killer whale's dorsal fin slicing through the air. While he was connecting with the past and finding reassurance about the future, his messages in the present were not always working so well.

*

There was a major project in the anthropology department at UBC in which, given his experience, Wilson might have played a large role, yet he did not. When he came to UBC in 1965 he knew that for some years Harry Hawthorn had a vision of a new Museum of Anthropology on campus. If the plans came to fruition, he expected that his museum knowledge would be called upon. At first it was. Vision and hope turned into concrete planning in 1971 when Prime Minister Pierre Trudeau, as part of the centennial celebration of British Columbia's entry into Confederation, announced a federal grant of $2.5 million toward building a new Museum of Anthropology at UBC. Arthur Erickson was to be the architect, and he worked closely with the Hawthorns. They had already made some basic decisions. The new museum would be an integral part of the Department of Anthropology and Sociology, and it would be based on the idea of visible storage. That is, as much as possible of the museum's collection would open to be seen by visitors rather than hidden away in back storage rooms. As with any university building project, committees were set to work and administrators made decisions. The museum took five years of work to complete.

In the early stages, Wilson was the chair of the program committee, the position from which, in many building projects, decisions about the shape and the use of the building would be made. In this case, with Hawthorn as director of the museum, decision-making went from him up into the university administration rather than from him down to the Department of Anthropology and Sociology. When Wilson questioned Hawthorn to get clarification on the role of his committee on the matter of the naming of one of the galleries, the response was that, while he would take advice, Hawthorn was the "locus of such decisions."[30] Then, in 1974, Hawthorn stepped down as director and many in the department assumed that Wilson would take over the position. But he had already seen the writing on the wall and indicated to the program committee that he would not be a candidate for the position. He knew that Hawthorn was not going to appoint him. Instead, Michael Ames, who was not a Northwest Coast specialist but was thought to be a better administrator, became the director. Ames had been a UBC graduate student and returned as a faculty member in anthropology after a Harvard PhD. He quickly became a favoured son in the department. "A power to be reckoned with," according to Hawthorn, who knew one when he saw one.[31] Wilson tried to get clarification about the role of the program committee from Ames, but with no better success than with Hawthorn, so he stepped down as chair. Ames was a strong and dominant personality and, while others who worked with him found him to be both demanding and encouraging, Wilson and Ames rubbed each other the wrong way. Ames's assertiveness did not work with Wilson's retiring disposition and uncertainties. The clash between the two was also a symptom of—in spite of the wishes of Hawthorn and Belshaw—a growing distance between the museum and the Department of Anthropology and Sociology. Ames replaced Wilson as chair of the program with a sociologist from the department, on the grounds that it was important to get the sociologists involved in the project. It was a slap in the face for Wilson, who rightly concluded that his expertise was not going to play much part in the new museum.

That conclusion played itself out as the planning for the museum continued. Wilson brought his experience-based ideas about the role of an anthropology museum into the early discussion. The primary functions, particularly of a university museum of anthropology, should be teaching both students and the public, and research. Both aspects should involve the Indian people whose cultures were represented in the museum. When the university received the federal funding for the new museum, it set off what Wilson described as "loud and healthy debates" around the planning. In an initial communication with the planning committee, he began by expressing the wish that "the collections had voices of their own, and equal time to speak." In the absence of that voice, he wanted to say a couple of things on behalf of the Northwest Coast collections. He argued that, while the new museum was correctly spoken of as an anthropology museum housing ethnographic collections, it was important to remember that large parts of the Northwest Coast material were now considered to be fine art, thus the museum would, in part, be an art museum. This designation as fine art had important implications for the dollar value of many pieces and, more importantly, how they should be displayed.

He was particularly concerned about the ancient totem poles that he described as not just "national treasures" but as having beauty as art as well as being "expressions of humanity in cultures" that made them. "It is our responsibility to provide a suitable public repository for them, and it will not be enough to stand them in corners and stairwells, or arrayed in rows like specimens in trays."[32] During the detailed planning, within that general framework and with those thoughts in mind, he advocated for two specific areas in the new building. On one, he had some success, but on the other his views were largely ignored.

The first matter was the importance and role of archaeology in the museum. There were now two archaeology faculty in the department, though Charles Borden, arguably British Columbia's leading archaeologist, had never been given a position in the Department of Anthropology and Sociology. The archaeologists needed an archaeology laboratory in the museum if they were to assemble and analyze artifacts there. They felt that they were not getting wholehearted support from those in authority. The archaeological specimens that came from digs on reserves were also becoming a bone of contention. Indigenous people, as they were entitled to do under their own tradition and by legislation, were asserting their ownership of the material. Several Indian communities and the Union of British Columbia Indian Chiefs were part of the discussion. Cyril Belshaw, as head of department, was more supportive of archaeology than Hawthorn and asked Wilson to clarify the situation. The issue of First Nations ownership was resolved by an agreement that the archaeological material would be held at the museum in trust for the owners. Wilson supported the archaeologists' research, and the archaeology lab became an integral part of the new museum. He still harboured the hope that archaeology would "come through the long night of intensive data-gathering into the morning of interpretation."[33]

The second matter in the new museum that greatly concerned Wilson was the treatment and placement of totem poles. He had for many years been worried about the preservation of the poles, or massive sculptures as they were now called, on the UBC campus. Over the past years he had repeatedly made the point that the poles would require a great deal of conservation work before they could be put on public display. Now his added concern was that they would be further damaged by the move from storage to display in the new museum. He had not been consulted in any way about the move. Many were poles that he had painstakingly salvaged from abandoned Haida villages twenty years earlier. Wilson was vibrating with rage when he wrote to Ames about his dismay: "I am shocked, angered and very much saddened by the needless deterioration some of these old sculptures have suffered because of neglect, and by the callous treatment which they are now receiving. Some of them are literally falling to pieces." He was ashamed as a museologist, angered as a citizen and outraged as one who respects the Indian cultural heritage. "As someone who was involved in salvaging the old poles to preserve them, and in helping to design the new museum which would honour them, I am all the more disheartened." He demanded that these "national treasures be given the standard of care they deserve." He threatened to convene a meeting of representatives of the relevant Indian bands to reconsider the museum's trusteeship of the poles. He also deplored the plan to attach some of the poles to the walls of the entry hall of the museum. He wrote that the poles were being displayed in a way that served the interests of architecture rather than art: "To bolt them to the walls in their present condition would be an insult and a desecration, both to the interested public and to the cultures they represent."

Michael Kew also wrote to Ames to say that Wilson's "anger and concern are quite justified." Kew had attended many meetings about the new museum but still felt uninformed about developments. As Wilson did, he recommended that an expert in preservation be hired at the museum to ensure that the poles remained intact. Along with Wilson, he recalled the work that they had done together in the 1950s to preserve the disappearing totem poles. Now it appeared that their experience was of no value. Ames did not give Wilson the courtesy of a reply. He responded to Kew's letter with a copy to Wilson, among others. He thanked Kew for the advice but was clear that he did not agree, and he added, worthy

successor to Hawthorn that he was, that it was his job to make the decisions. To add to the insult, he had appointed Carol McLaren, one of Wilson's graduate students, to consult with both Wilson and Kew about the
poles and "to brief you on recent developments." Kew did not think that
was "fair or proper to thrust the responsibility on an inexperienced student." By means of the copy of the letter to Kew, Ames invited Wilson to
contact him "if he wishes further information about our procedures." This
high-handed treatment over the totem poles that were so dear to his heart
and mind was the last straw for Wilson. He had told Ames that, unless
something was done to correct the situation, he would no longer be able
to remain associated with the museum. Some of the Ninstints poles were,
indeed, bolted to Erickson's concrete wall like "a pinned insect specimen,"
just as Wilson had feared.[34] He had little to do with the museum after that.

*

As would a prophet without honour in his own household, Wilson sought
opportunities to offer his talents and knowledge outside the UBC campus,
where they might be more appreciated. He and Gloria Cranmer Webster
had worked with Peter Macnair at the Provincial Museum on developing
The Legacy, an exhibition that featured the work of contemporary Indian
artists. The three visited Indian communities along the coast to meet with
artists and encourage them to submit work for the exhibition. The show
opened in Victoria in 1971 and, over the years, travelled to many parts of
Canada. It was another measure of the endurance of tradition and the
revival of Northwest Coast Indian art. In the fall of 1974, there was a Bill
Reid retrospective exhibition, though his career was hardly over, at the
Vancouver Art Gallery. As things were going haywire for Wilson at the
Museum of Anthropology, he was glad for the opportunity to contribute
an exquisite and thoughtful essay to the exhibition catalogue. He began
by writing that the "thing that is least in question here is Bill Reid's stature
as an artist." He recognized that Reid had, through Totem Park at UBC
and *Arts of the Raven*, played a major role in the redefinition of the classic

style of the Edenshaws from "primitive art" to "fine art." And yet, while new melodies had developed from old rhythms, the ideas behind the old Haida art remained elusive. "Art speaks to the eye, with only silent whispers, when the eye is closed, to the farthest reaches of the mind." That is where, in the mind, doubt about the deeper meaning of the art begins. The source of the doubt was not the artists and the galleries. They have made and presented the art so that people could see its form and representation. For Wilson, the place where the doubt belonged was in the university, where intuition was lacking. Where we "have not yet learned to grant full credence to the intellect that resides in Haida art." The questions that we ask "seem capable, at best, of reaching only half of the truth that is there." Universities needed new words with which to frame new thinking about the art, to recognize that, more than "pictorial representation," it is a system of visual logic. There needs to be a bridge, Wilson thought, between the minds of the Haida artists and those that seek to understand their meanings: "Then we will still need to listen, eyes closed, for the sharper words which only Raven seems to speak."[35]

Also in the fall of 1974, the position of director of the Provincial Museum in Victoria became available. Encouraged by the anthropologists at the museum, and after a lot of thought, Wilson applied for the post, although he remained in two minds about the possibility. The advertisement for the job expressed a preference for a PhD and it was a heavily administrative position. On the other hand, Wilson saw it as an opportunity to give back to the province that had given him so much. When he was interviewed for the role, he felt that the interview committee spent a lot of time on his limited administrative experience. His application was not successful, and the job went to Yorke Edwards, an internal candidate. Wilson was very disappointed, as the move back to the Provincial Museum would have been a chance to reinvigorate his career and, perhaps, his life. He did, however, have the opportunity for another triumph in the world of museums and galleries, this time doing what he did best: creative thinking. The show was called *images stone b.c.*

*

The initial idea for the exhibition came from Richard Simmins, who was then the director of the Art Gallery of Greater Victoria. He was struck by the power and beauty of what became known as the Sechelt Image when he saw it in the Centennial Museum (now the Museum of Vancouver) in Vancouver. The image was of a seated human figure embracing in its arms what could be either a child or a large phallus. Twenty inches high and weighing seventy pounds, the large "boulder" was likely used as a male strength-testing stone.[36] Simmins was drawn by the Sechelt Image to look at other Northwest Coast stone sculpture and then to the idea of an exhibition of the art. He turned to others to work with him to develop the idea into reality. Wilson's close friend Hilary Stewart visited museums large and small throughout Canada and the United States to catalogue and photograph all the stone sculptures from British Columbia that she could find. She developed an expertise in the making and the function of the artifacts. Based on her work, 136 "images" were selected for the exhibition according to the criteria that each one should be a singular and striking sculpture. Wilson was the academic and artistic leader on the selection of pieces and the setup of the exhibition, but his most enduring legacy was his thinking and writing. He had published on stone sculpture, in a very descriptive way, early in his time at the Provincial Museum.[37] *Images stone b.c.* showed how his thinking about Northwest Coast art had since evolved by light years rather than just a couple of decades. The text that he wrote for the exhibition catalogue is a classic piece of late-style Wilson Duff.

He began with this sentence: "Images seem to speak to the eye, but they are really addressed to the mind."[38] The images in the exhibition were grouped according to their meaning. There were images of strength, like the Sechelt Image; fonts of life that were life-form bowls and seated human–figure bowls; images of power like hammers, pile drivers, slave killers and clubs; paint dishes were classified as vessels of thought. Then there were pieces that could not be classified at all, like the little abstract "whatsit" that was pure form and "resists all specific suggestions as to use and image."[39] Most of the items were found through archaeological work. At one level, Wilson wanted his account of the images to "invite humanity back into archaeology: flesh, blood, fear, love, contemplation."[40]

But what did these images mean and what did they signify? He was clear that there was no way of knowing for sure and that surmises were the best that he could do. But, of course, he had some definite ideas. The *b.c.* in *images stone b.c.* stood for place, British Columbia, and time, before Christ. It was another affirmation that the Indigenous people of British Columbia had lived on the land for thousands of years. The second image in the show was the oldest: a tiny animal form image that was worn from thirty centuries of use. Stone art is unusual on the Northwest Coast, where most is made from wood. Even the medium had its message. Stone is the substance of eternity. In many cultures, statues and gravestones preserve the memory of those who have passed. "To select stone," Wilson thought, "was to deny time and reject death." Beings turned into stone live forever. For the artists who created the images, "the surest denial of death seems to have been in the celebration of the origins of life." Hence there are many images of sex, birth and death, and the ambiguities between them. Item 105 in the exhibition was a stone club collected in Hagwilget, on the Bulkley River near where it joins the Skeena, and now on display in the National Museum of the American Indian in New York. The blade is shaped like a Roman sword and is a death bringer or a life preserver, depending on whose hand grasps the handle. At the top of the handle is an enigmatic image of a human head that could either be a baby or an old man: an image of either birth or death.[41]

Wilson was increasingly interested in sexual imagery and meaning in Northwest Coast Indian art. In his earlier thinking about Haida art he believed that sexuality was usually not explicit because it was a taboo subject. So, when it was there, it was there by analogy and metaphor. Perhaps because the portrayal was not explicit, perception of sexual meaning was not common among those who wrote about Northwest Coast Indian art in Wilson's day. In the wider anthropological world, however, it was not unusual to see taboo subjects in the appreciation of Indigenous art. Wilson read, for example, Edmund Leach on the subject and made notes on his work. Leach argued that many, some would say most, artists deal with taboo subjects, though the question remains to what extent artistic thought can be appreciated across cultural boundaries. Can clearly expressed messages, let alone hidden ones, in the art of one culture be heard in another culture, and, if so, how?[42] Certainly Wilson believed that, by getting past simple seeing and into the realm of thinking and intuition, clearer listening and understanding were possible. He talked about the sexual imagery in more detail in the talks that he gave associated with the exhibition than he did in the publication. He was still thinking it through. In *images stone b.c.* he was assisted by the fact that several pieces had quite explicit sexual meaning, while with others it was possible to interpret the form in sexual terms even when it was not explicit. Thus Wilson described many of the pestles, mauls and clubs as *phalliform* and dishes and bowls as *vulviform*. Most of the images in the exhibition had their origins in a function, though some had evolved to the point where form had taken over function. Clearly the function of a pestle and mortar has sexual connotations. One could not argue that the form of some of the mauls and clubs wasn't phallic. Wilson took sexual interpretations of the images from those that were obvious into those that were more ambiguous.

The Sechelt Image was the number-one piece in the exhibition, and the culmination was numbers 135 and 136, two stone masks. The two Tsimshian masks were already known to be similar to anthropologists. One had been collected at Kitkatla and was now in the National Museum of Canada in Ottawa. The second was from either the Nass River or Metlakatla and was now in the Musée de l'Homme in Paris. The one at the National Museum was easy enough to secure for the exhibition. The one in Paris was more of a challenge, as the museum was reluctant to lend its treasure. Simmins, after considerable negotiation, got an agreement to borrow the mask if it were highly insured, and Wilson flew to Paris to collect it. During his short time in Paris, he had dinner with Lévi-Strauss before he flew back to Canada with the mask in a box on the seat beside him. He brought the box to his house, and a group of people watched as it was opened. It was a thrilling moment for Wilson. Hilary Stewart then took the mask to Victoria, where it was brought together with the similar mask from Ottawa. The joining of the two masks was a revelation. They were made to fit together and be worn at the same time. Wilson rushed over to Victoria to see the stunning discovery. He and Hilary were like a couple of kids. It was so exciting for Wilson: the high point of the whole *images stone b.c.* experience. Just as the Final Exam, Edenshaw's 4 × 4, was the culmination of *Arts of the Raven*, the twin stone masks were the capstone of *images stone b.c.* "The culminating image of thirty years of stone sculpture." Wilson even wondered if Albert Edward Edenshaw had made them.[43]

He called the two masks an "image of recognition." Both masks had a hint of the enigmatic smile of Frog. On other images there was Frog with a mouth that was so big it could eat itself. It seemed to Wilson that Frog could pass from life to life with no need for death. Frog was a "symbol of life pure and simple." One mask, to be held in front of the other, had its eyes closed, while the one behind had its eyes open. Perhaps "worn" in a sacred winter ritual, they could be switched "in the blink of an eye, to demonstrate the kind of power that logic alone finds incredible." Because they were made of stone, one has eyes that never open and the other eyes that can never close. One is about inward vision, the other about out- ward vision. They are about "sight and memory, seeing and imagining." One sees itself, the other sees the world. They are "two sides of a single profound equation": two things the same, but opposite at the same time. Wilson connected the thought that nothing comes only in halves with the creation story on Edenshaw's 4 × 4. In the end, he concluded that because sight and memory come together in recognition, the stone mask image was "really about the glint of recognition which is the purest pulse of life." For Wilson, another recognition that came out of the cumulative collection of images was that: "To the existing proof of the prior claim and Indian presence in Canada may be added, however poorly understood, this evidence of thirty centuries of hard thinking."[44]

The stone images exhibition opened in Victoria in March 1975 and travelled to Vancouver and three other Canadian cities. Bill Reid, returning the favour that Wilson had done for his exhibition, spoke at the opening of the show. In the past, Reid had written and spoken about the demise of Northwest Coast Indian art and culture, but now he said that *images stone b.c.* showed that that art had too much power to fade away, that the powerful old images were too strong to die. Robert Davidson spoke at the opening in Vancouver. He said that the art of those that went before him "encourages me to keep high standards in my own work." He was excited by Wilson's interpretations and admired his "ability to analyse and to share his ideas." Underneath the surface, he concluded, "there's a deeper meaning if you're willing to be open minded."[45] Wilson gave lectures in some of the cities where the show appeared and he elaborated on his sexual interpretations of many of the images. With a slide of a plainly phallic maul or club up on the screen, he would say to the audience, "You do not have to see sexual symbolism if you don't want to, but I do." When George MacDonald introduced Wilson at the National Museum, he noted that he had to revise his ideas about Northwest Coast art as a result of reading the *images stone b.c.* catalogue. He believed that the discipline of anthropology was now more open to ideas like Wilson's, referring, for example, to Carlos Castaneda's allegorical book on *The Teachings of Don Juan* and to Lévi-Strauss.[46]

Alas, MacDonald was only partially correct. The show and Wilson's ideas did receive positive responses from some. The director of the National Museum wrote to Wilson that his lecture "was just about perfect." Many of the written reviews in newspapers and magazines were positive, while other writers were perplexed. His colleague in anthropology at UBC, Robin Ridington, thought that the show was "amazing and brilliant." Roy Henry Vickers said that *images stone b.c.* was one of the most important publications that he had read. Even from afar, at the University of Sydney, Australia, a professor wrote that he was very impressed with Wilson's ideas and wanted to incorporate them into his lectures.[47] Others, quite decidedly, could not follow Wilson along his lines of thought. Visitors to the show were sometimes overheard making flippant and dismissive remarks about the images and the interpretation of them. Wilson took negative comments from colleagues much more seriously. Some expressed light-hearted amusement. When the Simon Fraser University archaeologist Roy Carlson heard that a documentary was being made of the exhibition, he wrote to Wilson: "I sincerely hope you can keep the film from being x-rated." Bill Reid was deeply moved by the art, but was not convinced by Wilson's interpretations of the images. For some anthropology colleagues it was all too speculative. When they said that Wilson was reaching beyond logic, they were correct—the problem, for them, was that he was going too far. Wilson perceived Michael Kew's response as being "Nah! Couldn't be…It violates the difference between one and two. It violates ordinary logic."[48] And Kew was not alone in that view. Naturally Wilson enjoyed the positive responses, and he understood when colleagues had straightforward disagreements with this thinking. Disagreement can be based on understanding, and Wilson wanted his ideas to be understood. At the same time, he was devastated by derision.

A downswing often follows the high of a major and successful project after it is over. *Images stone b.c.* was an exciting time for Wilson. He felt like he was making a contribution. People were seeing the images and think-ing about them. They were listening to his ideas even if they did not always agree with them. "The trouble with being high on inspiration," however, "is that it all seems so flat when you come down."[49] When it was over, Wilson crashed. It was like a belly landing in an aircraft with no under-carriage: survivable, but terrifying. With little that was positive to block them, his fears flowed in on him again.

*

He still did not find much peace in his private life. Though he continued to search, he could not find a relationship that worked. His love affairs were usually with younger women, often graduate students. They some-times called him *chinai*, the Haida word for grandfather, recognizing that he was the elder in both in years and insight. Their mutual enthusiasm for Northwest Coast cultures was the initial bond that led to romantic interest. Wilson wanted to believe that sleeping with someone was not just about sex, rather more about trust. Yet he could not attain that trust. Not surprisingly, there were two sides to the stories. In moments of frustration and disappointment, he would blame the other person. He once wrote of his latest girlfriend: "You are a pussy cat that is a puppy dog. Emotionally promiscuous." But when he looked at himself, which was most of the time, he could clearly see that he was the impediment: "I am giving you my eye, but not my heart," as he put it. He never found what he was looking for because he could not give enough of himself to make a romantic relationship work. His hopes ran along the lines of the songs that he listened to about love and need. The reality was, as he bounced from extremes of calm to frantic, that "Duff's song is equal parts lullaby and tarantella."[50] And, even more disturbing, Wilson was increasingly likening losing in love to death.

His most satisfying connections with women were with two to whom he related, one entirely and the other mostly, by letter. Both were intellectual relationships without the complications of romantic and sexual entanglement. Lilo Berliner was a reference librarian at the University of Victoria when she struck up a conversation with Wilson through the mail. Collyne Bunn was a student who got to know Wilson through taking one of his classes.

Lilo Berliner was a friend of Beth Hill, with whom she shared an intense interest in petroglyphs. She was prompted to write to Wilson after she read Beth Hill's copy of Wilson's essay "Levels of Meaning in Haida Art." After a couple of letters back and forth, they clicked and continued to exchange insights and intuitions. Lilo was a wide and eclectic reader in anthropology and philosophy. She sent Wilson suggestions of books to read, and he shared some more of his thinking with her. After Wilson had written her a few letters about his ideas on meaning Haida art, she responded that it "is as if you had given me a new pair of glasses" to see the art. She was thrilled when she received a copy of "Nothing Comes

Only in Pieces" and very excited about *images stone b.c.* Though she could not make the Victoria opening, she visited the show several times. After she read Wilson's catalogue, she wrote to him: "I do not understand how you could have written anything so beautiful." They also wrote about personal things. Wilson told Lilo about the joy that he was getting from his meeting of minds with Collyne. Lilo, though she felt like she might be breaking a taboo, wrote of her feelings when her best friend died of cancer. Her friend was full of ideas, wrote a lot, and tore most of it up. He was, by most measures of the world, a failure and had made three suicide attempts. "He must have been," Lilo concluded in the letter to Wilson, "your exact opposite."[51] Wilson and Lilo both believed in reincarnation. They shared many things, but they never met.

In the spring semester of 1974, Collyne Bunn, who is part First Nations from the Yukon, was uncomfortable living in the big city and bored with her program in education when she crossed the campus to take in Wilson's course, Anthropology 301. His thinking was a revelation to her. She responded to a written exercise in the class with a poem, and they connected. Wilson saw that she was very bright, "the only student to whom I have ever given the grade 150/150." Collyne worked as a research assistant in Wilson's faculty office and, when the semester was over, they spent time writing poetry. As Collyne's poetry blossomed, Wilson thought that it "was the nicest thing that has happened in my teaching career." When they were together they enjoyed the fun of playing with ideas, and Collyne understood his insights better than anyone. Then she went to Haida Gwaii for a while before she returned to the Yukon as a teacher. Wilson admired and respected that she loved the old traditional ways. She talked and wrote about concepts that he wanted to understand. The wisdom, for example, held in the belief that there is a living spirit in everything. People, animals, plants and even inanimate substances such as lakes, rocks, and mountains are all sentient beings in a universe of life, recognizing each other in each other. Collyne was reluctant to talk about it too much because she was worried about how deeply Wilson was dwelling on it. As she wrote,

It's not supposed to be.
We see, we hear, we feel,
We know,
We don't need that talking.[52]

Collyne was very perceptive. Wilson was dwelling on these ideas and wanted to know more. His reading prompted his thinking. Alan Watts, in *The Book*, downplays the role of the ego in favour of the idea of a connected universe of which each individual is a part. Because the universe continues, so does the individual. Or, as Wilson put it in one letter: "In some sense, each thing is the 'other half' of each other thing, and of all things." He also read Mircea Eliade, *The Myth of the Eternal Return*, who looks at new year and spring ceremonies that regenerate time and celebrate cosmic cycles, and considers how life can be recreated through repetition rather than historical linear time. In another letter to Collyne, he noted that when "the Kwakiutl refer to spirits and powers which we would call the supernatural, they say they are 'on the other side'...How do I visualise or conceptualize the other side?" he asked. It got to a point where Collyne would not go further on that subject. Still, she and Wilson stayed connected through the mail. He wrote letters about his work, his thinking and his love affairs. When *images stone b.c.* was nominated for a British Columbia book award, Wilson attended a reception for authors. He wrote to Collyne, "I'll let you know what authors look like."[53] They also exchanged poems, and Wilson amended hers and encouraged her by writing an introduction to a potential publication of her poetry. For Wilson, at a stage in his life when much was unsettling, it was reassuring to have someone who thought deeply on his wavelength.

Wilson and Lilo could have quite readily have met face to face. He was often in Victoria and she in Vancouver. But it seems that they preferred not to. They simply enjoyed the correspondence of ideas. Collyne and Wilson spent a short time together at UBC and then mostly shared their thoughts by letter. As a young man, Wilson had told his mother, when he was writing letters to her from India, that he shared more of himself with her by letter than when they were living in the same house. Now he was sharing his thinking, pieces of his private life as lovers came and went, and even some of his feelings, in letters to women who, by return letter, gave him the support and validation that had become so elusive.

*

Teaching was becoming increasingly stressful. Wilson was finding it more difficult to stand in front of a lecture theatre and a large crowd of students. He had to build himself up in the privacy of his office and then make the mental transition to lecture as he walked across campus to the Buchanan Building. He had a sabbatical leave during the 1974–75 academic year when he was working on *images stone b.c.*, then he struggled with returning to teaching in the fall of 1975. Over Christmas that year he was physically ill and mentally exhausted, and he missed several classes at the beginning of the new year's semester. His teaching assistant took the classes in his place. Collyne visited him over that Christmas break and thought that he seemed fragile and jaded. Teaching had become stale and he was fearful of audiences. He was not looking forward to going back to the classroom.

Even worse was his inability to write, at least as much as he wanted to, for publication. He was still thinking and writing furiously on his yellow pads. His ideas were now more often swirling in circles than following connected lines of thought. When it came to publication, he was busy with minor, if important, things, but not getting the major things done. He completed a few short, straightforward pieces for publication. He wrote an entry for the subarctic volume of the *Handbook of North American Indians* on the Tsetsaut, an Athapaskan-speaking group who had lived around the headwaters of the Nass River but were by then believed to be absorbed into surrounding groups. He also wrote two short biographies of Haida leaders in the early contact period for *The Dictionary of Canadian Biography*. But he had begged off writing some of the other articles that he had been assigned for the *Handbook of North American Indians, Volume 7: Northwest Coast*. He suggested that his colleague and PhD student

Marjorie Halpin be asked to write on the Tsimshian.[54] Wilson was much more engrossed in getting his thinking about Northwest Coast Indian art into print, but his anxieties were blocking his writing. Part of the problem was that he had too many writing projects in mind. He was planning books on meaning in Haida art, to be written with Bill Reid, on the Edenshaws and on argillite carving. Another challenge was that he was so deep into the complexities of his thinking, particularly about Haida art, that he could not bring his ideas up to the surface. He also worried that he lacked the expressive power to explain his thinking in a way that others could follow. And then he was disheartened and dismayed by the negative reaction to *images stone b.c.*

Wilson tried twice more to lay bare his ideas, particularly about sexual meaning in Northwest Coast Indian art, before his colleagues. The first attempt was at an academic conference in Victoria, and he tried again at a conference on Northwest Coast studies at Simon Fraser University in May 1976. The Simon Fraser conference was a gathering of many of the leading names in anthropology of the Northwest Coast: that is to say, Wilson's colleagues. Bill Holm and Wayne Suttles gave papers in the same session as Wilson. He dedicated his paper to his teachers from graduate school, Erna Gunther and Viola Garfield. The talk was anchored in a reference to Boas "who once said that it was essential to bear in mind the twofold source of artistic effect. The one based on form alone and the other on ideas associated with form." Wilson added that he thought that what Boas meant by "ideas associated with form" was what he meant by meaning.

At the same time, the acknowledgement of tradition, in the dedication to his mentors and the reference to Boas, served to highlight how far his thinking had come since he was a student. His presentation was entitled "The World Is as Sharp as a Knife: Meaning in Northern Northwest Coast Art" and was a summary of his thinking on the subject as best as he could explain it. It was delivered with a calm clarity that masked an inner insecurity.[55] He began and ended by reiterating his point that the understanding of meaning had lagged behind the understanding of form and, through the presentation, he elaborated his ideas about sexual imagery in the art. His last sentence confirmed his belief that "Northwest Coast Images have deep meanings, deep structures and some of them, deep time depth." There was an appreciative round of applause when he finished, but in the informal conversations that followed, he got the same range of reactions as he had to *images stone b.c.* Some thought that it was the most innovative and exciting paper at the conference, while others were sniggering behind their hands. The paper was later published in a volume edited by Roy Carlson on Northwest Coast art.[56] At the time, Wilson was gratified by those who tried to understand and enjoy his ideas. But he was becoming ever more sensitive to negative feedback. He was visibly upset after presenting that paper to his peers. Nearly thirty years earlier, Wilson had glided into anthropology, not so much like a duck as a swan. This was his swan song.

Two weeks later, across town on the UBC campus, the new Museum of Anthropology was opened. Once opened, the museum was by most standards a great success. It was a spectacular building that housed a stunning collection. It was innovative, particularly with the visible storage of almost the entire collection. It would soon attract large numbers of visitors and become a centre for research. Wilson received an official invitation and attended the opening with Marnie. It should have been an exciting event among friends and colleagues, but Wilson was very detached. He had a dream about refusing to take any role in the opening, much to Ames's displeasure. The museum director gave a speech at the opening based on his own written history of the museum, making no mention of Wilson as he thanked all and sundry who had been involved in the project.[57] Wilson had hoped that he would get an office in the new building, but that did not happen either as the slights continued.

The first visiting exhibition to come to the new Museum of Anthropology after it opened was *The Legacy*, from the Provincial Museum. Gloria Cranmer Webster spoke at the opening. Of the two besides herself who developed the exhibition, she gave full credit to Peter Macnair but did not mention Wilson. She compared *The Legacy* with *Arts of the Raven*.

She was very proud of *The Legacy* because it was "a completely North-west Coast Collection." Unlike *Arts of the Raven*, there were "no works by latter-day Kwagiutl or white people with Cherokee grandmothers who claim some sort of right to produce Northwest Coast-style art." It was a reference to Bill Holm and Don Lelooska Smith, who had pieces in the contemporary works gallery of *Arts of the Raven*, alongside the art of her brother, Douglas Cranmer. She went on to say that she actually objected to the label "Northwest Coast Indian art" because, prior to newcomer contact, the Indians did not produce art. They simply made objects to be used. Wilson conveyed his excitement about *The Legacy* show to his students and, with a greater generosity, shared his admiration for Douglas Cranmer's origin-myth screen as the most original and important piece in the exhibition.[58]

A few days after the new Museum of Anthropology opened, Ames did ask Wilson's advice on the value of a collection that he was consid-ering for acquisition by the museum. As a museum practitioner, Wilson had always been reluctant to put a monetary value on artifacts, because it brought the museum into the commercial art market and also tended to increase the value of items. He had taken that position again at a meet-ing of the Archaeological Sites Advisory Board just two months earlier. Wilson was not prepared to give Ames an evaluation, and Ames took it personally. Ames wrote to Marjorie Halpin about the conversation with Wilson: "Strange, strange conversation. He is crawling back in his shell, and it gives me the creeps."[59] There is no suggestion that Ames did any-thing to help Wilson, but perhaps he thought Halpin would provide him some support, as they were closer friends.

Unfortunately, there were accumulating signs that Wilson was also withdrawing from contact with friends. On the occasion of his fiftieth birthday, in March 1975, Marjorie Halpin hosted a party for him at her apartment and many of his friends were there. Wilson brought over one of the masks that he had carved and, after a few drinks, they all put it on in front of a big floor-to-ceiling mirror and experienced the incredible sense of transformation. They were looking at themselves, but themselves transformed. Bill Reid presented Wilson with a medallion that he had crafted with a human figure with an eagle-like nose on the front and, on the back, two large ovoids with the inscription "Wilson Survivor First Class." Bill and Wilson remained close friends, and, as Marion later observed, they had a thing between them about which one might outlive the other.[60] It was a wonderful evening.

Convivial social occasions became rarer for Wilson as he withdrew into himself and away from others. He told Kenelm Burridge that he was fearful of audiences, "even audiences of one, making communication difficult."[61] Friends fell by the wayside as he disengaged with people around him. His former bomber crewmate Art Skirrow visited Wilson at UBC to talk to him about a possible reunion, but Wilson had no interest in that prospect. A few weeks after the opening of the Museum of Anthropology, Harry and Audrey Hawthorn left UBC and began the first phase of their retirement in Kumeu, New Zealand. At that stage Wilson would not have confided in them about his deep state of mind, even though both had been strong supporters earlier in his career.

Martine Reid (then de Widerspach-Thor) was living in the basement of Wilson's house for the 1975–76 academic year. She recalls his desire for solitude and sensed that there was an inner tension within him. She thought that Wilson was very lonely. They sometimes did things together. Once Wilson drove Martine out to the family cottage at Point Roberts, which was still a place of refuge and some peace for Wilson. Louise Jilek-Aall was walking along the road through Tsawwassen as Wilson drove by, and they stopped for a chat. She thought that the look on Wilson's face said, "Help me," and she was very concerned about him. They did not talk for long, so she did not get beyond that initial impression. During the first half of 1976, others noticed that Wilson was different. He went to a show with his sister, Win, and her daughter, and they noticed that something seemed really wrong with him. He was perspiring and anxious and there was a tremor in his hands. He just seemed very upset. He was seeing Tyhurst again, but neither the therapy nor the antidepressants were helping. He was distracted and disengaged, and he knew that he was pushing people away. Some commented that his luminous blue eyes had lost their lustre. A friend sent him a card transcribed with the words of Bob Dylan's "A Hard Rain's a-Gonna Fall," a song of lost innocence and many ominous portents. She called it "a symbol of the beginning of our understanding."[62] The last verse of "Hard Rain" suggests that there is salvation for the singer through his song, but there were no redemption songs for Wilson. The world was dark and he felt that his life was of little value. He once wrote to himself, on his own at midnight, "my life right now? Leave of absence?"[63]

There were some moments when Wilson found some peace. Marnie had a boyfriend who attended Christ Church Cathedral, and in June 1976 they decided to have her daughter, Raven, christened there. Wilson and Marion attended, along with Win and her husband, Bill. Wilson suggested that he and Marion sit together. It was an important moment for Marnie. She remembers Wilson coming downstairs for coffee wearing a blue sweater and with bright blue eyes. He was looking good. Wilson, Marion, Win and Bill went out to Point Roberts that Sunday afternoon, sat in the sun, drank beer and had supper together. As the evening air got chilly, Wilson gave Marion his sweater. They were relaxed in each other's company, and Wilson said that he had felt the presence of his mother during the church service.[64]

Over the next few weeks, others observed that another change had come over Wilson. There was a calm about him that they had not seen for several months. He was, at that stage, capable of clear and precise thought about things from the past. On August 6 he responded to a request from Peter Macnair about the circumstances of the acquisition of the fifth of the Kitwancool totem poles in 1962. He clearly described how the pole was lying on the ground, who the owners were, and the detail of the purchase arrangements.[65] His mind was lucid and his memory explicit. He seemed more at peace, as if he were no longer struggling. He had found a solution to all that was troubling him.

On the evening of August 8, 1976, Wilson, as he often did, went for a walk on Kitsilano Beach. He ran into Marnie's boyfriend, who was working as a lifeguard, and stopped to chat for a few moments. In the fading light of the summer night, he drove in his beloved BMW up to UBC. He parked and went into his office in the Ponderosa Building. He spent some time at his desk writing letters and sorting papers into neat piles. He was wearing Bill Reid's medallion that designated him a survivor. By the eleventh hour the navigator had plotted his course. It was the eighth day of the eighth month or, to think of it another way, it was 4 × 4, Edenshaw's moment of creation. He called campus security and asked them to come over to his office. He then put the barrel of a loaded .22 rifle in his mouth and pulled the trigger. It was Raven's cry at the crack of dawn, as he burst through the darkness into the light.

10. Coming Back

On a housetop in Masset a raven ruffled up its feathers and made a clamour, as ravens do when someone of note passes. A visitor to Masset, thinking that they were bearing news, informed some of the people of Wilson's death. The people replied that they already knew that. The raven had told them.[1] Wilson Duff had passed over, yet he remained in many ways. He did not grow old as we grow old. Gwaaygu7anhlan's head was still resting on the island.

Halfway across the continent from Masset, in a small town in Iowa, Wilson's colleague in anthropology Jay Powell was staying in his father's apartment. His father had recently passed away. He woke at 2:30 in the morning and was compelled to sit in front of his father's old typewriter and type a letter of thanks to Wilson, who had been very supportive and helpful as he was beginning his career at UBC. Having written the letter, at 3:30 a.m., something prompted him to put on his bathrobe and slippers and go down to the main street just below the apartment to put the letter in the mail. Later that morning there was a call from a graduate student at UBC to say that Wilson had taken his life. Powell is convinced that Wilson passed by on his way out that evening. He had heard such legendary stories when working in the field, and knew others who had. In the past he had discounted them. Now "I live with that one," he said.[2]

That same Monday morning, in North Vancouver, there was a loud knocking on the door of the apartment where Marion and Marnie were living. Wilson's sister, Win, was there with the police. After they all sat down, Win told them that Wilson had been found dead in his office at UBC. Marion was surprised and shattered by the news, and Marnie remembers her father's passing as the worst thing that ever happened to her. Win and Marnie went over to Wilson's house near UBC to see if he had left any notes or instructions and to begin the process of trying to understand.

Bill Reid's panels that reproduced the four sides of the Final Exam were in his bedroom, where he worked, and one desk drawer contained many bottles of prescription drugs.[3] When suicide is the last act of an organized person, it is likely to be very well organized, and this was certainly true in Wilson's case. On his desk at home and in his UBC office he left letters to many people. At the top of the pile at the house was a note to Win about the disposition of some of his effects. He also left a long list of people to call. It was perhaps a lot to ask of a grieving family and not all the calls were made. Wilson had left all his financial affairs in order, and Marion was the beneficiary in a will that he had made in 1951 and never changed. Such details were no distraction from the shock waves that went through friends, colleagues and, particularly, family.

For most, when they heard the news of Wilson's passing, the immediate reaction was surprise and dismay. Very few had any inkling that Wilson might take his own life. Win later said that she was not entirely surprised. Kenelm Burridge, head of the department of anthropology, and Michael Ames, director of the Museum of Anthropology, both wrote to the Hawthorns in New Zealand to convey the tragic news. Audrey Hawthorn replied that she had "feared it would happen" as Wilson had become "more unreachable to human touch." Every time she congratulated him on his latest success, he would respond, in all seriousness: "But what can I do for an encore?"[4] With few exceptions, people who knew him, or thought that they knew him, were caught completely off guard by his suicide. It seemed to be a totally incomprehensible act. They could not believe it.

As they tried to fathom the unfathomable, many wanted to take some responsibility. What could they have done to help Wilson, to prevent such a terrible act? Suicide is usually an individual decision made by someone consumed by their own perception of their situation. An unwarranted feeling of guilt in those around the departed one is also very common. Though Wilson was probably unreachable, many now wondered how they could have reached out to him. None more poignantly than a close friend from the north who wrote a poem simply called "Chinai."

If I had known,
just known
your thoughts,
the loneliness, wishes, loss and ache,
I would have flown outside
and captured you.
Taken you away
from all universities,
research, the writing you found so hard.
I would have stolen you away from all your thinking.
I would have stolen all you
all that was Everything
You.
And I, Black Raven's Mother, could have done just that....
Wilson,
somehow
your pieces of Nothing
your pieces of Everything
got lost
but they were flying around
and
I, Black Crow Mother,
know we could have caught them,
gathered them into Life.[5]

While some wanted to take on responsibility, others were simply angry with Wilson for what they thought was a selfish act. Anger is also a common emotion in reaction to suicide. It is part of the "How could they?" response. And there is a real sense in which suicide is the act of someone who is absorbed with their own perceived shortcomings. Wayne Suttles took time to come to terms with Wilson's death, as he was angry and frustrated. "Such a needless waste of a good mind and a good human being."[6] Part of his response, as with others, was sadness and exasperation because of the knowledge that Wilson took with him when he departed—the insights that he would have revealed if he had remained. It took time for some people to remember all the knowledge and insights that he left behind.

*

Amidst all these different emotions, the question that most people asked was: Why? Suicide is such an individual act, often with so many layers of causes, that perhaps we never really know why. Suicide eventuates from a person's private life, and insights into a private life will always be limited. Certainly there is scarcely a measure of grace to be found in the literature on the subject. Interpretations of the act are many and various, but some are consistent. Suicide is much more common than we realize, it requires courage and, for the one departing, it is a rational response to an intolerable situation. Suicide is not often an impulsive act in the moment, but usually the outcome of factors that have built up over a long time. They often go back to early childhood. Men who commit suicide are often closer to their mother and have difficulties with their father, particularly if that father was the source of discipline in the family. For returning servicemen, emotions, or the shutting down of emotions, arising from combat in war is often a factor in the long buildup to suicide.

When Marnie went into Wilson's house after he died, she found, on a footstool in the downstairs den where Wilson often sat and read, a book called *The Male Climacteric*, written by two British Columbia authors, about the male mid-life crisis. Tyhurst had likely recommended it. The book described many of Wilson's symptoms and acknowledged that they sometimes led to suicide.[7] Suicides are more common among men; one statistical study shows that fifty-one, Wilson's age, is the average age at which men take their own lives.[8] Men are also much more likely to use a firearm, because it is the most effective method. "Completers," as they are called in the literature, intend the act to be final. Wilson was not attempting suicide as a way to send a cry for help; he intended it to be conclusive.

The lack of a fulfilling, stable relationship and being disconnected from social contacts and networks are also factors. Indeed, many who take their own lives feel that they are a burden to others who will be better off without them. There is a consensus in the literature that the chemical solutions sought in the drugs of the 1970s would not prevent, and likely enhanced, the possibility of suicide. The locus of suicide is in the social circumstances and the psyche of the individual rather than the chemistry of the brain. Losing the fear of death is a significant, often close-to-final step down the path to leaving by one's own hand. Generalizations about suicide provide some insights, but they only begin to explain an individual case.

Perhaps, after all, we should be satisfied with Wilson's own explanations. Just before he died, he wrote letters to a number of people, including family, friends and colleagues, usually to say that he was sorry for the hurt that he would cause. In many of those letters he absolved the other person of any responsibility, writing that he, and only he, was responsible. He gave the most detailed explanation in a letter written for Kenelm Burridge, dated August 8 (1976). The problem, he wrote, was his "own neurotic personality" that led to "chronic depression, anxiety, apprehensiveness." He noted that the side effects of the drugs he had been taking were bad and Tyhurst could explain the reasons for that. In another letter, he wrote that he thought that Tyhurst had done his best, but to no avail.[9] Wilson continued that his "personality has loused up my personal life" so he was "becoming more and more self-isolated." He was alone and lonely and could not find pleasure in anything: either serious thinking or mundane interests. "I am out of step with the times...I feel hollow. I am not what I am supposed to be." He believed that the insights that he was developing into Northwest Coast Indigenous art were real, but he was unable to get them into written, publishable form. Writing to the head of his department, he concluded that, "The worst thing is my inability to write." There is sad irony in the fact that Burridge, who was in Europe at the time, never received the letter in which Wilson explains so much.[10] Beyond all these explanations, Wilson, as might be expected, had another, much deeper level of belief that he did not convey to any of his colleagues, not even Burridge, though he would have been the most likely among them to understand. At this point, we should draw a lesson from the twin masks. We can look outward for the observable reasons for suicide, while the inward-looking mask tells us that death is not the end of life.

With the weight of their world upon them, many who choose to end their life believe that death will take them to a better place. For Wilson it was more than that. In the end, he did not fear death, because "the end is the beginning." He believed in reincarnation: that he would be coming back. Death was simply a door through which one passed to another life. He learned this "profound certainty" from the Haida. The belief that death is a threshold that you cross to reach a better life is a basic tenet of world religions such as Christianity and Islam, and yet we still have difficulty with the notion of reincarnation. Wilson attributed to the Haida philosopher-poet John Sky (or Skaay) the thought that "the white man" is afraid of death because of ideas about the agony of the crucifixion and the possibility of hell. "They don't seem to realise that life and death is the same thing, and when I die it isn't the end. I'll be back soon. There is no eternal hell fire, no eternal heaven, just temporary resting places before coming back." Wilson believed that reincarnation was about life because, in life, "you are a reincarnation" already.[11] He took great comfort from this knowledge in his last years, when he found little contentment elsewhere.

Wilson wished for a small, private celebration of life, involving family only, after his passing. His colleagues at UBC held a memorial service for him at the Museum of Anthropology at the end of August, before the start of a new academic year. There was some irony in remembering Wilson in the museum that had not been a particularly happy place for him toward the end. But, as usual, Burridge, the head of Anthropology, was tuned in to Wilson. He had found, pinned to the wall in Wilson's office, a note from Collyne about the people who have passed being part of everything. There were intimations of immortality in what Burridge had to say. The tradition in his culture, he said, was "the death of one in the community diminishes all… And death wins. Unless, that is, its pain and our diminution are transformed into, equated with and recognized as also birth pangs." He urged his colleagues to "recognize Wilson recognizing us. We can pursue the truth of things where he left off." He must have known that Wilson believed that "I am you. We exist only in our recognition of each other."[12] Such thoughts were immediate. In the longer term, people came to terms with Wilson's passing in different ways.

*

Wilson once wrote, in a poem called "The Mask in the Mirror,"

> That lonely man of art, the poet,
> keeps tossing his pebbles shaped of metaphor
> into the pond of analogy,
> delighting in the perfect circles he has caused to form,
> then closing his eyes to watch the ripples spread
> all the way across, and back.
> It is the restless lapping on the banks
> That feels so good,
> So...
> absolute.[13]

These lines of poetry were a premonition, for in the ripples that he made, Wilson drew people to him in death as in life.

In January 1977 Lilo Berliner was staying in a cottage on the grounds of Beth and Ray Hill's house on the shore of Ganges Harbour, on Salt Spring Island. Along the beach from the cottage, past the shell midden on a rocky promontory, there is a cultural bowl carved into the rock. It is now called Wilson's Bowl. Having left her letters from Wilson at the doorstep of the poet Phyllis Webb, Lilo walked down the beach as the full moon was reflected in the bowl, took off her clothes and walked into the sea. Some have said that she left a note saying that she had "gone to join Wilson."[14] Phyllis Webb later wrote a series of poems under the title *Wilson's Bowl*.[15]

Another who was close to Wilson had the opposite reaction. Roy Henry Vickers, like many others, was devastated by Wilson's passing. Several years later he sat in a cold, dark place, at a dark time in his life, with a pistol in his hand. He thought of Wilson and the way that had he closed the circle of his life, and a message came that "you have no right to do this." Life is a gift of the creator and must be lived. Wilson's example taught him that "we are mentors" and, if he were to be a mentor, it should be for his passion for life and his refusal to give in to addiction and depression. Vickers took steps to turn his life around and to be the person who could talk to me about Wilson, with such feeling, more than twenty years later.[16]

Collyne had written to Wilson about how the old people recognize themselves in others who have have passed away.[17] Then, one day, when she was living in a little town in the Yukon, Wilson did come to her. She was hanging some planters on the outside walls of the house. She went inside and Chinai was sitting at a desk in an alcove as if nothing had changed. She laid her hand on his shoulder and he was warm and alive. He was working on four "puzzles of thinking" that required using different types of thought processes, different parts of the mind, to solve each one. Collyne understood the solutions without a word passing between them. "We were thinking each other's thoughts." Chinai was comfortable and content, "part of the land there, part of the people," just as Collyne had wished. "It was real and Wilson was there."[18]

Those who end their lives are often consumed by their own situations more than they are thinking about the devastation for the people they leave behind. And most of those who remained did not share in Wilson's knowledge that he was coming back. In spite of his wish that it not be, Wilson's suicide was particularly painful and destructive for his family. Though they had been separated for seven years, Wilson and Marion never divorced and neither found another life partner. They had known each other since they were teenagers and remained in contact after they separated. Marion was devastated by Wilson's passing and, though her life went on, she never really recovered. She continued to work as a secretary and receptionist at International House at UBC. She was close to Wilson's memory, as International House was just across the road from the Museum of Anthropology. In her desk drawer she had a selection of Robert Davidson's screen prints that she sold at, by today's standards, ridiculously low prices. The one that I bought from her, entitled *Killer Whale Fin*, still hangs in my living room.[19] In time, Marion bought a house and moved to Hope to be closer to her parents. But life and health were closing in on her and, in 1983, Marion also took her own life: as silent as a killer whale fin slicing through the air. As with Wilson's passing, it was tough on those around her. Michael Kew wrote to Marnie remembering her mother's laughter and "far-out sense of humour." And yet added that "Dark times are upon us."[20]

Marnie and Tom were left with the painful legacy of both parents choosing to leave them by suicide. Tom was hurt and angry at his father's passing, but he tried to limit the impact on his life. He was even more angry when his mother left him. When Tom himself later died, at fifty-one, the same age as his father, of Lou Gehrig's disease (ALS), Marnie was left with no immediate family other than her daughter. She struggled with, and survived, the loss of both parents by their own hand. Her relationship with Wilson had always been fraught because, she said, "they baffled each other." In spite of all that, Marnie once wrote to me, "the thing about my dad, Robin, is that he was so beautiful."[21] It is a touching epitaph.

*

Wilson also came back in the academic evaluations of his contribution to the understanding of First Nations peoples and cultures. That assessment began immediately and then extended into the longer term. First off the mark was Michael Ames. Within two months of Wilson's passing, he wrote "A Note on the Contributions of Wilson Duff to Northwest Coast Ethnology and Art," published in *BC Studies* in the fall of 1976. One would not think of Ames as either the first or the best person to evaluate Wilson's work, and his article consists of faint praise and hasty judgments.

Perhaps he thought that he should get the first word out to set the agenda. The article did not indicate that Wilson had committed suicide. When Michael Kew was asked to comment on a draft, he responded that "It is my personal view that suicides are acts of communication & oughtn't to be censored." Kew also observed that Ames had written nothing about Wilson's personal style: that, for instance, that he enjoyed a beer above other drinks and that hockey was his favourite sport.[22] Ames then went on, through his career at the Museum of Anthropology, to write essays that described bold new developments in museum practice, particularly around involving First Nations people, many of which Wilson had already initiated when he was at the Provincial Museum.[23]

In time, others wrote more thoughtful and balanced assessments of Wilson's contribution. Charles Borden felt that Ames had not written enough about Wilson's archaeological work and so published an article that emphasized that part of his legacy. Robin Ridington wrote about Wilson's poetry and his careful use of words, particularly around *images stone b.c.* and the meaning of the twin masks.[24] Donald Abbott brought together and edited a collection of essays, recollections, art and poetry by Wilson's colleagues and friends, including a number of First Nations contributors. The volume also incorporates several of Wilson's own essays. The anthology was published by the British Columbia Provincial Museum under the title *The World Is as Sharp as a Knife*. That volume described, evaluated and celebrated the full range of Wilson's legacy of museum work, thinking and writing. One notable absence from the book was Wayne Suttles, who was still too upset by Wilson's death to contribute. He later wrote his own assessment of Wilson's career in a review article on the Abbott volume, also entitled "The World Is as Sharp as a Knife." Suttles was still bothered that none of the writing in the anthology made clear that Wilson had committed suicide. He endeavoured to explain Wilson's passing as he grappled with his partial understanding of Wilson's late-life thinking.[25]

Others also took time to come to terms with Wilson's passing through their own scholarship. Within two years of Wilson's death, Carol Sheehan McLaren, one of Wilson's graduate students, published an article on the image of Hawk on the Northwest Coast. She draws on the two different traditions of interpretative anthropology represented by Franz Boas and Claude Lévi-Strauss. There are also distinct echoes of Wilson's thinking and language in, for example, her use of the image of the Möbius strip. A fleeting reference to *images stone b.c.* is the only acknowledgement of her debt to Wilson. A few years later, in an exhibition at the Glenbow Museum and the accompanying catalogue, Wilson's influence is right up front. The title is *Pipes that Won't Smoke; Coal that Won't Burn*. The catalogue is dedicated "To Chinai." "Scholar, teacher and friend, Wilson Duff gave so much to me and to all his students." She draws on Wilson's ideas throughout and says that they had planned to write a book and develop an exhibition together.[26] There is no mention of that plan in Wilson's papers, so it must have been a conversation. Other scholars, writing about argillite, have taken Sheehan's book to mean that her ideas and Wilson's were not just linked, but identical.[27] That is a simplification.

Then there is the fiction—two operas and a novel. To be clear, these are works of imagination and so perhaps immune from a fact-based critique. And perhaps fiction is a safer place of refuge from which to contemplate a life and thinking as complex as Wilson's. These fictional accounts do present a view of Wilson that should be considered. The first opera was also called, by now without much imagination, *The World Is as Sharp as a Knife*. It did not make it to the stage, but the libretto, written by the then-land claims lawyer Leslie Pinder, was performed at the UBC Museum of Anthropology. It portrays a fictional character tormented over the removal of the SGang Gwaay poles. The second opera, written and produced by Bruce Ruddell, called *Beyond Eden*, was staged. In this case the relationship between fiction and fact is more slippery. While the opera is a work of imagination, there is no attempt to distance the depiction from the actual person, as in the printed program, at least for the Calgary performances, there is a brief account that purports to be about Wilson's career.[28] On stage, Lewis Wilson (Wilson Duff) is, again, tormented by the removal of the SGang Gwaay totem poles while the expedition is on Anthony Island in 1957. Removal of the totem poles is described as "an

Armageddon on the beach at Ninstints."[29] There is no evidence for that interpretation. Wilson's family and some colleagues were very upset by the characterization of him in *Beyond Eden*.[30]

Then Leslie Pinder wrote a novel, *Bring Me One of Everything*, in which a leading character, named Austin Hart, is a thinly disguised Wilson Duff. There is the usual disclaimer that "any resemblance to…persons living or dead, is entirely coincidental." All the same, Wilson and his contemporaries are quite recognizable. We are told early on in the novel that the reason Austin Hart killed himself was "the obvious guilt he must have felt about taking the poles."[31] The removal and restoration of the totem poles from SGang Gwaay was one of the few things in his life that Wilson did not feel guilty about. Just before he died, knowing that it would be his last word on the subject, he wrote again about that formative experience. In an article published posthumously in the *Smithsonian* magazine, he noted that "The time for collecting and preserving these sculptures is past," but he still believed in the value of preserving some poles as a record of the world that was lost in villages like SGang Gwaay. At the conclusion of the article, he used exactly the same paragraph as he had used twenty years before to describe his feelings about Ninstints:

> What was destroyed here was not just a few hundred individual human lives. Human beings must die anyway. It was something even more complex and even more human—a vigorous and functioning society, the product of just as long an evolution as our own, well suited to its environment and vital enough to participate in human cultural achievements not duplicated anywhere else. What was destroyed was one more bright tile in the complicated and wonderful mosaic of man's achievement on earth. Mankind is the loser. We are the losers.[32]

*

These accounts of Wilson's life and work each arose from personal experience and recollections of him, his published writing, museum displays and exhibitions, or a literary imagination. They are not based on a close reading of the voluminous manuscript record that he left behind.

Wilson's papers, in which he speaks for himself, have survived, although it was not a foregone conclusion that they would. Much of his manuscript record from the Provincial Museum days languished in boxes in Donald Abbott's office until, in 1979, Randy Bouchard and Dorothy Kennedy, of the British Columbia Indian Language Project, noticed them and made a preliminary inventory. They became the Wilson Duff papers in the BC Archives, now part of the Royal British Columbia Museum. The papers have been recently reorganized as the Department of Anthropology (Wilson Duff) records. Wilson's ethnographic notes and papers have been particularly valuable to Bouchard and Kennedy, among others, in their ethnographic and linguistic work with First Nations communities, which takes them into the courtroom as expert witnesses. Kennedy was shocked when, on one occasion as she was presenting in court and referring to Wilson's work, the opposing lawyer asked, "How could you rely on the evidence of a madman?"[33] It is not uncommon for the work of a creative person who takes their own life to be denigrated, as some still think that suicide is itself a sign of madness. Wilson was troubled toward the end of his life but always capable of lucid, rational thought. Perhaps all the courtroom incident tells us is that all is fair in love and law.

When Wilson died, he left a large collection of papers in his house. There was a box of papers in a wardrobe with a note instructing that they be destroyed since they would be of no interest to anyone but him.[34] Marnie took the view that, if Wilson had really wanted the papers destroyed, he would have done so himself, so she hung on to them and most of them are still in her personal collection. Other papers and books went to Hope with Marion and, in time, Marnie donated them to the Museum of Anthropology Archives at UBC. They constitute a rich, valuable collection that includes, among much else, what I have called Wilson's "Notes for Thinking."

Scholarship has continued based on these collections of papers. In an analysis of Wilson's ideas about Northwest Coast art, E.N. Anderson brought to light and analyzed a segment of those papers, the unpublished "Notes to Myself" that include writing about Northwest Cast art and some of Wilson's poetry.[35] Wilson bequeathed the Tsimshian file of Barbeau material to his student and "close colleague" Marjorie Halpin.[36] She had written her PhD dissertation on "The Tsimshian Crest System" under Wilson's supervision and continued to publish, using the Tsimshian files and remaining mindful of Wilson's ideas.[37] And it would not have been possible for Wilson to come back in this biography without Marnie Duff's collection of papers and the two major collections that are now in the Provincial Archives and the UBC Museum of Anthropology Archives. Every time I return to his papers, I find that Wilson has, through his thinking and writing, more to teach me.

Throughout his life and work as an anthropologist, Wilson took several different approaches to developing a conversation between First Nations people and newcomers, and then making it a better conversation. Since his passing, that conversation has taken many different turns. It is now such easy scholarship to lift his efforts out of their context and judge them to be wanting by today's standards. Thus, displaying items from another culture in a museum becomes appropriation, and the removal of totem poles from deserted villages is called theft. *The Indian History of British Columbia* is now old-fashioned anthropology because anthropologists have since become politically informed and engaged in more collaborative work rather than treating First Nations people as "simply objects in a curio cabinet."[38] Wilson's testimony in the *White and Bob* case in Nanaimo now simply illustrates "a shift in control of knowledge of traditional life from Native leaders and elders to academic experts."[39]

More recent scholars have carried out their slice and dice in an effort to diminish the importance of *Arts of the Raven*. It was not the first exhibition to make the point that Indigenous art could be fine art. It was appropriation to draw Indigenous art into the western orbit. And, in a slight to Bill Reid, it was said that non-Indigenous connoisseurs were making aesthetic decisions about Indian art. Moreover, the work of Bill Reid, Bill Holm and Wilson Duff did not signal a renaissance in Northwest Coast art because the art never declined to a point where a renaissance was necessary. And, of course, trying to understand meaning in Haida art, as Wilson did in his last few years, is culturally presumptuous. I daresay that some of these evaluations of particular pieces of Wilson's work contain a grain of truth. Wilson would even have acknowledged some up to a point. He was certainly well aware by the end of his life that we are "into a time when academic anthropology will be called into account by the people it has presumed to describe for the manner in which it has interpreted their cultures."[40] But presentist presumptions, along with a blinkered view of the past, do not lead to a fair assessment of Wilson's overall work and wisdom.

The one aspect of Wilson's life and work that has not been assailed by later commentators is his teaching. First at the University of Victoria and then at UBC, hundreds of students left his classes with a greater understanding of First Nations cultures and the consequences of settler colonialism in British Columbia. After he was gone, he continued to teach through other teachers. Wayne Suttles wrote to Marion, "when I teach Northwest Indians...he has been and will continue to be a constant presence. Much of what I talk about I have discussed with him, and much of what I describe I experienced with him..."[41] Wilson also believed that museums were places of learning, and thousands learned something when they walked through the doors of museums where he had worked on the presentation of cultures. He brought in First Nations people as teachers. He and Mungo Martin were partners who kept the thread of Northwest Coast art alive at a time when it was very tenuous. Their work still resonates today. Recently Mungo Martin's grandson, Richard Hunt, raised a restored totem pole at Thunderbird Park. He recalled Mungo's potlatch for the opening of Wawadit'la, saying, "This is where our culture was reborn."[42]

Wilson understood the meaning of appropriation and its impact on colonized people. Today, particularly in the museum world, we are preoccupied with appropriation and it is usually seen as operating in only one direction. If we look more carefully, however, history presents historians, and anthropologists, with other narratives. Sometimes there was reciprocity even in the midst of newcomer domination. Wilson certainly knew that cultural exchanges in British Columbia could be two way when he noted that, Indians were "collectors of the white man's products—else there would have been no trade!"[43] Scholars in other places have been able to get past the simple, one-way appropriation narrative and point out, as Douglas Cole did for the Northwest Coast many years ago, that First Nations people had interests, and sometimes even agency, in collecting, museum work and art.[44] Wilson did not simply appropriate the poles and stories of Gitanyow (Kitwancool). Rather, after taking no for an answer several times, he tactfully negotiated an exchange agreement on the poles and then he enabled the elders to tell their own stories in their own way to a wider audience.

At SGang Gwaay many poles still stand—only just—silent witnesses to the spirits of the people who once lived there. Soon they will be gone. All that will be left will be the few examples that Wilson collected and are now in the Provincial Museum and the Museum of Anthropology. Many objected, after the fact, to the removal of those poles, while others still think that it was the right thing to do. According to his wife, Martine, Bill Reid never regretted the salvage of some totem poles and would have done it all over again. Bill Reid's connection with Wilson and Haida Gwaii endured to the end. When he passed away in 1998, his ashes were taken in a replica of the Final Exam to be buried at T'anuu, the place of his ancestors. The poles in the museums encouraged the continued development of Haida art. Robert Davidson says the ancient examples in museums were a huge influence on his own understanding of the art: "I was absolutely blown away by the standard and quality of the work. I was in dreamland, seeing the endless possibilities of art." He learned from the old poles what could not be learned from new ones: the effect of weathering. He could then take the weathering process into account in his own carving.[45] Other Haida artists have also learned from the poles that Wilson restored.

The Indian History of British Columbia endures in spite of criticism. It is an obvious point that the book is of its time. Yet it can still be found, more than fifty years later, in its umpteenth printing, in bookstores and ferry terminals. People are still learning from it. Wilson's unpublished manuscript on prehistory, which was to be volume two of the series, is a model of clarity about a more distant past based on a range of sources: including archaeology, ethnography, art and mythology. Twenty years later, historians would embrace the value of these various sources to illuminate Canada's Indigenous past, and they would call it ethnohistory. His later publications and presentations on meaning in Northwest Coast art showed that his level of thinking was way ahead of his time, and it has not been reached since. In my view, the only book that approaches Wilson's way of thinking about Haida art is Colin Browne's *Entering Time*, which looks at the three Edenshaw argillite platters depicting Raven's hunt for *tsaw*.[46]

Wilson's role as a witness in *White and Bob* also needs to be seen in the context of its time. At that time the courts were not listening to elders like Joe Elliott, who attempted to speak at the first trial. Wilson understood the obligation. "In testifying as expert witnesses, anthropologists are playing a very serious game that deeply affects the lives and fortunes of the people they represent, and had better know the limits of their expertise."[47] When he spoke in that Nanaimo courtroom to confirm that the Snuneymuxw occupied and owned the land around them, he was also speaking to a settler audience. It was at a time when neither politicians nor lawyers were discussing, let alone taking seriously, the existence of First Nations title. After *White and Bob* that changed. In time, both courts and governments would recognize Aboriginal title in British Columbia. Though the road to recognition of title and sovereignty has been long, winding and ongoing, the Snuneymuxw lawyer and leader Douglas White III believes today that the case was a turning point.[48] And it does not appear that, in the process, First Nations elders and leaders have lost their ability to speak for themselves.

Subsequent scholars have performed their semantic gymnastics on the development of Northwest Coast Indigenous art during Wilson's time. Was it a revival, a resurgence, a renaissance, or was it none of the above because there was continuity? It is the kind of thing that infuriated Wilson: "playing games with words, until words set traps and you fall in."[49] So let's try to put it as simply as Wilson would have done. In 1950, when Wilson started at the Provincial Museum, Northwest Coast Indian art was at a very low ebb. It was not dead, as Mungo Martin, Bill Reid and Robert Davidson's work testified. Twenty-five years later, when Wilson passed away, the artistic tide had risen and he had contributed much to that flow of creativity.

Just as Wilson's life is far more significant than the manner of his leaving it, when all was said and done, his many different contributions add up to so much more than the sum of the parts that have been rejected by the niggling revisions of later scholars. The critiques usually come from focusing on one piece of Wilson's life and not the full range of his interests. How could one possibly maintain, knowing the full story, that he did not see the value of political engagement and collaboration with communities? There is a literal sense in which "Nothing Comes Only in Pieces" if we only focus on the individual pieces and cannot see the everything that lies behind them.

Wilson had taken the final exam. He recognized all the pieces and imagined their meaning. But the pieces are just a glimpse of the whole. He knew, as Raven found, that "when you are biting a piece off one thing. You don't know where the other is…When you are looking at its outside you don't know what's inside, and vice versa." Inside the box is the absence of everything that is present outside: that is, the world. Raven then creates the world by pecking at pieces, even though he makes mistakes in the process. "What then holds the whole system together, is the mind, memory, purpose of the artist…Order is in the mind," he concluded. Wilson asked, "on my death, put my two masks on my face." [50] The one held in front with the inward eyes of introspection and deep thinking; behind it the mask with open eyes that looked clearly at the world of First Nations people and their relations with newcomers. And the masks are a pair: opposites that are the same. Thinking of the end of this life, Wilson wrote:

> Let me wrap it all up
> And send it into time as message
> And receive it
> And take it on from there[51]

And so, did the wisdom of Wilson Duff endure, as he had hoped, after he passed over? Wilson's wisdom is to be found in his life, his thinking, his death and his coming back. Most of all, he gave us the gift of meaning, as he spoke to our imagination. And I am you. We can take it on from there.

Abbreviations

BCPM—British Columbia Provincial Museum

DAWD—Department of Anthropology (Wilson Duff) Records GR-3662, British Columbia Provincial Museum

MDP—Marnie Duff papers

PMC—Provincial Museum Correspondence, GR-0111, British Columbia Provincial Museum

UBCA—University of British Columbia Archives

UBC MOA—University of British Columbia, Museum of Anthropology

WD—Wilson Duff

WDF—Wilson Duff fonds, Museum of Anthropology Archives, University of British Columbia

WDF(2)—Wilson Duff fonds, University of British Columbia Archives

Bibliography

PRIMARY DOCUMENTARY SOURCES

Ames, Michael, fonds, UBCA.

Archaeological Sites Advisory Board, Minutes, 1969–1986, Museum of Archaeology & Ethnology, Simon Fraser University.

Bain, Don, Massive Carvings Documentation Project (Research Collection), UBC MOA.

Barbeau, Marius, fonds, Canadian Museum of History Archives.

Belshaw, Cyril, fonds, UBCA.

Borden, Charles E., fonds, UBCA.

British Columbia Centennial Committee (Historic Sites Sub-Committee), GR-1448, BCPM.

British Columbia Provincial Museum and Archives, Anthropology Correspondence, 1925–1970, GR-3662, BCPM.

Bunn, Collyne, papers in her possession.

Capes, Katherine H., fonds, Canadian Museum of History Archives.

Department of Anthropology (Wilson Duff) records, GR-3662, BCPM.

Directors fonds, UBC MOA.

Drucker, Philip, notes, MS-0870, BCPA.

Duff, Marnie, papers in her possession.

Duff, Wilson, faculty record, UBCA.

———, fonds, UBCA.

———, fonds, UBC MOA.

———. Images Stone BC, video presentation, Canadian Museum of History Archives.

———. Lecture on Images Stone BC, sound recording, Canadian Museum of History Archives.

———. "Report on an Archaeological Excavation at Marpole BC," Charles Borden Series, Laboratory of Archaeology, UBC MOA.

———. "Report on Archaeological Survey of Hope-Chilliwack Area," Reading Room Series, Laboratory of Archaeology, UBC MOA.

Garfield, Viola, papers, Special Collections, University of Washington Library.

Halpin, Marjorie, Museum of Anthropology, Curator fonds, UBC MOA.

———, private fonds, UBC MOA.

Hawthorn, Audrey, fonds, UBC MOA.

Hawthorn, Harry, fonds, UBCA.

———, fonds, UBC MOA.

Leechman, Douglas, fonds, Canadian Museum of History Archives.

MacNeish, Richard Stockton, fonds, Canadian Museum of History Archives.

President's Office, University of British Columbia, papers, UBCA.

Provincial Archives of British Columbia, correspondence, GR-1738, BCPM.

BIBLIOGRAPHY

Provincial Museum Correspondence—People, GR-0111, BCPM.

Northwest Indians: Bill Reid and Wilson Duff (On 1954 Expedition to Queen Charlotte Islands), tape recording, BCPM.

Registrar's Office, University of British Columbia, records, UBCA.

Royal British Columbia Museum, scrapbook, 94-8868, BCPM.

Stewart, Hilary, fonds, UBC MOA.

Vertical files (of newspaper clippings), BCPM.

Vancouver School Board, Archives and Heritage website.

———, student records.

Vancouver Technical Secondary School, student records.

Webb, Phyllis, papers, Library and Archives Canada.

Wilson, Solomon, interview, tape recording, Imbert Orchard files, BCPA.

INTERVIEWS

Abbott, Maria

Anderson, Eleanor

Anderson, Susan

Belshaw, Cyril

Berger, Thomas

Bouchard, Randy and Kennedy, Dorothy

Bunn, Collyne

Burridge, Kenelm

Buxton, Judith

Calcowski, Marcia

Captain Gold

Carlson, Roy

Carpenter, Jennifer

Chidley, Cyndy

Cranmer Webster, Gloria

Davidson, Robert

Davidson, Susan

Demmert, Jane and Dennis

Dewhurst, John

Donald, Leland

Duff, Helen

Duff, Marnie

Farber, Carole

Hilton, Susanne

Holm, Bill and Marty

Hoover, Alan

Jilek, Wolfgang and Louise Jilek-Aall

Jones, Roy

Keddie, Grant

Keenleyside, David

Kew, Michael

Laforet, Andrea

MacDonald, George

McMillan, Al

Macnair, Peter

McTaggert, Sheila

Malkin, Reeva

Mason, Helen

Matson, R.G.

Mills, Tonia

Mitchell, Donald

Moore, Leslie

Powell, Jay

Pritchard, John

Reid, Martine

Ridington, Robin and Jillian

Robinson, Michael

Romaine, Nancy

Rowan, Madeline

Rudell, Nancy

Sanger, David

Sendy, John

Simonsen, Bjorn

Skirrow, Art

Sparrow, Leona

Tuner, Nancy

Vickers, Roy Henry

Voneugen, Dick

White, Douglas III

Whittaker, Elvi

SELECTED WRITINGS BY WILSON DUFF

In chronological order. This list does not include minor items in, for example, the British Columbia Provincial Museum of Natural History and Anthropology Annual Report *or the* Anthropology in British Columbia series, publications that Wilson Duff edited.

1951. "Notes on Carrier Social Organization," *Anthropology in British Columbia no. 2* (Victoria: British Columbia Provincial Museum), 28–34.

1952. "The Upper Stalo Indians: An Introductory Ethnography" (master's thesis). Seattle: University of Washington.

———. *The Upper Stalo Indians of the Fraser Valley, British Columbia, Anthropology in British Columbia Memoir no. 1.* Victoria: British Columbia Provincial Museum.

———. "Gitksan Totem Poles 1952," *Anthropology in British Columbia no. 3* (Victoria: British Columbia Provincial Museum), 21–30.

———. *Thunderbird Park: Victoria British Columbia, Canada.* (Victoria: Queen's Printer).

1954. "Preserving the Talking Sticks," *Powell River Digester* 30, no. 6 (November–December), 10–12.

———. "A Heritage in Decay—The Totem Art of the Haida," *Canadian Art* xi, no. 2, 56–59.

———. With C.E. Borden. "A Scottsbluff-Eden Point from British Columbia," *Anthropology in British Columbia no. 3* (Victoria: British Columbia Provincial Museum), 34–35.

1956. "An Unusual Burial at the Whalen Site," *Research Studies, State College of Washington* 24, no. 1, 67–72.

———. With Herbert C. Taylor, "A post-Contact Southward Movement of the Kawakiutl," *Research Studies, State College of Washington* 24, no. 1, 56–66.

———. *Prehistoric Stone Sculpture of the Fraser Valley and Gulf of Georgia, Anthropology in British Columbia no. 5.* Victoria: British Columbia Provincial Museum.

1957. With Michael Kew, "Anthony Island, A Home of the Haidas," *Report of the Provincial Museum for 1957* (Victoria: Provincial Museum).

———. "Totem Poles Recall Vanished Seafarers," *The Crowsnest* 9, no. 3, 22–23.

1959. (ed.). *Histories, Territories and Laws of the Kitwancool, Anthropology in British Columbia Memoir no. 4.* Victoria: British Columbia Provincial Museum.

———. "Mungo Martin, Carver of the Century," *Museum News* 1, no. 1, 3–8.

1961. "The Killer Whale Copper," Provincial Museum of Natural History and Anthropology, *Report for the Year 1960* (Victoria: King's Printer), 32–36.

———. *Preserving British Columbia's Prehistory.* (Victoria: Archaeological Sites Advisory Board).

1963. "Stone Clubs from the Upper Skeena River," Provincial Museum of Natural History and Anthropology, *Report for the Year 1962* (Victoria: King's Printer), 27–38.

1964. "Contributions of Marius Barbeau to West Coast Ethnography," *Anthropologica* vi, no. 1, 63–96.

———. *The Indian History of British Columbia, Volume 1: The Impact of the White Man,* Anthropology in British Columbia Memoir no. 5. Victoria: Provincial Museum of Natural History and Anthropology.

1965. "Thoughts on the Nootka Canoe," Provincial Museum of Natural History and Anthropology, *Report for the Year 1964* (Victoria: King's Printer), 24–31.

1966. Review of "Northwest Coast Indian Art," *American Antiquity* 31, no. 6 (October 1966), 881–82.

1967. With articles by Bill Holm and Bill Reid. *Arts of the Raven.* Vancouver: Vancouver Art Gallery.

1969. "The Fort Victoria Treaties," *BC Studies*, no. 3 (Fall 1969), 3–52.

———. "(La Cote Nord-Ouest) The Northwest Coast," in Musée de l'homme, *Chefs d'oeuvre des arts indiens et esquimaux du canada: masterpieces of indian and eskimo art from Canada.* (Paris: Societe des Amis du Musée de l'Homme).

——— (ed.) With Jane Wallen and Joe Clark. "Totem Pole Survey of Southeastern Alaska, Report of Field Survey and Follow Up Activities, June–October 1969," typescript (Alaska State Museum).

1970. "On Wardwell's Partial Rediscovery of a Northwest Coast Monument," *Curator* 13, no. 4, 243–50.

1973. With Michael Kew. "A Select Bibliography of Anthropology in British Columbia," *BC Studies*, no. 19 (Autumn), 73–121.

1974. "An Act of Vision and an Act of Intuition," in Vancouver Art Gallery, *Bill Reid: A Retrospective Exhibition* (Vancouver: Vancouver Art Gallery), n.p.

1975. *images stone b.c.: Thirty Centuries of Coast Indian Sculpture.* anichton: Hancock House.

1976. "Mute Relics of Haida Tribes Ghost Villages," *Smithsonian* (September), 84–89.

1981. "Tsetaut," in June Helm, ed. *Handbook of North American Indians, Volume 6: Subarctic.* (Washington: Smithsonian Institution), 454–57.

1983. "The World Is as Sharp as a Knife: Meaning in Northwest Coast Art," in Roy Carlson, ed., *Indian Art Traditions of the Northwest Coast.* (Burnaby: Archaeology Press, Simon Fraser University).

PUBLISHED AND UNPUBLISHED SOURCES

Abbott, Donald N., ed. *The World Is as Sharp as a Knife: An Anthology in Honour of Wilson Duff.* Victoria: British Columbia Provincial Museum, 1981.

Adams, John W. *The Gitksan Potlatch: Population Flux, Resource Ownership and Reciprocity.* Toronto: Holt, Rinehart and Winston of Canada, 1973.

Ames, Michael M. *Cannibal Tours and Glass Boxes: The Anthropology of Museums.* Vancouver: UBC Press, 1992.

———. "A Note on the Contributions of Wilson Duff to Northwest Coast Ethnology and Art." *BC Studies*, no. 31 (Autumn 1976), 3–11.

Amoss, Pamela. *Coast Salish Spirit Dancing: the Survival of an Ancestral Religion*. Seattle: University of Washington Press, 1978.

Anderson, E.N. *Bird of Paradox: The Unpublished Writings of Wilson Duff*. Surrey: Hancock House, 1996.

Anderson, Margaret and Marjorie Halpin, eds. *Potlatch at Gitsegukla: William Beynon's 1945 Field Notebooks*. Toronto: UBC Press, 2000.

Arieti, Silvano. *The Intrapsychic Self: Feeling, Cognition, and Creativity*. New York: Basic Books, 1967.

Baime, A.J. *The Arsenal of Democracy: FDR, Detroit, and an Epic Quest to Arm an America at War*. Boston: Mariner Books, 2015.

Barbeau, Marius. *Alaska Beckons*. Caldwell: Caxton Printers, 1947.

———. *The Downfall of Temlaham*. Edmonton: Hurtig, 1973.

———. *Haida Carvers in Argillite*. Ottawa: National Museum of Canada, 1957.

———. *Haida Myths Illustrated in Argillite Carvings*. Ottawa: National Museum of Canada, 1953.

———. *Totem Poles*. Ottawa: National Museum of Canada, 1950.

———. *Totem Poles of the Gitksan, Upper Skeena River, British Columbia*. Ottawa: National Museum of Canada, 1929.

Barman, Jean and Robert A.J. McDonald. *Vancouver's Past: Essays in Social History Vancouver Centennial Issue of BC Studies*. Vancouver: UBC Press, 1986.

Belshaw, Cyril. *Bumps on a Long Road: Essays from an Anthropologist's Memory*. n.d.

———. *The Sorcerer's Apprentice: An Anthropology of Public Policy*. New York: Pergamon Press, 1976.

Berger, Thomas. *One Man's Justice: A Life in the Law*. Vancouver: Douglas & McIntyre, 2002.

Bering, Jesse. *Suicidal: Why We Kill Ourselves*. Chicago: University of Chicago Press, 2018.

Bird, F.C.C. *Nickel Trip*. Pemmican Publications, 2004.

Blackley, Roger. *Galleries of Maoriland: Artists, Collectors and the Māori World, 1880–1910*. Auckland: Auckland University Press, 2018.

Blackman, Margaret B. *During My Time: Florence Edenshaw*. Seattle: University of Washington Press, 1982.

Boas, Franz. *Primitive Art*. New York: Dover Publications, 1955.

Boelscher, Marianne. *The Curtain Within: Haida Social and Mythical Discourse*. Vancouver: UBC Press, 1958.

Bohannan, Paul and Mark Glazer, eds. *High Points in Anthropology*. New York: Knopf, 1973.

Bond, Douglas. *The Love and Fear of Flying*. New York: International Universities Press, 1952.

Borden, Charles. "West Coast Crossties with Alaska." *Arctic Institute of North America Technical Paper*, no. 11 (December 1962): 9–19 and 170–81.

———. "Wilson Duff (1925–1976): His Contributions to the Growth of Archaeology in British Columbia." *BC Studies*, no. 33 (Spring 1977): 3–12.

Bowman, Martin W. *Consolidated B-24 Liberator*. Ramsbury: The Crowood Press, 1998.

Bringhurst, Robert. *Solitary Raven: The Essential Writings of Bill Reid*. Vancouver: Douglas & McIntyre, 2000.

————. *A Story as Sharp as a Knife: The Classical Haida Mythtellers and Their World.* Vancouver: Douglas & McIntyre, 1999.

British Columbia. *Directories.*

————. *Papers Connected with the Indian Land Question, 1850–1875.* Victoria: Government Printer, 1875.

————. *Provincial Museum of Natural History and Anthropology, Report.* Victoria: King's/Queen's Printer, 1949–66.

British Columbia Court of Appeal. *Regina v. White and Bob, Appeal Book.*

Brown, Steven C. *Native Visions: Evolution in Northwest Coast Art from the Eighteenth through the Twentieth Century.* Vancouver: Douglas & McIntyre, 1998.

Browne, Colin. *Entering Time: The Fungus Man Platters of Charles Edenshaw.* Vancouver: Talon Books, 2016.

Burridge, Kenelm. *Someone, No One: An Essay on Individuality.* Princeton: Princeton University Press, 1979.

Carlson, Keith Thor. *The Power of Place, the Problem of Time: Aboriginal Identity and Historical Consciousness in the Cauldron of Colonialism.* Toronto: University of Toronto Press, 2010.

Carlson, Roy L. "Archaeology in British Columbia." *BC Studies*, no. 6 (Fall and Winter 1970): 7–17.

———— and Luke Dalla Bona. *Early Human Occupation in British Columbia.* Vancouver: UBC Press, 1996.

————, ed. *Indian Art Traditions of the Northwest Coast.* Burnaby: Archaeology Press, Simon Fraser University, 1983.

Carroll, Lewis. *Through the Looking Glass and What Alice Found There.* London: Bloomsbury, 2001.

Carter, Anthony. "In Memory of Mungo Martin." *The Beaver* (Spring 1971, Outfit 301:4): 44–45.

Castaneda, Carlos. *The Teachings of Don Juan: A Yaqui Way of Knowledge.* Berkeley: University of California Press, 1968.

Chalmers, John W. "Learning the Gen Trade." *Alberta History* 42, no. 3 (Summer 1994): 2–10.

———— and John J.N. Chalmers. *Navigator Brothers: The Story of Two Brothers in the RCAF.* Edmonton: Chalmers, 2008.

Clifford, James and George E. Marcus, eds. *Writing Culture: The Poetics and Politics of Ethnography.* Berkeley: University of California Press, 1986.

Cocking, Clive. "Indian Renaissance: New Life for a Traditional Art." *Alumni Chronicle* 25, no. 4 (Winter 1971): 16–19.

Codere, Helen. *Fighting with Property: A Study of Kwakiutl Potlatching and Warfare 1792–1930.* Seattle: University of Washington Press, 1950.

Cole, Douglas. *Captured Heritage: The Scramble for Northwest Coast Artifacts.* Vancouver: Douglas & McIntyre, 1985.

————. *Franz Boas: The Early Years.* Vancouver: Douglas & McIntyre, 1999.

————. "Tricks of the Trade: Some Reflections on Anthropological Collecting." *Arctic Anthropology* 28, no. 1, 48–52.

Collins, Robert. *The Long and the Short and the Tall: An Ordinary Airman's War*. Vancouver: Douglas & McIntyre, 1986.

Colombo, John Robert. *The Penguin Treasury of Popular Canadian Poems*. Toronto: Penguin Canada, 2002.

Condliffe, J.B. *Te Rangi Hiroa: The Life of Sir Peter Buck*. Christchurch: Whitcombe and Tombs, 1971.

Cook, Tim. *Fight to the Finish: Canadians in the Second World War 1944–1945*. Toronto: Penguin Random House, 2015.

——. *The Necessary War: Canadians Fighting the Second World War 1939–1943*. Toronto: Penguin Random House, 2014.

Cruikshank, Julie. *The Social Life of Stories: Narrative and Knowledge in the Yukon Territory*. Vancouver: UBC Press, 1998.

Dalzell, Kathleen E. *The Queen Charlotte Islands 1774–1966*. Terrace: C.M. Adam, 1968.

Darling, David and Douglas Cole. "Totem Pole Restoration on the Skeena: An Early Exercise in Heritage Conservation." *BC Studies*, no. 47 (Autumn 1980): 29–48.

Darnell, Regna. *Edward Sapir: Linguist, Anthropologist, Humanist*. Berkeley: University of California Press, 1990.

——, Michelle Hamilton, Robert L.A. Hancock, and Joshua Smith, eds. *The Franz Boas Papers, Volume I: Franz Boas as Public Intellectual—Theory, Ethnography, Activism*. Lincoln: University of Nebraska Press, 2015.

Davidson, Robert. *Four Decades: An Innocent Gesture*. Vancouver: Robert Davidson, 2009.

Davis, Chuck. *The Chuck Davis History of Metropolitan Vancouver*. Madeira Park: Harbour Publishing, 2011.

——. *The Vancouver Book*. North Vancouver: J.J. Douglas, 1976.

De Menil, Adelade and William Reid. *Out of the Silence*. New York: Harper Row, 1971.

Douglas, Stan, ed. *Vancouver Anthology: The Institutional Politics of Art*. Vancouver: Talonbooks, 1991.

Douglas, W.A.B. *The Creation of a National Air Force: The Official History of the Royal Canadian Air Force Volume II*. Toronto: University of Toronto Press, 1986.

Drew, Leslie and Douglas Wilson. *Argillite: Art of the Haida*. North Vancouver: Hancock House, 1980.

Dunmore, Spencer. *Wings for Victory: The Remarkable Story of the British Commonwealth Air Training Plan in Canada*. Toronto: McClelland & Stewart, 1994.

Duffek, Karen and Charlotte Townsend-Gault, eds. *Bill Reid and Beyond: Expanding on Modern Native Art*. Vancouver: Douglas and McIntyre, 2004.

——. *Robert Davidson: The Abstract Edge*. Vancouver: Museum of Anthropology at the University of British Columbia, 2004.

Dyen, Isidore and David F. Aberle. *Lexical Reconstruction: The Case of the Proto-Athapaskan Kinship System*. London: Cambridge University Press, 1974.

Eban, Dan, ed. *Art as a Means of Communication in Pre-Literate Societies: The Proceedings of the Wright International Symposium on Primitive and Precolumbian Art Jerusalem, 1985*. Jerusalem: The Israel Museum, 1990.

BIBLIOGRAPHY

Edwards, Elizabeth, Chris Gosden and Ruth B. Phillips, eds. *Sensible Objects: Colonialism, Museums and Material Culture*. Oxford: Routledge, 2006.

Eliade, Mircea. *The Myth of the Eternal Return or, Cosmos and History*. Princeton: Princeton University Press, 1965.

Fisher, Robin. *Contact and Conflict: Indian-European Relations in British Columbia, 1774–1980*. Vancouver: UBC Press, 1977.

Fladmark, K.R. "An Introduction to the Prehistory of British Columbia." *Canadian Journal of Archaeology*, no. 6 (1982): 95–156.

Forge, Anthony, ed. *Primitive Art and Society*. Oxford: Oxford University Press, 1972.

Francis, Martin. *The Flyer: British Culture and the Royal Air Force, 1939–1945*. Oxford: Oxford University Press, 2008.

Frazer, W.W. *A Trepid Aviator: Bombay to Bangkok*. Burnstown: General Store Publishing House, 1995.

Fry, Alan. *How a People Die*. Toronto: Doubleday, 1970.

Galois, Robert. *Kwakwaka'wakw Settlements, 1775–1920: A Geographical Analysis and Gazetteer*. Vancouver: UBC Press, 1994.

Garfield, Viola E. and Pamela T. Amoss. "Erna Guther 1896–1982." *American Anthropologist* 86, n.s., no. 2 (June 1984): 394–99.

——— and Linn A. Forrest. *The Wolf and the Raven: Totem Poles of Southeastern Alaska*. Seattle: University of Washington Press, 1948.

Gessler, Trisha. *the art of nunstints*. Queen Charlotte Islands Museum Society, 1981.

Gladwell, Malcolm. *Outliers: The Story of Success*. New York: Little, Brown and Company, 2008.

Glass, Aaron. "From Cultural Salvage to Brokerage: The Mythologization of Mungo Martin and the Emergence of Northwest Coast Art." *Museum Anthropology* 29, issue 1, 20–43.

Gosselin, Viviane and Phaedra Livingston, eds. *Museums and the Past: Constructing Historical Consciousness*. Vancouver: UBC Press, 2016.

Gough, Barry M. "New Light on Haida Chiefship: The Case of Edenshaw 1850–1853." *Ethnohistory* 29, no. 2 (Spring 1982): 131–39.

Greenberg, Laura J. "Art as a Structural System: A Study of Hopi Pottery Designs." *Studies in the Anthropology of Visual Communication* 2, issue 1 (Spring 1975): 33–50.

Greenhous, Brereton, Stephen J. Harris, William C. Johnston and G.P. Rawling. *The Crucible of War, 1939–1945: The Official History of the Royal Canadian Air Force Volume III*. Toronto: University of Toronto Press, 1994.

Griffen, George H. *Legends of the Evergreen Coast*. Vancouver: Clarke & Stuart, 1934.

Grodeck, Georg. *The Book of the It*. London: Vision Press, 1949.

Grof, Stanislav. *Realms of the Human Unconscious from LSD Research*. New York: Viking, 1975.

Gunther, Era. *Art in the Life of the Northwest Coast Indians*. Portland: The Portland Art Museum, 1966.

———. *Ethnobotany of Western Washington*. Seattle: University of Washington Press, 1945.

Guthe, Carl E. *So You Want a Good Museum: A Guide to the Management of Small Museums*. The American Association of Museums, n.s., no. 17 (1957).

Gwynne-Timothy, John R.W. *Burma Liberators: RCAF in SEAC*. Toronto: Next Level Press, 1991.

Hall, Edward T. *The Hidden Dimension*. New York: Doubleday, 1966.

Halpert, Sam. *A Real Good War*. London: Cassell, 1997.

Halpin, Marjorie. *Jack Shadbolt and the Coastal Indian Image*. Vancouver: UBC Press, 1986.

———— "The Tsimshian Crest System: A Study Based on Museum Specimens and the Marius Barbeau and William Beynon Field Notes" (PhD dissertation). University of British Columbia, 1973.

Harris, Christie. *Raven's Cry*. Vancouver: Douglas & McIntyre, 1966.

Harrison, Julia and Regna Darnell, eds. *Historicizing Canadian Anthropology*. Vancouver: UBC Press, 2006.

Harvey, J. Douglas. *Boys, Bombs and Brussels Sprouts: A Knees-Up Wheels-Up Chronicle of WWII*. Toronto: McClelland & Stewart, 1982.

Hatch, F.J. *The Aerodrome of Democracy: Canada and the British Commonwealth Air Training Plan, 1939–1945*. Ottawa: Directorate of History, Department of National Defence, 1983.

Hawker, Ronald W. *Tales of Ghosts: First Nations Art in British Columbia, 1922–61*. Vancouver: UBC Press, 2003.

Hawthorn, Audrey. *Kwakiutl Art*. Vancouver: Douglas & McIntyre, 1967.

———. "Mungo Martin Artist and Craftsman." *The Beaver* (Summer 1964, Outfit 295-1): 18–23.

———. "Totem Pole Carver." *The Beaver* (March 1952, Outfit 282) 3–6.

Hawthorn, H.B. and C.S. Belshaw. "Cultural Evolution or Cultural Change—the Case of Polynesia," *The Journal of the Polynesian Society* 66, no. 1 (1957): 18–3.

————, C.S. Belshaw and S.M. Jamieson. *The Indians of British Columbia: A Study of Social Adjustment*. Toronto: University of Toronto Press, 1958.

————, C.S. Belshaw and S.M. Jamieson. "The Indians of British Columbia: A Survey of Social and Economic Conditions A Report to the Minister of Citizenship and Immigration" (typescript). The University of British Columbia, 1955.

———. "The Māori: A Study in Acculturation." *American Anthropologist,* April 1944, 40, no. 2, part 2, no. 64 in Memoir Series of American Anthropological Association, 1944.

———— (ed.). "Report of Conference on Native Indian Affairs at Acadia Camp, UBC, Vancouver BC, April 1, 2, and 3 1948" (typescript).

———. Review of *Te Rangi Hiroa: The Life of Sir Peter Buck*, by J.B. Condliffe, *Native Indian Affairs* 47, no. 1 (Spring 1974): 111.

———— (ed.). *A Survey of the Contemporary Indians of Canada: A Report on Economic, Political, Educational Needs and Policies*. Ottawa: Indian Affairs Branch, 1967.

Hayes, E. Nelson and Tanya Hayes. *Claude Lévi-Strauss the Anthropologist as Hero*. Cambridge: MIT Press, 1970.

Heide, Lee. *Whispering Death: My Wartime Adventures*. Victoria: Trafford Publishing, 2000.

Helm, June (ed.). *Handbook of North American Indians, Volume 6: Subarctic*. Washington: Smithsonian Institution, 1981.

Hill, Beth and Ray. *Indian Petroglyphs of the Pacific Northwest*. Saanichton: Hancock House, 1974.

Hillary, Richard. *The Last Enemy*. London: Pimlico, 1997.

Hillenbrand, Laura. *Unbroken: A World War II Story of Survival Resilience and Redemption*. New York: Random House, 2014.

Holm, Bill. *Crooked Beak of Heaven*. Seattle: University of Washington Press, 1972.

———and William Reid. *Form and Freedom: A Dialogue on Northwest Coast Art*. Houston: Institute for the Arts, Rice University, 1975.

———. *Northwest Coast Indian Art: An Analysis of Form*. Seattle: University of Washington Press, 1965.

———. *Smoky-Top: The Art and Times of Willie Seaweed*. Seattle: University of Washington Press, 1983.

Hope and District Historical Society. *Forging a New Hope Struggles and Dreams 1848–1948: A Pioneer Story of Hope, Flood and Laidlaw*. Hope: Hope and District Historical Society, 1984.

Hopkins, Anthony. *Songs from the Front and Rear: Canadian Servicemen's Songs of the Second World War*. Edmonton: Hurtig, 1979.

Howe, K.R. *Nature, Culture and History: The "Knowing" of Oceania*. Honolulu: University of Hawai'i Press, 2000.

Howe, Michael J.A. *Genius Explained*. Cambridge: Cambridge University Press, 1999.

Hyde, Christopher. *Abuse of Trust: The Career of Dr. James Tyhurst*. Vancouver: Douglas & McIntyre, 1991.

Inglis, Richard I. and Donald N. Abbott. "A Tradition of Partnership: The Royal British Columbia Museum and First Peoples." *Alberta Museums Review*, Volume 17, issue 2, Fall/Winter 1991, 17–23.

Inverarity, Robert Bruce. *Art of the Northwest Coast Indians*. Berkeley: University of California Press, 1950.

Iverach, John A. *Chronicles of a Nervous Navigator*. Winnipeg: Iverach, n.d.

Jackness, Ira. *The Storage Box of Tradition: Kwakiutl Art, Anthropologists and Museums, 1881–1981*. Washington: Smithsonian Institution Press, 2002.

Jamieson, Eric. *The Native Voice: The Story of How Masie Hurley and Canada's First Aboriginal Newspaper Changed a Nation*. Halfmoon Bay, Caitlin Press, 2016.

Jenness, Diamond. *The Faith of a Coast Salish Indian Anthropology in British Columbia Memoir no. 3*. Victoria: British Columbia Provincial Museum, 1955.

Jilek, Wolfgang G. *Indian Healing: Shamanic Ceremonialism in the Pacific Northwest Today*. Surrey: Hancock House, 1982.

Johnson, Peter. *The Withered Garland: Reflections and Doubts of a Bomber*. London: New European Publications, 1995.

Joiner, Thomas. *Why People Die by Suicide*. Cambridge: Harvard University Press, 2005.

Jonaitis, Aldona and Aaron Glass. *The Totem Pole: An Intercultural History*. Seattle: University of Washington Press, 2010.

———. *A Wealth of Thought: Franz Boas on Native American Art*. Seattle: University of Washington Press, 1995.

Jopling, Carol F. (ed.). *Art and Aesthetics in Primitive Societies*. New York: E.P. Dutton, 1971.

Jordan, Group Captain (Lucky). *To Burma Skies and Beyond: An Airman's Story*. London: Janus Publishing, 1995.

Kan, Sergei. *Symbolic Immortality: The Tlingit Potlatch of the Nineteenth Century*. Washington: Smithsonian Institution Press, 1989.

Karp, Ivan and Steven D. Lavine.. (eds.). *Exhibiting Cultures: The Poetics and Politics of Museum Display*. Washington: Smithsonian Institution Press, 1991.

Kew, John Edward Michael. "Coast Salish Ceremonial Life: Status and Identity in a Modern Village" (PhD Dissertation). University of Washington, 1970.

Kew, Michael, "Reflections on Anthropology at the University of British Columbia." *BC Studies*, no. 193, Spring 2017, 163–85.

King, Thomas. *The Truth About Stories: A Native Narrative*. Toronto: Anansi, 2003.

Kirkness, Bill and Matt Poole. RAF *Liberators Over Burma: Flying with 159 Squadron*. Croydon: Fonthill Media, 2017.

Klassen, Pamela E. *The Story of Radio Mind: A Missionary's Journey on Indigenous Land*. Chicago: University of Chicago Press, 2018.

Kluckner, Michael. *Vancouver the Way it Was*. North Vancouver: Whitecap Books, 1984.

Koestler, Arthur. *The Act of Creation*. London: Hutchinson, 1964.

Kostova, Elizabeth. *The Historian: A Novel*. New York: Little Brown and Company, 2005.

Kubler, George. *The Shape of Time: Remarks on the History of Things*. New Haven: Yale University Press, 1962.

Kuper, Adam. *Anthropologists and Anthropology: The British School 1922–1972*. New York: Pica Press, 1973.

Kushner, Howard I. *Self-Destruction in the Promised Land: A Psychocultural Biology of American Suicide*. New Brunswick: Rutgers University Press, 1989.

Leach, Edmund. *Claude Lévi-Strauss*. New York: Viking, 1974.

Laforet, Andrea (ed.). "Cultural Heritage Project—report on Kasaan" (typescript).Alaska State Museum, 1971.

———. *Culture and Communication: The Logic By which Symbols are Communicated: An Introduction to the Use of Structuralist Analysis in Social Anthropology*. Cambridge: Cambridge University Press, 1976.

——— (ed.). *The Structural Study of Myth and Totemism*. London: Tavistock, 1967.

Lévi-Strauss, Claude. *Myth and Meaning*. Toronto: University of Toronto Press, 1978.

———. *The Raw and the Cooked: Introduction to a Science of Mythology*. New York: Harper & Row, 1969.

———. *The Way of the Masks*. Seattle: University of Washington Press, 1988.

———. *Tristes Tropiques*. New York: Atheneum, 1970.

———. *The Savage Mind*. Chicago: University of Chicago Press, 1966.

MacDonald, George F. *Haida Art*. Vancouver: Douglas & McIntyre, 1996.

———. *Haida Monumental Art: Villages of the Queen Charlotte Islands*. Vancouver: UBC Press, 1983.

McLennan, Bill and Karen Duffek. *The Transforming Image: Painted Arts of the Northwest Coast First Nations*. Vancouver: Douglas & McIntyre, 2000.

McLynn, Frank. *The Burma Campaign: Disaster Into Triumph*. London: Vintage Books, 2011.

Macnair, Peter, Alan L. Hoover and Kevin Neary. *The Legacy: Continuing Traditions of Canadian Northwest Coast Art*. Victoria: British Columbia Provincial Museum, 1980.

——— and Alan Hoover. *The Magic Leaves: A History of Haida Argillite Carving* Victoria: Royal British Columbia Museum, 2002.

Mandelbaum, David G., Gabriel W. Lasker and Ethel M. Albert (eds.). *The Teaching of Anthropology*. Berkeley: University of California Press, 1963.

Manual of RCAF. Drill and Ceremonial. Ottawa: King's Printer, 1941.

Manuel, George and Michael Posluns. *The Fourth World: An Indian Reality*. Don Mills: Collier, 1974.

Marcus, George E. and Michael M.J. Fischer. *Anthropology as Cultural Critique: An Experimental Moment in the Human Sciences*. Chicago: University of Chicago Press, 1986.

——— and Fred R. Myers (eds.). *The Traffic in Culture: Refiguring Art and Anthropology*. Berkeley: University of California Press, 1995.

Maris, Ronald W. *Pathways to Suicide: A Survey of Self-Destructive Behaviours*. Baltimore: The Johns Hopkins University Press, 1981.

Marshall, R.G. (Bob). "Air Force Memories—RCAF 1940–1945." In the possession of Dave Marshall (typescript).

Marshall, Yvonne. "Reading Images Stone b.c." *World Archaeology* 32, no. 2, October 2000, 222–35.

Matson, R.G. and Gary Copeland. *The Prehistory of the Northwest Coast*. San Diego: Academic Press, 1995.

Mauze, Marie, Michael E. Harkin and Sergei Kan. *Coming to Shore: Northwest Coast Ethnology, Traditions and Visions*. Lincoln: University of Nebraska Press, 2004.

Melnyk, T.W. *Canadian Flying Operations in South East Asia 1941–1945*. Ottawa: Directorate of History, 1976.

Miller, Bruce Granville (ed.). *Be of Good Mind: Essays on the Coast Salish*. Vancouver: UBC Press, 2007.

Miller, Jay and Carol M. Eastman (eds.). *The Tsimshian and their Neighbours of the North Pacific Coast*. Seattle: University of Washington Press, 1984.

Mills, Antonia and Richard Slobodin (eds.). *Amerindian Rebirth: Reincarnation Belief among North American Indians and Inuit*. Toronto: University of Toronto Press, 1994.

Morris, Rosalind C. *New Worlds: Film, Ethnography and the Representation of Northwest Coast Cultures*. Boulder: Westview Press, 1994.

Murdock, George P. *Outline of Cultural Materials*. New Haven: Human Relations Area Files, 1945.

New, W.H. "Writing Here." *BC Studies*, no. 147, Autumn 2005, 3–25.

Neumann, Erich. *The Great Mother: An Analysis of the Archetype*. Princeton: Princeton University Press, 1972.

Nowry, Laurence. *Man of Mana Marius Barbeau*. Toronto: New Canada Publications, 1995.

Nurse, Andrew. "Tradition and Modernity: The Cultural Work of Marius Barbeau" (PhD Dissertation). Queens University, 1997.

Nuytten, Phil. *The Totem Carvers: Charlie James, Ellen Neel, and Mungo Martin*. Vancouver: Panorama Publications, 1982.

Oberg, Kalervo. *The Social Economy of the Tlingit Indians* Vancouver: J.J. Douglas, 1973.

Otten, Charlotte. *Anthropology and Art: Readings in Cross-cultural Aesthetics*. Garden City: The Natural History Press, 1971.

Owram, Doug. *Born at the Right Time: A History of the Baby-Boom Generation*. Toronto: University of Toronto Press, 1996.

Panofsky, Erwin. *Meaning in the Visual Arts: Papers In and On Art History*. Garden City: Doubleday, 1955.

———. *Studies in Iconology: Humanistic Themes in the Art of the Renaissance*. New York: Harper Torchbooks, 1962.

Parr, A.E. *Mostly About Museums*. New York: The American Museum of Natural History, 1959.

Pearce, Joseph Chilton. *The crack in the cosmic egg Challenging constructs of mind and reality*. New York: Pocket Books, 1973.

Peden, Murray. *A Thousand Shall Fall*. Toronto: Stoddart, 1988.

Phillips, Ruth B. *Museum Pieces: Toward the Indigenization of Canadian Museums*. Montreal: McGill-Queens University Press, 2011.

Pinder, Leslie Hall. *Bring Me One of Everything: A Novel*. Marblehead: Grey Swan Press, 2012.

Plant, Byron King. "'A Relationship and Exchange of Experience': H.B. Hawthorn, Indian Affairs, and the 1955 BC Indian Research Project." *BC Studies*, no. 163, Autumn 2009, 5–31.

Price, Sally. *Primitive Art in Civilised Places*. Chicago: University of Chicago Press, 2001.

Ray, Verne F. *Cultural Relations in the Plateau of Northwestern America*. Los Angeles: The Southwest Museum, 1939.

Reid, Bill and Robert Bringhurst. *The Raven Steals the Light*. Vancouver: Douglas & McIntyre, 1984.

Report of the Royal Commission on National Development in the Arts and Letters 1949–1951. Ottawa: King's Printer, 1951.

Ridington, Robin. "The World Is as Sharp as a Knife: Vision and Image in the Work of Wilson Duff." *BC Studies*, no 38, Summer 1978, 3–13.

Ritchie, Margaret. *Denver Art Museum: Major Works in the Collection*. Denver: Denver Art Museum, 1981.

Roy, Patricia. *The Collectors: A History of the Royal British Columbia Museum and Archives*. Victoria: Royal BC Museum, 2018.

———. *Vancouver: An Illustrated History*. Toronto: James Lorimer and National Museum of Man, 1980.

Roy, Susan. *These Mysterious People: Shaping History and Archaeology in a Northwest Coast Community*. Montreal: McGill-Queens University Press, 2010.

Ruebsaat, Helmut J. and Raymond Hull. *The Male Climactic*. New York: Hawthorn Books, 1975.

Said, Edward W. *On Late Style: Music and Literature Against the Grain*. New York: Pantheon Books, 2006.

Sanders, Douglas. "The Nishga Case." *BC Studies*, no. 19, Autumn 1973, 3–20.

Scearce, Phil. *Finish Forty and Home: The Untold World War II Story of B-24s in the Pacific*. Denton: University of North Texas Press, 2011.

Seguin, Margaret. *The Tsimshian Images of the Past: Views for the Present*. Vancouver: UBC Press, 1984.

Serl, Vernon and Herbert C. Taylor. *Essays in Honour of Harry Hawthorn*. Bellingham: Western Washington State College, 1975.

Shahn, Ben. *The Shape of Content*. New York: Vintage Books, 1957.

Shadbolt, Doris. *Bill Reid*. Vancouver, Douglas & McIntyre, 1986.

Sheehan McLaren, Carol. "Moment of Death: Gift of Life A Reinterpretation of the NorthwestCoast Image of 'Hawk'." *Anthropologica* vol. 20, no. 1–2, 1978, 65–90.

———. *Pipes that Won't Smoke; Coal that Won't Burn: Haida Sculpture in Argillite*. Calgary: The Glenbow Museum, 1981.

Shephard, Ben. *A War of Nerves; Soldiers and Psychiatrists 1914–1994*. London: Pimlico, 2002.

Shorter, Edward. *Before Prozac: The Troubled History of Mood Disorders in Psychiatry*. New York: Oxford University Press.

Siwak, Dr, W.J. *My Times: An Autobiography*. Edmonton: ASAP Fincolour, 1992.

Smyly, John and Carolyn. *Saving the Silent Ones: The 1957 Totem Pole Salvage Expedition to Ninstints, World Heritage Site*. Victoria: Trafford Publishing, 2007.

Sorrenson, M.P.K. *Manifest Duty: The Polynesian Society Over 100 Years*. Auckland: The Polynesian Society, 1992.

———. "Polynesian Corpuscles and Pacific Anthropology: The Home-Made Anthropology of Sir Apirana Ngata and Sir Peter Buck." *The Journal of the Polynesian Society* 91, no. 1, March 1982, 7–27.

Sterrit, Neil J., Susan Marsden, Robert Galois, Peter R. Grant and Richard Overstall. *Tribal Boundaries in the Nass Watershed*. Vancouver: UBC Press, 1998.

Stewart, Hilary. *Robert Davidson Haida Printmaker*. Vancouver: Douglas & McIntyre, 1979.

———. *Totem Poles*. Vancouver: Douglas & McIntyre, 1990.

Stocking, George W. Jr. (ed.). *Colonial Situations: Essays on the Conceptualization of Ethnographic Knowledge*. Madison: University of Wisconsin Press, 1991.

———. *Objects and Others: Essays on Museums and Material Culture*. Madison: University of Wisconsin Press, 1985.

——— (ed.). *Observers Observed: Essays on Ethnographic Fieldwork*. Madison: University of Wisconsin Press, 1983.

——— (ed.). *Romantic Motives: Essays on Anthropological Sensibility*. Madison: University of Wisconsin Press, 1989.

Stonechild, Blair. *The Knowledge Seeker: Embracing Indigenous Spirituality*. Regina: University of Regina Press, 2016.

Stouck, David. *Arthur Erickson: An Architect's Life*. Madeira Park: Douglas & McIntyre, 2013.

Sturtevant, William. "Does Anthropology Need Museums?" *Proceedings of the Biological Society of Washington* 82, 1969, 619–49.

Suttles, Wayne. *Coast Salish Essays*. Vancouver: Talonbooks, 1987.

——— (ed.). *Handbook of North American Indians, Volume 7: Northwest Coast*. Washington: Smithsonian Institution, 1990.

———. "The World Is as Sharp as a Knife: A Review Article." *BC Studies*, no. 56, Winter 1982–83, 82–91.

Swanton, John R. *Contributions to the Ethnology of the Haida: Memoir of the American Museum of Natural History, Volume V.* New York: AMS Press, 1905.

———. *Haida Texts and Myths: Skidegate Dialect.* Washington: Government Printing Office, 1905.

Swift, Daniel. *Bomber Country: The Poetry of a Lost Pilot's War.* New York: Farrar, Straus and Giroux, 2010.

Szaz, Thomas. *Fatal Freedom: The Ethics and Politics of Suicide.* Westport: Praeger, 1999.

Tax, Sol. *Indian Tribes of Aboriginal America: Selected Papers of the xxixth International Congress of Americanists.* New York: Cooper Square Publishers, 1967.

Thom, Ian M. (ed.). *Robert Davidson: Eagle of the Dawn.* Vancouver: Douglas & McIntyre, 1993.

Thomas, Susan Jane. "The Life and Work of Charles Edenshaw: A Study of Innovation" (BA essay). University of British Columbia, April 1967.

Tippett, Maria. *Bill Reid: The Making of an Indian.* Toronto: Vintage Canada, 2004.

Townsend-Gault, Charlotte, Jennifer Karmer and Ki-ke-in (eds.). *Native Art of the Northwest Coast: A History of Changing Ideas.* Vancouver: UBC Press, 2013.

University of British Columbia. *Calendar Thirty-Third Session 1947–1948.* Vancouver: 1947.

University of British Columbia. *Calendar Thirty-Fourth Session 1948–1949.* Vancouver: 1948.

University of British Columbia. *Calendar Thirty-Fourth Session 1949–1950.* Vancouver: 1949.

Vancouver Art Gallery. *Bill Reid: A Retrospective Exhibition.* Vancouver: Vancouver Art Gallery, 1974.

Vancouver School Board. *Archives and Heritage.* Website.

The Van Tech (Vancouver Technical Secondary School yearbook). Vols. 17–24, 1939–45.

Vodden, Christy and Ian Dyck. *A World Inside: A 150-Year History of the Canadian Museum of Civilization.* Gateneau: Canadian Museum of Civilisation, 2006.

Wade, Jill. *Houses For All: The Struggle for Social Housing in Vancouver, 1919–1950.* Vancouver: UBC Press, 1994.

Waite, P.B. " Invading Privacies: Biography as History." *Dalhousie Review* 69, no. 4, 1990, 479–96.

———. *Lord of Point Grey: Larry MacKenzie of UBC.* Vancouver: University of British Columbia Press, 1987.

Warren, Jeff. *The Head Trip: Adventures in the Wheel of Consciousness.* Oxford: Oneworld Publications, 2007.

Watts, Alan. *The Book: On the Taboo Against Knowing Who You Are.* New York: Vintage Books, 1972.

Weaver, John C. *A Sadly Troubled History: The Meanings of Suicide in the Modern Age.* Montreal: McGill-Queens University Press, 2009.

Weaver, Sally. *Making Canadian Indian Policy: The Hidden Agenda.* Toronto: University of Toronto Press, 1981.

Webb, Phyllis. *Talking.* Dunvegan: Quadrant Editions, 1982.

———. *Wilson's Bowl.* Toronto: The Coach House Press, 1980.

Webster, Gloria Cranmer. "The 'R' Word." *Muse* vi, no. 3, October 1988, 43–44.

West, Robert Gerard. "Saving and Naming the Garbage: Charles E Borden and the Making of BC Prehistory 1945–1960" (MA thesis). University of British Columbia, 1992.

Weyler, Rex. *Greenpeace: How a Group of Ecologists, Journalists and Visionaries Changed the World*. Vancouver: Raincoast Books, 2004.

Wheeler, Rueben. *Man, Nature and Art*. Oxford: Pergamon Press, 1968.

Whitaker, Robert. *Anatomy of an Epidemic: Magic Bullets, Psychiatric Drugs and the Astonishing Rise of Mental Illness in America*. New York: Broadway Paperbacks, 2010.

Wickwire, Wendy. *At the Bridge: James Teit and an Anthropology of Belonging*. Vancouver: UBC Press, 2019.

———. "The Quest for the 'Real" Franz Boas: A Review Essay." BC *Studies*, no. 194, Summer 2017, 173–193.

Wike, Joyce. "Problems in Fur Trade Analysis: The Northwest Coast," *American Anthropolgist* 60, 1958, 1086–1101.

Wilcken, Patrick. *Claude Lévi-Strauss: The Poet in the Laboratory*. New York: Penguin, 2010.

The Working Lives Collective. *Working Lives: Vancouver 1886–1986*. Vancouver: New Star Books, 1985.

Wright, Robin and Diana Augaitis (eds.). *Charles Edenshaw*. London: Black Dog Publishing, 2013.

Wright, Robin K. *Northern Haida Master Carvers*. London and Seattle: University of Washington Press, 2001.

Young, David E. and Jean-Guy Goulet (eds.). *Being Changed: The Anthropology of Extraordinary Experience*. Peterborough: Broadview Press, 1998.

Notes

Preface

1   Wilson Duff, "Images Stone BC" lecture, recording, National Museum of History Archives.
2   Robin Fisher, *Contact and Conflict: Indian-European Relations in British Columbia, 1774–1890* (Vancouver: UBC Press, 1977).
3   Wilson Duff to M. Kew, June 27, 1975, Wilson Duff fonds, Museum of Anthropology Archives, University of British Columbia (WDF), box 30/5.
4   Wilson Duff, Notes for Thinking, WDF, box 51/10.
5   Wendy Wickwire, *At the Bridge: James Teit and an Anthropology of Belonging* (Vancouver: UBC Press, 2019), xv–xvii.
6   Wilson Duff, *The Indian History of British Columbia, Volume 1: The Impact of the White Man*, Anthropology in British Columbia Memoir No. 5 (Victoria: Provincial Museum of Natural History and Anthropology, 1964), 10.
7   The phrase is Wilson's in Wilson Duff and Michael Kew's "Anthony Island: A Home of the Haidas," *Report of the Year 1957* (Provincial Museum of Natural History and Anthropology), 63.
8   Interview with Roy Henry Vickers, March 18, 2015.

1. Vancouver Boyhood

1   Interview with Roy Henry Vickers, March 18, 2015.
2   Wilson Duff (WD), "Spirit Quest," Marnie Duff Papers (MDP). Also in Donald N. Abbott, ed., *The World Is As Sharp As a Knife: An Anthology in Honour of Wilson Duff* (Victoria: British Columbia Provincial Museum, 1981), 308.
3   Keith Ralston in The Working Lives Collective, *Working Lives: Vancouver 1886–1986* (Vancouver: New Star Books, 1985), 179; Patricia E. Roy, *Vancouver: An Illustrated History* (Toronto: James Lorimer and National Museum of Man, 1980), 112.
4   *British Columbia Directories*, 1925–1937
5   "History of Charles Dickens School," Vancouver School Board Archives and Heritage (website).
6   Ron Duff, Recollections, MDP.
7   Vancouver School Board, Progress Record Elementary for Wilson Duff.
8   For this picture of schooling at Charles Dickens Elementary School I have drawn particularly on Neil Sutherland, "The Triumph of Formalism: Elementary Schooling in Vancouver From the 1920s to the 1960s," in Jean Barman and Robert A.J. McDonald, *Vancouver Past: Essays in Social History Vancouver Centennial Issue of BC Studies* (Vancouver: UBC Press, 1986), 179.
9   Ron Duff, Recollections, MDP.

10 Mervyn Davis, Recollections, MDP.

11 W.H. New, "Writing Here," BC *Studies*, no. 147 (Autumn 2005): 4.

12 Ron Duff, Recollections, MDP, and interviews with Marnie Duff, June 25 and August 29, 2013.

13 WD, notes, WDF, box 47/1 and 45/3.

14 "The Principal's Message," *The Vantech* (1939): 9.

15 Vancouver Technical Secondary School, student record for Wilson Duff.

16 Ron Duff, Recollections, MDP.

17 *The Vantech* (1941): 25–26 and (1942): 24–28.

18 *The Vantech* (1941): 54.

19 "The Principal's Message," *The Vantech* (1942): 9.

20 Pierre and Justin Trudeau respectively.

21 Editorial, *The Vantech* (1941 and 1943): 7 and 8.

22 *The Vantech* (1942): 43.

23 *The Vantech* (1942): 43.

24 Vancouver Technical Secondary School, student record for Marion Barber.

25 *The Vantech* (1943): 24.

26 Ron Duff to Marnie Duff, November 3, 2003, MDP.

27 *The Vantech* (1942): 11, extracted from George H. Griffen, *Legends of the Evergreen Coast* (Vancouver: Clarke & Stuart, 1934), 19–21.

28 *The Vantech* (1939): 22.

29 WD to Mom, April 28, 1945, MDP.

30 Enrollment Services, University of British Columbia, student transcript for Wilson Duff.

31 WD, "Three Years in the R.C.A.F.," scrapbook, MDP.

32 *The Vantech* (1944): 8 taken, with some liberties, from Ecclesiastes 9:11.

2. I, the Navigator

1 WD to Mom, February 9, 1945, MDP.

2 Douglas Bond, *The Love and Fear of Flying* (New York: International Universities Press, 1952), 71–72. Bond was a Freudian psychiatrist who worked with a number of flyers after the war.

3 WD to Mom, January 6, 1945, MDP.

4 F.J. Hatch, *The Aerodrome of Democracy: Canada and the British Commonwealth Air Training Plan, 1939–1945* (Ottawa: Directorate of History, Department of National Defence, 1983), 182; W.A.B. Douglas, *The Creation of a National Air Force: The Official History of the Royal Canadian Air Force Volume II* (Toronto: University of Toronto Press, 1986), 293.

5 R.G. (Bob) Marshall, "Air Force Memories—RCAF 1940–1945," typescipt in the possession of Dave Marshall.

6 Hatch, 194.

7 Hatch, 83.

8 Robert Collins, *The Long and the Short and the Tall: An Ordinary Airman's War* (Vancouver: Douglas & McIntyre, 1986), 1.

9   Ibid., 39–41; Martin Francis, *The Flyer: British Culture and the Royal Air Force, 1939–1945* (Oxford: Oxford University Press, 2008), 4 and 34.

10 WD, "Three Years in the R.C.A.F."; WD to Folks, June 9, 1943; WD to Mom, June 13, 1943, MDP.

11 Rueben Wheeler, *Man, Nature and Art* (Oxford: Pergamon Press, 1968), 5–6. Wilson read and thought about Wheeler's ideas many years later.

12 *Manual of R.C.A.F. Drill and Ceremonial* (Ottawa: Kings Printer, 1941).

13 Collins, 24. For this picture of the Manning Depot experience I have also drawn on John W. Chalmers and John J.N. Chalmers, *Navigator Brothers: The Story of Two Brothers in the R.C.A.F.* (Edmonton: Chalmers, 2008); John A. Iverach, *Chronicles of a Nervous Navigator* (Winnipeg: Iverach, n.d.); Murray Peden, *A Thousand Shall Fall* (Toronto: Stoddart, 1988); and Dr A.J. Siwak, *My Times: An Autobiography* (Edmonton: ASAP Fincolour, 1992).

14 The quotations in this paragraph are from WD to Mom, June 1, 1943; WD to Folks, June 9, 1943; WD to Mom, June 13, 1943, MDP.

15 WD to Win and Chick, August 18, 1934 (1943), MDP.

16 WD to Folks, June 17, 1943; WD to Mom, July 13, 1943, MDP.

17 Spencer Dunmore, *Wings for Victory: The Remarkable Story of the British Commonwealth Air Training Plan in Canada* (Toronto: McClelland & Stewart, 1994), 76.

18 Lee Heide, *Whispering Death: My Wartime Adventures* (Victoria: Trafford Publishing, 2000), 7.

19 WD to Mom, n.d., July 25, 1943 and September 7, 1943, MDP.

20 WD, "Three Years in the R.C.A.F."

21 WD telegram to Mrs W. Duff, August 16, 1943; Wilson Duff, "Three Years in the R.C.A.F."; WD to Win and Chick, August 18, 1934 (1943), MDP.

22 WD to Mom, October 24, 1943, MDP.

23 Hatch, xviii.

24 WD to Mom, n.d.; September 25, 1943; October 13, 1943; October 24, 1943, MDP.

25 WD to Win, November 5, 1943, MDP.

26 *Manual of R.C.A.F. Drill and Ceremonial*, 1.

27 WD to Mom, December 11, 1943, MDP.

28 For this paragraph I found Chalmers and Chalmers, 94–103 and John W. Chalmers, "Learning the Gen Trade," *Alberta History* 42, no. 3 (Summer 1994): 2–10 particularly helpful.

29 WD to Mom, December 20, 1943, MDP.

30 Chalmers and Chalmers, 103.

31 WD to Mom, December 5, 1943; December 11, 1943; January 5, 1944, MDP.

32 WD to Mom, December 31, 1943; George Barr to Marnie Duff, June 18, 1984; Wilson Duff to Mom, January 21, 1944, MDP.

33 WD to Mom, March 11, 1944, and n.d.; WD to Mom and Dad, March 31, 1944, MDP.

34 WD, "Three Years in the R.C.A.F."

35 WD to Mom, January 21, 1944, MDP.

36 Bill Kirkness and Matt Poole, *RAF Liberators Over Burma: Flying with 159 Squadron* (Croydon: Fronthill Media, 2017), 36.

37 WD to Mom, February 24, 1945, MDP.

38 Interview with Art Skirrow, November 26, 2012.

39 Ibid.

40 A.J. Baine, *The Arsenal of Democracy: FDR, Detroit, and an Epic Quest to Arm America at War* (Boston/New York: Mariner Books, 2015), 234.

41 WD to Mom, n.d., MDP.

42 WD to Mom, n.d. and August 22, 1944, MDP; T.W. Melnyck, *Canadian Flying Operations in South East Asia 1941–1945* (Ottawa: Directorate of History, 1976). 109.

43 WD to Mom, n.d. and September 22, 1944, MDP.

44 WD to Mom, September 23, 1944, MDP.

45 Ibid.

46 WD to Mom, September 30, 1944, MDP.

47 WD to Mom, October 6–7, 1944 and October 13, 1944, MDP.

48 WD to Mom, October 16, 1944 and n.d., MDP.

49 This description is drawn from Kirkness and Poole, 154.

50 Melnyck, 106.

51 WD to Mom and Dad, December 7, 1944; WD to Mom, n.d., MDP.

52 Newspaper clipping in WD, "Three Years in the R.C.A.F.," MDP.

53 W.W. Frazer, *A Trepid Aviator: Bombay to Bangkok* (Burnstown: General Store Publishing House, 1995), 176.

54 Interview with Art Skirrow, November 26, 2012.

55 Frazer, 183.

56 Richard Hillary, *The Last Enemy* (London: Pimlico, 1997), 4.

57 For this paragraph I have drawn partly from Francis, 109, 118–119 and 197; Daniel Swift, *Bomber Country: The Poetry of a Lost Pilot's War* (New York: Farrar, Straus and Giroux, 2010), 178–79.

58 WD, "Polynesian and Micronesian Navigation," March 1950, WDF, box 1, file 3.

59 Bond, 15; Swift, 202.

60 See, for example, Kirkness and Poole, 103; Peden, 51.

61 John Gillespie Magee, "High Flight," in John Robert Colombo, ed., *The Penguin Treasury of Popular Canadian Poems* (Toronto: Penguin Canada, 2002), 53.

62 Swift, 14–15.

63 Interview with Art Skirrow, November 26, 2012.

64 WD to Mom and Dad, May 16, 1945, MDP.

65 WD to Mom and Dad, April 28, 1945; WD to Win, January 31, 1945, MDP.

66 WD to Dad, April 1945, MDP.

67 WD to Mom, n.d.; WD to Win, January 3, 1945, MDP.

68 WD to Mom and Dad, April 28, 1945, MDP.

69 WD to Mom and Pops, June 4, 1945; WD to Win, June 19, 1945, MDP.

70 WD to Win, August 9, 1945; WD to Folks, August 17, 1945, MDP.

71 John R.W. Gwynne-Timothy, *Burma Liberators: RCAF in SEAC* (Toronto: Next Level Press, 1991), 437.

72 WD to Folks, August 17, 1945, MDP.

73 WD to Folks, September 5, 1945, MDP.

74 Group Captain (Lucky) Jordan, *To Burma Skies and Beyond: An Airman's Story* (London: Janus Publishing, 1995), 151.

75 WD to Dad, August 1945; WD to Folks, August 1945; WD to Folks, August 21, 1945, MDP.

76 WD to Folks, August 21, 1945; WD to Folks, September 16, 1945; WD to Mom, September 28, 1945, MDP.

77 WD to Mom, October 15, 1945; and WD to Folks, October 25, 1945, MDP.

78 WD to Mom, October 30, 1945, MDP.

79 WD to Folks, November 15, 1945; WD to Mom, December 31, 1945, MDP.

80 WD to Mom, n.d.; WD to Mom, December 31, 1945; WD to Mom, January 3, 1946, MDP.

81 WD to Mom, January 3 and January 6, 1945, MDP.

82 Brereton Greenhous, Stephen J. Harris, William C. Johnston and William G.P. Rowling, *The Crucible of War, 1939–1945: The Official History of the Royal Canadian Air Force Volume III* (Toronto: University of Toronto Press, 1994), 890–909. The deficiency is somewhat made up by Melnyk, passim.

3. Learning Anthropology

1 Tim Cook, *Fight to the Finish: Canadians in the Second World War 1944–1945, Volume Two* (Toronto: Penguin Random House, 2015), 416; Ben Shepard, *A War of Nerves: Soldiers and Psychiatrists 1914–1994* (London: Pimlico, 2002), 332.

2 WD to Folks, September 5, 1945; WD to Mom, September 28, 1945; WD to Folks, November 15, 1945, MDP.

3 Robert Burns, "To a Mouse," in Henry W. Meikle and William Beattie, eds., *Robert Burns* (Harmondsworth: Penguin Books, 1946), 88–89.

4 P.B. Waite, *Lord of Point Grey: Larry MacKenzie of UBC* (Vancouver: University of British Columbia Press, 1987), 116.

5 WD to Mom, December 20, 1943, MDP.

6 Waite, 118 and 126; S.N.F Chant, "The Veteran Returns," University of British Columbia Archives (UBCA), website.

7 Enrollment Services, University of British Columbia, student transcript for Wilson Duff.

8 H.F. Angus to Hawthorn, July 22, 1946 and January 8, 1947; N.A.M. MacKenzie to Hawthorn, January 30, 1947, Michael Ames fonds, box 32/12, UBCA.

9 H.B. Hawthorn, "The Māori: A Study in Acculturation," *American Anthropologist*, n.s. 40, no. 2, part 2, (April 1944): Memoir Series of the American Anthropological Association, no. 64: 5.

10 M.P.K. Sorrenson, "Polynesian Corpuscles and Pacific Anthropology: the Home-Made Anthropology of Sir Apirana Ngata and Sir Peter Buck," *The Journal of the Polynesian Society* 91, no. 1 (March 1982): 7 and 17.

11 H. Hawthorn review of *Te Rangi Hiroa: The Life of Sir Peter Buck*, by J.B. Condliffe. *Pacific Affairs* 47, no. 1 (spring 1974): 111.

12 George W. Stocking Jr., *Objects and Others: Essays on Museums and Material Culture* (Madison: University of Wisconsin Press, 1985), 124–26.

13 Cyril Belshaw to Raymond Firth, November 1, 1955, Belshaw fonds, box 60/56, UBCA.

14 Hawthorn to Hugh Keenleyside, September 15, 1947, Hawthorn fonds, box 1/1, UBCA.

15 Belshaw to Hawthorn, August 11, 1952; Hawthorn to Belshaw, August 28, 1952, Hawthorn fonds, box 4/6 and box 61/22, UBCA.

16 H.B. Hawthorn and C.S. Belshaw, "Cultural Evolution or Cultural Change—the Case of Polynesia," *The Journal of the Polynesian Society* 66, no. 1 (1957), 18–35; M.P.K. Sorrenson, *Manifest Duty: The Polynesian Society Over 100 Years* (Auckland: The Polynesian Society, 1992), 105–6.

17 Hawthorn to Gordon Inglis, April 1, 1974, H. Hawthorn fonds, box 6/29, UBCA.

18 H.B. Hawthorn, ed. "Report of the Conference on Native Indian Affairs at Acadia Camp, UBC, Vancouver BC, April 1, 2, and 3 1948," typescript, 17–18 and 81.

19 MacKenzie to Hawthorn, February 7, 1950, Hawthorn fonds, box 2/11, UBCA; *Report of the Royal Commission on National Development in the Arts, Letters and Sciences 1949–1951* (Ottawa: King's Printer, 1951), 435; Audrey E. and Harry B. Hawthorn, "Report on Contemporary Art of the Canadian Indian, 1950," Ames fonds, box 26/8, UBCA.

20 H.B. Hawthorn, ed., *A Survey of the Contemporary Indians of Canada: A Report on Economic, Political, Educational Needs and Policies* (Ottawa: Indian Affairs Branch, 1967), 13.

21 Cyril S. Belshaw, *The Sorcerer's Apprentice: An Anthropology of Public Policy* (New York: Pergamon Press, 1976), passim.

22 Belshaw to Raymond Firth, November 20, 1956, Belshaw fonds, box 60/56, UBCA.

23 Harry Hawthorn to Gordon Inglis, April 1, 1974, Hawthorn fonds, box 6/29, UBCA.

24 Hawthorn to C.E. Beeby, April 8, 1948; Hawthorn to Horace Belshaw, April 23, 1954: Hawthorn to J.F. Leddy, February 14, 1963; Hawthorn fonds, box 1/2; box 1/10 and box 7/17, UBCA.

25 Hawthorn to Gordon Inglis, April 1, 1974, Hawthorn fonds, box 6/29, UBCA.

26 *University of British Columbia Calendar, 1948–1949*, 195; WD, Student Transcript, Enrollment Services, University of British Columbia; Hawthorn to H.F. Angus, January 24, 1949, Harry Hawthorn fonds, series 1, box 8, UBC MOA.

27 Charles E. Borden, "Wilson Duff (1925–1976): His Contributions to the Growth of Archaeology in British Columbia," *BC Studies*, no. 33 (Spring 1977): 4.

28 Wilson Duff, "Report on an Archeological Excavation at Marpole BC," Laboratory of Archaeology, UBC MOA.

29 Interview with Marnie Duff, November 7, 2013.

30 Douglas Owram, *Born at the Right Time: A History of the Baby-Boom Generation* (Toronto: University of Toronto Press, 1996), 12 and 24–29.

31 Hawthorn to H.F. Angus, January 24, 1949, Harry Hawthorn fonds, series 1, box 8, UBC MOA.

32 Wilson Duff, "Report on Archaeological Survey of Hope-Chilliwack Area," Laboratory of Archaeology, UBC MOA.

33 WD, Notes on the Stalo 1949, Department of Anthropology (Wilson Duff) Records, (DAWD), GR-3662, box 2/38, British Columbia Provincial Museum (BCPM); *The Native Voice* (November 1949): 15.

34 Hawthorn to Clifford Carl, May 17, 1949; WD Notebook, n.d., DAWD, box 8/26 and box 5/25.

35 Interview with Roy Carlson, July 4, 1913.

36 For a summary of the literature and thinking, for an against, about the Boas legacy see Wendy Wickwire, "The Quest for the "Real" Franz Boas: A Review Essay," *BC Studies*, no. 194 (Summer 2017), 173–93.

37 Interview with Bill and Marty Holm, December 1, 2014.

38 Interview with Roy Carlson, July 4, 1913, Leland Donald, December 21, 2018; Viola E. Garfield and Pamela T. Amoss, "Erna Gunther," *American Anthropologist*, n.s. 86, no. 2 (June 1984): 394–99; Viola E. Garfield and Linn A. Forest, *The Wolf and the Raven: Totem Poles of Southeastern Alaska* (Seattle: University of Washington Press), passim; Verne F. Ray, *Cultural relations in the Plateau of Northwestern America* (Los Angeles: The Southwest Museum, 1939): 1 and 145.

39 Wilson's graduate student essays are to be found in DAWD, box 1/35 and box 4/3; Wilson Duff, "Polynesian and Micronesian Navigation," March 1950, WDF, box 1/3.

40 Barbara Lane to WD, July 24, 1952, Provincial Museum Correspondence (PMC), GR-0111, box 9/7, BCPM.

41 George P. Murdock et al., *Outline of Cultural Materials* (New Haven: Human Relations Area Files, 1945).

42 WD, Notes taken on Anthropology 250 at the University of Washington, DAWD, box 2/1.

43 Erna Gunther, *Ethnobotany of Western Washington* (Seattle and London: University of Washington Press, 1945).

44 Patricia Roy, *The Collectors: A History of the Royal British Columbia Museum and Archives* (Victoria: Royal BC Museum, 2018): 118–20; Harry Hawthorn to A.E. Pickford, February 2, 1948, Hawthorn fonds, box 1/3, UBCA.

45 Wilson Duff, "The Upper Stalo Indians: An Introductory Ethnography" (master's thesis, University of Washington, 1952), preface.

46 Ibid.; Provincial Museum of Natural History and Anthropology, *Report for the Year 1950* (Victoria: King's printer, 1951), 14; WD to Erna Gunther, October 3, 1950, PMC, box 4/4.

47 WD to Erna Gunther, October 17, 1950, PMC, box 4/14.

4. Provincial Anthropologist

1 *Vancouver Sun*, March 8, 1952.

2 WD to H.D. Skinner, October 28, 1955, DAWD, box 7/4.

3 C. Carl to T.F. McIlwraith, March 12, 1946; Carl to Marion Smith, May 27, 1947; Douglas Leechman to WD, October 13, 1950, PMC, box 10/48, box 19/13 and box 10/02.

4 WD to Barbara Savadkin, June 27, 1950, DAWD, box 6/40.

5 Provincial Museum of Natural History and Anthropology, *Report for the Year 1950*, 14–15.

6 Gunther to WD, January 29, 1951; WD to Gunther, February 7, 1951, PMC, box 4/14.

7 WD to Hawthorn, September 5, 1950; WD to Hawthorn, November 1, 1950 and Hawthorn to WD, November 3, 1950, DAWD, box 8/26.

8 Marion to Folks, n.d., MDP.

9 WD, "History and Prehistory," DAWD, box 1/37; WD to Gunther, February 7, 1951; Gunther to WD, February 8, 1951, PMC, box 4/14; Duff, "The Upper Stalo Indians," passim.

10 WD to Viola Garfield, May 6, 1952, DAWD, box 8/22.

11 Wilson Duff, *The Upper Stalo Indians of the Fraser Valley, British Columbia, Anthropology in British Columbia Memoir no. 1* (Victoria: British Columbia Provincial Museum, 1952).

12 Alice Ravenhill to WD, September 2, 1950, PMC; Vancouver *Province*, July 10, 1958, Vertical Files, reel 41, no. 1056, BCPM; Firth to WD, September 23, 1953, DAWD, box 6/43.

13 WD Field Notes, notebook 13, 1953, DAWD, box 2/22; interview with Gloria Cranmer-Webster, March 4, 2014.

14 WD Field Notes, notebook 10, 1955, DAWD, box 3/9. For an account of Willie Seaweed and his art see Bill Holm, *Smoky-Top: The Art and Times of Willie Seaweed* (Seattle: University of Washington Press, 1983). Wilson's photos of the artist and his work are on pages 8 and 63.

15 WD, "The Southern Kwakiutl," DAWD, box 3/3; Robert Galois, *Kwakwaka'wakw Settlements, 1775–1920: A Geographical Analysis and Gazetteer* (Vancouver: UBC Press, 1994): 21.

16 WD, files of research notes, DAWD, box 1/24; Herbert C. Taylor and Wilson Duff, "A Post-Contact Southward Movement of the Kwakiutl," *Research Studies, State College of Washington* 24, no. 1 (1956): 56–66.

17 Suttles to WD, August 6, 1956, WDF, box 45/1.

18 Wilson Duff, "Unique Stone Artifacts from the Gulf Islands," Provincial Museum of Natural History and Anthropology, *Report for the Year 1955*, 45–55; Wilson Duff, *Prehistoric Stone Sculpture of the Fraser River and Gulf of Georgia, Anthropology in British Columbia Memoir no. 5* (Victoria: British Columbia Provincial Museum, 1956), 59 and 109.

19 Wilson Duff, "Stone Clubs from the Skeena River Area," Provincial Museum of Natural History and Anthropology, *Report for the Year 1962*, 27–38.

20 Bob and Barb Lane to WD, mid-July 1957, PMC, box 9/7; Hawthorn to WD, June 7, 1957, DAWD, box 8/28.

21 WD to T.F. McIlwraith, 1 Mat 1952, PMC, Box 10/48.

22 WD, "Anthro. Museum," undated typescript, WDF, box 13/13.

23 WD to Hawthorn, November 1, 1950, DAWD, box 8/26.

24 Michael Kew, "Reflections on Anthropology at the University of British Columbia," *BC Studies*, no. 193 (Spring 2017) 168–69; interview with Michael Kew, April 16, 2013.

25 Diane MacEachern Barwick, "'A Grand Old Man at 35': Wilson Duff as Curator," in Abbott, ed., 26.

26 Interview with Roy Henry Vickers, March 18, 2015.

27 Interview with John Sendy, December 28, 2018.

28 Interview with Maria Abbott, October 27, 2014, and recorded interview with Beth Hill in her possession; Beth and Ray Hill, *Indian Petroglyphs of the Pacific Northwest* (Saanichton: Hancock House, 1974).

29 WD to A.C. Davison, November 15, 1950, DAWD, box 6/40; Wilson Duff, "Thoughts on the Nootka Canoe," Provincial Museum of Natural History and Anthropology, *Report for the Year 1964*, 24–31.

30 *The British Colonist*, January 4, 1953, Museum Scrapbook, box 2, BCPM; WD to T.B. Upton, November 16, 1961, DAWD, box 7/11; Ed Meade to WD, July 20, 1960, and WD to Ed Meade, July 25, 1960, PMC, box 34/11.

31 WD to Alice B. Kasakoff, May 15, 1964, DAWD, box 7/16; John W. Adams, *The Gitksan Potlatch: Population Flux, Resource Ownership and Reciprocity* (Toronto: Holt, Rinehart

and Winston of Canada, 1973). Kasakoff and Adams were wife and husband and worked together in the Gitksan communities.

32 Wilson Duff, *The Indian History of British Columbia, Volume 1: The Impact of the White Man, Anthropology in British Columbia Memoir No. 5* (Victoria: Provincial Museum of Natural History and Anthropology, 1964), 54ff.

33 WD to Joyce Wike Holder, November 24, 1954, DAWD, box 8/35; Joyce Wike, "Problems in Fur Trade Analysis: The Northwest Coast," *American Anthropologist*, n.s. 60 (1958): 1097.

34 WD to L.H.J. Cook, February 25, 1957; WD to Victor P. Hall, May 8, 1956; WD to Donald E. Shultz, February 16, 1960, DAWD, box 7/7, 7/5 and 7/10.

35 Russell Potter to WD, February 17, 1954; WD to E.J. Ross, March 21, 1956; WD to Ken McKay, March 22, 1951, DAWD, box 7/1, 7/5 and 6/41.

36 Roy, *The Collectors*, 103–4 and 108.

37 Marion to Folks, n.d., MDP.

38 Audrey Hawthorn, "Totem Pole Carver," *The Beaver*, Outfit 282 (March 1952): 5.

39 Interview with Gloria Cranmer Webster, March 4, 2014.

40 Wilson Duff, "Mungo Martin, Carver of the Century," reprinted in Abbott, ed., 37–40. The essay was originally published in 1959.

41 *Reader's Digest* (March 1955) Museum Scrapbook, box 2; *British Colonist*, January 21, 1954, Vertical Files, reel 42, no. 1678; Victoria *Times*, Vertical Files, reel 190, no.0262, BCPM; Interview with Gloria Cranmer Webster, 4 March 2014.

42 Provincial Museum of Natural History and Anthropology, *Report for the Year, 1953*, 21–23.

43 Ibid., 23–24; Program for Opening Ceremonies of the Kawkiutl Indian House, DAWD, box 3/31; WD to Erna Gunther, November 30, 1953, PMC, box 4/14.

44 *British Colonist*, December 13, 1953, vertical Files, reel 142, no. 1668; *Times*, December 11, 1953, Vertical Files, reel 142, no. 1683; *Vancouver Sun*, December 14, 1953, Vertical Files, reel 142, no. 1686; Vancouver *News Herald*, December 15, 1953, Vertical Files, reel 142, no. 1687, BCPM.

45 WD Notes on Mungo Martin House Potlatch, n.d., DAWD, box 3/12.

46 Bill Reid to WD, May 21, 1956, and July 17, 1956, PMC, box 17/46.

47 WD to Harry Hawthorn, January 20, 1956, DAWD, box 8/27.

48 WD to Charles Borden, January 12, 1951, Borden Papers, UBCA, box 7/10.

49 Charles E. Borden, "A Uniform Site Designation Scheme for Canada," *Anthropolgy in British Columbia, No. 3* (Victoria: British Columbia Provincial Museum, 1952), 44–48.

50 Victoria *Times*, December 9, 1950, Museum Scrapbook, BCPM, box 1.

51 WD to W.T. Straith, December 9, 1950, Borden Papers, UBCA, box 7/10.

52 WD to Douglas Leechman, December 10, 1950, PMC, box 10/02.

53 Charles Borden, Lecture notes, Borden Papers, UBCA, box 28/26.

54 WD to Charles Borden, September 12, 1951, Borden Papers, UBCA, box 7/10.

55 WD to Charles Borden, May 21, 1952, Borden Papers, UBCA, box 7/10; Interview with Roy Carlson, July 4, 1913.

56 Charles Borden, "West Coast Crossties with Alaska," *Artic Institute of North America Technical Paper*, no. 11 (December 1962): 9–19 and 170–81; Charles Borden to Jill Willmot, November 24, 1966, Borden Papers, UBCA, box 17/7.

57 Interview with Nancy Romaine, November 20, 2017.

58 Duff, "The Upper Stalo Indians," 250–78; WD, notes, DAWD, box 2/25.

59 Ibid., 264–67; John Edward Michael Kew, "Coast Salish Ceremonial Life: Status and Identity in a Modern Village" (PhD dissertation, University of Washington, 1970), 154; Pamela Amoss, *Coast Salish Spirit Dancing: the Survival of an Ancestral Religion* (Seattle: University of Washington Press, 1978), 91.

60 Michael Kew in "Coast Salish Ceremonial Life," 332–35, makes this point with some caution. Writing a decade later, Wolfgang G. Jilek, *Indian Healing: Shamanic Ceremonialism in the Pacific Northwest Today* (Surrey: Hancock House, 1982), particularly pages 64 through 95, makes the case for the therapeutic role of spirit dancing more strongly.

61 WD, "The 1953 Dancing Season," DAWD, box 5/14; WD, "Salish Spirit Dancing," WDF, box 10/39.

62 Interview with Marnie Duff, June 28, 2019.

63 WD, Notes for Thinking, WDF, box 51/10.

64 David E. Young and Jean-Guy Goulet (eds.), *Being Changed: The Anthropology of Extraordinary Experience* (Peterborough: Broadview Press, 1998), 7–13 and 94.

5. Restoring Totem Poles

1 Marius Barbeau, *Totem Poles*, 2 volumes, (Ottawa, National Museum of Canada, 1950), passim; Marius Barbeau, *Totem Poles of the Gitksan, Upper Skeena River, British Columbia* (Ottawa: National Museum of Canada, 1929), passim.

2 For a detailed account of collecting see Douglas Cole, *Captured Heritage: The Scramble for Northwest Coast Artifacts* (Vancouver: Douglas & McIntyre, 1985), passim.

3 WD to H. Hartman, March 8, 1960, DAWD, box 8/44.

4 Wilson Duff, "Preserving the Talking Sticks," *Powell River Digester* 30, no. 6(November–December 1954): 12.

5 WD, Field Notes Queen Charlotte Islands 1953 and 54, Field Notebook 13, DAWD, box 2/22.

6 Maria Tippett, *Bill Reid: The Making of an Indian* (Toronto: Vintage Canada, 2004): 16–17.

7 WD, Clew, Haida Graveyard, DAWD, box 2/13.

8 WD, Skedans, WDF, box 45/4.

9 WD, Field Notes Queen Charlotte Islands 1953 and 54, Field Notebook 13, DAWD, box 2/22; Wilson Duff, "A Heritage in Decay—The Totem Art of the Haidas," *Canadian Art* xi, no. 2 (Winter 1954): 58.

10 *British Colonist*, October 16, 1953, Museum Scrapbook, BCPM, box 2.

11 WD, Field Notes, 1953, WDF, box 6/3; John R. Swanton, *Contributions to the Ethnography of the Haida: Memoir of the American Museum of Natural History, Volume V*, (New York: AMS Press, 1905): 34–37.

12 WD, Field Notes on the Queen Charlotte Islands, WDF, box 6/3; WD, Notes, WDF, box 4/14.

13 WD to Tilly Rolston, January 26, 1953, PMC, box 21/1.

14 Vancouver *Sun*, March 8, 1952, February 9, 1954, February 16, 1954; *The Native Voice*, July 1954.

15 H.B. Hawthorn, "Proposal to the Canada Council," H.B. Hawthorn fonds, UBC MOA, box 1/15; N.A.M. MacKenzie to H. Hawthorn, February 16, 1958, Audrey Hawthorn fonds, UBC MOA, box 37/15.

16 *The Native Voice*, February 1954.

17 WD, Arrival at Anthony Island, DAWD, box 2/14.

18 Molly Stewart to Mr. Anfield, October 30, 1956, DAWD, box 2/14.

19 WD to Skidegate Band Council, December 19, 1956; WD to Molly Stewart, December 3, 1956, DAWD, box 8/32 and 7/6.

20 Skidegate Band Council resolution on Anthony Island Totem Poles, DAWD, box 2/24; WD to Peter Kelly, April 23, 1957, PMC, box 8/14.

21 W.S. Arneil to WD, May 9, 1957; WD to W.S. Arneil, April 23, 1957 and May 15, 1957, DAWD, box 2/14 and 8/7.

22 For a day-to-day account of the expedition see John and Carolyn Smyly, *Saving the Silent Ones: The 1957 Totem Pole Salvage Expedition to Ninstints, World Heritage Site* (Victoria: Trafford Publishing, 2007), passim.

23 Wilson Duff, "An Act of Vision and an Act of Intuition," in Vancouver Art Gallery, *Bill Reid: A Retrospective Exhibition* (Vancouver: Vancouver Art Gallery, 1974): n.p.

24 "The Silent Ones," British Columbia Recreation and Conservation; "Totem," CBC Vancouver.

25 Wilson Duff and Michael Kew, "Anthony Island, A Home of the Haidas," Provincial Museum of Natural History and Anthropology *Report for the Year 1957* (Victoria: Provincial Museum, 1957), 63.

26 Duff, "An Act of Vision," n.p.

27 Robert Markson to W.C.R. Jones, November 5, 1956; WD to Markson, November 15, 1956, DAWD, box 7/6.

28 Interview with Captain Gold, August 7, 2015.

29 Interview with Roy Jones, April 6, 2017.

30 Ronald Hawker, *Tales of Ghosts: First Nations Art in British Columbia, 1922–1961* (Vancouver: UBC Press, 2003): 154.

31 Tippett, *Bill Reid*, 265; Bill Reid to WD, February 22, 1954, PMC, box 17/46.

32 WD, Notes for Thinking, WDF, box 45/6 and 47/1; Interview with Robert Davidson, January 17, 2014.

33 WD to Bill Reid, February 23, 1954, PMC, box 17/46.

34 Marius Barbeau, *Totem Poles of the Gitksan*, passim; Wilson Duff, "Gitksan Totem-Poles, 1952, Anthropology in British Columbia Memoir no. 3*, (Victoria: British Columbia Provincial Museum, 1952), passim.

35 Duff, "Gitksan Totem-Poles," 21.

36 Ibid., 24.

37 WD, "Interview with Albert & Walter Douse," WDF, box 3/6; WD to R.G. Large, September 4, 1953, PMC, box 9/18.

38 WD, Field Notebook 16, October 1957, DAWD, box 6/7; Barbeau's ideas are in Marius Barbeau, *Alaska Beckons* (Caldwell: Caxton Printers, 1947), 187ff and 80.

39 WD, Field Notebook 16, October 1957, DAWD, box 6/7.

40 WD to Viola Garfield, November 7, 1957, DAWD, box 8/22.

41 WD, Field Notebook 16, 1958, DAWD, box 6/7.

42 "An Agreement between the People of Kitwncool and the Provincial Museum of British Columbia," Bain Collection, UBC MOA, file A 500019.

43 Peter Williams etc. to WD, March 23, 1965, DAWD, box 5/27.

44 Walter Koerner to WD, April 21, 1958, DAWD, box 5/33; WD to Walter Koerner, May 5, 1958, PMC, box 8/33; Cyril Belshaw to WD, July 14, 1954, Borden Papers, UBCA, box 7/10.

45 WD to Peter Williams, May 14, 1858; WD to the People of Kitwancool, n.d., DAWD, box 5/33.

46 Wilson Duff, ed., *Histories, Territories and Laws of the Kitwancool, Anthropology in British Columbia Memoir no. 4* (Victoria: British Columbia Provincial Museum, 1959): 3.

47 Constance Cox to Micheal Kew, November 7, 1958, DAWD, box 5/33.

48 George MacDonald to Borden, October 4, 1966, Borden Papers, UBCA, box 11/6; Walter Koerner to WD, April 13, 1960, DAWD, box 5/33; Interview with Peter Macnair, July 17, 2014; Peter Williams, "Tribute of the Kitwancool," in Abbott, ed., 47.

6. Museums and Beyond

1 WD, Notes for Thinking, WDF, box 10/9.

2 WD, "Anthro. Museums" and "Notes for Thinking," WDF, box 13/13.

3 A.E. Parr, *Mostly About Museums* (New York: The American Museum of Natural History, 1959): 26–27 and 62–64. The copy of this book inscribed to Wilson and with his underlining and marginal notes is in the UBC Museum of Anthropology Library.

4 WD, "Anthro. Museums" and "Notes for Thinking," WDF, box 13/13.

5 Ibid.

6 WD, "Museum Roles," WDF, box 13/13.

7 WD, "Notebook no. 16," 1957, DAWD, box 6/7; see also Roy, *The Collectors*, 137–38 on these initiatives.

8 WD to Suttles, September 27, 1957, PMC, box 20/14; Carl E. Guthe, "So You Want a Good Museum: A Guide to the Management of Small Museums," *The American Association of Museums*, n.s. (number 17, 1957): i and 1.

9 Provincial Museum of Natural History and Anthropology, *Report for the Year 1960*, 13.

10 Marius Barbeau to Jacques Rousseau, August 16, 1957, Marius Barbeau fonds B–F 621, Canadian Museum of History Archives.

11 H. Hawthorn to WD, December 10, 1957; WD to Barbeau, November 20, 1957, DAWD, box 8/28 and 8/8.

12 J.E.A. Parnell to WD, September 3, 1958 and November 3, 1958; WD to Parnell, n.d.; Hawthorn to WD, September 16, 1958 and November 26, 1958, Hawthorn fonds, UBC MOA, series 1, box 1.

13 WD to Hawthorn, August 1, 1958; WD, "Progress Report on Tsimshian Social Organisation," Hawthorn fonds, UBC MOA, series 1, box 1.

14 WD to Hawthorn, September 23, 1958, undated (November 1958), and December 29, 1958, Hawthorn to WD, November 8, 1958, Hawthorn fonds, UBC MOA, series 1, box 1; Wilson Duff, "The Role of the Human History Branch with Special Reference to Ethnology," WDF, box 39/3.

15 Hawthorn to WD, December 9, 1958, Hawthorn fonds, UBC MOA, series 1, box 1.

16 WD to Hawthorn, September 23, 1958, Hawthorn fonds, UBC MOA, series 1, box 1; Wilson Duff, "The Role of the Human History Branch with Special Reference to Ethnology," WDF, box 39/3.

17 WD to Hawthorn, May 1, 1959, Hawthorn fonds, UBC MOA, series 1, box 1.

18 Interview with Maria Abbott, October 27, 2014.

19 Provincial Museum of Natural History and Anthropology, *Report for the Year 1961*, 9.

20 D.B. Turner to C. Carl, April 7, 1961, PMC, box 23/ 02. Subsequent files from 02 to 05 contain further instructions.

21 WD to William Taylor, December 9, 1959, PMC, box 32/06.

22 WD to C. Carl, October 3, 1961, PMC, box 23/02.

23 Wilson Duff, "The Role of the Human History Branch," WDF, box 39/3.

24 Wilson Duff, "Contributions of Marius Barbeau to West Coast Ethnography," *Anthropologica* VI, no. 1, 1964, 63–96.

25 WD to Hawthorn, May 12, 1961, DAWD, box 8/28.

26 V. Garfield to WD, June 27, 1964; WD to Garfield, July 6, 1964, DAWD, box 8/22.

27 Barbeau to WD, June 6, 1961, DAWD, box 8/8; WD to Ernest Cote, June 8, 1961, PMC, box 32/04.

28 WD to Tom McFeat, March 8, 1962, PMC, box 32/04.

29 WD to Tom McFeat, May 25, 1962, PMC, box 32/04.

30 Interviews with Peter Macnair, July 17, 2014 and George MacDonald, May 1, 2015; WD to Barbeau, May 12, 1961, DAWD, box 8/8.

31 Wilson Duff, *The Indian History of British Columbia, Volume 1: The Impact of the White Man, Anthropology in British Columbia Memoir No. 5* (Victoria: Provincial Museum of Natural History and Anthropology, 1964).

32 Art Stott, "Talking About Indians," unidentified newspaper clipping, WDF, box 49/18.

33 Duff, *Indian History*, 67, 9 and 107.

34 WD, Preface (Prehistory), DAWD, box 2/3.

35 WD, "History and Prehistory," DAWD, box 1/37.

36 Ibid.

37 Ibid.; WD, Summary (Prehistory), DAWD, box 1/39.

38 WD, Prehistory, DAWD, box 5/11.

39 WD to Tom McFeat, March 8, 1962, PMC, box 32/04.

40 Interview with Donald Mitchell, July 14, 1915.

41 Victoria *Times*, August 13, 14, 15, 17, 18, 19, 20, 21 and 29, 1959.

42 WD to Borden, March 18, 1960; Borden to WD, March 19, 1960, Borden Papers, UBCA, box 7/11; WD to R.S. McNeish, March 18, 1960, PMC, box 32/06.

43 "Preserving British Columbia Prehistory: A Guide for Amateur Archaeologists," Provincial Archives of British Columbia Correspondence, GR 1738, BCPM, box 6/9.

44 WD, Notes, WDF, box 1/1.

45 British Columbia, *Papers Connected with the Indian Land Question, 1850–1875* (Victoria: Government Printer, 1875), 5–11.

46 WD to Tom Berger, December 12, 1963, DAWD, box 7/15.

47 British Columbia Court of Appeal, *Regina v. White and Bob, Appeal Book*, 52; Thomas R. Berger, *One Man's Justice: A Life in the Law* (Vancouver/Toronto: Douglas & McIntyre, 2002), 100.

48 In this and the previous two paragraphs I have drawn on an interview with Tom Berger, March 31, 2016; Berger, *One Man's Justice*, 87–119; and Thomas R. Berger, "Wilson Duff and Native Land Claims," in Abbott, ed., 49–63.

49 Hawker, 137 and 171; Aldona Jonaitis and Aaron Glass, *The Totem Pole: An Intercultural History* (Seattle: University of Washington Press, 2010): 184.

50 Berger, *One Man's Justice*, 102.

51 Roy, *The Collectors*, 138.

52 Hawthorn to WD, 6 April 1961, DAWD, box 8/28.

53 Carl to Arnold Webb (deputy minister of public works), September 18, 1961, PMC, box 22/06.

54 WD "Museum Acquires Mungo Martin Collection," DAWD, box 3/12.

55 WD to Lillian Breen, n.d. (1963), DAWD, box 8/46.

56 Gunther to Carl, July 22, 1963, PMC, box 4/14; WD to Clarke Brott, August 26, 1963, DAWD, box 7/15.

57 Interviews with Judith Buxton, June 14, 1918, Eleanor Anderson, June 22, 2019, and David Keenlyside, June 22, 2018.

58 Clifford Carl, "A Post War Program for the Provincial Museum," January 1944, PMC, box 26/2.

59 Victoria *Colonist*, January 21, 1954.

60 Moncrieff Williamson in the Victoria *Times*, November 14, 1959; Guthe quoted in the Victoria *Times*, September 13, 1961.

61 Roy, *The Collectors*, 178–79.

62 Interview with Peter Macnair, July 17, 2014; Carl to D.B. Turner, October 28, 1964, PMC, box 22/11.

63 WD, "Provincial Museum: A General Exhibit Programme" and "Overall Exhibit Sequence," Provincial Archives of British Columbia, BCPM, Correspondence, GR 1738, box 79/2.

64 WD to H. Hawthorn, January 8, 1965, and H. Hawthorn to WD, January 11, 1965, DAWD, box 8/28.

65 WD to Frederica de Laguna, February 24, 1965, PMC, box 8/43.

66 Interview with Judith Buxton, June 16, 2018.

67 Interview with Michael Kew, May 29, 2013.

68 George Manuel and Michael Posluns, *The Fourth World: An Indian Reality* (Don Mills: Collier-Macmillan, 1974): 158.

69 Bill Reid, "Foreword," in George F. MacDonald, *Haida Monumental Art: Villages of the Queen Charlotte Islands* (Vancouver: UBC Press, 1983): viii.

7. Teaching Anthropology

1 Hawthorn to Belshaw, September 23, 1965, Belshaw fonds, box 35, UBCA; Elvi Whittaker and Michael M. Ames, "Anthropology and Sociology at the University of British Columbia

from 1947 to the 1980s," in Julia Harrison and Regna Darnell, eds., *Historicizing Canadian Anthropology* (Vancouver: UBC Press, 2006): 162.

2 Whittaker and Ames, 165.

3 Hawthorn to John Graham, September 17, 1963, Hawthorn fonds, UBCA, box 6/11.

4 Unidentified faculty member to Belshaw, February 14, 1966, Belshaw fonds, UBCA, box 35.

5 Hawthorn to Belshaw, September 23, 1965; Bill Willmott to Belshaw, September 22, 1965, Belshaw fonds, UBCA, box 35.

6 Audrey Hawthorn to Jill Willmott, February 4, 1966, Audrey Hawthorn fonds, UBC MOA, box 27/18.

7 Hawthorn to Henry Zenter, October 24, 1960, Hawthorn fonds, UBCA, box 11/17.

8 Interview with John Pritchard, November 29, 2017; Isidore Dyen and David F. Aberle, *Lexical Reconstruction: The Case of the Proto-Athapaskan Kinship System* (London: Cambridge University Press, 1974): xiv.

9 M. Stott to Marnie Duff, March 24, 2004, MDP; interview with R.G. Matson, February 28, 2018.

10 Carl to D.B. Turner, January 25, 1966, PMC, box 22/10.

11 Interview with Marnie Duff, July 8, 2013.

12 Raymond Firth, "Aims, Methods, and Concepts in the Teaching of Social Anthropology," in David G. Mandlebaum, Gabriel W. Lasker and Ethel M. Albert, eds., *The Teaching of Anthropology* (Berkeley: University of California Press, 1963): 127–40; WD, seminar notes, WDP, box 11/8.

13 WD, "Approach to Teaching" and "Who's Doing the Teaching here, Anyway?" WDF, box 9/35 and 17/3.

14 Student paper files, WDF, box 19/26 and 36.

15 Interview with John Pritchard, November 29, 2017.

16 Interview with Michael Robinson, January 28, 2017.

17 Christie Harris, *Raven's Cry* (Vancouver: Douglas & McIntyre, 1966); Alan Fry, *How A People Die* (Toronto: Doubleday, 1970).

18 WD, Parable of Civil Disobedience, WDF, box 8/24.

19 WD, "A Proposal to Settle the BC Indian Land Question," and undated lecture notes, WDF, box 11/30 and 10/3.

20 WD, undated lecture notes, WDF, box 7/6 and 10/3.

21 Marius Barbeau, *Haida Myths Illustrated in Argillite Carvings* (Ottawa: National Museum of Canada, 1953): 117–29. Wilson's copy of Barbeau has many careful annotations. Reid, Bill and Robert Bringhurst, *The Raven Steals the Light* (Vancouver: Douglas & McIntyre, 1984): 63–73.

22 Wilson Duff, "Lecture on Women and Bears," recording, MAN-97, WDF, series 14–12; WD, Bear Mother, WDF, box 44/18. I am grateful to Collyne Bunn, who heard Wilson give this talk, for her help with this paragraph.

23 WD, lecture notes for Anthropology 301, WDF, box 9 /21; Adelade DeMenil and William Reid, *Out of the Silence* (New York: Harper Row, 1971), 114; Michael Kew to Michael Ames, June 4, 1975, Directors fonds, UBC MOA, box 23/4–C-21; *The Native Voice*, January 1973; interview with Marcia Calkowski, October 20, 2016.

24 Interview with Gloria Cranmer Webster, March 4, 2014.

25 Interviews with Collyne Bunn, December 3, 2013; Suki Anderson, October 16, 2015; Leslie Moore, November 25, 2016; and Nancy Ruddell, July 9, 2015; WD, Notes for Thinking, WDF, box 47/2; Shirley Haycock, "A critical Review of the Presentation of North-West Coast Art (Haida)," 5, WDF, box 19/6.

26 WD, draft outlines of Anthropology 502, WDF, box 11/7 and 11/8.

27 Interview with Susan Davidson, November 5, 2018; Susan Jane Thomas, "The Life and Work of Charles Edenshaw: A Study of Innovation," (B.A. essay, University of British Columbia, April 1967), passim.

28 Interview with Wolfgang Jilek and Louise Jilek-Aall, May 5, 2016; Wolfgang G. Jilek, passim.

29 Interview with Martine Reid, December 16, 2014.

30 Audrey Hawthorn to WD, January 25, 1968, Audrey Hawthorn fonds, UBC MOA, box 6/17.

31 WD, Functions and Scope of the Vancouver Centennial Museum, and Vancouver Centennial Museum Exhibit Planning, WDF, box 22/18 and 19.

32 Vancouver *Sun*, February 23, 1968 and Vancouver *Province*, February 24, 1968, WDF, box 8/34.

33 Interviews with Robin Ridington, October 27, 2014, and Elvi Whittaker, February 18, 2015.

34 British Columbia, Indian Advisory Act, 1960, Chap 186.

35 Minutes of the British Columbia Indian Advisory Committee, November 15, 1968, and May 9, 1969, WDF(2), box 6/2.

36 Ibid.; Interview with Susanne Hilton, July 8, 2015.

37 "Ethics in Anthropological Field Work" symposium at the Northwest Anthropological Conference, April 5, 1969, WDF, box 14/10; Recording of proceeding, MAN-97, WDF, series 14–12.

38 Wilson Duff, "Foreword," in Kalervo Oberg, *The Social Economy of the Tlingit Indians* (Vancouver: J.J. Douglas, 1973): vii.

39 Wilson Duff, "The Fort Victoria Treaties," *BC Studies*, no. 3 (Fall 1969): 3–57.

40 Bill Holm, *Northwest Coast Indian Art: An Analysis of Form* (Seattle: University of Washington Press, 1965): vii–ix; Wilson Duff, review of "Northwest Coast Indian Art," *American Antiquity* 31, no. 6 (October 1966): 881.

41 Interview with Bill and Marty Holm, December 1, 2014.

42 Vancouver Art Gallery, *Arts of the Raven: Masterworks by the Northwest Coast Indian* (Vancouver: Vancouver Art Gallery, 1967), unpaginated.

43 Robin Wright and Daina Augaitis, eds., *Charles Edenshaw* (London: Black Dog Publishing, 2013): 151–61.

44 *Arts of the Raven*, unpaginated.

45 Ibid.

46 Ira Jacknis, *The Storage Box of Tradition: Kwakiutl Art, Anthropologists and Museums, 1881–1981* (Washington: Smithsonian Institution Press, 2002): 176.

47 Bill Holm and William Reid, *Form and Freedom: A Dialogue on Northwest Coast Art* (Houston: Institute for the Arts, Rice University, 1975), passim; Bill Reid, "A New Northwest

Coast Art: A Dream of the Past or a New Awakening?" Harry Hawthorn fonds, UBC MOA, box 3/9.

48 Minutes of Alaska conferences on totem poles, July 13–14, 1967, and November 17, 1967, WDF, box 3/11.

49 Andrea Laforet, ed., *Cultural Heritage Project—Report on Kasaan*, (Alaska State Museum, 1971): 70.

50 WD, Alaska Field Notebook, June 8–27, 1969, in the possession of the author.

51 Wilson Duff, ed., Jane Wallen and Joe Clark, *Totem Pole Survey of Southeastern Alaska, Report of Field Survey and Follow Up Activities, June–October 1969*, (Juneau: Alaska State Museum, 1969): 16 and 41.

52 Laforet, ed., passim; interview with Andrea Laforet, June 16, 2016.

53 Interview with Jane and Dennis Demmert, March 16, 2015.

54 Interview with Marnie Duff, July 8, 2013.

55 WD to Jane Wallen, July 22, 1969, WDF, box 2/39.

56 Interview with Robert Davidson, January 14, 2014.

57 WD, Notes for Thinking and Resurgence of Haida Culture, lecture notes, WDF, boxes 45/6 and 10/16.

58 Interview with Robert Davidson, January 14, 2014; Robert Davidson, *Four Decades: An Innocent Gesture* (Vancouver: Robert Davidson, 2009): 2–4 and 87.

59 Interview with Michael Kew, May 29, 2013.

60 Wilson Duff, *images stone b.c.: Thirty Centuries of Coast Indian Sculpture* (Sannichton: Hancock House, 1975): 13.

8. Meaning in Haida Art

1 WD, Notes for Thinking, WDF, box 45/6.

2 See Edward W. Said, *On Late Style: Music and Literature Against the Grain* (New York: Pantheon Books, 2006), passim.

3 Kenelm Burridge, *Someone, No One: An Essay on Individuality* (Princeton: Princeton University Press, 1979): 144.

4 WD, Notes for Thinking, WDF, box 45/2, 45/3 and 45/6.

5 WD, Notes for Thinking, WDF, box 47/4, 45/6, 45/3 and 51/10.

6 Stanislav Grof, *Realms of the Human Unconscious: Observations from LSD Research* (New York: Viking, 1975): xvi, 3 and 11.

7 For example, WD, "Images Stone BC," lecture, recording, National Museum of History Archives.

8 WD, Notes for Thinking, WDF, boxes 47/5 and 45/4.

9 Interview with Cyril Belshaw, March 25, 2015.

10 Georg Groddeck, *The Book of the It* (London: Vision, 1949); Koestler, *The Act of Creation* (London: Hutchinson, 1964).

11 George Kubler, *The Shape of Time: Remarks on the History of Things* (New Haven: Yale University Press, 1962): 17. The copy of this book in the UBC Museum of Anthropology Library has Wilson's underlining and marginal notes.

12 For a summary of his thought see George Devereux, "Art and Mythology: A General Theory," in Carol F. Jopling, ed., *Art and Aesthetics in Primitive Societies* (New York: E.P. Dutton, 1971): 193–224.

13 Joseph Chilton Pearce, *The Crack in the Cosmic Egg: Challenging Constructs of Mind and Reality* (New York: Pocket Books, 1973); WD, Notes for Thinking, WDF, box 45/7.

14 Claude Lévi-Strauss, "The Story of Asdiwal," in Edmund Leach, ed., *The Structural Study of Myth and Totemism* (London: Tavistock, 1967): 1–47; Claude Lévi-Strauss, *The Raw and the Cooked: Introduction to a Science of Mythology* (New York: Harper Row, 1969), passim.

15 Claude Lévi-Strauss, *Myth and Meaning* (Toronto: University of Toronto Press, 1978): 9 and 12.

16 David Maybury-Lewis, "Science by Association," in E. Nelson Hayes and Tanya Hayes, eds., *Claude Lévi-Strauss: The Anthropologist as Hero* (Cambridge: MIT Press, 1970): 136.

17 Edmund Leach, *Claude Lévi-Strauss* (New York: Viking, 1974): 13 and 65; a similar thought is expressed in the title of Patrick Wilcken, *Claude Lévi-Strauss: The Poet in the Laboratory* (New York: Penguin, 2010).

18 Susan Sontag, "The Anthropologist as Hero," in Hayes and Hayes, eds., 186.

19 Hawthorn to WD, April 8, 1960, DAWD, box 8/28; Interview with Gloria Cranmer Webster, March 4, 2014.

20 Aldona Jonaitis, *A Wealth of Thought: Franz Boas on Native American Art* (Seattle: University of Washington Press, 1995): 324.

21 Lévi-Strauss, *The Raw and the Cooked*, 16–32; Lévi-Strauss, *Myth and Meaning*, 44 and 53.

22 Malcolm Gladwell, *Outliers: The Story of Success* (New York: Little, Brown and Company, 2008): 47ff.

23 Lévi-Strauss, "Three Memories of Wilson Duff," in Abbott, ed., 260.

24 WD, Notes for Thinking, WDF, box 45/2.

25 WD, The Art of Conducting Public Business, WDF, box 44/18.

26 See, for example, Erna Gunther, *Art in the Life of the Northwest Coast Indians* (Portland: The Portland Art Museum, 1966), passim.

27 Boas, *Primitive Art*, 185–298; Holm, passim.

28 WD, Iconics of Haida Art, and Levels of Meaning in Haida Art, WDF, box 44/18 and 46/18.

29 Ibid.

30 Ibid.; Erwin Panofsky, *Meaning in the Visual Arts: Paper In and On Art History* (Garden City: Doubleday, 1955); Silvano Arieti, *The Intrapsychic Self: Feeling, Cognition and Creativity* (New York: Basic Books, 1967).

31 WD, Notes for Thinking, WDF, box 45/2.

32 Abbott, ed., 307.

33 WD, General on Haida Art, Haida Art and Architecture, and Notes for Thinking, WDF, box 44/21 and 46/1.

34 WD, Notes for Thinking, WDF, box 45/4, 44/22, 45/6 and 47/2.

35 WD, Notes for Thinking, WDF, box 45/4.

36 WD, Notes forThinking, WDP, box 47/4, 45/7, 47/2, and 44/18.

37 WD draft letter to "Dear Erna," undated, WDF, box 45/5.

38 Franz Boas, *Primitive Art* (New York: Dover Publications, 1955): 275–76.

39 WD, Notes for Thinking, WDF, box 4/11.

40 WD, Notes for Thinking, WDF, box 44/18.

41 This suggestion is made by Bill McLennan and Karen Duffek, *The Transforming Image: Painted Arts of the Northwest Coast First Nations* (Vancouver: Douglas & McIntyre, 2000): 141.

42 Bill Reid, "The Box Painting by the 'Master of the Black Field'," in Abbott (ed.), 300–301.

43 WD, Notes for Thinking and draft letter to "Dear Erna," undated, WDF, box 47/3 and 45/5.

44 WD, Haida Art Was For Thinking, WDF, box 46/20.

45 WD, What is the Box Design About? WDF, box 45/2 and 45/8.

46 WD, Notes for Thinking, WDF, box 48/8.

47 John R. Swanton, *Haida Texts and Myths Skidegate Dialect* (Washington: Government Printing Office, 1905): 110–12. Swanton has other versions of this story in other books but this is the one that Wilson read and used for his story.

48 Wilson Duff, "Nothing Comes Only in Pieces," MDP; WD, Notes for Thinking, WDF, box 45/2. A version of "Nothing Comes Only in Pieces," is published in Abbott, ed., 315–324.

49 WD, Notes for Thinking, WDF, box 45/6.

50 Bob (Robert) Davidson, "Mighty Mouse Lives," in Abbott, ed., 294–95; Robert Davidson, "Kuugan Jaad, Mouse Woman," in Robin Wright and Daina Augaitis, eds., *Charles Edenshaw* (London: Black Dog Publishing, 2013): 51.

51 WD, "Frog's Mirror," MDP; also in Abbott, ed., 310; WD to Daphne, March 10, 1975, MDP.

52 Kathryn Bunn-Marcuse, "Eagles and Elephants: Cross-Cultural Influences in the Time of Charles Edenshaw," in Wright and Augaitis, eds., 175; Leslie Drew and Douglas Wilson, *Argillite: Art of the Haida* (North Vancouver: Hancock House, 1980): 11.

53 WD, Notes for Thinking, WDF, box 45/2.

54 WD, Sense and Nonsense on Haida Panel Pipes, WDF, box 46/7.

55 Lewis Carroll, "Jabberwocky," in *Through the Looking Glass and What Alice Found There* (London: Bloomsbury, 2001): 25; WD, Sense and Nonsense on Haida Panel Pipes, WDF, box 46/7.

56 WD, Sense and Nonsense, WDF, box 46/7, and Panel Pipes—Ribald Sculpture, WDF, box 47/4.

57 WD, Raven Comport, WDF, box 4/12, 47/2 and 47/5.

58 Swanton, *Haida Texts and Myths*, 126.

59 WD, Notes for Thinking, WDF, box 4/11 and 47/5.

60 Terri-Lynn Williams-Davidson, "How Raven Gave Females their Tsaw," in Wright and Augaitis, eds., 61; Colin Browne, *Entering Time: The Fungus Man Platters of Charles Edenshaw* (Vancouver: Talon Books, 2016): 31–36 and passim.

61 WD, Art of Acculturation, WDF, box 11/31.

62 WD, Is it Haida? Is it Art? and Notes for Thinking, WDF, boxes 19/9, 8/40 and 10/3.

63 WD, Notes for Thinking, WDF, box 13/4.

64 WD to R.G. Matson, August 1975, WDF, box 1/4.

9. Negative Spaces

1 Swanton, *Contributions*, 37; WD, Notes for Thinking," WDP, box 45/2.

2   Interview with Bill Holm, December 1, 2014.

3   Interviews with Michael Robinson, January 28, 2017 and Jay Powell, February 18, 2015.

4   WD, Notes for Thinking, WDF, box 45/6.

5   WD, Notes on NWC Religion, WDF, box 7/15.

6   WD, Notes for Thinking, WDF, box 45/6.

7   WD to Collyne Bunn, November 30, 1974 and October 11, 1975, Collyne Bunn, Papers, in her possession; Robin Riddington, "The World Is as Sharp as a Knife: Vision and Image in the Work of Wilson Duff," *BC Studies*, no. 38 (Summer 1978): 12–13.

8   WD, Notes for Thinking, WDF, box 45/3.

9   WD, Notes for Thinking, WDF, box 4/11 and 46/18.

10 Christopher Hyde, *Abuse of Trust: The Career of Dr. James Tyhurst* (Vancouver: Douglas & McIntyre, 1991), 11–21.

11 WD to Majorie Halpin, August 8, 1976, Marjorie Halpin, Private Fonds, box 20/55, UBC MOA; Rex Weyler, *Greenpeace: How a Group of Ecologists, Journalists and Visionaries Changed the World* (Vancouver: Raincoast Books, 2004): 209.

12 WD, Notes for Thinking, WDF, box 47/1.

13 Interview with Cyril Belshaw, March 24, 2015.

14 WD to Marnie, Wednesday (undated), MDP.

15 K.O.L.B. to WD and Ken Burridge to WD, both undated, WDF, box 51/10 and 44/18; Elvi (Whittaker) to WD, undated, MDP.

16 WD, Notes for Thinking, WDF, box 47/4; interview with Michael Kew, May 29, 2013.

17 Interview with Gloria Cranmer Webster, March 4, 2014; Elizabeth Edwards, Chris Gosden and Ruth B. Phillips, eds., *Sensible Objects: Colonialism, Museums and Material Culture* (Oxford: Berg, 2006): 1.

18 Dan Eban, ed., *Art as a Means of Communication in Pre-Literate Societies: The Proceedings of the Wright International Symposium on Primitive and Precolumbian Art Jerusalem, 1985* (Jerusalem: The Israel Museum, 1990): v, 4–6.

19 Interviews with Bill and Marty Holm, December 1, 2014 and Martine Reid, December 16, 2014.

20 WD, Notes for Thinking, WDF, box 47/3 and 4.

21 WD, Notes for Thinking, WDF, box 45/6.

22 Swanton, *Contributions*, 117; WD, Notes for Thinking, WDF, box 47/4.

23 WD, Notes for Thinking, WDF, box 45/6.

24 Marianne Boelscher, *The Curtain Within: Haida Social and Mythical Discourse* (Vancouver: UBC Press, 1988): 153.

25 WD, Notes for Thinking, WDF, box 45/2 and 47/5.

26 WD, Notes for Thinking, WDF, box 10/9; Interview with Marcia Calcowski, October 20, 2016; Ron Hamilton, "Some Thoughts about Wilson Duff," in Abbott, ed., 46. "The old man" was not the younger Charles Edenshaw as Hamilton suggests.

27 WD, Notes for Thinking, WDF, box 45/6.

28 WD, "Death is a Lie," MDP; a slightly different version of the poem is in Abbott, ed., 308.

29 WD, Notes for Thinking, WDF, box 45/3.

30 Minutes of program committee, January 24, 1974, Directors fonds, UBC MOA, box 10/1-F-4.

31 Hawthorn to Belshaw, January 1, 1966, Belshaw fonds, UBCA, box 35.

32 WD, Memo to Museum Planning Committee, November 10, 1971, WDF, box 22/17.

33 WD to R.G. Matson, August 1975, WDF, box 1/4.

34 WD to Ames, May 29, 1975; Kew to Ames, June 4, 1975; Ames to Kew, June 11, 1975, Directors fonds, UNC MOA, box 23/4-C-21,; WD, Totem Poles, WDF, box 4/8.

35 Wilson Duff, "Bill Reid: An Act of Vision and an Act of Intuition," in Vancouver Art Gallery, *Bill Reid*, unpaginated.

36 Wilson Duff, *images stone b.c.*, 28 and 29.

37 Wilson Duff, *Prehistoric Stone Sculpture*, passim.

38 Wilson Duff, *images stone b.c.*, 12.

39 Wilson Duff, *images stone b.c.*, 34–35.

40 WD, Notes for Thinking, WDF, box 45/4.

41 Wilson Duff, *images stone b.c.*, 12–25 and 120–121.

42 Edmund Leach, "Levels of Communication and Problems of Taboo in the Appreciation of Primitive Art," in Anthony Forge, ed., *Primitive Art and Society* (Oxford: Oxford University Press, 1973): 221–34.

43 Wilson Duff, *images stone b.c.*, 164–165 and 22; Hilary Stewart, "Stone Mask Reunion," in Abbott, ed., 261–264; interview with Roy Henry Vickers, March 18, 2015.

44 Wilson Duff, *images stone b.c.*, 149, 164–166 and 25; WD, Notes for Thinking, WDF, box 45/5 and 7 and 46/1.

45 Bill Reid, Opening Remarks, Hilary Stewart fonds, box 4/7, UBC MOA; Robert Davidson, Opening Remarks, from *Vanguard*, June and July 1975, WDF, box 29/9.

46 George MacDonald, introduction, Images Stone BC lecture, National Museum of History Archives; Carlos Castaneda, *The Teaching of Don Juan: A Yaqui Way of Knowledge* (Berkeley: University of California Press, 1968), passim.

47 Bill Taylor to WD, November 27, 1975, WDF, box 38/28; Interview with Robin Riddington, October 27, 2014; Interview with Roy Henry Vickers, March 18, 2015; John Clegg to WD, WDF, box 1/4.

48 Interview with Leslie Moore, November 25, 2016; Roy Carlson to WD, August 12, 1975, WDF, box 44/2; Interview with Martine Reid, December 16, 2014; WD, Notes for Thinking, WDF, box 47/5.

49 WD to Lilo Berliner, January 13, 1975, MDP.

50 WD, Notes for Thinking, WDF, box 45/2, 45/3 and 51/10.

51 Lilo Berliner to WD, July 26, 1974, March 6, 1975, and April 12, 1974, Phyllis Webb, Papers, Library and Archives Canada.

52 WD to Lilo Berliner, July 17, 1974, MDP; Collyne Bunn, "Poems by Collyne" in Abbott, ed., 329.

53 WD to Collyne Bunn, June 25, 1975, December 5, 1975, and March 27, 1976, Collyne Bunn, Papers in her possession; Allan Watts, *The Book: On the Taboo Against Knowing Who You Are* (New York: Vintage Books, 1972): especially 141–143; Mircea Eliade, *The Myth of the Eternal Return or, Cosmos and History* (Princeton: Princeton University Press, 1965): 52–81 and 130–57.

54 WD to Burridge, August 8, 1976, MDP; Wilson Duff, "Tsetsaut," in June Helm, ed., *Handbook of North American Indians, Volume 6: Subarctic* (Washington: Smithsonian Institution, 1981): 454–57; WD to William Sturtevant, 3 December 1971, WDF, box 44/12.

55 WD, "The World Is as Sharp as a Knife: Meaning in Northern Northwest Coast Art," paper given at Simon Fraser University, May 14, 1976, recording, MDP. The opening reference to Boas is in the recorded version of the talk but not the published one.

56 Wilson Duff, "The World Is as Sharp as a Knife: Meaning in Northern Northwest Coast Art," in Roy L. Carlson, ed., *Indian Art Traditions of the Northwest Coast* (Burnaby: Archaeology Press Simon Fraser University, 1983): 48–66. A version of the paper can also be found in Abbott, ed., 209–224, but the version in the Carlson volume is closer to the spoken presentation.

57 WD, Notes for Thinking, WDP, box 48/1; Michael Ames, Speaking Notes at the Opening of the Museum of Anthropology, Directors fonds, box 23/4-C-24, UBC MOA.

58 Gloria Cranmer Webster, Opening of the Legacy, June 8, 1976, Marjorie Halpin, Curator fonds, box 15/2, UBC MOA; WD, "Resurgence & Art," WDP, box 7/6; Peter Macnair, Alan L. Hoover and Kevin Neary, *The Legacy: Continuing Traditions of Canadian Northwest Coast Indian Art* (Victoria: British Columbia Provincial Museum, 1980): 121 and 160.

59 WD to Ames, June 10, 1976, and Ames to Marjorie Halpin, n.d., Michael Ames fonds, box 14/37, UBCA.

60 Interview with Jay Powell, February 18, 2015; Bill Reid, "Prologue" in Abbott, ed., 13–14; Interview with Robert Davidson, January 14, 2014.

61 WD to Burridge, August 8, 1976, MDP.

62 D---- to WD, undated, including a handwritten copy of "A Hard Rain's a-Gonna Fall," MDP.

63 Interviews with Art Skirrow, November 26, 2012, Martine Reid, December 16, 2014, Wolfgang Jilek and Louise Jilek-Aall, May 5, 2016, Susanne Hilton, July 8, 2016 and Sheila McTaggert, January 24, 2014; WD, "Thoughts on Today," WDF, box 47/3.

64 Interview with Marnie Duff, July 8, 2013; Marion Duff to Dave and Lee, September 1, 1976, MDP.

65 WD to Peter Macnair, August 6, 1976, Marjorie Halpin, Curator fonds, box 5/11, UBC MOA.

10. Coming Back

1 Swanton, *Contributions*, 27; interview with Wolfgang Jilek and Louise Jilek-Aall, May 5, 2016.

2 Interview with Jay Powell, February 18, 2015.

3 Interview with Marnie Duff, May 28, 2015.

4 Audrey Hawthorn to Ames, September 2, 1976, Ames fonds, UBCA, box 32/10.

5 Collyne Bunn, "Chinai," Collyne Bunn papers in her possession.

6 Interview with Gloria Cranmer Webster, March 4, 2014; Suttles to Belshaw, 5 October 4, 1976, Borden papers, UBCA, box 16/3.

7 Helmut J. Ruebsaat and Raymond Hull, *The Male Climacteric* (New York: Hawthorn Books, 1975), 165–166.

8 Ronald W. Maris, *Pathways to Suicide: A Survey of Self-Destructive Behaviors* (Baltimore: The Johns Hopkins University Press, 1981): 43 and 65. The following books were particu-

larly helpful for this paragraph: Thomas Joiner, *Why People Die by Suicide* (Cambridge: Harvard University Press, 2005); Howard I. Kushner, *Self-Destruction in the Promised Land: A Psychocultural Biology of American Suicide* (New Brunswick: Rutgers University Press, 1989); Thomas Szasz, *Fatal Freedom: The Ethics and Politics of Suicide* (Westport: Praeger, 1999) and John C. Weaver, *A Sadly Troubled History: The Meanings of Suicide in the Modern Age* (Montreal: McGill-Queens University Press, 2009).

9 WD to Win, n.d., MDP.

10 WD to Burridge, August 8, 1976, MDP; interview with Kenelm Burridge, July 4, 2013.

11 WD, Notes for Thinking, WDF, box 45/2, 47/2 and 48/1.

12 K.O.L. Burridge, "Epilogue: The Eulogy Given at Wilson Duff's Memorial Service," in Abbott, ed., 341; WD, Notes for Thinking, WDP, box 45/2.

13 Wilson Duff, "The Mask and the Mirror," MDP, and in Abbott, ed., 309.

14 Phyllis Webb, *Talking* (Dunvegan: Quadrant Editions, 1982), 131 and 147–48; interview with Grant Keddie, January 18, 2017.

15 Phyllis Webb, *Wilson's Bowl* (Toronto: The Coach House Press, 1980), 61–73.

16 Interview with Roy Henry Vickers, March 18, 2015.

17 Burridge in Abbott, ed., 341.

18 Collyne Bunn, personal communication, 27 September 2017.

19 Hilary Stewart, *Robert Davidson Haida Printmaker* (Vancouver: Douglas & McIntyre, 1979): 69.

20 Kew to Marnie Duff, July 22, 1983, MDP.

21 Interview with Helen Mason, December 6, 2017; Interview with Marnie Duff, August 19, 2013; Marnie Duff, personal communication.

22 Kew to Ames, September 28, 1976, Ames fonds, UBCA, box 14/37.

23 Ames, "A Note," 3–11; Michael Ames, *Cannibal Tours and Glass Boxes: The Anthropology of Museums* (Vancouver: UBC Press, 1992), passim.

24 Robin Ridington, "The World Is as Sharp as a Knife," 3–13.

25 Borden, "Wilson Duff," 3–12; Abbott, ed., passim; Suttles, "The World Is as Sharp as a Knife," 82–91.

26 Carol Sheehan McLaren, "Moment of Death: Gift of Life A Reinterpretation of the Northwest Coast Image of 'Hawk,'" *Anthropologica* xx, n.s., nos. 1–2 (1978): 65–90; Carol Sheehan, *Pipes That Won't Smoke; Coal that Won't Burn: Haida Sculpture in Argillite* (Calgary: The Glenbow Museum, 1981): 10 and 7.

27 Peter Macnair and Alan L. Hoover, *The Magic Leaves: A History of Haida Argillite Carving* (Victoria: Royal British Columbia Museum, 2002): 151.

28 Bruce Ruddell, *Beyond Eden* (Theatre Calgary, February 16–March 7, 2010).

29 Bruce Ruddell, draft script for *Beyond Eden*, 58, MDP.

30 Interviews with Marnie Duff, August 29, 1913, Sheila McTaggert, January 24, 2014, and Jay Powell, February 18, 2015.

31 Leslie Hall Pinder, *Bring Me One of Everything: A Novel* (Marblehead: Grey Swan Press, 2012): n.p and 32.

32 Wilson Duff, "Mute Relics of Haida Tribes Ghost Villages," *Smithsonian* (September 1976): 84 and 89.

33 Interview with Randy Bouchard and Dorothy Kennedy, April 21, 2016.

34 WD, Note, WDF, box 49/8.

35 E.N. Anderson, passim.

36 WD to Burridge, August 8, 1976, MDP.

37 Majorie M. Halpin, "The Tsimshian Crest System: A Study Based on Museum Specimens and the Marius Barbeau and William Beynon Field Notes," (PhD dissertation, University of British Columbia, 1973); Marjorie Halpin, "'Seeing' in Stone: Tsimshian Masking and the Twin Stone Masks," in Margaret Seguin, *The Tsimshian Images of the Past: Views for the Present* (Vancouver: University of British Columbia Press, 1984): 281–307; and Margaret Anderson and Marjorie Halpin, eds., *Potlatch at Gitsegukla: William Beynon's 1945 Field Notebooks* (Vancouver: UBC Press): 2000.

38 Charles Menzies, review of *The Indian History of British Columbia, BC Studies*, no. 121 (Spring 1999): 130–31.

39 Daniel L. Boxberger, "Whither the Expert Witness: Anthropology in the Post-Delga-muukw Courtroom," in Marie Mauze, Michael E. Harkin and Sergei Kan, eds., *Coming to Shore: Northwest Coast Ethnology, Traditions and Visions* (Lincoln: University of Nebraska Press, 2004): 336

40 Wilson Duff, "Foreword," in Oberg, p.v.

41 Suttles to Marion Duff, September 30, 1976, MDP.

42 *Tofino-Ucluelet Westerly News*, December 20, 2021 and *Victoria Times Colonist*, December 21, 2021.

43 WD, The Collectors, WDP, box 4/20; for my work, supervised by Wilson, on reciprocity in the fur trade see Fisher, 1–48.

44 Roger Blackley, *Galleries of Maoriland: Artists, Collectors and the Māori World, 1880–1910* (Auckland: Auckland University Press, 2018); Douglas Cole, "Tricks of the Trade: Some Reflections on Anthropological Collecting," *Arctic Anthropology* 28, no. 1: 49–50.

45 Davidson, *Four Decades*, 2; interview with Robert Davidson, January 14, 2014.

46 Browne, *Entering Time*, passim.

47 Wilson Duff, "Foreword," in Oberg, viii; For a positive assessment of Wilson Duff's contribution in this area see Robert L.A. Hancock, "Franz Boas, Wilson Duff, and the Image of Anthropology on the North Pacific Coast," in Regna Darnell, Michelle A. Hamilton, Robert L. A. Hancock and Joshua Smith, eds., *Franz Boas as Public Intellectual: Ethnography, Theory, Activism.* (Lincoln: University of Nebraska Press, 2015): 248–54.

48 Interview with Doug White, March 30, 2020.

49 WD to Norman Newton (CBC Prince Rupert), July 12, 1962, DAWD, box 7/14.

50 WD, Notes for Thinking, WDP, box 45/2 and 51/5.

51 WD, Notes for Thinking, WDF, box 51/10.

Index